THE SYSTEMIC DIMENSION OF GLOBALIZATION

Edited by **Piotr Pachura**

The Systemic Dimension of Globalization
Edited by Piotr Pachura

Published by InTech

Janeza Trdine 9, 51000 Rijeka, Croatia

Publishing Process Manager Niksa Mandic

Technical Editor Teodora Smiljanic

Cover Designer InTech Design Team

Additional hard copies can be obtained from orders@intechopen.com

The Systemic Dimension of Globalization, Edited by Piotr Pachura
p. cm.
ISBN 978-953-307-384-2

For EU product safety concerns:
IN TECH d.o.o., Prolaz Marije Krucifikse Kozulić 3, 51000 Rijeka, Croatia,
info@intechopen.com or visit our website at intechopen.com.

Meet the editor

Piotr Pachura (assoc. prof. dr. hab.), European academic and scientist, the reader at Częstochowa University of Technology (Poland) and University of Presov (Slovak Rep.). Academic degrees achieved in: social science (MA), economic sicence (PhD) and geograpy (dr hab.). Consultant in regional innovation policy and practice. Author of over 80 books and articles, participant in many international research projects, originator of several scientific international journals as e.g.: Springer Journal of Innovation and Entrepreneurship: A Systems View Across Time and Space and Polish Journal of Management Sudies. Engaged in interdyscyplinary research on: network and global economy, glocalization, economic geography, theory of regional and local change and development.

Contents

Preface

Steward Kauffman remarks that the 21st century science will head towards ordered complexity, also in the field of theories concerning social and economic sciences (*The orgins of Order: Self-Organizations and Selection in Evolution*, Oxford univ. Press, 1993). Efforts will be made to attempt to "crystallize" complex systems, that is to transform them into structures characterized by a high degree of order.

This book *The Systemic Dimension of Globalization* that consists of a variety of approaches and topics was connected throughout the main message - the system conception. System approach can be counted among most explored theories in the contemporary science, including social and socio-economic sciences. It seems that such concepts as *catastrophe theory, chaos theory, synergetic theory or fractal theory* will constitute a strong inspiration for research in contemporary global world.

The main common element of these theories is that according to them, systems are *non-linear* and *unstable* complexes. Other characteristics of system thinking is a changing "routine" of scientific approaches: from *reistic thinking* to *phenomenological thinking* (thing – phenomena); from *mechanistic* thinking to *process* thinking; from *linear models* to the creation of *network models;* from scientific metaphor such as *"tower"* to scientific metaphor such as *"network".*

The genesis of this release results from *INTECH* mission of interdisciplinarity in scientific publications. Today science is moving in the direction of synthesis of the achievements of various academic disciplines. The idea to prepare and present a multidimensional and systematic approach to the globalization phenomenon to the international academic milieu was an ambitious undertaking.

The book *The Systemic Dimension of Globalization* consists of 14 chapters divided into three sections: *Globalization and Complex systems; Globalization and Social systems; Globalization and Natural systems.* The Authors of respective chapters represent the great diversity of disciplines and methodological approaches as well as a variety of academic culture. I am convinced that this is the value of this book and I hope that it will be appreciated by a global scholar audience.

As editor of this book I would like to express gratitude for the trust was endowed by the Publisher, but most of all I would like to express my appreciation for the Authors of all chapters.

June 2011.

Piotr Pachura
Częstochowa

Part 1

Globalization and Complex Systems

1

Sustainability by Interrelating Science, Society and Economy in Embedded Political Economy – an Epistemological Approach

Masudul Alam Choudhury[1] and Lubna Sarwath Mohammad[2]
[1]*College of Commerce and Economics, Sultan Qaboos University, Muscat, Sultanate of Oman and International Chair, Postgraduate Program in Islamic Economics and Finance, Trisakti University, Jakarta,*
[2]*Faculty of Economics (Islamic Economics and Finance), Trisakti University, Jakarta, Indonesia*

1. Introduction

Sustainability is a far wider concept than in the environment context. Besides, when ecology is invoked to establish sustainability the concept assumes a wider field of ethical and social evaluation. Such an evaluative domain involves embedding among a wide field of interactive subsystems. The systems learn by synergy and unify in the midst of the good things of life. The learning and choice of the good things of life through the interactive systemic synergy conveys the essential meaning of ethicality. Systemic learning as an embedded phenomenon in a unification framework of human ecological setting establishes the substantive meaning of sustainability (Hawley, 1986). Indeed, the South Commission (1990, p.13) defines development as such an embedded process in the following words: "To sum up: development is a process of self-reliant growth, achieved through participation of the people acting in their own interests as they see them, and under their own control."

Yet the context of learning by synergy is not prevalent in this definition of development. The process of choice by participating individuals in the light of their own interests could very well be a ruthless experience in competition and self-interest -- if not of individuals then of collusive groups. In the sustainability debate we find such a conflict to be entrenched. Consider the conflict between global corporation and small enterprises. One complains of the other for their individual impediments to growth (Barbier, 1986). Yet it is a fact that enterprises must necessarily survive within the reality of markets, an institutional regulatory framework, and participatory mechanism (Kim & Mauborgne, 2005). Besides, there is also the conflict between the present and future generations, whereby the magnitude of financial and physical resource allocation problem between the present and future generations remains indeterminate. The savings problem is unresolved in the intertemporal case (Phelps, 1989).

In fact, there is no participation between the present and far future generation. These two are not contiguous, and hence cannot co-determine, participate and interrelate. Thereby, there does not exist a discounting for such indeterminate future preferences and the resource allocation linked with such out-of-bound resource allocation points beyond overlapping generations (Choudhury, 2011). Consequently, the expressed ethical problem of intertemporal resource allocation to maximize the associated discounted utilities of future non-overlapping generations fails in the methodological problem of valuation of a resource bundle. Only the mystical shade of ethical feeling at the cost of ethical reality prevails (Inglott, 1990). Neither the South Commission Report nor the Brundtland Report on sustainable development addresses the intergenerational ethical problem of resource allocation even though a certain form of collusive participation involving community, national and social collusion, namely between the North and the South, is emphasized. Globalization as a result assumes the façade of conflict and individuating transnational cultural identities (Sklair, 2002).

The theme of sustainability invoked in this paper is premised on the episteme of unity of knowledge and its impact on unified social reconstruction. This approach involves a substantive methodology and a specific perspective of application. The research investigation in the epistemological basis of sustainability by synergistic learning process involves an endogenous ethical symbiosis. It is extensively embedded in ever-expanding domains of social activities for the common good of all. We explain below the underlying methodology as such a complex learning process.

2. Objective

Three principal undertakings comprise the objective of this paper. Firstly, we will establish the epistemic methodological formal expression for the model of unity of knowledge and the sustainability criterion under the emergent symbiotic system perspective. The internal dynamics of the inter-systemic embedded domains in the study of sustainability with endogenous ethical dynamics between science and society including the global economic order will be explained in the context of political economy. The idea of political economy in this context will be explained in terms of the epistemic dynamics of unity of knowledge and its symbiotic process of systemic learning between social and scientific, hence socio-scientific, diversity. Secondly, the emergent methodological formalism of sustainability will be contrasted with other ones of similar types in received literature. This is a deeply epistemological issue on the theme of selecting the correct premise for unity of knowledge, thereby defining the unified world-system as a social construction enabled by invoking the episteme of unity of knowledge. Thirdly, we will apply the emergent sustainability worldview to the institutional political economy of the Copenhagen Summit on Climatic Change.

3. Explanation of key concepts as the building blocs of the learning model of sustainability in this paper

This section defines and explains some key terms and concepts that are to be used in the construction of the generalized system model of unity of knowledge as the episteme and its application to the theme of sustainability.

Sustainability

In mainstream literature of economic development, sustainability is defined as the growth and progress of the economy in keeping with non-inflationary economic advancement in real output. Economic development is also construed as the conveying of the fruits of such growth for the benefit of labor and enterprise big and small, and the attainment of environmental preservation and social justice derived from the consumption, production and distribution of goods and services to all of the present and future generations.

In this paper, sustainability is the entirety mentioned above. But the attainment of such a compendium of wellbeing is not taken in the sense of economic optimization of these possibilities. Rather, the paper addresses sustainability as learning process established by organic complementary interrelations between the good things of life. Indeed, such an idea of complementarities out of choices of the good things of life is the meaning of wellbeing. We will expand on this idea below.

Ethics

In received literature ethics is understood as humanly driven behavior to attain utilitarian objectives that may be collectively derived though they exist as individual objectives. The foundation of such an understanding of ethics is the rational process that emanates distantly in the metaphysical moral law, but is utterly changed to assume a humanistic character.

In this paper, the meaning of ethics is equivalent to the learning process premised on the evaluation of an existing degree of unity of knowledge in the examined system of sustainability. This is then followed by the formalism of social reconstruction to gain the state of complementarities between the variables representing the good things of life. These bundles of variables as vectors are like Rawls' primaries (Rawls, 1971). Thus the following chain of relations prevails in the understanding of ethics in the context of our explanation of sustainability:

Episteme of Unity of knowledge	learning process in unity of knowledge and its evaluation and construction of the world-system	evaluation of the problem of the world-system: estimating existing state followed by social reconstruction	simulation of the wellbeing objective criterion	
		↓ the ethical consequence In given learning process	continuity across continuum of knowledge, time and space dimension (Choudhury, 2009a)	(1)

The meaning of ethics so understood is similar to how Nozick (2001) explains ethics in his following words (p. 240):

Our actions are mutually connected when my actions are connected with yours and yours with mine. Frequently, the actions of different people are mutually connected and the outcomes are nontrivially affected. This is the background that gives rise to ethics.

Episteme

We adopt the meaning of episteme given by Foucault (trans. Scheffler, 1972, p. 191) as follows:

By *episteme* we mean the total set of relations that unite, at a given period, the discursive practices that give rise to epistemological figures, sciences, and possibly formalized systems The episteme is not a form of knowledge (*connaissance*) or type of rationality which, crossing the boundaries of the most varied sciences, manifests the sovereign unity of a subject, a spirit, or a period; it is the totality of relations that can be discovered, for a given period, between the sciences when one analyses them at the level of discursive regularities.

In a like sense of the concept of episteme in this paper, we mean by episteme the totality of the ontological and phenomenological precept and formalism premised on the epistemology of unity of knowledge. This primal concept is followed by its inductive capability out of the deductive premise. This primal precept of unity of knowledge denotes the episteme. It is subsequently followed by the entire system of learning experiences in evolving processes of unity of knowledge. The episteme of unity thereby induces the variables and entities of sustainability.

Functional ontology and epistemology

Ontology according to Heidegger (trans. Hofstadter, 1988, p. 128; Kant,) is encapsulated in this passage:

Transcendental knowledge relates not to objects, not to beings, but to the concepts that determine the being of beings. 'A system of such concepts would be called transcendental philosophy.' Transcendental philosophy denotes nothing but ontology.

Yet in our paper ontology assumes a functional, i.e. an engineering meaning (Gruber, 1993). In this perspective, the universe assumes a mathematical form in which symbolization acts as reflective soul of reality of specific issues and problems, of the nature of the universe that we want to study as a world-system. The universe and sustainability as continuous learning by epistemic unity in it across 'everything' (Barrow, 1991) is a mathematical semiosis (Heiskala, 2003) of the socio-scientific order. Thus we will use the meaning of functional ontology as opposed to the metaphysical conception of ontology to mean the formalism of a specific idea. This is the being of becoming of an idea, which means (*functional*) ontology in this paper.

According to the functional meaning of ontology, the theory of knowledge (epistemology) and the ontological principle are made up of two parts that encircle and evolve in the continuum of knowledge, time, space dimension. These two parts are firstly, the epistemic derivation of unity of knowledge from a primal premise. Secondly, such an epistemic knowledge flow develops the concrescence (Whitehead, trans. Griffin & Sherburne, 1978, pp. 20-30) of the world-system of unified forms representing the ontological formalism of the socio-scientific order. Sustainability as explained earlier in the domain of organic complementarities (i.e. participation = organic unity) *res extensa* is the cause and effect circularity of the above-mentioned two parts across continuum of systems and over time.

In light of the above definition and explanation of ontology and the ontological principle of being and becoming, epistemology, the theory of knowledge, and ontology as theory of functional forms as description of the dynamics of being and becoming of the socio-scientific universe – its semiosis -- are juxtaposed. Episteme as totality of the phenomenological content of meaning emerges from epistemology (idea) and leads to functional ontology; *and* ('and' -- this meaning here is taken in the sense of mathematical intersection) ontology leads into evolutionary epistemology across continuum of systems and knowledge, time and space dimension. Such is the consequential vintage of sustainability. See below for further explanation on this dynamics of creativity.

Socio-scientific world-system

The epistemological-ontological delineation of the model emergent from expression (1) is of the universal and unique type in respect of its possibility for explanation and application to the widest possible domain of systems, issues, and problems *res extensa*. (Descartes, trans. Commins & Linscott, 1954, p. 176). Hence, despite the diversity of problems addressed for systems under consideration, the meta-model of epistemic unity and sustainability remains invariant. That is because the primal cause, the consequential effect, and the recursive and evolutionary continuity of the same relations are uniquely premised on knowledge simultaneously with its induction of variables, entities and events. The totality of such diversity of systems and events by knowledge induction of a unified order is the idea of the unified world-system. The fact that such unifying systems span across all domains -- the meaning of universality by virtue of the epistemic role of unity of knowledge -- causes science, ecology, society and economy to interact, integrate and evolve by organic symbiosis. The resulting embedding domain is the wider field of social valuation comprising our scope of political economy.

Political economy

Political economy is a discipline of thought -- but not the pedagogical study -- of power and conflict in states of production, ownership and distribution. These activities together assume a meaning of systemic concrescence in embedding political economy. The domains of science, society and economy are now integrated together out of systemic interaction and the learning spaces of evolutionary epistemological dynamics.

Staniland (1985, p. 33) invokes reference to Lionel Robbins on the concern with the scientific (epistemological) as opposed to the institutional (pedagogical) approach to the definition of political economy in the following words: "Lionel Robbins acknowledged that the logical basis of welfare economics was flawed, that it was impossible to arrive at a scientific definition of the general good from an examination of individual preferences. But governments had to make judgments about such matters, and values were inescapably involved in such judgments. Therefore Robbins proposed dividing the field into 'political economy', which dealt with such important but essentially unscientific matters, and 'economic science', which would continue the central, normatively neutral tasks of analyzing the facts of economic behavior"

The understanding and application of the theme of political economy are different in this paper. We define political economy in the scientific framework of interaction, integration and evolutionary epistemology of unity of knowledge caused by the convergence to unification of 'everything' according to the methodology of learning processes *res extensa* differentiating truth and falsehood. The scientific universality and uniqueness of this methodology are preserved while bringing together what in the above quote means unscientific institutionalism. Scientific formalism of the meaning of institutionalism is fired by its own dynamics of preferences, structures and creative futures. The resulting symbiotic worldview is the essential characteristic of our definition of political economy. Within such a worldview is subsumed the opposing study of conflict and cooperation on the theme of production, consumption, ownership and distribution of wealth and resources, and all the opportunities that emerge there from.

On such a systemic spanning perspective of the field of political economy the organic model of interrelationship between epistemology and development (Koizumi, 1993) can be adopted to explain our systemic and unification concept of political economy. It integrates 'everything' within a modeled framework of human reality partitioned between truth and choices of the good things of life on the one side; and falsehood and differentiation of life on the other side.

Evolutionary learning process

The meaning of process in the sense of the ontological principle rests on the principle of being and becoming (Prigogine, 1980). Process breeds sustainability by virtue of the unified nexus of organic relations between diversity. This idea of sustainability and learning process is represented in expression (1). In this regard, Whitehead (op cit, p. 80) writes: "The philosophy of organism extends the Cartesian subjectivism by affirming the 'ontological principle' and by contrasting it as the definition of 'actuality'. This amounts to the assumption that each actual entity is a locus for the universe."

The consequence interrelating epistemology and functional ontology along the reproduction of knowledge and its constructed world-system of unity of knowledge is the essential meaning of learning. Sustainability is borne by and of itself in continuum of the knowledge, time, and space dimension. The universe takes its form and reshaping in such a continuity and systemic continuum of organic forms and their inter-relations.

To configure the study of the learning process and the forms of sustainability and ethics embedded in it this paper brings out definitive functions inherent in the meaning of evolutionary epistemology. The idea is emphatically explained by Campbell (1974, pp. 413-463): "The central requirement becomes an epistemology capable of handling *expansions* of knowledge, *breakouts* from the limits of prior wisdom, *scientific discovery*." In our paper such a permanent characteristic of learning process assumes a universal and unique socio-scientific construction.

Interaction

Interactions arise from the diversity of organic relations and their immanent forms that agencies, entities, variables and their relations assume in the study of specific problems, subject to pervasive inter-organic complementarities. Imbuing interactions with their legitimacy emanates from the epistemic foundation of unity of knowledge, whereby the immanent organisms - human and non-human ones - are construed as being pairs of complements. Yet the idea of pairing is one of unity between the good things of life. Oppositely, pairing in modes of competition is the permanent characteristic of the domain of organic competition. Thus a logical contradiction arises from the former kind of unified worldview and the latter kind of social Darwinism (Darwin, 1985, p. 115).

The meaning of interaction in the sense of sustainability by virtue of the learning process means the initial recognition of the legitimacy of paired complementarities as the sure sign of unity of knowledge that is embedded in the systemic domains of diversity. In the social Darwinian sense the contradictory explanation of interaction is worded as Natural Selection by way of competition, marginalism, and association among similar organisms that compete to dominate.

Integration

Integration necessarily breeds as the consequence of interaction. Integration is the process-determined stage of realized unity of being out of its becoming through the interactive process. Integration marks order out of diversity of interactions that search for symbiosis. Integration follows interactions because only discursive, relational and divergent learning situations can yield to consensual order in the socio-scientific domain, and similarly to symbiosis in the inanimate domain of 'everything'. Any consensus that precedes interactions conveys a denial of freedom of participation. Participation is essential in forming a unified world-system by the episteme of unity of knowledge.

How does integration arise out of a system of interaction? In the social domain the bundle of interactions denote possibilities of unity of knowledge in respect of particular issues that altogether interrelate to unify together in forming a mapping of the possibilities onto the unified ensemble (Hubner, 1985). In the physical domain, biological diversities unify together to form unified bundles of types conforming to specific categories. But central to such interaction leading to integration is the fact that knowledge remains the be-all and end-all of the unification process, and hence of the learning process defining sustainability across the knowledge, time and space dimension of reality.

Consequently, inter-systemic diversity is able to unify in the knowledge-relational sense to form the organizational structure of the diverse entities that now become unified -- not by forms in the primal, but by the basis of knowledge. Two examples are given here:

The unification of the North and South geopolitical world-systems into a unified world order is the good form of globalization (Behrman, 2003). So-called Darwinian biological primates converge with human beings in terms of the knowledge organization to share coexistence of the planet earth. Such a process is different from the type of social Darwinism of the selfish gene (Dawkin, 1976).

The above-mentioned are examples of sustainability reflected in entities, but not by the evolution of species by way of competition and replacement of survival of the fittest. Sustainability here means the knowledge that enables coexistence to participate and to share in the resources of the planet earth.

The principle of pervasive complementarities is thereby the simulated normative consequence of improving on all relations of the positivistic nature, either of competition or coexistence. The endemic social reconstruction in the transformation of unwanted positivistic situations into simulated normative possibilities of complementarities, hence unity of being, is a function of knowledge. The episteme of unity of knowledge establishes the functional ontology of knowledge through the social derivation of knowledge flows. These knowledge-flows form the laws and preferences of the socio-scientific order at large. The consequential representations of the resulting world-system are thus knowledge-induced. These induced entities and relations are now capable of learning further on, as explained by expression (1). The result is generating sustainability across continuous learning processes in knowledge, time, and space dimension.

Evolution

Evolution is a function of knowledge-flows causing the bursting of new knowledge-flows from the previously attained ones through the process of learning in unity of knowledge across specific experiences. Such experiences occur at specific points of the knowledge, time and space dimension. Evolutionary epistemology arising from the sequential process of interaction leading to integration is thereby continuous across continuum of knowledge, time and space dimension.

We need to ask how evolution arises from (interaction to integration) and cannot arise in any other juxtaposition. In the knowledge, time and space dimension of the learning world-system, knowledge precedes the occurrence of event. Hence knowledge in its foundational epistemic stage, subsequently followed by the simulation of derived knowledge-flows by means of the discursive mechanism, is firstly a spatial experience. It is then followed by its evolutionary continuity over time.

The knowledge-formation stage of the learning continuum, hence evolutionary epistemology in the continuum of space at a point of time marks the interaction-integration dynamics. This stage of knowledge formation and the simulation process at a given point of time thus establishes the continuum phenomenology (knowledge-induced transformation at a point of time). Next the interaction-integration continuum of phenomenology is protracted over time.

Sustainability thereafter continues by the joint protraction of (interaction-integration) over time, forming thus the logical and cognitive forms across continuums of timal continuity. This phase of continued learning marks emergence of domains of evolutionary epistemology in the res extensa of systems, entities, variables and relations. On such a coevolutionary phenomenological experience in continuum and over time, namely, the representation of the total dynamics over knowledge, time and space dimension pertaining to the episteme of unity of knowledge and its unification relationship with the world-system writes Primavesi (2000, p. 110): "… the evolutionary possibility of our interacting peacefully, fruitfully and happily with other organisms cannot be ruled out".

The feature of continuous and discrete timal coevolutionary learning processes is found in Nozick's argumentation (2001, p. 43). But we remove the relativism of truth in Nozick by the permanence of truth existing as exogenous foundation outside time-space, though truth de facto relates with time-space events to actualize evolutionary epistemology and forms of the world-system. In our terms therefore, truth as knowledge of the foundational episteme is not relativistic. It is the cement in the overarching totality between the derived and discoursed knowledge-flows and the unifying world-system actualized out of social transformation.

Thus epistemic knowledge is the exogenous factor of cause in space-time dimension of the world-system. This is the fundamental origin of sustainability. Without this strong implication we disagree with Nozick who says, "Our theory places truth *within* space-time". Obviously, the meaning of epistemic knowledge is different between the relativistic knowledge, which to us means temporal knowledge-flows. But such knowledge-flows are foundationally derived by the combination of absolutist truth based on text and history of the good things of life, and the discourse of the enlightened society. Braudel (1995) referred to this kind of worldview as the consciousness of history of the long dure. Now in regards to expression (1), sustainability takes a multidimensional meaning. It involves in it res extensa the socially converged structures of science, society, and economy; hence of the embedding political economy as the coordinated unified, interactive, integrative and evolutionary system that we have pronounced.

In the coevolutionary phase of the learning process there is no binding prediction for the evolutionary processes to be definitely truth-knowledge directed. It is possible that contradictory scenarios of evolutionary epistemology can emerge and continue, or they can revert again to the socially constructed path of change. An example is that of the absolutist episteme of unity of knowledge (truth) disintegrating into Darwinian evolutionary processes (Popper, 1988), and then again reverting to the autopoiesis of Gaia, which refers to "the dynamics, self-producing and self-maintaining network of production processes within live organisms" (Primavesi, p. 2).

A note needs to be made on the nature of absolutism contra relativism in the truth-knowledge amalgam. Unlike the many speculative philosophers of all times, in our paper there is no relativism of truth and the epistemic knowledge. We make the argument that, if this was the case then the world and reality would descend into an endless spiral of void and nothingness. There is no basis; everything remains relative, changeable, and hence unfounded. Now to emanate two streams of truths from disparate epistemic origins means the reign of perpetual competition, marginalism and differentiation of existence. In this kind of reality there cannot prevail coexistence, coordination, unity and sustainability. Unfortunately, such a competing and marginalizing dichotomous worldview is the basis of all of western science of nature and society. The resulting political economy then is seen as the study of conflict and competition between unsustainable opposed groups that oppositely claim power over the production, consumption, distribution and ownership of wealth.

Contrary to the idea of relativism of truth, the absolutism of the unitary episteme means irreducibility of certain laws and the socio-scientific implements derived there from by a regressive method of argumentation and belief. Such a truth that is solely premised on the episteme and functional nature of the precept of oneness is absolutely inexorable, implacable. Socio-scientific sustainability now becomes uniquely and universally attainable by means of the extension of unity across nexus of cohering systems res extensa.

In the end, there is no relativism of truth. At the epistemic level the identity of topological mappings causes Truth ≡> Epistemic Knowledge of Oneness ≡> Truth, in the sense of equivalence of relations denoted by ≡>.[1]

Wellbeing

Unlike utility and welfare functions, which are neoclassical concepts of optimum economic objective criteria for the individual and household, and community and government,

---

[1] If possible, let Ω_1 and Ω_2 be two origins of relative truths, if possible. Then $\Omega_1 \cap \Omega_2 = \phi$. Consequently, by the topological property of each and all the mappings (Maddox, 1970), $\{f_i\}$, i=1,2,..,n; the domains of these mappings denoted by $\{x_s\} \cap (x_q\} = \phi$, plus their functional relations taken in bundles have the property, $\{f_p(x_s)\} \cap (f_r(x_q)\} = \phi$; with i, p, q, r, s with assigned numbering either over finite, infinite, discrete or real sets. Hence truths and their consequences over entities, variables, relations and domains remain differentiated. No interaction is possible. Hence integration through the interactive learning process and evolutionary epistemology is impossible. Consequently, ethics and causal interrelationships remain impossible. There is no embedding as of science, society and economy within political economy. Sustainability is permanently denied to such a differentiated system.

Contrarily, if Ω_1 and Ω_2 are relational, then say, $\Omega_1 \cap \Omega_2 \subset \Omega \neq \phi$. In the denumerable case of all numbered topological mappings of variables as mentioned above, it is possible to find an associated non-zero and non-identity scalar factor α, such that $\Omega_1 \bullet \Omega_2 = \alpha.I \subset \Omega \neq \phi$, with I as the identity set. Consequently, Ω_1 and Ω_2 are only near relational inverses of each other with a convergence towards Ω, but with an α-scalar margin of identity.

The conclusion is that with Ω_1 and Ω_2 as disparate knowledge, both of them are encompassed by the law (topology) of Ω. Therefore, $\Omega \equiv$ Truth. Besides, Truth is epistemic Knowledge because it has functional essence displayed by the topological mappings emanating from Ω and routing through Ω_1 and Ω_2. Thus, $\Omega \supseteq$ Truth ≡ Knowledge. But Truth ≡ Knowledge $\subseteq \Omega$. Thereby $\Omega \leftrightarrow \Omega$. Hence, Ω self-references. Likewise, the epistemic Truth ≡ Knowledge self-references (Choudhury & Zaman, 2009). This is the temporal consequence of sustainability as the learning process over continuum and in continuity of the knowledge, time and space dimension. The topological subsets in this sustainability concept is the embedding of science, society, economy in political economy with its relational power of ethicality gained by learning, i.e. interaction, integration and coevolutionary epistemic unity.

The special case is that of the metaphysical ontology of 'being' in unity as Truth equivalent to Knowledge, when α=0. That is error in relative relationalism is zero. Then $\Omega_1 \cap \Omega_2 = \phi$. We now term Ω_1 and Ω_2 as Truth and Falsehood, respectively. Thereby, Truth and Falsehood or Relative Truths become perfectly disjoint.

In the end altogether, sustainability is attainable at a margin of deflection (error) in our mundane experience; sustainability as the perfection of Truth and Knowledge in the epistemic sense remains optimally attained. Consequently, the world-system established on the basis of the epistemic unity of being and becoming does not stand on the relativity of truth. In the mundane sense only, as in the case of science, society, economy embedding in political economy, evolutionary knowledge is simulated by discursive learning on the premise of the epistemic unity and its unified social reconstructions.

wellbeing is a simulative objective criterion function. It conceptualizes and measures the degree to which organic complementarities, reflecting unity of knowledge in the systemic organic relations between the good things exist, or simulative social reconstructions can be improvised.

The social welfare function of welfare economics is defined as a mathematical mapping from the domain of socially selected states to their outcome in the social space. Such a functional map has the following mathematical properties to make it viable for analytical work (Quirk and Saposnik, 1968, pp. 105-108): Social choices comprise vector-bundles X_1 and X_2, such that either X_1 is preferred to X_2 or vice-versa, or these are indifferent to one another at the individual level. These directions of social choices at the individual level are mapped on to the social level while the axioms of economic rationality are preserved. That is preferences remain unchanged along the mapping from the individual to the social level. Transitivity of preferences over bundles of goods (variables) in rational choice at the individual level is preserved at the social level as well.

Social welfare function involving the preservation of the properties of the mapping from the individual to the social level needs a dictator to impose attainment of social welfare level by a given set of social choices. Irrelevant preferences hold for a subset of society, where a truncated form of the welfare function can be extended to the whole of society (Hammond, 1987). It is equally possible to replicate the social welfare function in terms of bundles of social choices, e.g. economic growth, distributive justice, employment and price stability, or in terms of individual utility functions in terms of these variables individually chosen. They are then aggregated socially.

Thus, the principal rationality property of individual utility function and its effect on private choices to make up aggregated order-preserving social choices, namely by means of the postulate of marginal substitution and exogenous preferences and ethical implication, remain in tact both at the individual and social levels. This is the idea of pervasive substitution and marginalism, scarcity of resources, economic rationality in choices, non-dynamic preferences and full information (or bounded rationality as in Simon (1957)). Consequently, the idea of sustainability in the sense of social embedding of interacting, integrating and creatively evolutionary systems is never prevalent in mainstream conception and applications of science, society and economics.

On the other hand, wellbeing function is a mapping from the social space of states with endogenous ethical induction of the variables on to the space of social outcome as measured by the degree of complementarities between the social choices of the good things of life as they are represented in the social variables with ethical induction. In the social wellbeing space ethics is parametrically estimable for which simulation possibilities exist to arrive at better social reconstructions.

A social wellbeing function does not stand alone. It is there for purposes of evaluation of the prevalent state that can lead into simulated states of social reconstruction. Hence the social wellbeing function is estimated and simulated with respect to a system of circular causation interrelations between the variables, all of which are endogenously ethically induced.

There is no substitution between the variables and functional inputs (e.g. consumer utility indexes) in the wellbeing function, as it is otherwise found in the case of the welfare function. The implication of these two properties is this: There is permanent substitution between social choices in the welfare function; and pervasive complementarities or social reconstruction of social choices in the wellbeing function. Sustainability explained by the embedding of science, society and economy in the social political economy by way of continuous learning process in unity of knowledge as the episteme is never a possibility in the order of substitution between possibilities. Possibilities are always to be complemented for augmenting knowledge-flows and their material inductions as ethically-induced resources for human development and reproduction of resources, rather all kinds of resources for life-sustenance.

With the continuous augmentation of resource as the result of the growth of knowledge-flows and their induction of social variables into evolutionary discovery of possibilities, the contrary core postulate of scarcity in received economic theory, or Darwinian conception of biology and anthropology, and optimization concepts of scientific theories are all replaced by the theory of coevolutionary symbiosis. A theory for this kind of dynamics is uniquely and universally explained by the Interaction-Integration-Evolutionary (IIE) phases of the learning processes, as explained earlier.

While the problem of sustainability is seen in the eyes of scarcity in the case of mainstream common understanding by science, society and economics (Coombs, 1990; Martinez-Alier, 1987), scarcity is abandoned in a logical way in the sustainability concept of complementary learning processes (Daly et al, 1992). The postulate of diminishing marginal returns to scale of received economic and social theory does not exist in the knowledge-induced learning space and its model of organic unity of knowledge (Romer, 1986). Yet coexistence is the possibility, unlike the evolutionary process models of Darwinian type of social choice (Myrdal, 1987) and science (Hull, 1988).

Indeed, knowledge for participation and sharing is power. When knowledge-flows continue under this epistemic framework of induced possibilities, the latter artifacts become the bastion of rediscovered resources ad-infinitum. Now the wellbeing function becomes exclusively an objective criterion of learning processes and interactive-integrative-evolutionary (IIE) systems premised on epistemic unity of knowledge.

Therefore, pervasive complementarities are inherent in the systemic interrelations between the variables chosen to describe the wellbeing function. The feedback relations that emanate from the estimation followed by the simulation of the wellbeing function in terms of the interrelations between the variables that are pervasively complementary to each other form a system of circular causation relations.

The system of circular causation relations are used for dual purpose. Firstly, they are estimated by using positivistic data from the 'as is' state of the sustainability problem under examination. The unity dynamics of being and becoming towards attaining a semblance of social reconstruction of a unified world-system requires coefficients to be simulated into better values to exhibit inter-variable complementarities. This simulated change in the coefficients convey the idea of social reconstruction or social simulation from a positivistic order of 'as is' reality into a normative aspired transformation for an 'ought-to-be' better world of sustainability. The latter world-system is gained by unity of knowledge induced in its unity of the problem under study. In such a context, the social political economy takes its meaning of embedding between the synergies of science, society and economy (Choudhury, 2003, 2007). The conformable meanings of systemic globalism and globalization follow. See later.

Social (re-) construction

The empirical and applied part of the theory of unity of knowledge on the issues and problems of the world-system res extensa is established by the estimation followed by simulation of the wellbeing function, subject to the system of circular causation relations.

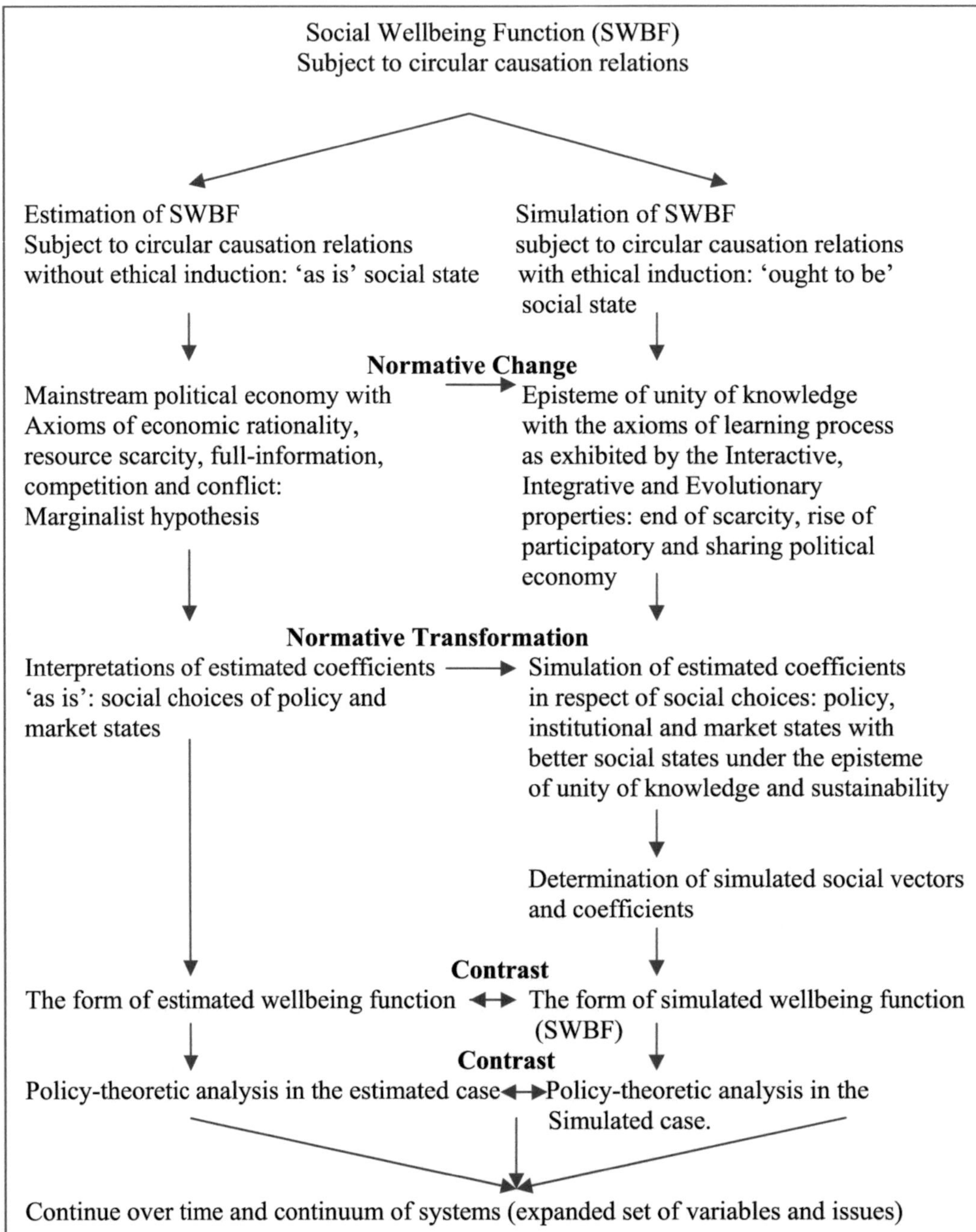

Fig. 1. Schema of social reconstruction out of estimated leading to simulation

For further details see the next section. The meaning of social reconstruction is that of normatively recommending structural change, biodiversity, policy diversity, and program developments for sustaining a coexisting, participatory and endogenously knowledge-induced world-system of possibilities. The result is simulation of social wellbeing towards attaining better states out of the fallen states of marginalism, differentiation and resource paucity that mainstream idea of sustainability otherwise conveys through its constricted models of science, society and economy.

Despite the process-oriented structure of the learning world-system for sustainability, the foundational episteme, theory, dynamics and consequences of our wellbeing simulation subject to circular causation results are opposed to the dialectical process-oriented worldview of mainstream political economy. The dialectical process of the unification dynamics is based on unity of knowledge as the power enabling sustainability. The dialectical process of conflict and power in mainstream science, society and economy studies do not establish a unified world-system. Even the idea of consciousness attained by creative evolution and learning in the framework of unity of knowledge, time and space dimension is opposed to the idea of consciousness and the universe in space-time dimension. The latter form is conveyed by Quantum Physics (Kafatos & Nadeau, 1990), Relativity Physics (Einstein, trans. Lawson, 1960), and political economy (Wallerstein, 1998).

The following figure shows the template of social reconstruction from 'as- is' to 'as-it-ought-to-be' social state. Further details on the social reconstruction perspective are given in the next section on the construct of the learning-process model of sustainability.

4. The knowledge-induced formalism of learning process in unity of knowledge as the episteme

The various characteristics, definitions and explanations of critical terms presented in the preceding sections are now assembled in the following model representation of the learning process of unity of knowledge and the knowledge-induced unified world-system. The precept of unity of knowledge that grounds the entire study of sustainability in its embedded social sense is pervasive in the model shown by expression (2).

Firstly, there is unity at the foundational epistemic origin by way of enunciating the law. This primal stage is denoted by $[\Omega \to_S \{\theta\}] \equiv \{\theta$; given the epistemic law, $(\Omega,S)\}$. The epistemic law denoted by (Ω,S) defines the conception formed by knowledge-flows that are socially discoursed. Knowledge-flows that set up the conception of the derived worldview are denoted by ordinally assigned $\{\theta\}$-values in the discursive forums of science, society and economy embedding. S is the mapping of the epistemic Law into functional discourse, and onwards into material and cognitive concrescence of reality.

The functional ontology $\mathbf{f}(.)$ denoting logical formalism unravels extended unity between the knowledge-induced variables pertaining to the problem under study. The knowledge-induced variables are denoted by $\{\mathbf{x}(\theta)\}$. The networked and participative nature of causality between the knowledge-induced variables is denoted by the vector of relations, $\mathbf{f}(\theta,\mathbf{x}(\theta))$.The bold notations denote vectors.

The limiting value of θ in the discursive $\{\theta\}$-space is the result of yet another unity process of learning, the critical characteristics of the learning process in unity of knowledge. It comprises the total phase of Interaction, Integration coming together and leading up to the point of creative Evolution to establish sustainability by continuity across continuums of systems.

Unity of the knowledge-induced world-system with particularity of the problems under investigation is shown by the evaluation of the wellbeing function $W(\mathbf{x}(\theta))$. Unity between the variables and evaluation of systemic unity of the induced world-system under study is sought at any stage of learning by simulating $W(\mathbf{x}(\theta))$, subject to circular causation relations between the $\mathbf{f}(\theta,\mathbf{x}(\theta)$-relations.

Thus the principle of pervasive complementarities between the variables explained by their interrelations in the circular causation system establishes the measured degree of unity between the variables in the problem under investigation. The principle of pervasive complementarities (hence systemic participation) is an empirical representation of unity of the knowledge-induced cognitive phenomena.

Unity is also shown by the recursive nature of coevolutionary learning processes that carry evolutionary epistemology involving $(\theta_N, \mathbf{x}_N(\theta_N), f(\theta_N, \mathbf{x}_N(\theta_N))$ across new knowledge-flows and their induced forms subscripted by N. Now there come about expanding organic unity (symbiosis) across systemic continuums and continuity of knowledge, time and space dimension.

The formal model of learning process in unity of knowledge and the knowledge-induced world-system is now formalized in expression (2).

(Ω,S,θ): $[\Omega\rightarrow_S\{\theta\}] \rightarrow \mathbf{x}(\theta)$

$\downarrow(\theta,\mathbf{x}(\theta)) \rightarrow$ Simulation $W(\mathbf{x}(\theta))\rightarrow$ subject to, circular caudation relations denoted by vector of interrelations $\mathbf{f}(\theta,\mathbf{x}(\theta)$ $\rightarrow$ determination of θ-ethical index as the simulated value of wellbeing $\rightarrow$ evolution into new θ_N-ethical i.e.knowledge-flows and knowledge-induced values $\downarrow$ continuity of learning across symbiotic continuums (2)

5. A brief review of the literature on the process concept of sustainability

Our interest in this paper being on sustainability as a medium of social reconstruction, we therefore focus our review of the literature on the process modeling of systemic learning. This is a new field of inquiry and properly belongs to the area of systems and cybernetics (Choudhury & Hossain, 2007, 2010). Though we make a brief coverage of a review of the literature in this field, our focus lies on the Gaia concept of process-oriented change leading to sustainability as an embedding concept of participative worldview (Primavesi, op cit).

Along the lines of the Gaia concept of sustainability as embedded participative formalism in science and society, there are the important works of Maturana and Varela (1998), Margulis (1998), Lovelock (1990, 2000). These authors have a unique message regarding the symbiosis of our relational existence that is reflected in their version of the microbiological Gaia. The common message is well-expressed as one of physical and relational coexistence contra bloody competition and marginalizing power of the strong over the weak, as per social Darwinism.

The important note in this theory is paid to microcosms that form the large scale universe of macrocosm. It is in this area that the Gaia shares a distinctive commonness with the learning worldview of epistemic unity of knowledge. But the epistemic worldview we propound in this paper is not constricted by material limitation as exhibited, explained and delimited by the microbiological phenomenon. The micro-organism of knowledge, mind and matter do continue to play important cohesive roles in defining the social political economy as a world-system embedding of the organic interrelations between science, society and economy. This kind of organic unity in diversity of subsystems also conveys the idea of globalism (and globalization) that we will refer to below. The microcosmic order indeed is at the core of the building blocks that rise accumulatively in emergent hubs of interactively integrated and evolved entities.

There is no macrocosmic order as a system separate from the microcosmic one. There is no microcosmic disaggregating of the macrocosmic order into microcosmic entities. There is no lateral addition of the microcosmic subsystems and their variables into a microcosmic totality. There is only a complex aggregation and organization of coordinated forms from the microcosmic level to the macrocosmic level. Everything borrows such a complex systemic and cybernetic meaning of symbiosis, change, freedom and organization resting on the fundamental episteme of unity of knowledge.

At the present time, a gentle flow of papers is appearing in the systems and cybernetic treatment of complementary learning phenomenon. Despite this intellectual advancement in a new field, it is noted that the concept of complementarism is not understood as organic unity of being through the process of becoming in unity of knowledge.

Prigogine (op cit) formulates the idea of cognitive being and becoming in view of the idea of interrelatedness, as in social phenomenon and biological thermodynamics in the following way: Entropy is the inevitable property of change over time. This causes systems of chemical interaction to become highly unstable. Chemical states can be discerned only with probabilistic laws (Boltzmann's law of thermodynamics). When applied to the theme of sustainability, which involves biological and ecological processes of change, consideration of entropy is of much interest. According to the probabilistic nature of entropy in the process of change over time, sustainability becomes a phenomenon in entropy. Sustainability is thereby never attained except with a degree of probability attached to the states of perturbations around an equilibrium point. In the broader sense of the term such evolutionary equilibrium characterized by perturbations and increasing entropy describes dissipative states of the thermodynamic world. Likewise, there occur probabilistic states of dissipated sustainability in the natural order system. We can extend this explanation to the social and economic world of perturbations and process (Georgescu-Roegen, 1971).

Yet this is not the conclusion of our paper in which the epistemic origin of unity can lead into probabilistically determined evolutionary equilibriums of perturbation, but still a state of reverse-entropy can be gained (Choudhury et al, 1998). The resulting state of sustainability with knowledge-induction is a heightened state of denseness in equilibrium. Hence points are gravitated towards dense equilibrium points. The distanced points of dissipative energy away from the dense equilibrium points are reduced in number. Consequently, there exists a high probability of attaining sustainability around densely gravitated knowledge-induced equilibriums that are evolutionary in nature. This is the case of reverse entropy in accordance with the model of bifurcations in fields that are gravitated towards the densely equilibrium points.

Yet bifurcations occur profusely in such learning fields by virtue of the diversity of states that occur out of interactions. Examples of such states in political economy are risk and production diversifications leading to resource augmentation, investments and production; and thereby enabling ownership and distribution of resources, income and wealth. Consumption too, following product diversification, becomes diversified. All of the above consequences taken together, though with bifurcation between possibilities of wellbeing, yield effective sustainability by way of systemic embedding.

The model of knowledge-formation by way of Hegelian type dialectics is process-oriented. Carchedi (1991) presents such a model of dialectics in respect of the Marxian concept of money and goods across stages of social transformation. The resulting Money-Commodity-Money model (MCM), on which Heilbroner (1986) expounds his version of a Marxian dialectical model of the monetarist political economy emulates the dialectical dynamics in it. Money now is seen as a process of financial resource accumulation that arises by recycling a quantity of money back and forth between capital accumulation and interest rates creating intertemporal savings.

The learning model of epistemic unity of knowledge also displays dialectical dynamics (Choudhury, 2009b). But the dialectics is premised on the renewal of knowledge-flows and the induced wellbeing of variables of the unified world-system. Money and output, and thereby production, consumption, ownership and distribution are all together symbolic variables that are unified together by recursive causality between them. Consequently, the MCM model explains the evolutionary dynamics of unification by interrelationship between money and the real economy in the wellbeing function that is simulated subject to the circular causation relations in the variables. Now money as an independent and exogenous economic variable loses its meaning.

Sztompka (1991) presents a dialectical model of social evolution in the learning space of the Marxist type. Yet the human consciousness in this model is derived from the premise of rationalism as the episteme. In this regard Sztompka writes (p. 115) : "Our model is certainly 'anthropocentric'; it is founded on the assumption that the irreducible component of society, its only ultimate ontological substratum, is people. Therefore we cannot but seek the ultimate, primary mover of society in their traits and properties - in brief, in human nature." Consequently, power and conflict become the defining characteristics of the society that Sztompka describes. The case is similar to Carchedi's description of Marxist political economy. The normative implication of such a model is that sustainability remains a failed hope. Such a dismay is expressed emphatically by Heilbroner (1991, p. 20) in his following words: "Thus to anticipate the conclusions of our inquiry, the answer to whether we can conceive of the future other than as a continuation of the darkness, cruelty, and disorder of the past seems to me to be no; and to the question of whether worse impends, yes."

In the episteme of unity of knowledge in our paper, the social order is a unified systemic whole. Society is the result of integrative preferences of participating individuals and groups, communities and nations. The integrative preferences arise out of their interactive preferences through the medium of discourse and self-institution-market circular causal interrelationships. Preferences are thereby dynamic, evolutionary and complex in nature, though they are guided into symbiosis by the consciousness of self-organization, institutions, science, society and economy.

In respect of the theme of sustainability and complex aggregation of preferences, Hawley's model (op cit) of human ecology stands out as an example. Ecology is explained as a system of organizations inter-relating the human organizational world-system and the environmental world-system. To this I will add the significant place of markets and institutions, ethics and behavior in the ecological convergence process to its well-definition as a human system and a cybernetic field of study. This is also how Johannessen (1998) presents his idea of organizations as social system in search of a system and cybernetic theory of adaptive behavior.

Hawley presents the characteristics of his human ecological model as comprising three significant properties. These properties agree with the procedural aspects of the learning model of epistemic unity of knowledge that we propound in this paper.

Firstly, the adaptation stage is one of recognizing diversity of interactions between the members; likewise participating and complementary entities. These can also be taken as formal representations of states by means of mathematical and statistical variables.

The second stage is Hawley's maximum stage of adaptation. In the case of the learning-process epistemic worldview this stage is signified by integration in the holistic sense, consensus in the social sense, and equilibrium in the scientific sense. There is no optimum in the learning process of continuous simulation of knowledge and its induced possibilities. Only evolutionary equilibriums exist, like Thurow's (1996) punctuated equilibriums and Grandmont's (1989) temporary equilibrium.

Hawley's third stage of human ecology model is resumption of the first two stages by continued development and burst of new information. Subsequently, the renewed capacity for the movement of material artifacts continues.

Hawley ascribes these three stages as the adaptive, growth, and evolutionary stages. When placed in the framework of knowledge-sharing of the epistemic origin, the learning model is in agreement with Hawley's. But Hawley's model is limited to the environmental and social ecological dimensions.

Even with large extant of stochastic variations and uncertainty in the ecological order, either of the biological type -- hence environment and systemic globalism -- or of the type of embedded political economy, hence globalization (Thurow, op cit), the worrisome concern is voiced, as by Maurer (1999, p. 23). On the emergent problem of complexity Maurer writes, "The inability to determine causality ultimately arises from a lack of information about the system being considered". This problem is then associated with Maurer's concern with stochastic largeness of the population size, intensive variability caused by inter-member causality, and uncertainty in the behavior of the population membership.

These large-scale complexity problems are resolved in the case of the empirical description of the epistemic learning model -- at least theoretically. The system of circular causation relations based on evolutionary epistemology configures the evolving system in processes. Processes and the empirical evaluation of causality within time-periods depend on the availability of knowledge and its unifying impact on the ecological members. The limits to this kind of evolutionary and overarching systemic configuration are due to the constraints on the availability of systemically generated information along evolutionary processes, lack of appropriate computer-assisted algorithm, and indeterminacy of formalism for the functional ontology of the system, beyond a discursive approach to qualitative modeling of stochasticity.

6. Sustainability question in systemic globalism and globalization

Globalism is the phenomenology of intensively interactive, integrative and evolutionary domains of all forms of systems spanning conceptual ones and entire human experience. Such is also the idea of system ensemble advanced by Hubner (op cit) in respect of his theory based on a criticism of linear understanding of history and science. Is globalism in its systemic, evolutionary and unifying perspective a semblance of postmodern thought that bases it worldview on non-foundationalism? I raise the modern-postmodern contrasting ideal in reference to the IIE perspective explaining globalism by raising the following question (Choudhury, 1999, p. 3): "What is post-modernity in the context of a changing world order in respect to its economic, social and scientific dimensions? To answer this question one needs to fathom the complexity of interrelationships among human systems. A perspicuous explanation of such a vast web of systemic interrelationships had hitherto remained unexplained in the methodology of modernism. Post-modernity is a response to this modernist incompleteness. It is seen as a methodological questioning of the individualistic worldview of capitalist economic theory underlying modernity by a process-oriented possibility in human experience". Our epistemological explanations in this paper have amply established the direction of post-modernist thought in the framework of the episteme of unity of knowledge and its impact on the unified world-system.

Globalization that is of the capitalist genre is either of the following kinds of interactively aggregated world-system: Either the individual rational preferences, even though of individualized groups, aggregate in the linear way to establish a utilitarian society and economy and the attenuating scientific formalism, or the interactive aggregation of such preferences occur as dialectical evolution of power and hegemony for governance ad-infinitum. The episteme of unity of knowledge is absent for a conscious understanding of a relational world-system. This idea of methodological individualism is pervasive in the globalism of science, society and economy, hence in the capitalist political economy of globalization. In the sciences as well, Herman Weyl (2009, p. 202-203) voices his concern regarding the episteme of unity of knowledge: "Being and Knowing, where should we look for unity? I tried to make clear that the shield of Being is broken beyond repair. .... Only on the side of Knowing there may be unity.". The dichotomy of being and becoming remains in this kind of scientific thought.

But globalization if conceptualized, established, and pursued by a globally accepted ethical standard (Commission on Global Governance, 1995) need not be a denigrated human experience. The preferences of interacting participants in unifying globalism remain entrenched in complexity. Globalization is now an experience in globalism with a human face. It is expressed by convergence to the commonly determined ethical goals. International discourse and consensus, paradigmatic shift, and awareness to raise consciousness in and of 'everything' become the determining and sustaining factors of globalization with a human experience (Dunning, 2003). We turn now to one such global experience for the wellbeing of the human race and the ecological entirety spanning intergenerational future.

7. Climatic sustainability by the discursive model of unity of knowledge: The Copenhagen Summit 2009[2]

Copenhagen Summit 2009 is where representatives from 192 nations assembled to conduct UN Climate talks with the objective of achieving a binding document towards saving the planet from climatic problems and the fallouts of climate change. The summit concluded at a document called 'Copenhagen Accord' after seeing sharp differences between rich and poor countries, as also differences amongst the highest polluting nations.

---

[2] This section is extracted from Dr. Lubna Sarwath Mohammad's doctoral thesis entitled, "Institutional political economy – Islam and the occident: methodology with a case study of Sultanate of Oman", Faculty of Economics (Islamic economics and finance), Trisakti University, Jakarta, Indonesia. The section applies the methodology of unity of knowledge as explained in this paper to an important example of the institutional case of political economy in global discourse.

What have been portrayed as the positive developments at the summit are fund mobilization from industrialized nations to meet the challenges of climate change for developing countries to the tune of $100 billion by the year 2020. This is expected to cope with adverse climate changes, drought and floods. Also a short-term fund of $30 billion over 3 years by 2012 has been provided for adapting to climate changes and shifting to clean energy. A method of verification of greenhouse gas emission cuts has been agreed upon. Countries are to list actions taken to cut global warming pollutants by specific amounts. A target has been set to limit average temperature increase to below 2 degrees centigrade.

Provisions of Accord	Failures
- $100 billion fund mobilization for developing nations by 2020; - $30 billion short term funds over 3 years beginning 2010 for developing nations; - adopting a method of verification of green house gas polluter cuts; - target set to contain average global temperature rise by 2 degree C; - countries to list actions taken to cut carbon emissions; - industrialized nations under Kyoto 1997 to face possible sanctions upon failure to meet emission-cut targets;	- no binding carbon emission cuts on industrialized nations and big polluters; - no trajectory to contain global warming - no plan for protection of world's rain forests; - no agenda for containment of large-scale deforestation of Indonesia and Brazil; - USA not covered under Kyoto 1997 and hence not under sanction threat for failure to meet emission-cut targets;

Chart 1. Failures and success of the accord reached at the Copenhagen Summit 2009

The accord though failed to conclude on binding greenhouse gas emission cuts to reach the target of 2 degree centigrade. The agreed upon cuts in July 2009 fall short of avoiding dangerous effects of adverse climate change. Method of verification was the key demand from the USA and was not acceptable to China. Industrialized nations covered under Kyoto Protocol 1997 can face possible sanctions, if failing to meet the emission cuts and the USA is not covered under the Kyoto 1997. No plan has been drafted to protect the world's rain forests vital for healthy climate. There was no payment for 40 poor tropical countries to protect their woodlands. Non-industrial pollution by way of deforestation for logging, cattle-grazing and crops has made Brazil and Indonesia third and fourth largest carbon emitters after China -- and USA was not highlighted.

Having tabled the salient features of the Copenhagen Summit 2009 in terms of failures and the accord contours, we will now examine the functionality of Consultative Participatory interactive, integrative and evolutionary (IIE) learning process by simulating the Copenhagen Summit of December 7-18, 2009 as Copenhagen Consultative Participatory Summit 2009.

The under-mentioned points form the foundation of the psychological setup of an envisioned Copenhagen Consultative Participatory (IIE) discourse:

- Knowledge-building as a learning process is at the core of the IIE-learning process and is conceptualized on a particular pragmatic axiom.
- IIE-learning process admits of 'impossibility of certainty of knowledge'; learning is simulacra of possibilities.

- There is absoluteness of the epistemic stock of knowledge, viz., unity of knowledge to form the substance or theme of the Summit.
- The vastness of unknown knowledge cannot be fully exhaustible in our worldly learning experience.
- The method of optimality is replaced by evolutionary learning form of simulation of values and realistic targets.
- Transparency, accountability, judicious responsibility and broad-based development as the standard for conduct of decision-making and decision-taking prevail, or are aimed for.
- Realization of unity of knowledge and unity of systems through participatory development, pervasive complementarities, and circular causation organic linkages is the method.
- A degree of unity of systems and knowledge as criteria for wellbeing is evaluated.
- Ensuring wide representation and broad participation for large interactions and consensus for eventual implementation is institutionally necessary.

The participants of our proposed Copenhagen Consultative Participatory Summit would then work with a consciousness that permeates towards realization of the epistemic organic unity in the systems. The theory of political economy of institutionalism does not underestimate the role of psychology in socio-scientific and economic study. These reckon the intention and attitude of shared participation as a component IIE-process variable.

We argue that the natural systems are interacting with the world-systems, even as the natural systems and the world-systems are interacting among themselves as well. These result in intra- and inter- systemic synergies leading to organic symbiosis. Yet, environmental issues and ecological factors have been rendered exogenous at strategic policy designing for economic growth and development in Copenhagen Summit. In the Consultative Participatory type Copenhagen Summit, the entities representing technology, production, geo-political strategies, and capturing of markets are made to mutually interact.

The proposed Copenhagen Consultative Participation in this paper would have the in-built IIE-learning process. The knowledge-building proposals in such a Copenhagen Consultative Participatory institution would follow the methodological function of the IIE-recursive learning process. At each round of the discourse, the entities would be interacting with the epistemic premise of unity of knowledge. Under repeated recursive discourses on the serious concerns of climate change, the devastating repercussions are addressed in the light of the complaints of the developing countries and the historical faults of developed nations.

At Copenhagen Consultative Participatory body each round of discourse is having a mechanism to recall the episteme of organic unity. The knowledge deduced and the simulated levels of common wellbeing of the participating entities and the corresponding variables in this regard would go through a circular causation knowledge-gaining process.

The interactive, integrative and evolutionary form of learning in unity of knowledge in our proposed Copenhagen Consultative Participatory institutional model is shown in Figure 2.

8. Conclusion

This paper has broken new grounds on the theme of social reconstruction of globalization by examining the epistemological roots of thought, model conceptualization and application underlying the science, society and economy embedding. The theme of social political economy in this epistemic sense was laid down in a synergistic model of embedding

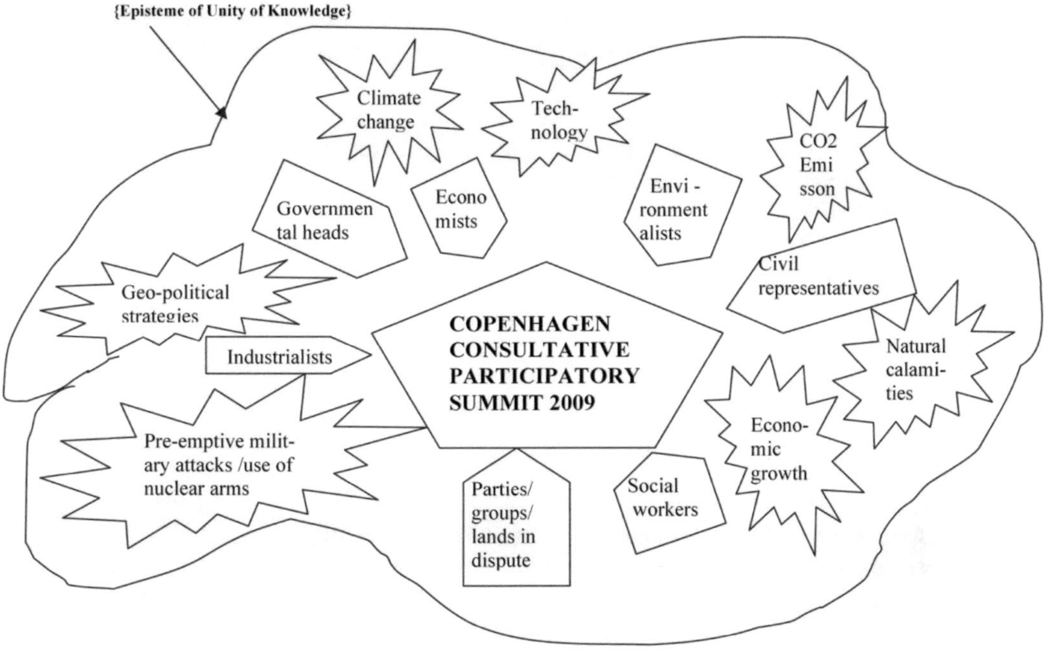

Fig. A representation of the proposed Copenhagen Consultative Participatory Summit 2009

between the interacting, integrative and evolutionary domains of human activities. The substantively new idea of political economy in this social sense was thus established. Such a definition recognizes the traditional one on conflict and power in the ownership, distributional and production of resources. But it extends to the moral and ethical foundation of unity of knowledge and its epistemic influence on the construction of politico-economic issues under study. The theme of globalization was thus placed in the midst of this worldview.

The paper also formulated a non-mathematical textual version of a model of extensive participation. The premise of unity of knowledge and its structural representation in the global world-system involving science, society and economics were thus explained. Such a path towards moral and ethical reconstruction of the social question was considered as the way towards a new social contract under globalization with human face.

The application of the model of unity of knowledge and its discursively driven organic participation to the case of the Copenhagen Summit on Climate Change was done. In this way the future model of global political economy with embedded synergy in it was exemplified for political and institutional consideration.

9. References

Barbier, E. 1986, "Economic growth: the political economy of resource misallocation", in Ekin, P. ed. *The Living Economy, a New Economics in the Making*, London, Eng: Routledge and Kegan Paul, pp. 10-12.

Barrow, J.D. 1991, *Theories of Everything, the Quest for Ultimate Explanation*, Oxford, Eng: Oxford University Press.

Behrman, J.N. 2003, "Transformation of society: implications for globalization", in Dunning, J.H. ed. *Making Globalization Good,* Oxford, UK: Oxford University Press, pp. 108-144.

Braudel, F. 1995, *A History of Civilizations,* New York, NY: Penguin Books.

Campbell, D.T. 1974, "Evolutionary epistemology", in Schilpp, P.A. ed. *The Philosophy of Karl Popper,* LaSalle: Open Court, pp. 413-463.

Carchedi, G. 1991, *Frontiers of Political Economy,* New York, NY: Verso.

Choudhury, M.A. 1999, *Comparative Economic Theory, Occidental and Islamic Perspectives,* Norwell, MA: Kluwer Academic Publishers.

Choudhury, M.A. 2004, *The Islamic World-System, a Study in Polity-Market Interaction,* London, Eng: RoutledgeCurzon.

Choudhury, M.A. 2007, *The Universal Paradigm and the Islamic World-System, Economy, Society, Ethics and Science,* Singapore: World Scientific Publication.

Choudhury, M.A. 2009a, "Which of the two? – knowledge or time", *Philosophical Papers and Review,* 1:1.

Choudhury, M.A. 2009b, "Dialectics in socio-scientific inquiry: Islam contra Occident", *International Journal of Sociology and Social Policy,* 29:9/10.

Choudhury, M.A. 2011, "Overlapping generation model for Islamic asset valuation: a phenomenological application", Chapter 8 of his *Islamic Economics and Finance, an Epistemological Inquiry,* West Yorkshire, UK: Emerald Publication.

Choudhury, M.A. M. Shahadat Hossain & M. Mohiuddin 1998, "Violent effects of deforestation and watershed management on wave and ocean current cybernetical relationships: an empirical study with respect to Bangladesh ecology", *Kybernetes: International Journal of Systems and Cybernetics,* Vol. 27, No.5.

Choudhury, M.A.& Hossain, M.S. 2007, *Computing Reality,* Tokyo, Japan: Blue Ocean Press for Aoishima Research Institute.

Choudhury, M.A.& Hossain, M.S, 2010, "Neuro-Cybernetics of socio-Scientific systems", *Mind and Society,* Vol. 9, pp. 59-83.

Choudhury, M.A. & Zaman, S.I. 2009, "Self-referencing as socio-scientific methodology in contrasting paradigms", *Kybernetes, International Journal of Cybernetics, Systems and Management Studies,* 38:6.

Committee on Global Governance, 1995, *Our Global Neighbourhood,* Oxford, UK: Oxford University Press.

Coombs, H.C. 1990, *The Return of Scarcity,* Cambridge, UK: Cambridge University Press.

Daly, H.E. 1992, "From empty-world to full-world economics: recognizing an historical turning point in economic development", in R. Goodland, H.E. Daly, S. el-Serafy & B. von Droste Eds. *Environmentally Sustainable Economic Development: Building on Brundtland,* pp. 29-40, Paris, France: UNESCO.

Darwin, C. 1985 [1859] ed. J.W. Barrow, *The Origin of Species by Means of Natural Selection,* London, Eng: Penguin.

Dawkins, R. 1976, *The Selfish Gene,* New York: Oxford University Press.

Descartes, R. 1954, "Discourse on method", in S. Commins & Linscott, R.N. Eds. *Man & the Universe: The Philosophers of Science,* pp. 163-220, New York, NY: Pocket Books, Inc

Dunning, J.H. 2003, "The moral imperatives of global capitalism: an overview", in Dunning, J.H. ed. *Making Globalization Good,* Oxford, UK: Oxford University Press, pp. 11-40.

Einstein, A. 1960, *Relativity, The Special and the General Theory* (London, Eng: Methuen.

Foucault, M. trans. A.M. Sheridan 1972, *The Archeology of Knowledge and the Discourse on Language*, New York: Harper Torchbooks.

Georgescu-Roegen, N. 1971, *The Entropy Law and the Economic Process*, Cambridge, MA: Harvard University Press.

Grandmont, J-M. 1989, "Temporary equilibrium", in Eatwell, J. Milgate, M & Newman, P. eds. *New Palgrave: General Equilibrium*, W.W. Norton, New York, NY

Gruber, T.R. 1993. "A translation approach to portable ontologies", *Knowledge Acquisition*, Vol. 5, No. 2, 199-200.

Hammond, P.J. 1987, "Social choice: the science of the impossible", in Feiwel, J.R. (ed.) *Arrow and the Foundations of the Theory of Economic Policy*, London, UK: Macmillan Press Ltd. Pp. 116-134.

Hawley, A. 1986, *Human Ecology*, Chicago, IL: University of Chicago Press.

Heidegger, M. trans. A. Hofstadter, 1988. *The Basic Problems of Phenomenology*, Bloomington & Indianapolis, IN: Indiana University Press.

Heilbroner, R.L. 1986, "The ideology of capital", in his *The Nature and Logic of Capitalism*, Chapter 5, New York, NY: W.W. Norton.

Heilbroner, R.L. 1991. *An Inquiry into the Human Prospect*, New York, NY: W.W. Norton. Heiskala, 2003

Hubner, K. trans. P.R. Dixon, Jr. & H.M. Dixon 1985, "Foundations of a universal historistic theory of the empirical sciences", in his *Critique of Scientific Reason*, pp.105-
122, Chicago, IL: The University of Chicago Press.

Hull, D.L. 1988, *Science as a Process, an Evolutionary Account of the Social and Conceptual Development of Science*, Chicago, IL: University of Chicago Press.

Inglott, P.S. 1990, "The rights of future generations: some socio-philosophical considerations", in S. Busuttil, E. Agius, P.S. Inglott & T. Macelli Eds. *Our Responsibilities Towards Future Generations*, pp. 17-27, Malta: Foundation for International Studies & UNESCO.

Johannessen, J-A. 1998, "Organizations as social systems: the search for a systemic theory of organizational innovation processes", *Kybernetes, the International Journal of Systems and Cybernetics*, 27: 4&5, pp. 359-387.

Kafatos, M. & Nadeau, R. 1990. "The road untraveled: enlarging the new logical framework of complementarity", in their *Conscious Universe*, New York, NY: Sringer-Verlag.

Kim, W. C & Mauborgne, R. 2005, *Blue Ocean Strategy*, Boston, MA: Harvard Business Press.

Koizumi, T. 1993, *Interdependence and Change in the Global System*, Lanham, Maryland: University Press of America.

Lovelock, J. 1990, "Gaia and the balance of nature", in Schrift, A.D. (ed.) *The Logic of the Gift*, London, UK: Routledge.

Lovelock, J. 2000, "Foreword", in Primavesi, A. *Sacred Gaia*, London, Eng.

Maddox, I.J. 1970, *Elements of Functional Analysis*, Cambridge, Eng: Cambridge University Press.

Margulis, L. 1998, *The Symbiotic Planet*, London, UK: Weidenfield and Nicolson.

Martinez-Alier, J. 1987, *Ecological Economics: Energy, Environment and Society*, Oxford, UK: Basil Blackwell.

Maturana, H.R. and Varela, F.J. 1998, The Tree of Knowledge, Boston, USA: Shambhala.

Maurer, B.A. 1999, "Communities as non-linear systems", in his *Untangling Ecological Complexity*, Chicago, ILL: The University of Chicago Press.

Myrdal, G. 1987. "Utilitarianism and modern economics", in Feiwel, G.R. *Arrow and the Foundations of the Theory of Economic Policy*, London, Eng: Macmillan, pp. 273-278.

Nozick, R. 2001, *Invariances, the Structure of the Objective World*, Cambridge, MA, USA.

Phelps, E.S. 1989, "Distributive justice", in J. Eatwell, P. Newman & M. Milgate eds. *New Palgrave: Social Economics*, New York, NY: W.W. Norton.

Popper, K. 1988, "Natural selection and the emergence of mind", in G. Radnitzky & W.W. Bartley, III Eds. *Evolutionary Epistemology, Rationality, and the Sociology of Knowledge*, pp. 139-54, La Salle, IL: Open Court.

Prigogine, I. 1980. *From Being to Becoming*, San Francisco, CA: W.H. Freeman.

Primavesi, A. 2000, *Sacred Gaia*, London, Eng: Routledge.

Quirk, J. and Saposnik, R. 1968, *Introduction to General Equilibrium Theory and Welfare Economics*, New York, NY: McGraw-Hill Book Co.

Rawls, J. 1971, *A Theory of Justice*, Cambridge, MA: Harvard University Press.

Romer, P.M. 1986, "Increasing returns and long-run growth", *Journal of Political Economy*, Vol. 94, pp. 1002-37.

Sarwath, L.M. 2011, *Institutional political economy – Islam and the occident: methodology with a case study of Sultanate of Oman*, unpublished doctoral thesis, Faculty of Economics (Islamic Economics and Finance), Trisakti University, Jakarta, Indonesia.

Simon, H. 1957, *Models of Man*, New York, NY: John Wiley & Sons.

Sklair, L. 2002. "Transnational corporations and capitalist globalization", in *Globalization, Capitalism and Its Alternatives*, Oxford, Eng: Oxford University Press, pp. 59-83.

South Commission, 1990, *The Challenge to the South*, Oxford, Eng: Oxford University Press.

Staniland, M. 1985, "The fall and rise of political economy", in *What is Political Economy? A Study of Social Theory and Underdevelopment*, pp. 10-35, New Haven, CT: Yale University Press, 1985.

Sztompka, P. 1991, *Society in Action, the Theory of Social Becoming*, Chicago, IL: University of Chicago Press.

Thurow, L.C. 1996, "New games, new rules, new strategies", in his, *The Future of Capitalism*, London, Eng: Nicholas Brealey Publishing.

Wallerstein, I. 1998, "Spacetime as the basis of knowledge", in O.F. Borda Ed. *People's Participation, Challenges Ahead*, pp. 43-62, New York: The APEX Press.

Weyl, H. 2009, "The unity of knowledge", in his *Mind and Nature*, Princeton, NJ: Princeton University Press, pp. 194-203.

Whitehead, A.N. 1978, *Process and Reality*, D.R. Griffin & D.W. Sherburne Eds. New York: The Free Press.

2

Globalization of Software Development Teams

M. Rita Thissen, Susan K. Myers, R. Nathan Sikes,
Jean P. Robinson and Valentina Grouverman
RTI International, Research Triangle Park, North Carolina
USA

1. Introduction

The effects of globalization reach into almost every aspect of the software development business. Computers have become nearly ubiquitous in technically advanced societies, whether embedded in household appliances or supporting international data libraries. In parallel with the demand for new computer systems and functions, there is a growing need for highly productive software development teams who can work in the global market. For this reason, there are practical benefits to examining the factors of globalization that influence the success of software teams.

Predictably, advances in communication technologies and transportation draw the business sector into ever greater interaction around the globe (Vardi, 2010), a phenomenon termed "globalization." As commercial ventures, nonprofit organizations, and other agencies establish offices worldwide, the teams that develop software for their use have changed to accommodate the global viewpoint. Many teams experience a need for staff, advisors, and customers from around the world, creating a "globalized" team, and some aspects of software teamwork are changing as a result of the new pressures. What makes a good software team? What makes a good globalized software team? This chapter examines the characteristics of these technical teams, the obstacles to their success, and the various tools available for their use in coping with the demands of globalization.

We focus here on the effects of globalization on team composition and performance, considering technological aids to counteract teamwork challenges that are introduced or heightened by globalization.

1.1 Categorizing development teams by their composition

Not all software teams are alike in composition. We can classify the majority of them into one of three groups, and we use these terms throughout the chapter:

a. **traditional teams**, located in proximity to each other and with knowledge of each other as individuals, sometimes called "collocated teams" (Teasley et al., 2002);
b. **distributed teams**, working from multiple locations, but aware of the identities of team members, sometimes called "virtual teams" (Andres, 2002); and
c. **crowds**, unknown to each other as individuals and located anywhere, such as open-source development teams (crowds may also be considered to be virtual teams because their communication is largely electronic).

Our discussion centers on the first two types. Traditional and distributed teams are formed deliberately for the most part, and stakeholder organizations have some degree of control over composition and expectations for performance, as opposed to crowds, which may form haphazardly. Because the approach to "crowdsourcing" (see Howe, 2006) differs sharply from traditional or distributed teams, we leave that discussion for another publication. Like crowds, distributed teams may sometimes form spontaneously or from a need expressed by team members rather than by managers. Such grassroots teams soon take on the characteristics of teams formed by directive, and so we do not treat them separately.

Aside from geographic location, a second important dimension of teams is that of affiliation. Traditional and distributed teams may comprise individuals from a single organization or from many. When multiple employers are involved, the teams may be described as **collaborative**, indicating a common set of goals but not a common source of support. When all members belong to a particular organization, the team may be designated as **proprietary**, indicating a unity of purpose and support. For team members and leaders, the collaborative arrangement may add organizational diversity to an already heterogeneous team.

A third important component is the mix of skills, experience, and abilities that members provide. In the following sections, we discuss the interaction of globalization and technical composition, such as the increased opportunity for selecting team members according to capabilities as opposed to geographic proximity.

1.2 Categorizing success factors and barriers to team performance

Not all teams perform alike, even when tasked with similar jobs under similar conditions. How does globalization affect the performance of software development teams, and what tools exist to help the team perform better? Consider what makes a traditional software development team productive, without regard to the effects of globalization or location. Based on our experience, we identify the critical success factors as follows for both traditional teams and for those that are distributed regionally or globally:

a. selection of the people who make up the team,
b. team management,
c. effectiveness of communication,
d. adequacy of tools, and
e. control of external factors.

The topic of the first two items, the selection of team members and their management, can determine the effectiveness of any team. Yet the "right" people for a distributed team may be different from the "right" people for a traditional team, and project management can be more challenging because of the distributed nature of the team. To ensure the success of distributed teams, one must consider explicitly the pressures and barriers to teamwork that occur when the team members are not located in proximity to one another and may have very different cultural and working environments. New global challenges relate to the behavior and expectations of the people assigned to the team, their management, the work itself, and the tools and technologies routinely employed in their tasks.

The next two items seem equally important. In our experience, software team managers who promote communication and provide appropriate aids in the form of software tools are more likely to reach their goals and maintain good working relationships. We explore some of the reasons underlying this statement in the sections on management and tools, with particular emphasis on software tools. The same technological advances that promote globalization on a grand scale can facilitate globalization within a distributed team, particularly in a technically adept group such as software developers.

The last item bears examination in that it differs from the others in character. Regardless of the makeup of the team, success may be influenced by external factors, such as network disruptions, poorly defined requirements, budgetary pressures, and the nature of the work itself. Managers of any team, distributed or collocated, encounter these constraints and events, and successful managers achieve control through various means. It is not our intent to examine team management in general, only in the context of globalization.

In the sections that follow, we offer the knowledge that has been gained by the authors and by others who have reported their experiences in the technical literature. Our goal is to encourage examination and discussion of globalization as it affects the practice of software development, along with the technologies available to improve results.

2. Team formation and management

2.1 Selection of team members

The needs or mission of a project will often dictate the choice of whether to have a distributed or traditional software development team. Software development managers may be more comfortable with traditional or collocated teams when the end product is to be used in a local or in-house environment at a single location. If the software is run within the confines of a smaller organization, then the development team may also take on the same characteristics. Thus, when developing software for use within a limited geographic area, common sense often calls for a team from that same area.

At times, team formation may need to break with tradition to help resolve some difficulty. For example, an essential skill may be needed that cannot be found within the same locale, or deployment of the software may be planned outside the confines of the organization or to other countries, thereby requiring adherence to laws of a specific locale, a software interface design that incorporates specific cultural or language features, or technical support across widespread time zones. A manager of a project or a loosely organized group of people with a common goal may determine the need for the formation of a distributed team to provide the sought-after skills, cultural awareness, or presence in multiple time zones. A recent and highly publicized example of this was formation of the international team that won the "Netflix prize," a computing challenge to improve the probability of anticipating Netflix subscribers' interests. The Netflix prize was awarded to a group of teammates from many academic backgrounds, including computer science, machine learning, and engineering, bringing into play different perspectives and skills. The prize was first offered in 2006 for $1 million U.S. dollars and awarded in 2009 to a team that included Americans, Austrians, and Canadians (Bell et al., 2010).

However, solving one problem can initiate another. For example, a person with a highly unique skill-set who can address a project need may work and live in another time zone, which is inconvenient for other team members and may not easily communicate in the same language as others on the team. Distributed software development teams may encounter impediments to productivity resulting from the same reasons that led to their formation in the first place. Forming a distributed team to provide skills or cultural knowledge not available locally may force team members to work with people who have different technical backgrounds or languages. They may be accustomed to various work environments, legal restrictions, and political situations, and they may use disparate methods or styles of communication or rely on different technical infrastructure. As the physical distance grows between team members, often these cognitive challenges grow as well. Members of a distributed team who are located in the same geographic area or within a single country may readily become comfortable with each other's cultural, language, and communication nuances. Members of a distributed team that crosses geographic boundaries, especially at great distances, and particularly from multiple organizations in different countries, may find a significant challenge in understanding each other. Thus, forming a team based solely on members' knowledge may introduce operational difficulties as the work gets under way.

Aside from the practical benefits of assembling necessary skills within a team, there is another bright side to including distributed participants. Members may bring a diversity of skills, attitudes, personalities, and even cultures to a project, creating an interesting, exciting, and educational mix. The specialized attributes of the team members can be used to advantage in creating a software product with wide appeal because each team member contributes the point of view of his or her own background. This diversity can foster a natural mind-set of "thinking outside the box" because each team member is already "outside of the box" compared with the others (Hinds & Bailey, 2003). In an atmosphere of openness and acceptance, a programmer in a different geographic region often brings a different viewpoint, which in turn improves the universality of product design and can offer multiple avenues of problem-solving. Each team member can be encouraged to embrace the differences and strengths of other team members to maximize successful results for the team.

2.2 Team management

Many books have been written about team management in general and software team management in particular. See, for example, Covey (1989), DePree (1989), Guaspari (1991), Harragan (1977), Hill (1992), and Humphrey (2010) for general discussions of management, and Brooks (1975), Chrissis et al. (2004), Humphrey (2000), Krames (2005), McConnell (1998), and Wiegers (1999) for ways to manage software development. Many of the principles, practices, and advice can be applied to distributed software development teams although written with traditional teams in mind. Yet some special circumstances involved in directing globalized teams may take a team manager by surprise or cause the team to function with less than full efficiency and productivity. In the following paragraphs, we have merged the cited writers' general principles with some of our own experiences and comments about managing distributed teams.

As mentioned earlier, distributed and traditional teams have commonalities that should be exploited to full advantage. In both types of teams, the team leader brings focus to the group by firmly establishing the mission of the team's project. The leader directs and enforces the use of written specifications for the software with specific protocols for establishing boundaries for the software and assigning each person to specific tasks on the project. Those who lead by consensus seek agreement from all team members as to the scope of their work. Communication guidelines set by the team leader foster a cooperative environment and favorable work relationships. The team leader manages not only the team members and scope of work, but also the hardware and system environment, according to the project's specifications or other factors. The team leader is the final decision maker when judgment calls are needed by the team. Additionally, the team leader manages common tasks, such as project scheduling, labor forecasting, expense reporting, time reporting, and acquisition of needed software or hardware. These responsibilities and roles can be seen in both traditional and distributed teams. Table 1 gives an overview of the similarities and differences between traditional and distributed teams that may influence their management.

Additional responsibilities fall to the manager of a distributed team. The effective team leader feels comfortable communicating with team members whom he or she cannot see face to face. Because of the likelihood of cultural or lifestyle differences in a distributed team, and the low level of personal contact, global development team managers must be results-oriented, judging on clearly defined criteria, such as expected quality level, adherence to schedule and budget, and the degree to which individuals and their products integrate well with the work of the team as a whole.

Trait/aspect	**Traditional team**	**Distributed team**
Location	The traditional team is commonly located in same locale and often within same building.	The distributed team can traverse many different locales, time zones, and countries.
Familiarity with team members	Traditional team members often know one another and may be used to seeing one another in casual or business settings.	Members of distributed teams usually only engage one another for the sake of the project goals and may never meet one another face to face. The only contact they may have with one another is for the sake of the project.
Work environment and communication	Traditional team members work in close proximity to one another allowing for face-to-face communication. E-mails, telephones, and shared project documentation supplement the communication environment.	Face-to-face communication is rare. In-person meetings are replaced with telephone conferences and electronic white board sessions. E-mails and phone calls are likely more frequent, and project documentation can be more crucial in defining goals for the project.
Development (hardware, software, network) environment	The development environment is often set by the organization and is rigid and often cannot be easily adapted for software projects out of the ordinary.	The development environment may be as diverse as its team members. Members may be responsible for their own hardware, software, and network setup, requiring creative solutions for integration.
Project management	The manager of traditional teams has the ability to visually oversee work as it is being conducted by team members.	The manager of distributed teams must rely on review of deliverables, status reports, and other nonvisual communication to oversee projects. A greater degree of trust of team members is essential.

Table 1. Comparing traits and aspects of the traditional team versus the distributed team

The able manager of a distributed team seeks strength and advantage in the team members' differences. For example, sometimes hardware and software differences are likely among widely distributed teams as specific hardware, operating systems, or software tools are required by the project (e.g., an application needs to be migrated from the Windows platform to Linux or to the Apple OS environments). In this scenario, the needs of the software product dictate the hardware and software environment needed by its members, yet it may be possible to divide the work such that one individual works on one platform, creating a platform-independent or portable package to be tested by another team member. The team leader will recognize the talents and environments of his or her team members and exploit such differences to successfully reach the team's goals. Effective distributed team leadership requires that the team leader recognize and value the varied characteristics of team members. To overcome the challenges of diversity, the team leader fosters teamwork regardless of differences, promotes the mission of the project, and ensures that each team member benefits from successful completion of the goals. The team leader monitors work fairly regardless of individual personalities or cultural differences to ensure that results meet schedule milestones, relying on a focus on the work to address and overcome any issues between team members.

The leader of the distributed team can assure success by maintaining an atmosphere of responsibility for work results and schedule. Rewards, however, may be challenging to define. Cultural differences may influence whether rewards for meeting milestones would best be monetary or otherwise or whether the reward ought to come as public praise for work performed well or private comments. Section 3 goes into more depth on some of the cultural differences that may affect teamwork and productivity.

2.3 Practical guidelines for monitoring distributed teams

Effective management of global software development teams occurs best if the manager proactively maintains a watchful presence. The need for oversight can be more pronounced while working with distributed teams than with traditional teams because the isolation of one individual from another may allow irritation to fester unnoticed. At the same time, it can be more difficult.

For the greatest probability of success, try to do the following: (a) select staff who will adapt well to the distributed environment; (b) maintain accountability for the team as a whole and for individual staff members; (c) build an attitude of teamwork, trust, and collegiality; and (d) monitor staff availability and work progress.

We recognize that the personal characteristics needed for staff to be effective in a global team may differ from the characteristics of those who do well in traditional teams (Baruch & Nicholson, 1997; Guimaraes & Dallow, 1999). Traditional team members and managers are normally located in close proximity, and the manager or team leader can ascertain the presence of the team member at most any time by dropping in on them physically to see the progress of their work. Although managers of traditional teams can literally "stand over" their team members and their work, managers of distributed teams are deprived of this luxury. Consequently, the manager of a distributed team needs to select team members who can work independently and responsibly and who take it upon themselves to proceed with subsequent steps in a project once they have completed milestones if moving ahead is appropriate. Often the best team members are those who are self-reliant and are good problem-solvers who take the initiative to address challenging issues in their physical or technical environment before asking the team leader to intervene. These team members also recognize when to ask and receive help if the need arises. In general, such people are experienced because a novice team member requires more oversight and direction or training. Although these characteristics are valuable in any teamwork, they become even more important when team members must work independently at widespread locations, coming together on occasion virtually or indirectly to achieve the team's goals.

The effective manager maintains accountability by setting milestone goals and quality expectations for both the team and for its individual members. The goals should be announced internally so that the team can keep them in mind and self-monitor while developing their software. Each team member then knows the expectations for all and can plan accordingly. The individual team member should be encouraged to communicate with the manager and affected team members when they may not be able to meet the schedule with the desired results or if they are not available to work at the expected pace. Managers can then intervene with additional resources or other alternatives in order to meet the project goals. Being proactive in maintaining accountability is essential to good management of distributed teams.

The effective manager imparts a sense of camaraderie to the team and fosters a reliance on one another to stay on schedule and produce the desired results in a timely fashion. For some teams, it is effective to praise or reward individuals and the team as a whole when they have achieved their goals. The manager can set the tone by encouraging and welcoming praise for one another in communication among team members. These actions will foster desired camaraderie and even help maintain accountability of the team. Underscoring the need for cohesiveness as an antecedent to success, Denning et al. (1989) identified seven universal values and associated practices for coordination in a diversified team: (1) proficiency, (2) capacity to articulate a vision of the team's value, (3) capacity to enter into binding commitments and fulfill them, (4) capacity to spot and eliminate waste, (5) capacity to share real-time assessments of performance, (6) capacity to observe one's own history and how it interacts with others, and (7) capacity to *blend* (i.e., to align with others). These values must be promoted by the team manager to be fully adopted by the team as a whole.

It is essential for the manager to maintain knowledge of the progress of the work assigned to team members in nontraditional teams. For the team to achieve milestone dates and maintain a schedule, the manager should review software results on a periodic basis. This can be achieved by having team members post their work to a common storage location for the manager to review. Work results can be reviewed by using screen-sharing tools between the manager and the team member, as described in Section 6. While reviewing the software, a good practice is for the team leader to be in direct communication with the team member so that the manager can provide real-time feedback and explanation of the software deliverable being reviewed. It should also be a practice to turn the software deliverable directly over to one or more team members chosen specifically as testers to review and test the software for accuracy and completeness of the software as expected. Trust in the team member is always desired, but accountability for the results using software testers ensures the desired results.

3. Cultural effects on teamwork

Cultural diversity has both positive and negative effects on distributed team effectiveness and success. By employing team members from anywhere in a world, organizations can have access to a larger pool of skills and combine the best expertise available in the field regardless of members' geographic locations, thereby improving team quality and reducing development time. However, as noted earlier, distributed teams face greater communication challenges than traditional teams, especially teams that are not homogeneous with respect to cultural composition. Understanding the impact of cultural differences is one of the keys to distributed-team success in the global environment.

In one study, participants in global teams described challenges associated with intercultural communication and positive effects due to a potential for better decision-making (Shachaf, 2008). The negative impact came from increased complexity of communication, due in part to team differences and in part from working at multiple locations. Cultural and language differences often resulted in miscommunication, which undermined trust, cohesion, and team identity. Study participants mentioned challenges, such as lack of accuracy in both written and spoken communications, requiring team members to invest more time and effort in producing and understanding messages.

Yet cross-cultural diversity can enhance project team experience as a source of innovative thinking that improves the project design and enhances its chances for success through different approaches to solving problems. Because of a wider range of perspectives, cultural diversity can increase creativity and generate innovative ideas and alternative solutions.

Increased globalization is forcing a growing number of managers and employees to interact across linguistic and cultural boundaries that have demonstrable but unnoticed impact. Language differences are generally obvious, but other differences also affect teamwork. Often without people's realization, culture influences how closely they stand, how loudly they speak, how they make decisions, how well they handle conflict, or even their styles of participating in meetings. These differences present a unique challenge to management and teamwork, potentially reaching throughout the organizational structure (El Guindi & Kamel, 2003).

Consider the differences within a single language. In the English-speaking world, American, English, Canadian, Indian, Nigerian, Australian, and other cultures have their own differences of accents and vocabulary. Spoken language versions may range from easily understandable to incomprehensible among a group from around the world, if some team members have very strong accents. There are also regional differences of expression, and it may not be easy to understand colloquialisms. For example, an Australian may say "sticky beak" for a nosy person, and Americans may refer to someone having "horse sense," meaning a practical view of the world. Also, based on the context and tone used, a word or phrase can have several different meanings. A common language helps to overcome cultural barriers and sort out misunderstandings, but it is not necessarily enough; for those who learned a language as nonnative speakers, a common language can be very puzzling (Noll et al., 2010).

Although Western culture currently dominates much of the business world, Asian markets are expanding rapidly. This is particularly true in the software industry, in which the Indian communities of Bangalore and Hyderabad now play a strong role (Glaeser, 2010), but also in China, the Middle East, and other areas. Differences exist in body language, attitude toward age and rank, directness of speech, and attitude toward the passage of time. For example, Americans say, "Time is of the essence," which means that time is of the utmost importance in American business. In the United States, delay or slow pace may be seen as a lack of respect for one's employer, team members, clients, and business partners, and it is very important to get to the point, particularly during business meetings.

Some norms of body language accepted in the West convey the exact opposite of meaning in the East. For example, direct eye contact during conversation in the West is a sign of honesty, while in many Eastern countries it is disrespectful and can be even seen as a threat or hostile behavior. In a distributed development team, body language messages are muted because of the rarity with which team members may encounter each other. However, it is valuable for team members to recognize such differences if they do meet and to be open with each other about their expectations and understanding. Differences in Western and Eastern communication styles may cause dilemmas because so much of a distributed team's interactions depend on written or spoken communication. Western people often prefer clear instructions and direct talk. On the other hand, many Eastern cultures use "coded" speech (Krishna et al., 2004), and a lot is left to the intellectual "decoding" by team members, which enables them to correctly interpret a vague comment that is full of nuanced meaning. Straightforward statement from some Western team members could be misjudged by others, especially by those who are from an Asian background and who might find it disrespectful to their knowledge and ability to understand the underlying meaning.

Cultural background influences how people express themselves and with whom they are willing to share personal issues. For example, although many people in some nations may feel comfortable talking openly about their personal problems, people in Middle Eastern and Asian cultures generally discuss such personal only issues with very close friends. One study found that an American-Israeli team struggled at first with this concept. The Americans reported that Israeli team members were "all business" and never spoke of personal matters (Quinones et al., 2009).

Apart from the issues inherent in interpersonal communication, culture also has a major impact on approaches to problem-solving and strategic decision making. A lengthy consensus-building process is usual in Eastern cultures for making a decision that would be acceptable to all team members. They all would share the responsibility for this decision, and every member of the team needs to feel comfortable with a proposed way to move forward. There is an obvious benefit of such an approach that team members implementing this decision are actively involved in the project design, a concept sometimes referred to as "ownership." The converse also requires adaptation: Asian team members may need to realize that statements by Americans or other Westerners that seem abrupt or excessively pointed may actually be intended as an efficient use of time (Salacuse, 1998).

It is also very important for the entire development team to understand communications correctly, especially when a decision is being made. In Japan, for example, people are reluctant to say "no" or disagree with others, especially those who outrank or are older than themselves, because it is a sign of disrespect. It can be very difficult to be completely confident that a decision or agreement has been finally reached with support from all team members because of this. On the other hand, verbal agreements in Japan would have as much weight as written and signed contracts, while in the United States, they may simply be an indication of willingness to pursue a question further (Chui, 2005).

In today's globalized world, travel restrictions in the form of entry or work visas play an important role in controlling the movement of foreign nationals across borders, which may prevent multinational software development team members from meeting each other in person. Almost all countries now require visas from certain nonnationals who wish to enter their territory. Although visa restrictions are primarily based on citizenship, the holding of a residence permit may also be of importance. For example, a resident of any European Union country that is part of the Schengen zone may travel visa-free throughout that zone

(European Union website, http://Europa.eu). Therefore, on some occasions, team members working within that zone might be able to meet with each other in spite of working across national boundaries.

Geographic location, physical distance, and government policies may separate management and employees within a global team. The separation may require a change in management practices and also a different approach to treating transfer of services, products, and tools across international borders. In many cases, this type of activity may require interaction with government agencies. A manager may need a great deal of information related to international export/import restrictions in order to supply his or her team with materials and equipment. Security concerns are evolving along with the global workforce. In third-world countries, a shortage of hardware and abundant labor may promote hardware sharing, raising the risk of loss or damage to work products stored on the same machine. Data repositories generally cannot be located within countries whose governments may compromise confidentiality or security. To address security concerns, global teams may be required to follow enhanced security procedures, such as using a virtual private network, encryption, and antivirus or anti-malware software.

4. Tools for communication

4.1 The right tools for the team

As noted in the team formation and management section, communication is paramount for good teamwork, but not necessarily easy for distributed teams. For software teams, the specialized languages of programming, platforms, and tools may reduce misunderstanding

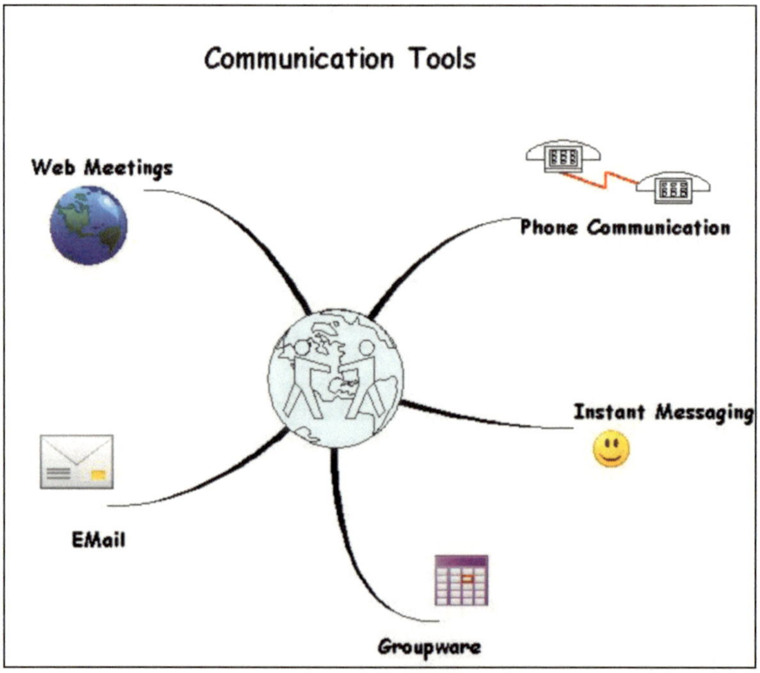

Fig. 1. Conceptual view of global communication tools (used with permission from Thissen et al., 2007)

because of the precise nature of the terms, but the process of communicating over long distances may still be daunting. For this reason, most teams rely on tools and products to aid communication.

Technology-mediated social participation supports closer coordination among larger groups of people, making it possible to address the problems of distributed workgroups in new ways. Kraut et al. (2010) described such team formations as "collaboratories" where collections of researchers who are not collocated work together to address a common problem, coordinating work through technology and social practice.

Communication tools can be divided into three groups: (a) synchronous, (b) asynchronous, and (c) knowledge transfer. Synchronous tools are dynamic or "real time." Asynchronous tools allow information to be transferred or received over a period of time, not requiring simultaneity. A knowledge transfer tool can be a collection of information or a tool that aids in using a collection of information. Depicted conceptually in Figure 1 (Thissen et al., 2007), all of these types of tools contribute to successful distributed teamwork, each in its own way.

4.2 Synchronous communication

Synchronous communication tools for software developers are much the same as those for any other type of far-flung working group. Some forms of communication take place with all participants involved at the same time, such as a telephone conversation or other real-time interactions. Tools that aid this form of communication are called synchronous. We describe here how these tools can help teams share thought processes and therefore boost quality and productivity among a software team.

Table 2 provides examples of the types of synchronous tools that may be of use to such teams. Some of these tools are physical devices, but most are software. Also, most of them

Tool	Examples	Features	Primary advantage
Telephone	"Plain Old Telephone Service" (POTS), Voice over Internet Protocol (VoIP)	Direct calls, conference calls	Familiar to everyone, provides instant interaction
Instant messaging and chat, video chat	Yahoo Messenger, MSN Messenger, AOL Instant Messenger, Internet Relay Chat, Skype	Instant interaction, less intrusive than a phone call	Provides instant interaction, can be used in asynchronous mode if all parties remain connected, with video chat conveying facial expressions for richer communication
Web casts	NetMeeting, WebEx, Citrix, GoToMeeting, ATT ConnectMeeting	Live audio, dynamic video, whiteboard, application sharing	Real-time interaction, augments speech with images and live action displays
Online translators	Google, Yahoo, various other free and commercial varieties available	Instant translation of words, paragraphs, and entire documents	Real-time translation

Table 2. Communication tools: synchronous

rely on the Internet connectivity. Global distributed teams are heavily dependent on the Internet; in fact, the entire growth of globalization for software development has been made possible by the existence of the Internet.

Many teams still rely on telephone communication for direct immediate conversations. The Internet has brought about advances in how distributed teams can benefit from a different type of phone—the Voice over Internet Protocol (VoIP) phone. This technology makes it possible for team members in any location to have a number in the same area code as other team members, reducing long distance or international calling costs. VoIP can also be used to put team members on the same phone network, meaning that a team member in a different location could still be reached by typing an extension versus entering in the entire sequence of area code, and so on. Simple things like being on the same phone network can make teams feel more cohesive.

Instant messaging (IM) can be a quick real-time way to get an answer from a teammate without the disruption of a phone call. Most IM software allows each person to set his or her status, indicating availability. If the person is not available, then IM could be considered asynchronous and function similar to sending an e-mail. If he or she is available, communication can be quick with little disruption. One-on-one communication is referred to as IM; when there are two or more participants, it is referred to as "chat." Some of the IM software allows for the use of web cams and voice along with typed conversation.

"Webcast or webinar, what's the difference?" The difference varies by who is using the term, but most often, a webcast refers to an online presentation, where the audio is only one way. Webinars generally allow two-way or multiway communication. They are similar to seminars and are like a short class or discussion session, but instead of all of the participants looking at a classroom's blackboard, each participant is in front of a computer screen. Some webinars include voice capability through VoIP, while others provide a telephone dial-in number for vocal communication. Webinars are useful for discussions or show-and-tell where all of the team can look at the same information at the same time. Webcasts are useful for one-way sharing, such as updates of information or status reports.

Online automated translation services and locally installed translation software can provide some timely information to a distributed team because the services are readily available and accessible when needed. Global teams sometimes need to work out differences between languages. If there are simple item labels in a software tool being developed, such as a command button with simple commands that needs to be rendered in different languages, these translation tools could provide the basic translation immediately. They could also be used to translate pieces of a message or a document shared by the team for brief or informal communications. If team members are not fluent in a language, these tools could clarify the meaning. Although these tools can help out "in a pinch" (i.e., temporarily or in an emergency), language translation can be fairly complicated because meaning sometimes depends on context and ambiguities may not be resolved correctly. The message may lose coherence in the translation.

Many distributed teams rely on synchronous tools, but there are situations within teams where real-time communication just does not work well. Global or distributed teams have to deal with varying time zones and different work schedules, and so not all of the team can be available at the same time. Even collocated teams find situations where synchronous tools are not right for the situation. Deadlines can make disruptions such as phone calls and e-mail messages undesirable. These types of situations create an opening for asynchronous tools to fill the gap.

4.3 Asynchronous communication

In the globalized workforce, one significant problem is that of time zone differences because it can be difficult for team members to find a common time of day at which all are available for meetings or other forms of communication. And yet, time zone differences can benefit a software development team's productivity because they let the combined team work around the clock. Asynchronous tools are therefore an asset to distributed teams because they facilitate communications without respect to time zone.

Many of the current tools that support asynchronous communication recognize the fact that they may be used by people whose schedules are not well aligned (see Table 3). One team member may be available while the next one is busy. Some of the tools provide indicators as to the user's current state, such as online, busy, unavailable, away from desk, and on the telephone. These software features can be used to advantage by team members to communicate without interrupting or disturbing their coworkers.

Tool	Examples	Features	Primary advantage
E-mail	Numerous vendors and free applications	Send messages or files	Simple way to share information that team members can read when time permits
Groupware/ shared services	Lotus Notes, Microsoft Exchange, Novell Groupwise	Calendars, contact lists, arrange meetings	Takes into account different time zones when scheduling a meeting
Issue trackers	Bugzilla, Mantis, Trac, Redmine, Request Tracker, OTRIS, EventNum, Fossil, Bug Genie, Issues, numerous others	Varies by package: Project Wiki, time tracking, Lightweight Directory Access Protocol (LDAP) authentication, reports	Clear ownership of issues, great for any type of team
Recordings	Recorded meetings, VoIP tools, Skype add-on software, AT&T Connect Meeting option	Audio and/or video recording	Archived record of communication can be made available to nonparticipants

Table 3. Communication tools: asynchronous

Familiar tools of traditional teams, such as e-mail and online calendars, help to fill the need for managing basic team communications across these differences in time zone and schedules. File transfer, issue trackers, and recordings put information within reach of the team members when it is needed. Whether the team is distributed or traditionally collocated, communication and sharing of information need to happen for the team to be successful. Asynchronous communication tools allow the team to choose the right time to access the information, minimizing disruption to any individual's schedule.

E-mail has been around long enough now that almost everyone is aware of what it is. In 2002, the number of e-mail users worldwide was around 890 million (Gwizdka, 2002) and by 2009 approximately 1.4 billion (Radicati Group, Inc., 2009). It has become a standard form of communication within teams and is hard to replace. With the flexibility of e-mail, a team member or leader can send messages to a single individual or to the entire group and can include file attachments if needed. Beyond the basics of sending and receiving, e-mail software can be used to organize and archive information for ready access. Many e-mail systems have calendars that allow users to set reminders, keep track of tasks, and take advantage of a variety of other features. Messages can be sent without perfect knowledge of the language or perfect pronunciation, aiding teams whose members have differing native languages. For many distributed teams, e-mail is the communication channel of choice.

Groupware or shared calendars are useful tools for keeping up with the availability and commitments of team members. Each member keeps up with his or her own calendar and sets limits on who has access to entries. Other team members can see who is available, who is on vacation, or when they might be available to meet. With shared calendars, each can see this information at a glance for individuals or a whole team. When working with distributed teams, a view of the team's shared calendar is as close as one might get to a traditional team's option of walking down the hall to see which programmers are at their desks.

One of the complexities of writing software as a team is determining who is currently responsible for a specific task, class, build, or package. For programmers, the question may be who is working on a particular bug. This issue crosses into both global and collocated teams, so issue trackers can be a great answer. An issue tracker can be a simple tracking system for one project, a single system for multiple projects, or a part of an integrated project management system. These systems allow issues or bugs to be assigned to a specific team member, with others on the team notified as needed. Viewing bugs by who has been assigned, by team, by category, and by project are desirable features with this type of software.

Often, a team meeting via web or conference call may occur at a time that is inconvenient for one or more staff. When that happens or when critical and complex information is being exchanged, the team manager may choose to record the call, creating an archival record that can be referenced later. Recordings could be viewed in the same way as webcasts, but webcasts most often provide live-streaming information. By recording the webcast or call, the information can be grouped with online training materials or text-based minutes for asynchronous review.

4.4 Knowledge transfer

Knowledge transfer is a specialized form of communication, and it can be difficult to do at a distance. For global software development teams, whose members need to coordinate their activities closely and ensure that their products integrate well, knowledge transfer can present a challenge. In response to that challenge, several products have been introduced and adopted in the marketplace, particularly by distributed teams.

What is knowledge transfer? In any team, some people have greater expertise in one domain than in another. For example, in a software development team, there may be roles for a specialist in gathering requirements, designing a database, determining the best user interface, or evaluating the appropriate platform. These roles may be held by one individual or shared by several people. It can be very important for each specialist to explain some of the concepts, constraints, or implications of his or her knowledge and understanding. What kinds of tools exist to support the communication of that expertise?

Table 4 shows examples of many tools that can be used to share knowledge in a routine informal way or for more controlled and planned training processes. The table gives a sampling only, and should not be seen as endorsement by the authors nor their organization. Each category of tool is discussed in the paragraphs following the table, based on the authors' experience.

Tool	Examples	Features	Primary advantage
Wiki	WikiPedia, PBWiki, TikiWiki, DocuWiki, MediaWiki	Information in many languages on many topics, constantly updated by contributors, easy to create a custom wiki for a team	Open sharing of information, anytime
Electronic library, institutional repositories	BRICKS, Fedora, Greenstone, Invenio, Refbase, and numerous others	Immediate access to library-type information, books, journals, graphics	Open sharing of information, anytime
Search tools	Google, Yahoo, Bing, Ask.com	Specialized search libraries, such as Google Scholar; access to worldwide extensive information sources	Open sharing of information, anytime
e-learning	Articulate Online, Adobe Elearning Suite, Moodle, SnagIt	Audio/video capture, develop tutorials, learning management systems, image capture (classroom)	Create once, and reuse any time, web-based presentation for easy access

Table 4. Communication tools: knowledge sharing and training

File transfer is commonly linked with data exchange, but when software teams need to communicate, large documents or files can be an important part of that communication. Some programmers may use a File Transfer Protocol (FTP) site as a drop-box location. When items are complete or ready for the next step, they are dropped to the FTP site. The communication is clearly visible as the presence of a file, indicating that this item is ready for the next step. Another team member can pick it up and continue work on it.

What is a wiki? A wiki is a website that anyone can contribute to by using built-in editing tools that post directly back to the web pages. Wikipedia, the free encyclopedia, is a well-known example offered in many languages (http://www.wikipedia.org/). Distributed teams can create and use a wiki site to share information on a new tool, on a package they are developing, or anything they want to collaborate on—the list could be endless. A wiki is a place to keep information organized in a central location where everyone can add to it or learn from it. Ward Cunningham, one of the creators of the wiki software, calls it, "The simplest online database that could possibly work" (Leuf & Cunningham, 2001).

How often do software developers search online for some piece of information they need to know? Programmers make extensive use of online search tools when they need an answer or an example. Electronic search engines, such as Google and Yahoo, are frequently a programmer's greatest resource because of the immediacy of information and access to technical posts from around the world. For a distributed team, who cannot ask questions to the person at the next desk, online search tools are a common resource to turn to. This ability to search by topic and keyword is a form of knowledge sharing with the rest of the world. Team members can share the knowledge with each other without having to copy or store it; they simply share or pass along the web location.

There many software packages for groups to use when creating their own training materials. They range from simple capture of voice and computer screen input, all the way to learning-management systems that track training progress and full classroom-type image capture. The simple desktop tools, such as SnagIt or Captiva, allow teams to record, save, and share information easily and informally. The first person to learn a new tool could record a quick how to or beginner guide, and the other members could review it when they need it. More complex tools, such as Moodle, offer the ability to create a more formal presentation, quizzes for certification, and shared training materials. For a large and highly organized international team, such as an organizational division that spans the globe, it may be worthwhile to develop training materials in multiple languages and post them on a centralized site.

Electronic libraries have many names, including digital library, virtual information services, institutional repositories, and many other variations, but they all serve the same purpose. These libraries are electronic repositories for reference materials, documents in preparation, regulatory materials, specifications, software lifecycle documentation, and other types of written information. They store most of this information in digital formats or scanned images rather than printed versions. Having access to search through these types of data can open doors for global team members enabling them to find information and share it. For a distributed software team, a library can provide support at each stage of development, from conceptual architecture through design and finally as a host for final product documentation. The ability to search across a wide range of articles, search within an article, and interact with multiple levels of information objects are significant features of electronic journals (Liew et al., 2000).

In the formative stages of the team, or in the design phase of software development, team members often need to expand their specialized skills, understanding of systems, awareness of confidentiality rules, and other topics that may not be easily learned as an individual. E-learning tools offer a way to provide customized, standardized training to the team, without requiring travel. E-learning is any type of learning that is done using some combination of a computer and/or Internet access. It generally includes web-based learning, computer-based learning, or a virtual classroom arrangement. Information is most often delivered via the Internet via recorded package or streaming video, or from a CD or DVD. These can be self-paced or led in real-time by an instructor. E-learning has the major advantage of being accessible from any location and having a variety of formats available from which to choose.

Social network software, such as Facebook, MySpace, LinkedIn, and other public-access websites, now play a growing role in society. To our knowledge, their penetration into software development teams is slight from a business perspective. Although team members may be active participants for their private connections, these sites tend to be frequented by less-focused groups. For business purposes and day-to-day work, members of a distributed software team typically use less open means of communication and transfer, such as those listed in Table 4. As security controls improve and the population becomes accustomed to these cloud-based systems, they may become more prevalent in the future.

5. Software development tools

Software development is a wide and diverse field. A simple breakdown of the types of software reveals three groups: (a) *platform- or device-specific tools*, such as software drivers, operating systems, or hardware-specific products; (b) *commercial or open-source application software*, such as word processors, development languages and environments, research applications, software for creating installation packages, or other independent applications; and (c) *custom user-developed add-on software*, such as document templates, macros, scripts, or command files.

Distributed teams may have different equipment and configurations depending on what type of development they are doing. It may or may not be critical to have the same software, perhaps even the same release, on each team member's workstation. As mentioned in the discussion on team management, the team leader or manager may need to provide and coordinate the development environment according to the needs of the specific project. Coordinating the development environment may be straightforward for small traditional teams, but the effort becomes more complex as the team size grows, the geographic distribution grows, and the number of home countries increases. In one study of computational science, "58% of scientists reported that they do development on their own; 17% work with one other person, and 18% work in teams of 3 to 5 people, while only 9% work in larger groups" (Wilson, 2009).

If development is geared toward a specific platform, and not all team members have the same platform, the team may have to reorganize who is responsible for doing what. If the development is not platform-specific, having development occur on multiple platforms could improve the robustness of the software being developed. The more platforms and equipment the software is tested on, the more reliable the product becomes.

Once development is under way, another type of tool is needed for tracking the versions of the work products and documentation. Most software teams follow a standardized life cycle for development, and many of the formalized approaches, such as the Capability Maturity Model–Integrated process levels (Chrissis et al., 2004), require a significant amount of version-controlled documentation. That voluminous work, in addition to monitoring configuration and build versions, can best be handled by a commercial or open-source revision-control package. There are two basic methods of version control—centralized and distributed. Version control using a centralized model places the code in a shared location, and allows only one person at a time to check out a piece of code. This is the most common approach, and a variety of tools are available to help manage it, such as Microsoft's Visual Source Safe. The other method is a distributed version control system, which allows a programmer to get a full copy of the source and only pass in updates as needed or when an

Internet connection is available, such as the open-source SVK. Some integrated development environments have a version control system integrated within them.

6. Collaborative software for exchanging materials

As Herbsleb pointed out in his paper for *The Future of Software Engineering*, the key phenomenon of global software development is coordination over distance (Herbsleb, 2007). Collaborative software allows people to work together on the same documents and projects over local and remote networks. One of the fundamental needs of any project is the ability to store and share documents, data, test reports, user manuals, and other electronic files among team members, including the software itself. At the most basic level, every team needs to have a centralized location for software, data and documentation, accessible to all. For some teams, this function is served by revision-control software described in Sections 4.3 and 5 while for other teams it may be as simple as a network-level shared disk or folder. Others may use more specialized tools, as described here.

Traditional and distributed teams have different dependencies on the collaborative exchange of materials because of the distance among team members. We mention here some of the available tools and indicate which ones may be more effective in various scenarios. At the simplest level, a traditional team from a single organization may or may not have all of the tools listed in Table 5, depending on the size and complexity of the institution. However, a traditional team is likely to share intranet disk space and therefore may function well without additional tools for exchanging materials. In distributed teams, the Information Technology (IT) infrastructure of organizations may not be compatible among all of the team members' sites and may need a cloud or Internet site with exchange tools, such as web forums, or other universal-access tools. We explore here some options for these teams and also touch upon the project requirements that drive the decision process.

The premise of "cloud" computing has reached most of the world with access to the Internet. It is a viable solution for many collaborative efforts, but there are differing opinions on what constitutes a cloud. For this chapter, we define it as a configuration of scalable IT services that allows for centralized document storage and management. In other words, the cloud offers a way for anyone to use an Internet-enabled computer from any location to access files stored there. Because the concept of cloud storage can underlie many of the tools presented here for discussion, we are not referring to any specific tools as being in the cloud.

As discussed earlier, teams in a globalized environment need to communicate and also to exchange materials among themselves. Although informal written and oral communications are important, it is also critical that teams have the tools to facilitate transfer and collaborate on formal documentation, source code, presentations, and so on.

Many types of collaborative software are used by software development teams to exchange materials. We categorize them according to their general purpose and potential use by teams. Both commercial and open-source products are presented, but we do not differentiate them in our discussion. Collaborative software is a rapidly growing market, and new products are introduced at an amazing rate. The list presented in Table 5 is representative, not comprehensive, and it is not an endorsement by the authors or their organization. Some categories and products appear here and in the communications section because the same software may be used for multiple purposes. We talk about each category of tool in the following paragraphs.

Tool category	Examples of commercial or open-source products	Selected features	Primary advantage
E-mail	Outlook, Gmail, Yahoo Mail	Attached files, shared folders	Ability to converse between e-mail servers
File transfer	FTP, Filezilla, CrossFTP, WebDrive, WINSCP, SSH	Secure, access permissions	Security
File transfer	SecureFX, CuteFTP, WSFTPPro, PSFTP, WebDrive, WINSCP, FileZilla, FIRE FTP	Varies by package: directory compare, syncing directories, SSL encryption, search/filtering, integrity checks, remote editing, drag & drop	Very useful when more than a few files or very large files need to be downloaded or transferred
Collaboration platforms	eRoom, WorkZone, Central Desktop, HyperOffice	Alerts, discussion, version control, access permissions	Centralized
Document sharing and management	MS SharePoint, Drop Box, GoogleDocs, CloudPointe, Network Servers, Visual SourceSafe, custom solutions	Cloud storage of files and materials, version control, access permissions	Easy deployment, templates
Instant messaging, chat	Google Chat, Skype, AIM	Available anywhere, attached files	Informal
Shared desktops	Skype, Netmeeting	File transfer, electronic whiteboard, virtual conferencing	Real-time collaboration, compatible across Windows operating systems
Content management	Alterian, MediaValet, Liferay	Librarianship for the web, workflow approval process	User friendly

Table 5. Selected collaboration tools for material exchange and their capabilities

As noted before, e-mail has been at the center of project communications for decades. It can serve as a messaging system, work as a file transfer system, and provide shared folders for archival purposes. It provides a basic form of data dissemination; information may be embedded in the e-mail text, provided as a link to a shared location, or included as an attachment. Although e-mail serves its purpose well, it has many drawbacks. Duplication of documents and version control both present problems that can affect projects greatly; who has not received large attachments on each message in an e-mail chain, overwhelming the mailbox and making it nearly impossible to reconcile the versions? Any savings in using e-mail over a dedicated tool for document exchange may be diverted to storage costs incurred for multiple copies filed by each e-mail recipient. Although e-mail has its drawbacks, it does remain a very useful and worthwhile tool for project teams. Even in the most widely distributed team, members may send documents via e-mail attachments across e-mail platforms. The attachments may be in any format and if encrypted can allay security concerns. One major drawback is the limitations in some systems for the size of attached files, and teams need to be aware of the impact that large attachments have on e-mail servers or controlled-size mailboxes. Another growing concern is the use of e-mail to spread viruses and other malware, resulting in restrictions and filters on many e-mail systems that prohibit executables and other types of attachments. Regardless of the concerns and limitations, e-mail remains extremely popular as a means of exchanging electronic materials.

A classic method of Internet-based file movement is FTP (mentioned earlier). Several forms are used by institutions, and these packages have varying levels of security. For simple transfers of materials with no security concerns, Anonymous FTP may be employed, while more sensitive material may need to be transferred with or without encryption via products, such as FileZilla. Another feature offered within FTP systems is the ability to add a structure and access levels to the structure. Not all products support all operating systems, so teams need to choose a system that will handle the needs of the team. CrossFTP is one of the most flexible systems and is compatible with Windows, Mac OS X, Linux, BSD, Unix, and AmigaOS. FileZilla can handle all of these except AmigaOS. Collaborative teams may or may not share operating systems, so some forms of FTP may not be a viable tool for exchanging documents.

SSH File Transfer Protocol, otherwise known as Secure File Transfer Protocol (SFTP), is another file transfer protocol that offers file transfer capabilities. Although it is similar to FTP systems, it is based on a different underlying protocol and is more platform independent. In addition to file transfer, SFTP also provides file access and management.

In the past decade, collaboration platform products have emerged as important tools to enable successful teaming across any boundary. Although collaborative software has been available since the mid- to late 1990s, in recent discussions "cloud computing" references have become commonplace. For distributed teams, an option has arisen of storing shared files "in the cloud," that is, at a location accessible through the Internet, but not explicitly known to the user. The cloud provides a solution for a centralized location of project documents and discussions. Some of the commercial cloud platforms offer a wide array of tools. For example, eRoom has discussions, version control on documents, search features, and security access. Another of its key features is the ability to send alerts to team members. Distribution lists are maintained, and the user may send a notice when documents are updated or action is requested. The notices are via e-mail and sent from the server. Although packages like this are very useful and convenient for multiorganization teams, they do come at a cost. The software for some of them must be installed locally and can also be quite expensive.

Document sharing and management is a need as long as a project consists of more than one person, and cloud computing services have had a remarkable effect on software development teams. As long as members have access to the web, materials may be disseminated and updated from any locale. Services such as Google Docs are great choices when teams have access to the Internet and need to collaborate with a document format available to all members. Because the services are housed in the cloud and access to the Internet is required, work will be slowed when connections are interrupted. Unexpected problems, such as natural disasters, power outages, and political uprisings, can result in Internet service interruption. These situations serve as a reminder that teams that depend on cloud-based services can be adversely affected by outside factors. Other systems, such as Lotus Notes or Microsoft (MS) Sharepoint, may be a more reasonable choice in some environments. For example, teams that are users of MS Office may select MS Sharepoint. Licenses are required, but integration with MS Office is an advantage in many situations. Other features, such as wikis, searches, and bulletin boards, make it a product to be considered. For highly confidential exchange, or for teams with very specific needs, a custom website with document-exchange features may be more cost-effective than a commercial choice (Sattaluri & Thissen, 2005).

If the team is proprietary in affiliation, its document sharing and management needs may be met by the use of the organization's own network servers or intranet. The use of software packages that track changes and materials stored on network servers allow multiple users to work on a central file; changes are marked for team members to accept or reject. This is a simple solution and may be very secure depending on the architecture of the server database. Further security may be achieved by controlling access within the server. Another advantage of network servers is that no access to the public Internet is needed, a very valuable feature at times when Internet service is interrupted.

IM was mentioned earlier as a communications tool. At a glance, IM services may not seem like a reasonable choice for an exchange of materials. However, they do serve a purpose and are used by many. They may be viewed as abbreviated forms of e-mail because files may be sent as attachments. With IM services or chat rooms, team members can have a spontaneous conversation about shared documents, software, or data files. A downside is that with some messaging software, there is no record kept of the conversation unless the participants actively save it.

There are several considerations when selecting tools for materials exchange, including team type, team size, team location, operating systems, security, budget, time constraints and project timelines, and the size and type of files.

Software development teams often need to view prototypes of products and systems as modifications are made. For collocated proprietary teams, this may result in an impromptu meeting in an office to do the viewing. For distributed teams, this may not be an option, and services that enable desktop sharing may fit the need. Desktop sharing provides an effective and impromptu way to demonstrate software systems as development progresses. Although products such as Netmeeting are commonly used for video conferencing and chatting over the Internet, they are also used for file transfer. By simply dragging a file icon to a Netmeeting window, the file may be globally transferred to all conference members. Similar to IM, there is no record of the meeting, but it is a quick and inexpensive way to collaborate on project materials.

For very large teams, or for teams that prepare a large volume of documentation, there may be value to designating a specific person as the librarian, someone who keeps track of the versions and content of each document. Typically, the documents will reside in a common location, and often the librarian may employ an organizing tool, such as content management software. Products such as Liferay offer a platform for web application development and content management. A key feature of Liferay for software developers is the Application Programming Interface (API) with a built-in rules engine, and enhanced Workflow APIs support integration with external workflow engines. This type of tool is particularly valuable for distributed teams, but may also aid traditional teams.

How does one determine what a specific software development team needs? As indicated above, there is a wide variety of choices and approaches. Careful planning and review of project-specific characteristics must be the driving force in choosing tools for successful teams. Determine how much exchange of materials will take place, and evaluate the barriers to sharing project files and documents. Define security and confidentiality requirements for storage, then evaluate software and storage options. Budget constraints may influence a choice between commercial and open-source software. Finally, select products and ensure that team members know how to use them.

7. Conclusion

In this chapter, we have examined the nature and functioning of software development teams that include members who work at locations distant from one another, a type of team that is becoming more common as globalization reaches into all parts of the world economy. These distributed teams may include telecommuters, staff from regional offices of a company, collaborators from various organizations, or even workers at worldwide locations. Regardless of the reasons for team delocalization, the practices of long-distance work take on a different flavor from those of teams who work together at a single site.

What is the impact of this transformation of the software development team structure? What are the driving forces behind team formation, and what are the factors that lead to their success? What are the implications for management and productivity? The topic is an important one for observation, discussion, and analysis in the coming years as globalization rises.

We have attempted to address these questions from a practical perspective with realistic examples to inform the broader community of software development professionals. We believe that distributed teams, already commonplace, may soon become the norm, and those who enter the globalized market unaware will be at a disadvantage. We hope to have increased the readers' level of knowledge of the contributing pressures, benefits, challenges, and obstacles and to have provided some common ground by way of examples to aid others in the software development domain.

8. References

Andres, H.P. (2002). A Comparison of Face to Face and Virtual Software Development Teams. *Team Performance Management*, Vol. 8, pp. 39-48, ISSN 1352-7592

Baruch, Y., & Nicholson, N. (1997). Home, Sweet Work: Requirements for Effective Home Working. *Journal of General Management*, Vol. 23, No. 2, pp. 15-30, ISSN 0306-3070

Bell, R.M., Koren, Y., & Volinsky, C. (2010). All Together Now: A Perspective on the Netflix Prize. *Chance*, Vol. 23, No. 1, pp. 24-29, ISSN 0933-2480

Brooks, F.P. (1975). *The Mythical Man Month*, Addison-Wesley, ISBN 0201835959, New York

Chrissis, M. B., Konrad, M., & Shrum, S. (2004). *CMM: Guidelines for Process Integration and Product Improvement*, Addison-Wesley, ISBN 0321279670, New York

Chui, K. (2005). Managing Projects in Asia: The Challenge of Cultural Diversity, *PMI Global Congress Proceedings*, Singapore, Republic of Singapore

Covey, S.R. (1989). *The 7 Habits of Highly Effective People*, Simon & Schuster, ISBN 0671663984, New York

Denning, P.J., Flores, F., & Luzmore, P. (1989). The Profession of IT: Orchestrating Coordination in Pluralistic Networks, *Communications of the ACM*, Vol. 53, No. 3, pp. 30-32, ISSN 0001-0782

DePree, M. (1989). *Leadership Is an Art*, Dell Publishing, ISBN 0385512465, New York

El Guindi, A., & Kamel, S. (2003). The Role of Virtual Multicultural Teams in Corporate Culture, In: *Advanced Topics in Global Information Management*, F.B. Tan (Ed.), 62-86, IGI Publishing, ISBN 1591400643, Hershey, Pennsylvania

Glaeser, E.L. (2010). *Making Sense of Bangalore*, Legatum Institute, ISBN 978-1-907409-05-9, London, England

Guaspari, J. (1991). *The Customer Connection*, American Management Association, ISBN 0-8144-5837-8, New York

Guimaraes, T., & Dallow, P. (1999). Empirically Testing the Benefits, Problems and Success Factors for Telecommuting Programmes. *European Journal of Information Systems*, Vol. 8, No. 1 (March 1999), pp. 40-54, ISSN 0960-085X

Gwizdka, J. (2002). Reinventing the Inbox: Supporting the Management of Pending Tasks in Email, In: *Proceedings of CHI EA '02, Human Factors in Computing Systems*, pp. 550-551, ISBN 1-58113-454-1, ACM, New York

Harragan, B.L. (1977). *Games Mother Never Taught You*, Warner Books, ISBN 0892560193, New York

Herbsleb, J.D. (2007). Global Software Engineering: The Future of Socio-technical Coordination. In: *Future of Software Engineering, 2007 (FOSE '07)*, L.C. Briand & A. Wolf (Eds.), pp. 188-198, ISBN 0-7695-2829-5, IEEE Computer Society, Washington, DC

Hill, L.A. (1992). *Becoming a Manager: Mastery of a New Identity*, Penguin Books, ISBN 0875843026, New York

Hinds, P.J., & Bailey, D.E. (2003). Out of Sight, Out of Sync: Understanding Conflict in Distributed Teams. *Organization Science*, Vol. 14, No. 6, (November–December 2003), pp. 615-632, ISSN 1047-7039

Howe, J. (2006). The Rise of Crowdsourcing. *Wired Magazine*, Vol. 14, No. 6, p. 06, ISSN 1059-1028

Humphrey, W.S. (2000). *A Discipline for Software Engineering*, Addison Wesley, ISBN 0201546108, New York

Humphrey, W.S. (2010). *Reflections on Management: How to Manage Your Software Projects, Your Teams, Your Boss, and Yourself*, Addison Wesley, ISBN 032171153X, New York

Krames, J.A. (2005). *Jack Welch and the 4 E's of Leadership: How to Put GE's Leadership Formula to Work in Your Organization*, McGraw-Hill, ISBN 0071457801, New York

Kraut, R., Maher, M.L., Olson, J., Malone, T.W., Pirolli, P., & Thomas, J.C. (2010). Scientific Foundations: A Case for Technology-Mediated Social-Participation Theory. *Computer*, Vol. 43, No. 11, pp. 22-28, ISSN 0018-9162

Krishna, S., Sahay, S., & Walsham, G. (2004). Managing Cross-Cultural Issues in Global Software Outsourcing. *Communications of the ACM - Human-Computer Etiquette*, Vol. 47, No. 4 (April 2004), pp. 62-66, ISSN 0001-0782

Leuf, B., & Cunningham, W. (2001). *The Wiki Way: Quick Collaboration on the Web*, Addison Wesley, ISBN 0-201-71499-X, New York

Liew, C.L., Foo, S., & Chennupati, K. R. (2000). A Study of Graduate Student End-Users' Use and Perception of Electronic Journals. *Online Information Review*, Vol. 24, No. 4, pp. 302-315, ISSN 1468-4527

McConnell, S. (1998). *Software Project Survival Guide*, Microsoft Press, ISBN 1-57231-621-7, Redmond, Washington

Noll, J., Beecham, S., & Richardson, I. (2010). Global Software Development and Collaboration: Barriers and Solutions. *ACM Inroads*, Vol. 1, No. 3, ISSN 2153-2184

Quinones, P.-A., Fussell, S.R., Soibelman, L., & Akinci, B. (2009). Bridging the Gap: Discovering Mental Models in Globally Collaborative Contexts, *Proceeding of the 2009 International Workshop on Intercultural Collaboration*, pp. 101-110, ISBN 978-1-60558-502-4, Association of Computing Machinery, Palo Alto, California, February 20-21, 2009

Radicati Group, Inc. (2009, May 6). *Email Statistics Report, 2009-2013: Including Statistics for Email, Instant Messaging, and Wireless Email* [press release]. Available from: http://www.radicati.com/?p=3237

Salacuse, J.W. (1998). Ten Ways That Culture Affects Negotiating Style: Some Survey Results. *Negotiation Journal*, Vol. 14, No. 3, (July 1998), pp. 221–240, ISSN 1571-9979

Sattaluri, S., & Thissen, M.R. (2005). Cross-Organizational Collaboration Using Web Based Technologies. Presented at the 2005 International Field Directors and Technology Conference, Miami Beach, Florida. Listed at http://www.ifdtc.org/pc2005.html

Shachaf, P. (2008). Cultural Diversity and information and communication technology impacts on global virtual teams: An exploratory study, *Information & Management*, Vol. 45, pp. 131-142, ISSN 0378-7206

Teasley, S.D., Covi, L.A., Krishnan, M.S., & Olson, J.S. (2002). Rapid Software Development Through Team Collocation, *IEEE Transactions on Software Engineering*, Vol. 28, No. 7, (July 2002), pp. 671-683, ISSN 0098-5589

Thissen, M.R., Page, J.M., Bharathi, M.C., & Austin, T.L. (2007). Communication Tools for Distributed Software Development Teams, *Proceedings of the ACM-SIGMIS CPR '07 Conference: The Global Information Technology Workforce*, pp. 28–35, ISBN 978-1-59593-641-7, St Louis, Missouri, USA, April 19-21, 2007

Vardi, M.Y. (2010). Globalization and Offshoring of Software Revisited. *Communications of the ACM*, Vol. 53, No. 5, p. 5, ISSN 0001-0782

Wiegers, K.E. (1999). *Software Requirements*, Microsoft Press, ISBN 0-7356-0631-5, Redmond, Washington

Wilson, G. (2009). How Do Scientists Really Use Computers? *American Scientist*, Vol. 97, pp. 360-362, ISSN 0003-0996

3

Bilateral Home Bias: New Perspective, New Findings

Crina Pungulescu
Université de Toulouse, Toulouse Business School - Barcelona Campus (ESEC)
Spain

1. Introduction

While it is generally agreed that international diversification improves portfolio performance, many countries hold puzzling low levels of foreign assets. The difference between optimal and observed (far too low) foreign holdings is known as the home bias puzzle (see French & Poterba, 1991). The academic literature has proposed several possible explanations for the home bias puzzle. The prime targets were transaction costs such as fees, commissions and higher spreads (see Glassman & Riddick, 2001; Tesar & Werner, 1995; Warnock, 2001) and direct barriers to international investment (see Black, 1974; Errunza & Losq, 1985; Stulz, 1981). Evidence in Tesar & Werner (1995) and more recently Glassman & Riddick (2001) and Warnock (2001), however, rules out transaction cost as an important driver of the equity home bias. Moreover, the home bias puzzle persists even in times when most direct obstacles to foreign investment have disappeared. Important contributions focus on differences in the amount and quality of information between domestic and foreign stocks (see Brennan & Cao, 1997; Gehrig, 1993; Veldkamp & Van Nieuwerburgh, 2006), on hedging of non-traded goods consumption as a motive for holding domestic securities (see Adler & Dumas, 1983; Cooper & Kaplanis, 1994; Stockman & Dellas, 1989), and more recently on psychological or behavioral factors (see Coval & Moskowitz, 1999; Grinblatt & Keloharju, 2000; Huberman, 2001). However, also these alternative explanations do not fully account for the observed home bias in international financial markets (see Ahearne et al., 2004, among others).

A relatively new surge in cross-border equity holdings works towards narrowing the gap and the documented decline in home bias (see Baele et al., 2007) suggests that countries are taking steps towards optimizing their international equity portfolios.

Until recently, available data only allowed for a comparison between domestic equity holdings and (aggregated) rest-of-the-world foreign holdings. The International Monetary Fund's Coordinated Portfolio Investment Survey (CPIS) collects information regarding the foreign equity holdings of 74 countries and territories, detailed by issuing country. Fidora et al. (2007) use this database available for the years 1997, 2001, 2002 and 2003 in order to compute bilateral home bias and show the contribution of real exchange volatility to explaining the well-known preference for local assets.

This chapter combines the (increasingly extensive) CPIS database for the period 2001-2009 to compute bilateral home bias together with a new perspective on optimal investment "benchmarks" in order to explore the dynamics of bilateral home bias and the importance of the host market performance. This first such exploratory exercise uncovers the phenomenon of "partner bias" (i.e. consistent overinvestment in specific target countries, regardless of market performance considerations) and suggest several hypotheses for further study.

A prime issue when measuring home bias, as the deviation from optimal international investment, is the choice of "benchmark", i.e. the "correct" mix of domestic and foreign equity. Traditionally, in the home bias literature it is assumed that the optimal portfolio weights equal each country's share in the world market capitalization. This result is valid only to the extent that the generating model, the International Capital Asset Pricing Model (I-CAPM) is an accurate description of the returns data. If this is the case, the I-CAPM investor should hold the market portfolio. Each country is expected therefore not to hold a larger proportion of domestic assets than its own share in the world market. At the same time, the optimal portfolio weights in foreign equity of all other countries are given by their respective market shares. No country raises to the challenge.

Given the rather strict assumptions of the I-CAPM, it is natural to question the validity of its investment prediction. The alternative to the I-CAPM optimal portfolio weights, the so-called 'model-based' approach was until recently, a pure 'data-based' approach (see Pástor, 2000). Discarding completely the I-CAPM assumption, purely 'data-based' optimal weights are calculated in a standard mean-variance framework using the sample moments of the return data. However, the sample mean and variance of asset returns are notoriously unreliable estimates of the true expected returns and variance (see Britten-Jones, 1994; Jenske, 2001; Merton, 1980). The resulting optimal weights take extreme and volatile values, of little use as optimal investment "benchmarks". Thus, the wide use of the 'model-based' approach is not necessarily evidence for the pertinence of the I-CAPM but more for the lack of a viable alternative.

Alternatives to the debatable I-CAPM prediction have been recently made possible, through the Bayesian portfolio selection framework developed by Pástor & Stambaugh (2000), Pástor (2000) and the Multi-Prior volatility correction method of Garlappi et al. (2007) that provide different sets of optimal portfolio weights and consequently, alternative measures of home bias. Pástor (2000) investigates to what extent optimal portfolio weights vary with various degrees of mistrust in the asset pricing model. In this Bayesian framework, the investor is neither forced to accept unconditionally the pricing relation nor discard it completely in favor of the data. As the degree of scepticism about the model grows, the resulting optimal weights move away from those implied by the 'model-based' approach to those obtained from the 'data-based' approach. While this methodology typically produces weights that are much more stable over time compared to the 'data-based' approach, its reliance on sample data for higher levels of model uncertainty means, however, that extreme and volatile weights cannot be ruled out. This can be addressed by applying the volatility correction technique developed by Garlappi et al. (2007). Their methodology introduces estimation risk in the standard mean variance framework by restricting the expected return for each asset to lie within a specified confidence interval around its estimated value, rather than treating the point estimate as the only possible value, i.e. they allow for multiple priors.

This methodology is also applied directly to returns data for a large set of countries to obtain volatility corrected 'data-based' benchmarks for optimal weights and alternative to the I-CAPM market share weights. This innovative perspective on optimal investment "benchmarks" results not only in alternative values of home bias, but also facilitates a deeper understanding of the international investment decision. A mean-variance investor might be more attracted by gains from investing in well performing markets (based on available data

on asset returns) than by the wisdom of the I-CAPM. In this case, and especially in the bilateral framework made possible by the CPIS data, the compelling performance of home versus host markets might be instrumental in explaining the investors' international portfolio decisions.
The purpose of the present exercise is therefore to provide a first exploration of the above hypothesis using country data on returns and bilateral foreign holdings. The 'data-based' and (to a certain extent) the Bayesian approaches allow for alternative rankings of the countries' attractiveness as well-performing investment destinations, compared to the I-CAPM prediction. More specifically, this approach makes it possible to distinguish the countries whose performance (from a mean-variance perspective) allows them to optimally "hold in" more domestic capital and conversely, which countries "deserve" a higher share of foreign capital. By comparing the Bayesian and 'data-based' sets of optimal weights with observed bilateral allocations, we can infer whether home bias is essentially affected by the relative performance the home versus host country.
The patterns uncovered by this first look into the dynamics of home bias across country pairs start with the first documenting of a phenomenon uncovered here: the existence of a partner bias, driven possibly by geographical closeness and cultural or historical ties. The partner bias is exhibited by both developed and emerging markets and endures across years where market performance suggests suboptimality of such a strategy. Secondly, there are noticeable differences from developed to emerging countries with respect to the adequacy of their equity investment strategies, in favor of the former. The converse of the proximity hypothesis also appears true, as countries that are less developed and/or further apart are consistently more home biased. Last but not least, this chapter raises the question of a possible crisis effect (eroding the process of market integration) that, together with the dynamics of bilateral home bias warrant further study.
The remainder of this chapter is organized as follows. Section 2 reviews the three alternative decision frameworks provided to the investors and discusses the chosen measure for bilateral home bias and section 3 presents data issues arising from the use of the Coordinated Portfolio Investment Survey (CPIS). The main patterns apparent within the bilateral home bias data are introduced in section 4, while section 5 concludes by reviewing the initial findings and the agenda for future research in this field.

2. Optimal portfolio weights and home bias measures

This section gives a brief presentation of three alternative frameworks available to a mean-variance investor to compute his optimal portfolio weights: (1) the traditional I-CAPM framework of Lintner (1965), which is the overwhelming choice in the home bias literature; (2) the Bayesian framework developed by Pástor (2000) and (3) the Multi-Prior framework of Garlappi et al. (2007).[1]

2.1 Three alternatives for the mean-variance investor

An investor making his portfolio decision under the mean-variance framework of Markowitz (1952) and Sharpe (1963) chooses to divide his investment budget across the available assets such that the ensuing portfolio gives the highest expected returns for his acceptable level of risk. When short sales are allowed and a budget constraint is enforced, the investor's maximization problem has an analytical solution expressed as a function of the mean and

[1] For more detailed discussion and an application of these techniques to the home bias problem, see Baele et al. (2007).

variance of excess returns. Under strict assumptions, the I-CAPM provides a clear portfolio decision to the mean-variance investor. The I-CAPM is valid in a perfectly integrated world, where the law of one price holds universally and markets clear (total wealth is equal to total value of securities). The world market portfolio can then be defined as the sum of all individual portfolios weighted by the positions held by mean-variance investors. The portfolio implication of the CAPM is that the average mean-variance investor holds the market portfolio (Lintner, 1965). In an international setting, the optimal investment weights of a country according to this so-called 'model-based' approach, are given by the relative shares of domestic and foreign equities in the world market capitalization. This implies that the optimal portfolio weights are given by the relative shares of each country in the world market and regardless of his domestic market, the average investor should hold about 40% of his budget in US stocks, 10% in stocks of Japan and respectively UK, 5% in French stocks and less in the other equity markets according to their relative weights. The home bias literature follows these assumptions and compares domestic and foreign holdings to show the well-known preference to domestic assets.
The I-CAPM results in the well-known linear beta relationship between risk premium on the domestic portfolio and the expected excess return on the world market benchmark [2]:

$$E(r_d) - r_f = \beta \left[E(r_w) - r_f \right], \tag{1}$$

where r_d is the real return on the domestic market portfolio, r_f is the risk free rate, $\beta \equiv \frac{cov(r_w, r_d)}{var(r_w)}$ is the world market beta of the domestic market and r_w is the return on the world market portfolio. The empirical counterpart of equation 1 is given by

$$r_d - r_f = \alpha + \beta \left(r_w - r_f \right) + \varepsilon, \tag{2}$$

where α and ε are respectively the intercept and the error term. The I-CAPM is considered valid if estimates of the intercept, $\hat{\alpha}$ are zero.
The debate of the validity of the I-CAPM, naturally casts a shadow on the results of home bias computed as the deviation of actual portfolio weights from world market shares. The traditional alternative to using the I-CAPM predictions about optimal weights would have been to plug in the sample mean and variance of a time series of asset returns in the analytical solution to the mean-variance maximization problem. Notoriously noisy (see Merton, 1980), the expected returns estimated by the sample mean perturb the final results for "optimal" weights into chaotic predictions alternating heavy short sales with large long positions in any given asset. The home bias literature's choice for the world market shares as optimal portfolio weights is rather a reaction to the lack of merit of the data alternative rather than an endorsement of the I-CAPM as the data generating model. Recent developments in the portfolio selection literature allow smoothing of the 'data-based' solution into relevant investment guidelines. Pástor (2000) uses a Bayesian updating approach by which optimal weights are the result of combining the initial prediction of the I-CAPM with 'data-based' information in amounts depending on the investor's degree of mistrust in the validity of the model. In this framework, when there is mistrust in the I-CAPM, the data becomes informative and is involved in the portfolio allocation decision. The degree of trust (i.e. the belief that the intercept $\hat{\alpha}$ is zero) is expressed in values of the standard errors of the intercept

[2] This model makes the additional assumption that currency risk is not priced. See De Santis & Gérard (2006) and Fidora et al. (2007) for an analysis of exchange rate risk on home bias measures.

σ_α. A small value indicates a strong belief that the theoretical model is valid and results in optimal portfolio weights that closely correspond to the 'model based' approach. A higher value involves data to a larger extent in the computation of optimal weights leading thus to a different set of optimal weights and brings us closer to the results of the 'data based' approach. Full mistrust in the model (i.e. $\sigma_\alpha \to \infty$) coincides with the 'data based' optimal weights. This Bayesian interpretation is an insightful reconciliation of the 'model' and 'data-based' approaches. For instance, a nonzero value for $\hat{\alpha}$, even if insignificant according to a standard t-test (and therefore failing to reject the I-CAPM), could become instrumental in explaining why observed allocations deviate from the model prescriptions.

The larger the mistrust in the I-CAPM results in a stronger reliance on data in order to obtain optimal portfolio weights which makes the investment prediction all the more vulnerable to data volatility. This can be corrected to a certain extent by applying the Multi-Prior technique of Garlappi et al. (2007). Garlappi et al. (2007) extend the mean-variance optimization problem by incorporating the investor's aversion to uncertainty over the estimate of expected returns. This changes the standard mean-variance problem in two ways: (1) it binds the expected returns to a confidence interval around their estimate, thus taking into account the eventual estimation error and (2) it allows the investor to minimize over the choice of expected returns, thus manifesting its aversion to uncertainty. The result of this extended mean-variance optimization is to obtain considerably smoother optimal portfolio weights using only time series of data.

By applying these techniques, the relative market performance as embodied in the data on asset returns can be meaningfully used in the portfolio decision.

This chapter computes and compares three sets of optimal weights: (1) I-CAPM weights (i.e. relative world market shares); (2) weights obtained by combining the I-CAPM with available returns data using the Bayesian updating technique of Pástor (2000)[3] and further corrected by Multi-Prior technique of Garlappi et al. (2007) and (3) weights obtained from available returns data smoothed by directly applying the same Multi-Prior volatility correction of Garlappi et al. (2007).

2.2 Bilateral home bias measure

The measure of bilateral home bias results from the relative difference between actual and optimal holdings of country j equity by country i:

$$HB_{ij} = \frac{OPT_j - ACT_{ij}}{max\left(|OPT_j|, |ACT_{ij}|\right)}, \tag{3}$$

where HB_{ij} represents the bilateral home bias of country i with respect to host country j, OPT_j is the optimal portfolio weight of destination country j computed under one of the three frameworks presented in Section 2.1 and ACT_{ij} measures the actual holdings by country i of equity issued in country j.

Virtually all the literature on home bias, limited by data availability contents itself with comparing domestic with foreign (rest-of-the-world) holdings. Without exception, this aggregate perspective shows that the actual and optimal weights are positive and actual

[3] The degree of mistrust in the model - used to determine the degree to which the data is used to update the prior belief in the I-CAPM - is chosen based on the standard errors of the intercept in the I-CAPM regression.

weights are lower than optimal weights. In this case, equation 3 becomes the well-known formula:

$$HB_i = 1 - \frac{ACT_i}{OPT_i}, \quad (4)$$

where ACT_i is the actual share of foreign holdings in country i's portfolio and OPT_i, its optimal foreign equity investment. This measure is therefore bound between 0 (when actual holdings are optimal) and 1 (when the country is fully invested in domestic equity).

This chapter uses recently available data on actual holdings (from the Coordinated Portfolio Investment Survey conducted by the International Monetary Fund) in order to take the analysis of home bias to the bilateral level and applies the techniques outlined in Section 2.1 to compute three sets of optimal weights. In this perspective, both actual and optimal weights can be negative (short sales being allowed) and countries may be overinvested in some of their investment destinations. If equation 4 were applied here, the (much lower) optimal weights in the denominator might result in extreme values for home bias that are practically irrelevant for subsequent analysis. Equation 3 redefines the formula for computing home bias in such cases, maintaining therefore the scale of the resulting home bias. In their paper linking home bias to exchange rate volatility, Fidora et al. (2007) make the same choice when computing bilateral home bias.

3. Data issues

The current exercise on bilateral home bias is made possible by the initiative of the International Monetary Fund (IMF) to conduct the Coordinated Portfolio Investment Survey (CPIS) in which 74 economies volunteer information about the geographical distribution of their foreign assets. The first trial was successfully conducted in 1997 and starting with 2001, the CPIS takes place every year. This chapter uses the 9 years of data on cross-border stocks available since 2001.

While the value-added in information brought about by such detailed statistics is substantial, it has to be noticed that several possible bias are in-built in this database. If for instance, country A uses a broker company in country B in order to ultimately invest in a third country C, the database will not allow us to uncover country A's holdings of country C's equity. Also, participating economies may (and do) on occasion choose to withhold information on the amounts of their holdings.

Data on market index prices and market capitalization is obtained from Datastream. Monthly US$-denominated total returns have been computed for 58 of the 74 economies covered by the CPIS. Where available (34 cases) Datastream's total market indices have been used. The coverage starts in January 1973 for the more established markets and as late as 2006 for Uruguay and Luxembourg. The world market index has been computed as a weighted average of the available market indices at each point in time. In order to compute Bayesian and 'data-based' optimal weights every period, only the countries with 120 monthly observations of returns data available prior to the year-end observation, have been taken into consideration.

The risk-free rate is the one-month Treasury Bill rate from Ibbotson and Associates Inc., available on Kenneth French's website[4].

[4] http://mba.tuck.dartmouth.edu/pages/faculty/ken.french/data_library.html

4. Results and patterns

The available data collected results in the following coverage for bilateral home bias: 15,423 observations are obtained for the I-CAPM home bias, pairing each year between 48 and 58 investing countries and 53 to 58 destination countries, 13,054 observations for Bayesian home bias (48 to 58 investing countries and 33 to 49 destinations) and 13,385 observations for 'data-based' home bias (48 and 58 investing countries and 34 to 52 destinations). The differences in coverage across the three measures come from the different data requirements for their computation, specifically the availability of market capitalization figures and/or long enough series of asset returns data.

4.1 From home bias to partner bias

The bilateral nature of this database allows a particular refinement of the notion of home bias. While most previous studies are forced to an aggregate view that suggests invariably that countries underinvest with respect to the rest of the world, zooming in to the level of individual destination countries uncovers a non-negligible amount of instances of overinvestment (negative home bias). Apart from their traditional home bias, many countries exhibit exceeding preferences for some destination countries in their equity portfolios. Otherwise put, many countries are partner biased.

Figure 1 shows for the I-CAPM home bias that while underinvestment (positive home bias) remains the dominant pattern, the examples of overinvestment are systematic. For each year from 2001 to 2009, all available figures for bilateral home bias are arranged in ascending year, with visible increases in the share of negative observations from year to year. The instances of negative home bias account from 12 to 18% of observations in any given year.

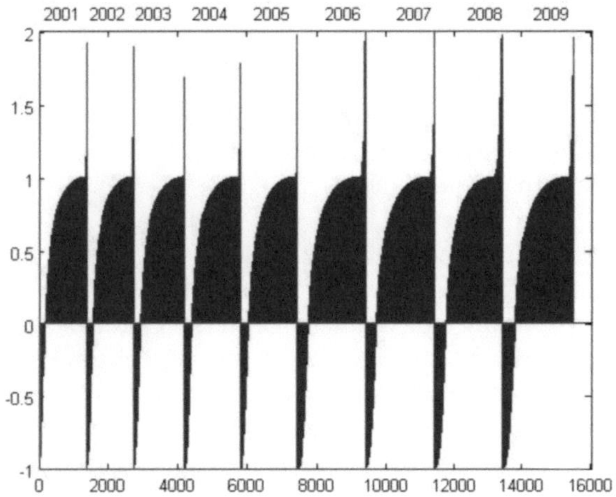

Fig. 1. I-CAPM Bilateral Home Bias
The figure shows bilateral home bias figures computed under the I-CAPM framework, arranged in ascending order for each year from 2001 to 2009.

When refining the I-CAPM optimal investment policy by taking into account the dynamics of asset returns, the amount of foreign holdings that exceed the optimal "benchmark" (from the Bayesian perspective) range from 50 to 65% of the observations (see Figure 2). However, the figure also suggests that the Bayesian framework is a more realistic representation of the optimization decision of investors, a substantial part of the observations appear close to the optimal zero home bias.

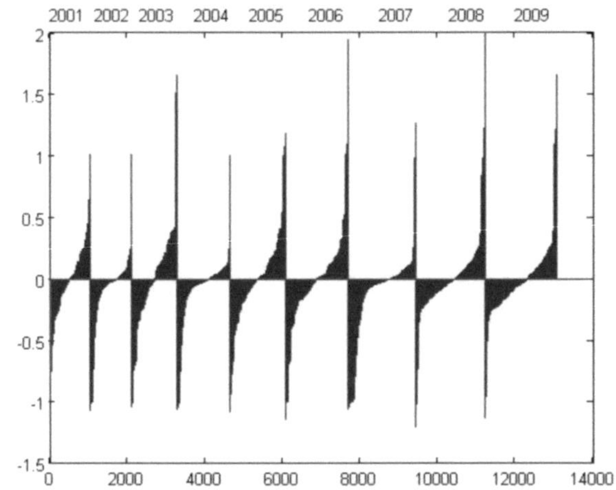

Fig. 2. Bayesian Bilateral Home Bias
The figure shows bilateral home bias figures computed under the Bayesian framework, arranged in ascending order for each year from 2001 to 2009.

Focusing only on market performance in deriving optimal portfolio weights under the 'data-based' framework, offers the most extreme view on home bias, with the largest values both on the negative and on the positive side. Figure 3 shows that few countries seem to follow an entirely data driven objective, as most of the observations fall far from 0. However, under this optimization framework as well, underinvestment is balanced by overinvestment and the share of negative figures ranges from 44 to 55%.
Having uncovered the phenomenon of partner bias, the following endeavours to extract a first set of hypotheses and patterns underlying it.

4.2 The importance of financial centers

The observation of a partner bias is linked to an important caveat present in this database, which is the particular importance of financial centers. Countries whose financial markets are actively intermediating cross-border capital flows, report foreign assets and liabilities in amounts disproportionate to their market capitalizations and/or the performance of their domestic asset returns. Some of the overinvesment observed in the data is bound to occur due to the presence of such markets, whose main activity is undergone on behalf of investors from (unidentifiable) third countries.
One way to determine whether the negative home bias is exclusively due to the presence of financial centers among the countries analyzed, is to identify the countries that appear as overinvestors or destinations of overinvestment in the majority of their bilateral relationships. Across the three measures of home bias, Ireland, a recognized financial center, appears to constantly overinvest in the equity of its partner countries (with the largest share - 60 to 70% - of negative positions in total investing observations). Together with other financial hubs such as Luxembourg and Bermuda, Ireland is also one of the preferred destinations for overinvestment. Other countries that also tend to be part of relationships with predominantly

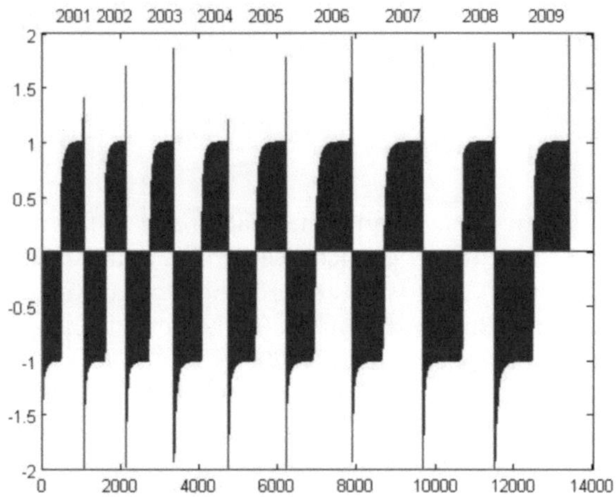

Fig. 3. 'Data-based' Bilateral Home Bias from 2001-2009
The figure shows bilateral home bias figures computed under the 'data-based' framework, arranged in ascending order for each year from 2001 to 2009.

negative home bias to some extent for possibly similar financial intermediation activities are Malaysia, The Netherlands, UK, Mauritius and Cyprus.
However, the presence of negative home bias is not an exclusive indication of financial intermediation. Countries like Colombia, Egypt, Norway are consistent overinvestors under at least one of the three optimality frameworks provided. Other countries too are overweighed in some foreign portfolios, especially when their market performance is taken into account. Bayesian and 'data-based' home bias measures suggest that many countries have not been a wise investment for the large majority of their partners: South Africa, Korea, Brazil, Indonesia, Latvia, Argentina, Hungary, Poland, Romania a.o.
Despite the (perturbing) effect of financial intermediation on the data, there are reasons to believe the data truly uncovered a previously undocumented phenomenon of partner bias.

4.3 Deviations from optimality and crisis effect

A second caveat to be taken into account due to the substantial negative home bias is that descriptive statistics of raw figures of bilateral home bias would result in the canceling out of positions of opposite signs. This situation occurs by default in all traditional studies of home bias that compare domestic and foreign holdings. For comparison, this section reports aggregate figures of bilateral home bias per investing as well as per destination country.
For a more accurate representation of bilateral home bias, the deviation from optimality is defined under the three measurement frameworks, first regarding each country's position as an investor:

$$DI_{it} = \sqrt{\frac{\Sigma_{j=\overline{1,n}} {HB_{ijt}}^2}{n}}, \tag{5}$$

where D_{it} represents for any year t, the deviation from optimality of bilateral home bias of investing country i averaged over the n available host countries j.

Similarly, DD_{jt} represents the deviation from optimality of bilateral home bias of destination country j, averaged over the m investing partners for any year t:

$$DD_{jt} = \sqrt{\frac{\Sigma_{i=\overline{1,m}} HB_{ijt}{}^2}{m}}. \tag{6}$$

Since the time frame includes the recent financial crisis, the sample is divided in three subperiods to observe possible differences occurring in the final subperiod which corresponds to the 2007-2009 crisis. Descriptive statistics are provided for averaged bilateral home bias and deviations from optimality for three subsamples: (1) the period 2001 - 2003, (2) the period 2004 - 2006 and (3) the financial crisis period, 2007 - 2009.

First, descriptive statistics for bilateral home bias and deviations from optimality are provided for data aggregated by investing countries. Table 1 provides results that would be comparable to aggregate home bias results discussed in previous literature. Consistent with Baele et al. (2007), for instance, the results suggest still a substantial I-CAPM home bias, corrected almost completely when data on asset returns is allowed to play a role in the investment decision. Bayesian and 'data-based' bilateral home bias are on average close to 0. However, the large ranges and standard deviations suggest especially for the I-CAPM and 'data-based' measures that in aggregation significant information has been lost through canceling out. The Bayesian measure, however, stands out as considerably smoother (lower range and standard deviation), suggesting that indeed a combination of the I-CAPM prediction and market performance is a better optimization framework.

	I-CAPM			BAYESIAN			DATA		
	(1)	(2)	(3)	(1)	(2)	(3)	(1)	(2)	(3)
	2001 - 2003	2004 - 2006	2007 - 2009	2001 - 2003	2004 - 2006	2007 - 2009	2001 - 2003	2004 - 2006	2007 - 2009
Mean	0.61	0.58	0.58	-0.05	-0.05	-0.05	-0.05	0.04	-0.01
Median	0.69	0.73	0.67	-0.06	-0.06	-0.07	-0.25	0.09	0.17
Minimum	-0.62	-0.76	-0.66	-0.35	-0.58	-0.32	-1.30	-1.16	-1.08
Maximum	0.95	0.95	1.01	0.68	0.71	0.72	1.00	1.00	1.00
Standard Deviation	0.30	0.36	0.37	0.19	0.19	0.15	0.93	0.88	0.82

Table 1. Descriptive Statistics of Bilateral Home Bias of Investing Countries
This table shows descriptive statistics for bilateral home bias aggregated by investor countries, across the three measures: I-CAPM, Bayesian and 'data-based' home bias and three periods: (1) 2001 - 2003, (2) 2004 - 2006, (3) 2007 - 2009.

Table 2 presents the same descriptive statistics for deviations of optimality aggregated by investing countries. The results confirm the appropriateness of the Bayesian optimization framework. Consistent with results for aggregate home bias presented by Baele et al. (2007), at the bilateral level, as well, deviations from optimality under the Bayesian perspective are dramatically decreased (by as much as 70%). The 'data-based' optimization framework is consistently furthest from the actual decisions of investors, with its large positive and negative positions in bilateral home bias resulting in the largest deviations from optimality.

The only statistically significant difference for the crisis period occurs for the deviations from I-CAPM optimality, which suggests that the crisis might be associated with possibly lower foreign holdings, leading to higher home bias. Under the interpretation of Baele et al. (2007)

that present the home bias as a relevant proxy of market integration, this raises the hypothesis that the financial crisis acted as a deterrent of the process of market integration.

	I-CAPM			BAYESIAN			DATA		
	(1)	(2)	(3)	(1)	(2)	(3)	(1)	(2)	(3)
	2001 - 2003	2004 - 2006	2007 - 2009	2001 - 2003	2004 - 2006	2007 - 2009	2001 - 2003	2004 - 2006	2007 - 2009
Mean	0.84	0.84	0.88	0.24	0.24	0.27	1.01	1.01	1.01
Median	0.84	0.84	0.89	0.23	0.22	0.25	1.00	1.00	1.00
Minimum	0.69	0.71	0.74	0.02	0.02	0.04	0.86	0.86	0.89
Maximum	0.97	0.94	1.03	0.64	0.93	0.80	1.39	1.15	1.16
Standard Deviation	0.06	0.05	0.06	0.13	0.16	0.15	0.09	0.06	0.04

Table 2. Descriptive Statistics of Deviations from Optimality of Bilateral Home Bias of Investing Countries
This table shows descriptive statistics for deviations from optimality aggregated by investor countries, across the three measures: I-CAPM, Bayesian and 'data-based' home bias and three periods: (1) 2001 - 2003, (2) 2004 - 2006, (3) 2007 - 2009.

Tables 3 and 4 provide the same descriptives for bilateral home bias and deviations from optimality, aggregated by destination countries. They present a similar picture, for the first time from the perspective of destination countries. In the case of the I-CAPM home bias, the larger ranges for deviations from optimality (compared to the ones reported for investing countries in Table 2) bring forth the idea that that some countries are preferred and others discriminated against, by most of their investing partners. These preferences act in direct breach of the asset pricing model. The statistics for deviations from Bayesian optimality, show that the deviations per destination countries, albeit higher, tend to be less volatile than the deviations of investing country home bias (with lower ranges and standard deviations during the three subperiods). This suggests that destination countries are chosen by most of their investing partner based on similar considerations regarding the performance of their stock returns. The deviations are consistently highest for the 'data-based' bilateral home bias, once again proving to be off-mark.

While at this stage the data only raises the hypothesis of a crisis effect (possibly deterring to some extent the previously documented phenomenon of market integration), with further analysis needed in order to settle the question, the dominant finding here remains the evidence that investors make an optimizing portfolio decision across a large number of foreign assets, in a manner not unlike the Bayesian updating methodology proposed by Pástor (2000).

4.4 Pairing and regional patterns

This section adds a first set of possible patterns and hypotheses regarding the bilateral home bias, extracted from examining the behavior of country pairs.

A first finding is that for both the I-CAPM and the Bayesian measures of home bias, a strongly significant positive correlation exists between the figures for the pairs Country A investing to Country B and reciprocally Country B investing to Country A. For the 'data-based' measure, the correlation is not statistically significant. It should be noted that the results for the 'data-based' measure (even after having applied the volatility correction mechanism of Garlappi et al. (2007) remain the least smooth. This suggestion of reciprocity in bilateral investment policies reinforces the idea of a partner bias, shared by pairs of countries and invites further analysis.

	I-CAPM			BAYESIAN			DATA		
	(1)	(2)	(3)	(1)	(2)	(3)	(1)	(2)	(3)
	2001 - 2003	2004 - 2006	2007 - 2009	2001 - 2003	2004 - 2006	2007 - 2009	2001 - 2003	2004 - 2006	2007 - 2009
Mean	0.66	0.66	0.59	0.04	-0.01	-0.04	0.06	0.02	-0.11
Median	0.71	0.70	0.61	-0.03	-0.02	-0.04	-0.04	-0.02	-0.08
Minimum	-0.04	-0.16	-0.33	-0.23	-0.25	-0.35	-0.27	-0.31	-0.43
Maximum	1.19	1.26	1.34	1.54	0.49	0.45	1.00	0.66	0.36
Standard Deviation	0.24	0.27	0.30	0.31	0.13	0.12	0.28	0.20	0.14

Table 3. Descriptive Statistics of Bilateral Home Bias of Destination Countries
This table shows descriptive statistics for bilateral home bias aggregated by destination countries, across the three measures: I-CAPM, Bayesian and 'data-based' home bias and three periods: (1) 2001 - 2003, (2) 2004 - 2006, (3) 2007 - 2009.

	I-CAPM			BAYESIAN			DATA		
	(1)	(2)	(3)	(1)	(2)	(3)	(1)	(2)	(3)
	2001 - 2003	2004 - 2006	2007 - 2009	2001 - 2003	2004 - 2006	2007 - 2009	2001 - 2003	2004 - 2006	2007 - 2009
Mean	0.85	0.86	0.88	0.30	0.38	0.35	1.01	1.01	1.00
Median	0.85	0.87	0.88	0.30	0.35	0.32	1.01	1.00	1.00
Minimum	0.48	0.48	0.54	0.15	0.21	0.21	0.93	0.95	0.78
Maximum	1.24	1.17	1.34	0.56	0.74	0.66	1.07	1.07	1.08
Standard Deviation	0.12	0.11	0.13	0.09	0.10	0.10	0.02	0.03	0.03

Table 4. Descriptive Statistics of Deviations from Optimality of Bilateral Home Bias of Destination Countries
This table shows descriptive statistics for deviations from optimality aggregated by investor countries, across the three measures: I-CAPM, Bayesian and 'data-based' home bias and three periods: (1) 2001 - 2003, (2) 2004 - 2006, (3) 2007 - 2009.

In order to gain more insight, the pairs of countries in the data are ranked according to the following criteria: (1) optimality of their foreign equity holdings; (2) consistent overinvestment (negative home bias) and (3) consistent underinvestment (home bias in the traditional acception).
For all three criteria, the pairs of countries that are, in any given year in the upper 10% are individually identified. The most relevant relationships are identified in the following.

4.4.1 Optimality of foreign holdings

The idea of reciprocity receives further support when investigating the pairs of countries that consistently appear in the top 10% of countries with low home bias. With respect to the I-CAPM home bias, the following pairs benefit reciprocally from (close to) optimal partner equity holdings: Austria - The Netherlands, Switzerland - Austria, Switzerland - Germany, Germany - France, Germany - The Netherlands, UK - The Netherlands, The Netherlands - Finland, France - The Netherlands, The Netherlands - Belgium. In other cases, consistent optimal investment behavior by the investing countries is not mimicked by the host countries. The most relevant examples involve the following pairs of investor to destination countries: Germany to Austria, Spain and Finland; France to Belgium, Finland, Spain and Italy; Finland to Norway and Denmark; The Netherlands to Switzerland, Norway to Switzerland, UK and The Netherlands; Sweden to Denmark and Switzerland. A possible pattern suggests itself. Developed European markets that have long standing trading traditions and are geographically close, follow and achieve (close to optimal) diversification benefits.

With respect to the Bayesian home bias, the best performers make for a different pattern and suggestion. It seems that combining data with the I-CAPM prediction, vindicates the (lower) investment decisions of several developed countries with respect with some (recurrent) emerging countries. The (under)investments (under the I-CAPM framework) of Belgium, Canada, Switzerland, France, Greece, Japan, Germany and Singapore to Turkey, as well as of Germany, France, Denmark, Japan, The Netherlands, Norway, Belgium and Spain to Argentina appear now justified.

An all market performance driving factor of investment decision (under the 'data-based' framework), appears to justify (to some extent) several countries' decisions to underinvest (based on I-CAPM standards) to the larger host markets such as USA (with repeated lower deviations of Austria, Switzerland, Argentina, Australia, Canada, Germany, Denmark, Netherlands, Norway, New Zealand, Sweden, UK, Finland, Japan and Singapore) as well as the UK (whose assets have closer to optimal weights in the portfolios of Canada, Germany, Denmark, Finland, France, Ireland, Norway, Sweden, USA, South Africa, Austria, Belgium and Singapore).

The most important patterns uncovered with respect to the optimality of investment strategies are firstly, the possible reciprocity of investment strategies for countries that benefit from cultural, historical and/or geographical proximity and secondly, the fact that market performance appears to play a more important role in the investment decision when the destination is an emerging country.

4.4.2 Negative home bias

In analyzing the negative observations for the I-CAPM home bias, further evidence adds to show the importance of financial centers in this data. The two consistent destinations of overinvestment are Bermuda (from Hong Kong, Singapore, USA, Ireland, South Africa, Austria, Bahrain, Brazil, Cyprus, Norway) and Luxembourg (from Belgium, Germany, Italy, Estonia, Hungary, Latvia, Iceland).

However, other pairs stand out for their consistent and reciprocal overinvestment. Estonia - Latvia, Czech Republic - Slovakia, Slovakia - Hungary. While these countries are small, they share not only a border but also historical and cultural ties that might explain why their partner equity weights exceed substantially the weight of the destination countries in the world market capitalization.

Financial centers are a relevant presence in the top 10% of overinvestment under the Bayesian framework, as well. Ireland appears as a dominant destination country for capital from Austria, Italy, Finland, UK, The Netherlands, Portugal and South Africa, followed by Switzerland with exceeding capital from Ireland, Germany, Denmark, The Netherlands, Norway, Sweden and Austria. Ireland is also a typical overinvestor, with preferred destinations being UK, Switzerland, Korea, Australia, Germany, Portugal, Brazil, Spain, The Netherlands, Belgium, Finland, Hong Kong, Sweden and Japan.

Reciprocity in overinvestment, a partner bias at work, is present here as well for the pairs Ireland - Italy, Finland - Sweden and Germany - Switzerland, with (excluding Ireland) clear implications of proximity driving investment and enduring even when confronted with (repeated) underperformance. The same hypothesis fits other bilateral relationships

consistently exhibiting overinvestment, such as those of: Estonia to Finland, Argentina to Brazil, Austria to Germany, New Zealand to Australia, Singapore to Hong Kong, Slovakia to Hungary, Belgium to France, France to Germany and to Spain, Cyprus to Greece, Portugal to Brazil and to Spain, Czech Republic and Slovakia to Austria, Belgium to The Netherlands.
A similar view emerges from the analysis of the 'data-based' negative home bias. Overinvestment persists from Denmark to Sweden, Finland to Sweden, Singapore to Hong Kong, Argentina to Brazil, Austria to Germany, Hungary to Poland, Ireland to Italy, Norway to Sweden, Belgium to Spain, France and The Netherlands, Germany to Spain, France and UK to Spain, Portugal to Brazil and Spain, Slovakia to Hungary, Chile to Brazil, Czech Republic to Ireland, Germany to France, Denmark to Finland.
When market performance considerations are dominant, Japan stands out as a consistently unwise destination from Australia, Austria, Canada, Switzerland, Germany, Denmark, Finland, France, Italy, The Netherlands, Norway, New Zealand, Singapore, Sweden and USA.

4.4.3 Positive home bias

The traditional view on home bias (represented by the positive observations in this data) shows on one hand a pattern of financial centers such as Bermuda and Luxembourg underinvesting in many of their counterparts, but also consistent underinvestment of some emerging countries with respect to larger, developed destination countries, such as Turkey to Sweden, Spain, France, Italy, Denmark, UK and USA; Argentina to Belgium; Bulgaria to Canada; Brazil to Japan and Thailand and Chile to Denmark, Hong Kong and Italy.
Under the Bayesian framework, USA (representing about 40% of the world market capitalization) stands out as the large destination that consistently receives comparatively too small weights in the portfolios of all its partners. Bermuda and Luxembourg continue to exhibit persistent home bias with respect to many partners, but also the pattern of inadequacy of emerging (or distant) countries' foreign holdings is maintained as for instance, in the cases of Argentina to Belgium, Australia to Belgium, Brazil to UK, Chile to UK, Cyprus to Russia.
The 'data-based' home bias provides further substantiation to the same claim, as countries further apart or less developed tend to exhibit higher home bias, as in the examples of Argentina to Belgium, Germany to Chile, Japan to Chile, Korea to Belgium, Brazil to Austria, Korea to Denmark.

5. Concluding remarks

This chapter provides a first analysis of the dynamics of bilateral home bias computed due to a recently available dataset covering 74 economies during the period 2001-2009. Disaggregating the well-documented phenomenon of home bias at the level of country pairs over time, uncovers several patterns and suggests hypotheses for further research. First, a partner bias (i.e. overinvestment, 'negative' home bias) appears to play an important role in the forming of international equity portfolios, driven possibly by geographical, cultural or historical proximity. Establishing causality remains the most important aim of subsequent research in this topic. A second pattern, regards a difference between emerging and developed countries in the optimality of their investment decisions, in favor of the former. Conversely pairs of countries that are less developed and further apart tend to exhibit higher bilateral home bias. Finally, the hypothesis of a crisis effect, in the sense of a possible temporary setback of the process of market integration deserves further analysis.

6. References

Adler, M. & Dumas, B. (1983). International portfolio choice and corporation finance: A synthesis., *Journal of Finance* 38: 925–984.

Ahearne, A. G., Griever, W. L. & Warnock, F. E. (2004). Information costs and home bias: An analysis of U.S. holdings of foreign equities, *Journal of International Economics* 62: 313–336.

Baele, L., Pungulescu, C. & Ter Horst, J. R. (2007). Model uncertainty, financial market integration and the home bias puzzle, *Journal of International Money and Finance* 26: 606–630.

Black, F. (1974). International capital market equilibrium with investment barriers, *Journal of Financial Economics* 1: 337–352.

Brennan, M. J. & Cao, H. H. (1997). International portfolio investment flows, *Journal of Finance* 52: 1851–1880.

Britten-Jones, M. (1994). The sampling error in estimates of mean-variance efficient portfolio weights, *Journal of Finance* 54: 655–671.

Cooper, I. & Kaplanis, E. (1994). Home bias in equity portfolios, inflation hedging, and international capital market equilibrium, *Review of Financial Studies* 7: 45–60.

Coval, J. D. & Moskowitz, T. J. (1999). Home bias at home: Local equity preference in domestic portfolios, *Journal of Finance* 54: 2045–2073.

De Santis, R. A. & Gérard, B. (2006). Financial integration, international portfolio choice and the European Monetary Union, *ECB Working Paper No. 626* .

Errunza, V. & Losq, E. (1985). International asset pricing under mild segmentation: Theory and test, *Journal of Finance* 40: 105–124.

Fidora, M., Fratzscher, M. & Thimann, C. (2007). Home bias in global bond and equity markets: The role of real exchange rate volatility, *Journal of International Money and Finance* 26: 631–655.

French, K. R. & Poterba, J. M. (1991). Investor diversification and international equity markets, *American Economic Review* 81: 222–226.

Garlappi, L., Uppal, R. & Wang, T. (2007). Portfolio selection with parameter and model uncertainty: A multi-prior approach, *Review of Financial Studies* 20: 41–81.

Gehrig, T. (1993). An information based explanation of the domestic bias in international equity investment, *Scandinavian Journal of Economics* 95: 97–109.

Glassman, D. A. & Riddick, L. A. (2001). What causes home asset bias and how should it be measured?, *Journal of Empirical Finance* 8: 35–54.

Grinblatt, M. & Keloharju, M. (2000). The investment behavior, and performance of various investor types: A study of Finland's unique data set, *Journal of Financial Economics* 55: 43–67.

Huberman, G. (2001). Familiarity breeds investment, *Review of Financial Studies* 14: 659–680.

Jenske, K. (2001). Equity home bias - can information cost explain the puzzle?, *Economic Review* 86: 31–42.

Lintner, J. (1965). The valuation of risky assets and the selection of risky investments in stock portfolios and capital budgets, *Review of Economics and Statistics* 47: 13–37.

Markowitz, H. M. (1952). Portfolio selection, *Journal of Finance* 7: 77–91.

Merton, R. C. (1980). On estimating the expected return on the market, *Journal of Financial Economics* 8: 323–361.

Pástor, L. (2000). Portfolio selection and asset pricing models, *Journal of Finance* 55: 179–223.

Pástor, L. & Stambaugh, R. F. (2000). Comparing asset pricing models: An investment perspective, *Journal of Financial Economics* 56: 335–381.

Sharpe, W. (1963). A simplified model for portfolio analysis, *Management Science* 9: 277–293.

Stockman, A. C. & Dellas, H. (1989). International portfolio nondiversification and exchange rate variability, *Journal of International Economics* 26: 271–289.

Stulz, R. (1981). On the effects of barriers to international investment, *Journal of Finance* 36: 923–934.

Tesar, L. L. & Werner, I. (1995). Home bias and high turnover, *Journal of International Money and Finance* 14: 467–492.

Veldkamp, L. & Van Nieuwerburgh, S. (2006). Information immobility and the home bias puzzle, *Working Paper* .

Warnock, F. E. (2001). Home bias and high turnover reconsidered, *International Finance Discussion Paper No. 702* .

4

Globalization and Global Innovations

Hassan Danaeefard and Tayebeh Abbasi
Tarbiat Modares University
Iran

1. Introduction

One of the main phenomena to which societies are confronted and that has influenced all aspects of social life of people living in the earth is globalization. Globalization is a multi-facet phenomenon which leads to disappearance of the borders between economic, social, cultural and political relations and shapes a modern relation and communication between nations (within countries and among countries)

Due to the significance of this phenomenon in the life, it has been the focus of the attention of scholars so that most scholars consider globalization as a factor for development, welfare and integration among nations which lead to the distribution of global benefits among people. Despite this perspective, some theorists consider it a discriminative force which makes the poor, poorer and the rich, richer. In their views, many people of developed and advanced counties would benefit of globalization while developing and undeveloped countries would drop behind developed countries due to lack of facilities to compete in this area.

So based on this, the proponents of globalization consider it as a positive phenomenon in all respects and the opponents consider it as the destructive factor of regional and national cultures due to overcoming the capitalism and the increase in economic and political dimensions. Because of this, the consequences of globalization on different aspects of human life and different matters lead to dissolution of interpretations.

The aim of this chapter is to examine the relation of globalization and innovation. So first the concept of globalization and its origin are reviewed and then for better investigation of this relation, the effect of globalization on different aspects of innovation would be analyzed. The authors believe that globalization reduces innovation following the reduction of variety in different aspects of the society including economic, social, political and cultural dimensions and inclination toward integration and unification and it has negative effect on innovation.

2. The concept of globalization

The term "globalization" has not a clear meaning and different definitions are provided to it under the influence of ideological backgrounds of researchers. Some consider globalization the same as communication revolution, other has considered it as a form of post-modernism and some other has regarded it as a new form of states without border. The optimistic view toward this phenomenon has considered it as a factor for growth, peace and friendship and the proximity of nations, also abundance of blessings and the pessimistic view equals it to crisis poverty and the disappearance of weak communities and unequal competition (Alvani, 2004).

Abushouk (2006) has classified the provided definitions for globalization into five groups considering the points which have been confirmed it them:

The first definition considers globalization synonymous with internationalization assuming that globalization leads to closer relation between nations within the framework of flowing of trade and investment and easier and faster communications (Hirst and Thompson, 1996).

However this definition has been criticized by some scholars such as Jan Art Scholte. He believes that cross-border relation between nations has existed long before the term "globalization" entered in international relation dictionary. Based on it, such definition does not provide a convincing meaning of globalization.

The second definition considers globalization as de-terrorization and liberalization and describes it as an integration process of international economy and reduction of legal limitation of import and export of goods, services, cash and financial tools. In this view, globalization refers to a movement in nations which leads to liberalization of negotiations between them and other nations and creates a borderless space for economic and financial affairs (Sander, 1996).

On the other hand, critics of this definition reject the general identity of these two terms (globalization and liberalization) and argue that this integration process for connecting the nations has appeared long before, especially at the time when imperial powers of Europe preserved their control on third- world countries (Abushouk, 2006).

Third definition assumes globalization as universalization; the proponents of this definition consider globalization as the process of spreading the topics, experiences and values all over the worlds and between people living in the earth (Abushouk, 2006; Alvani, 2004). In other words, the universalization informs of the combination of cultures and the experiences of people. In confirmation of samples globalization is referred to as the spreading of TV, automobile and etc. and the same trends of life and government of organizations. However some critics have criticized this definition. They argue that the transcontinental spreading of religions and trades have been long before globalization. So that the term "Universality" is proper for describing the spread of experiences and values and it should be confined to new global activities which have emerged from second half of the 20th century (Abushouk, 2006).

The forth definition regards globalization as synonymous with westernization and modernization and considers it as the dynamic factor which mentions the development of modernized social structure (capitalism, rationalism, industrialization, bureaucracy) and destructs non-westernized nations' identities and cultures. As an evidence for globalization Hollywood culture and McDonald fast food restaurant can be mentioned.

The critics of this definition describe the spread of such western values under concepts such as colonization, westernization and modernization. In this area there is no need to create the term "globalization" for describing western ideas and values in third world countries (Khor, 1996).

The fifth definition is offered by Jan Art Scholte. He defines globalization as deterritorilization. In this definition the geographical borders disappear and lose their significance. The social space is not defined within the traditional borders and geographical borders change and they would become super-territorial.

The above-mentioned definitions are among the most common definitions of globalization, each of which view globalization from a particular perspective. Although all of them suggest that a governing and organizing method would be created in form of comprehensive globalization which includes all powers which direct the world toward global village, reduce the distances, make convergence in cultures and reduce political borders. As Mazrouei (2002) asserts globalization is "Villagization of the World".

3. The origin of globalization

Historically, globalization is not a new phenomenon but its changes can be investigated in terms of scale, speed and cognition (Kinnvall, 2004). Within scale framework, economic, political and social relation between nations have become more than before. Globalization has experienced a kind of temporal and spatial compression in terms of speed which had not experienced it before. Within the framework of cognition it considers the globe as a smaller space where every phenomenon and event has some consequences on economic, social and political life (Kinnvall, 2004).

This means de-territorialization of time and space which affects our lives (Kinnvall, 2004). Anyway, the term globalization has been offered and coined by Reiser and Davise in 1994 and it becomes a catchword for most scholars from all parts of the world after collapse of Soviet Union and the end of cold war in late 20th century (Abushouk, 2006). In the 1970s, this term developed as "Global Village" which reflected the progress of technology which has made the international exchanges and trade easier and faster.

The publication of *War and Peace in the Global Village* written by Marshall McLuhan and *Berjinski* propagated the term globalization formally in 1970. In addition, the political and economic agreements after world war provided the ground for international collaboration and became the leader of globalization. The establishment of United Nations Union in 1945 and the proceeding economic and political agreements, the establishment of International Monetary Fund, General Agreement on Tariff and Trade and its first negotiation with 23 other participating countries in 1947 all have provided the ground for globalization. On the other hand, the establishment of some organizations such as World Trade Organization and the joining of countries to this organization are considered as the start of accepting globalization. Especially the wonderful growth of technology in some areas such as transportation, telecommunication and more importantly, informatics revolution in 80s and following spread of internet and network provided proper tools for development of this phenomenon.

4. Theoretical perspectives toward globalization

Different views have been offered about globalization. Farazmand (2001) in his paper entitled "Globalization, The State and Public Administration, A Theoretical Analysis with Policy Implication for Development States" has provided four theoretical perspectives for globalization. The first perspective is an optimistic one; the optimistic proponents of globalization speak of its advantages. While the critics and opponents refer to its negative consequences, the destructive effects that can influence the life of majority of people. For example, the proponents assert that the growth of transnational collaboration develops global capitalism in which the states are considered indifferent or improper and they create a de-territorialized world whose characteristic is mutual dependency, general order and governance of market. Thomas Friedman, the proponent of globalization, regards it as "herd" which directs all matters with its unique method and nothing can stop it (Farazmand, 2001). In his view, this phenomenon is not a choice but a fact. Farazmand (2001) refers to this fact that resistance toward globalization would charge huge costs. He believes that states can resist it but they would incur huge costs.

The second view is a critical one and in contrast with globalization. The opponents of globalization warn against the consequences and the negative effects of this phenomenon on national economy, human values, the benefits of democratic communities, national government and especially on third world countries (Farazmand, 2001). This group of opponents of globalization focuses on the vanishing and destruction of civil power, financial crisis in developing countries; governance crisis and economic problem (see Mele, 1996; Cox, 1993; Brecher and Costello, 1994; Kregel, 1998).

The third view refers to the fact that globalization would make the nations and states stay in their governing position. According to this view, globalization is an unavoidable fact and it is improper to fear it. Some socialists (such as Hirst and Thompson, 1996; Zysman, 1996) who believe in this idea, consider the negative consequences and effects of globalization less significance and argue that globalization would not decrease the power of nations. In fact, states would be more powerful in local and international areas (Farazmand, 2001).

However, Farazmand believes that the fourth view about globalization provides deeper analysis of this phenomenon. According to this view, even realists-pragmatists agree with the idea that globalization has important and considerable effects on the identity and characteristics of nations and states. Those theorists, who support this view, argue that globalization has positive/ negative effects on the economy of states and nations through changing world economy and with domination of transnational companies that has organizational, political and financial power (Farazmand, 1994).

This phenomenon can be examined from different perspectives considering different views toward globalization and different views toward globalization phenomenon.

5. Dimensions of globalization

It is worth noting that globalization is not a one-dimensional phenomenon. It has different dimensions and it can be divided into several complicated and interrelated dimensions (Hsiao and Wan, 2007; And United Nations, 2000). These dimensions have been examined from different aspects in several researches.

For example, Andreas Theophanous, 2011 has referred to four dimensions of globalization in his paper: 1. Economic, 2. Political. 3. Social and 4. Cultural. These four dimensions include different factors such as communications, transportation, technology, population mobility and life style.

Furthermore, he asserts that the consequence of each factor might be related to more than one dimension. For example, we make use of a particular dimension, in the first view, it might have economic applications, and meanwhile the technology affects the production, employment and the use of standard and life style (Theophanous, 2011). Robert Kcohance and Joseph Nye (2000) have also distinguished four dimensions of globalization that are economic, military, cultural and social (Taylor, 2005). In this chapter, these four dimensions have been considered and examined in detail.

6. Economic dimension

In definition of globalization, economic perspective is of great importance and is dominant in contrast to political, scientific, cultural and social dimensions (Krasner, 1976). The reason is the evolution of this dimension of globalization rather than other dimensions and time priority. This is why globalization is viewed mostly from economic point of view. The origin of economy globalization and its development is Breton Woods conference in 1944. However, the economy crisis of the 1970s facilitated globalization through creation of new drivers in neoliberal economic ideology and increase of Regan and Thatcher powers. On the other hand, advances in technology that reduced the transportation and communication costs reinforced this trend (Tiemstra, 2007). One of the other significant factors in development of economic globalization is the role of multinational companies and the emergence of networks of companies (Crevoisier, 1999) which act independent of particular geographical areas or state's policies (Ollapally, 1993).

Globalization is composed of two sub- processes from economic dimension (Oppenhein, 2003): the first one is the merging of distinct and isolated parts of global system which includes the spread of active forces and capital all over the world. Free trade agreements are the main part of this process due to the fact that they make legislation which facilitates the flow of work and capital. The second process is development of communication including telecommunication, internet etc. which facilitate the flow of labor and capital.

The agreement on free trade is the main part of this process due to the fact that they make some regulations which facilitate the flow of labor and capital. The second process is the development of communications including telecommunication, internet etc. that all facilitate the intra-national and international relations. Multifaceted trade agreements such as The Genera Tariff And Trade GATT negotiation have led to the formation and construction of World Trade Organization, The North American Free Trade Area and recently, Free Trade Area of Americas, all are part of globalization process (Farazmand, 1999a, b, 2005).

In economic dimension, one of the fundamental goals of globalization is the destruction of economic borders and removal of legal barriers and creation of free market system in a way that make the capitals flow freely. The other point in economic dimension of globalization is the removal of custom duties' barriers and globalization of competitions. Fukuyama and Hantington are among the proponents of globalization. They consider globalization as a process that leads to evolution and generalization of modern capitalism (Mir, Mohammadi, 2002).

6.1 Political dimension

Globalization as a political phenomenon means that the construction of political plays is not determined within distinct and independent units (independent organized structures and hierarchy of states). Therefore, that globalization is the process of political structuration. Political globalization is the reconstruction of political experiences and institutionalized structures for coordinating and removing the deficiencies of state (Cerny, 1997).

In political dimension, the state as the welfare provider has been removed from most communities under the influence of globalization and because of the reduction of state's collaboration in economic section. New groups and leaders have emerged for creating welfare and security. Such leaders are challenging for states and governments (Kinnvall, 2004).

On the other hand, according to some of theorists, globalization reduces the control of states and governments of their nations. So social liberation, democracy, civil attitudes and political culture are promoted (Bollen, 1979, 1983; Bollen And Jackman, 1985; Cutright, 1963; Cutright And Wiley, 1969; Hannan And Carroll, 1981; Jackman, 1973; Lipsert, 1959; Imai, 2002). Despite this, some theorists believe that regardless of cultural or regional differences between states (national economies integration within global market) globalization is a catalyzer for political liberalization of states. However, this idea is rejected by some thinkers of international policy due to the general effect of economy globalization of policy (Dupont, 1996; Fukuyama, 1989, 1995; Huntington, 1991; Jones, 1995; Kauhkan, 1993). This can be seen in the reduction of globalization effect in Asian countries (due to their unique political culture). However, one cannot ignore the great effects of globalization in political area within global level. The distribution of cosmopolitism relation, the growth of political culture, the transformation of traditional power of societies to competitive powerful power, the increase in citizen rights and awareness within civil society and institutionalization of liberty in selection within the political development models are a great part of globalization effect in political zone at global level which are mentioned in political dimension in globalization.

6.2 Social dimension

Social dimension of globalization is related to the globalization effect on the life and work of individuals, their families and communities. This dimension is related with the effect of globalization on employment, work condition, income and social support. The social dimension beyond labor world refers to security, culture, identity and the coherence of families and communities (Gunter and Hoeven, 2004).

Historically, this dimension of globalization is alongside with neoliberal ideology. The changes in the policies facilitated in late 1970s within liberalization framework. The movement from Keynesian economy to monetarist macroeconomic in developed countries which was followed through structural adaptation in developing countries in 1980s and 1990s, their aim was privatization and the increase of global competition which is a tool for making stable and promote civil society. However, in most countries, due to removing of occupational security from middle classes and below, it has reverse effect because of severe social stress (Kinnvall, 2004). Furthermore, the main effect of globalization that has worried most people all over the world is the possibility of increase in unemployment rate because of joining to organizations like World Trade Organization.

6.3 Cultural dimension

The effect of globalization of cultural dimension is different and globalization of culture had different reactions. However, the specification and identity of these reactions depend on those societies where it has occurred, in a way that the reaction of western and modern societies has been different from that of developing countries and especially Muslim countries. Two factors have been effective in this phenomenon: first: the economic and financial effect of globalization and modernity, the emergence of modern consumption goods, the effect of mass media (TV, Satellite, Film and internet…) has been effective.

Second one is western values including scientific argumentation, secularism, individualism, freedom of speech, political pluralism, ruling of law, equalization of women and minorities (Lieber And Weisberg, 2002; Howard, 2002). Theorists have different view toward the influence of globalization on culture. Proponents believe that although globalization leads to integration and removal of cultural barriers, it is an important step toward more stable world and better life for individuals (Rothkoph, 997). However, others consider globalization of culture improper due to fear from universal power and the continuance of multinational collaborations with international institutions such as International Monetary Fund (IMF) (Lieber and Weisberg, 2002).

According to these views, the idea of globalization is controversial form cultural point of view (Vair, 2004). More specifically, the views toward globalization of culture are based on two theories of convergence and divergence (Pin Goh, 2009). However, the review of related literature shows three flow of globalization that is indicative of social, cultural and political: Polarization, And Hybridization Homogenization (Holton 2000). Homogenization argues that globalization leads to cultural convergence, most discussions such as John Tomlinson's Cultural Imperialism (1991), Reinhold Wagnleitner's 'Coca-Colonization' (1994) And George Ritzer's 'Mcdonaldization' (2001) considers global culture as indicative of capitalism culture, necessarily, the culture which is inclined toward local cultures. Such culture penetrates in global economy. Furthermore, the emergence of transnational elites who are trained with western values and are committed to homeland values, helps in the construction of a dominant culture that is inspired from capitalism values (Hsiao and Wan, 2007).

The proponents of convergence theory assume that as the modernity level increases, the level of structural integration of modernized communities increases, too. On the other hand, the main changes that occur in structural uniformity of culture in modernized communities might lead to similar consequences, innovation, industrialization and modernization affect through converging the effects of technology on all aspects of social life and labor (Webber, 1969).

Ploralization theory offers an opposite view against this. Localities react differently due to external powers of the world due to various cultural and historical heritages. Some communities, particularly Muslim communities, resist westernized or American culture. Based on this, the feature of today's world is ethno-nationalism and the conflict between cultures (Tusicisny, 2004). There is cultural dichotomy between western and non- western life styles, east and west, east and Islamic Confucian Axis (Hsiao and Wan, 2007).

Ploralization theorists such as Adler and Bartholomew, 1992; Yuki and Falbe, 1990 argue that the cultural variation and resistance toward western norms assert that pluralism theory provide an interesting and more attractive picture of global culture development. They argue that it is simplistic to assume that behaviors, preferences and tests from all over the world are converging (Akkah, 1991) because cultures are changing and conform differently.

On the other hand, the third group of theorists that are known as hybridization believes that the previous outstanding theories do not include the complicated and multifaceted global culture. They argue that cultures adapt from one another and combine some elements from different sources within their own particular cultural experiences (Pin Goh, 2009).

Hybridization theory asserts that cultures have some elements and components specific to themselves (Kraidy, 2005). New terms such as globalization and hybridization are created for expressing the dynamic relation and link between globalization and localization (Hsiao and wan, 2007). These are main dimensions that are of great importance in the examination of the effect of globalization. On the other hand, they are helpful in determining the main discussion of this chapter which is the examination of the effect of globalization on innovation; this will be focused in what follows.

7. Globalization and innovation

What has been mentioned so far is for better determination of globalization process and the examination of its consequences in different cultural, social, political and economic dimensions. Nevertheless, the main topic of this paper is the consequences and effects of globalization on innovation and regardless of the positive and negative effects in different aspects, how globalization affects innovation. As it was mentioned previously, the researchers have offered different explanations and analysis about globalization and its consequences. Each of these scholars and theorists has tried to examine different dimensions of this phenomenon. Despite most of them, the overall effect of globalization is to move toward convergence and integration. As an example, Aldous Huxleyin his book, *Wonderful New World*, draws globalization in such a way that within it, human beings are surrounded in a world that control and supervise everything with its rhythmic order within which self-awareness and world- awareness link together and human being, thought world and culture transmute. Emanuel Wallenstein, German sociologist, believes that "globalization is the process of shaping some networks within which the societies which were isolated in this world merge in mutual dependency and global unity". Mentioning the global system theory, he draws the relation between nations a kind of convergence and integration between nations. Francis Fokoyama considers globalization as "the spread and development of western culture and dominance of American civilization on the world and interprets it as 'the end of history'".

Such theories reflect the orientation of globalization toward integration. However, such integration can have different influences from different dimensions. Economically, the world is being transformed to a unique economic creature very quickly, an undeniable creature within which all components and parts are dependent to one another.

From political and social perspectives, the results of globalization is the construction of transnational society which if it is done on all aspects, the political and cultural role of states is reduced and the transnational rules and values would govern the economic, political, cultural and social structures. Furthermore from cultural point of view, it leads to universal culture beyond local and national borders, the common and shared culture within the framework of which local cultures are defined and if this culture has the ability to collaborate in such culture, it would stay stable (Turki, 1383). Based on this, most of scholars regard globalization as the unification of all cultures and extension of westernized civilization's patterns that is in fact a cultural imperialism (Davoodi, 2009).

Considering these consequences of globalization, the main discussion of this paper is that globalization reduces innovation and it has a negative effect on innovation through removing the variation. In order to discuss this effectiveness, we should assert that of main consequences of globalization is the movement toward convergence and integration in all political, economic, social and cultural dimensions. It is obvious that the consequence of such phenomenon is disappearance of variety in these dimensions. In economic dimension, globalization is an economic phenomenon whose feature is the spread of capitalism and market mechanism all over the world. Since different countries have different social and political systems and their economies are in different level of growth and development, the obligations and necessities of economy globalization (liberation of trade and capital flow), the execution of social regulations (those emerged from global organizations like world trade organization, ...) have different effects on nations (Gengshen, 2001). Such discussion in globalization embeds this idea that the prerequisites of globalization destruct variation in all dimensions and due to fact that variation has positive effects on improving innovation and creativity and is considered a source of innovation, globalization phenomenon destructs innovation through destruction of variation and with inclination toward convergence and integration. For example in economy, some critics of globalization believe that the growth and development of market globalization reduces variation and necessitates the policy of support (The Economist, 1994, 1995, 1998; Waxman, 1998; Baughn And Buchanan, 2001; Kull, 2001; Francois And Vanypersele, 2002).

Klein (2000) has mentioned such concern in globalization and asserts that market- oriented globalization doesn't necessitate variation. For better elaboration of this topic, he refers to the growth of sport industry (Nike), the entertainment and child tools (Disney and Mattel) and software industry (Microsoft).

In culture dimension, the negative effects of globalization have been considered in eradicating variety. The critics of globalization assert that globalization is somehow imposition of western culture on non- western world. This theory that is mentioned within cultural imperialism follows the idea that although cultural globalization appears as trans-historical and transnational or as a supreme global power, it is nothing more than the issuance of goods, values and priorities of western life style.

What is spread in global level of culture are believes and constructs and generally identities which are offered by western culture industries. These theorists speak about the construction of cultural dominance on other cultures within the framework of globalization that endangers the cultural identity, believes, values and even the language of most countries using communicative and technological tools (Gol Mohammadi, 1381).

David Held (2000) regards culture globalization as a form of imperialism that is followed by western countries. Furthermore, he asserts, "cultural imperialism is a goof method and procedure for understanding culture globalization. The dominant culture of western countries disappears through the main trend of homogenization of local cultures disappear and this is an applicable matter for economic benefits of western countries".

Fukuyama is among scholars of globalization who reject the idea that globalization leads to convergence, removes tradition from cultures and destructs cultural variation (national and local). However, he asserts that although globalization creates convergence in some grounds, there are other deeper components in the culture of countries that make convergence a difficult task. He believes that the communities preserve their individual characteristics in spite of economic collaborations.

Nkosinathi Sotshangane (2002) speaks of cultural variation as an undeniable and important fact in "Global Village". While the rich value of it is ignored and most countries have some deficiencies in realizing the cultural values, most people have experienced the negative effects of globalization. In a way that from late 20 century, there have been some protest

movements against globalization and its effect on the economic, cultural, political, technological and religious order (Sotshangane, 2002).
Such measures and perspectives make some negative effects of globalization more important. For example, UNESCO has provided a broader definition to pay much attention to variation in culture and show its significance. After world conference 1983, culture was defined as the collection of material, intellectual, cultural and emotional characteristics and features of a society or social group to focus the attention on culture variation and its significance so that this definition includes the ways for living together, value system, traditions and believes in addition to art, literature and life style (UNESCO, 2002). In 2001, in Universal Declaration on Cultural Diversity, cultural variation was defined as "the source of exchange, innovation and creativity" and its positive side was confirmed (CHAN-TIBERGIEN, 2006).

8. Discussion and conclusion

Globalization is one of the topics which have been considered by different theorists and researchers and different contradictory views have been provided considering its significance and influence on different aspects of human life (economic, social, political and cultural).
On one hand, the proponents of globalization try to focus more on the benefits of this phenomenon and emphasize on economic and social development of communities and regards it a positive matter. In contrast, the opponents of globalization believe that globalization is good for developed and advanced countries and communities and it has negative consequences in other communities (developing countries). However, some believe that beyond the identity of societies and communities, globalization has different consequences for topics and phenomena. For example, the effect of globalization of the development of technology, science can be positive or negative. In this chapter, the authors try to examine the effect of globalization on innovation. They believe that globalization has some negative consequences on innovation through destruction of variety and with inclination toward convergence in all areas and eliminates variety.
Due to the fact that convergence and orientation toward integration occur in all dimensions including economic, social, political and cultural dimensions, in other words, moving in one dimension affects other dimensions, so it can be concluded that the negative effect of globalization on innovation occur in all dimensions.

9. References

Abushouk, A.I. (2006). Globalization And Muslim Identity Challenges And Prospects, The Muslim World, Vol.96. Pp.487-551.

Adler, N. J. (1983). Cross-Cultural Management Research: The Ostrich And The Trend. Academy Of Management Review, 8(2), 226–232.

Akaah, I. P. (1991). Strategy Standardization In International Marketing: An Empirical Investigation Of Its Degree Of Use And Correlates. Journal Of Global Marketing, 4, 39–62.

Baughn, C. C. And M. A. Buchanan (2001), 'Cultural Protectionism', Business Horizons، 44, 5–15.

Bollen,K., (1983). World System Position, Dependency And Democracy: The Cross-National Evidence, American Sociological Review, 48: 468-479.

Bollen,K., 1979, Political Democracy And The Timing Of Development, American Sociological Review, 44, 572-587.

Bollen,K., And Jackman, R. (1985). Political Democracy And The Size Of Distribution Of Income, American Sociological Review, 50: 438-457.

Brecher, Jeremy And Tim Costello. (1994). Global Village Or Global Pillage: Economic Reconstruction From The Bottom Up. Boston, MA: South End Press.

Cerny., P.G. (1997).Paradoxes Of The Competition State: The Dynamics Of Political Globalization, Government And Opposition, 32(2), Pp: 251-274.

Chan-Tibergien. J. (2006).Cultural Diversity as Resistance to Neoliberal Globalization: The Emergence of a Global Movement and Convention, Review Of Education (2006) 52:89-105.

Cox, R. W. (1993). "Structural Issues Of Global Governance." In S. Gill (Ed.), Gramci. Historical Materialism And International Relations. Cambridge, UK: Cambridge University Press, 259–289.

Crevoisier.C. (1999). Two Ways To Look At Learning Regions In The Context Of Globalization: The Homogenizing And Particularizing Approaches, Geojournal 49: 353–361, 1999

Curight, P. (1963). National Political Development: Measurement And Analysis, American Sociological Review, 28, Pp: 253-264.

Cutright, P., And Wiley., J.A. (1969), Modernization And Political Representation: 1927-1966, Studies In Comparative International Development, Vol.5, Pp: 23-44.

Dupont, A. (1996). Is There An Asian Way?, Survival, 38(2), Pp: 13-33.

Farazmand, A. (1999a). "Globalization And Public Administration." Public Administration Review, 59(6), 509-522.

Farazmand, A. (1999b). "Privatization Or Reform: Public Enterprise Management In Transition." International Review Of Administrative Science 65(4), 551-567.

Farazmand, Ali. (1994). "The New World Order And Global Public Administration: A Critical Essay." In Garcia-Zamor, Jean-Claude And Khator Renu (Eds.), Public Administration In The Global Village. Westport, CT: Praeger, 62–81.

Farazmand. A. (2001). Globalization, the State and Public Administration: A Theoretical Analysis with Policy Implications for Developmental States, Public Organization Review: A Global Journal 1: 437–463.

Farazmand. A. (2005).Role Of Government In An Era Of Total Quality Management (TQM) And Globalization: Challenges And Opportunities, Public Organization Review: A Global Journal 5: 201–217.

Francois, P. And T. Van Ypersele (2002), 'On The Protection Of Cultural Goods', Journal Of International Economics 56, 359–369.

Fukuyama, F. (1989). The End Of History?, The National Interest, Issu.16, Summer.

Fukuyama, F. (1995). Confucianism And Democracy, Journal Of Democracy, 6(2), Pp: 20-32.

Gengshen, Z. (2001). The Challenge Of The Social Dimensions Under Globalization For Social Security In China The Chinese Economy, 34(5), Pp. 71–90.
Goh., J. W. P. (2009).Globalization's Culture Consequences Of MBA Education Across Australia And Singapore: Sophistry Or Truth?, High Education, 58:131 155
Gunter., B.G. And Hoeven., R.V. D. (2004).The Social Dimension Of Globalization: A Review Of The Literature, International Labour Review, Vol. 143 (2004), No. 1-2.
Hannan, M.T., And Carroll, G.R. (1981). Dynamics Of Formal Political Structure: An Event-History Analysis, American Sociological Review, Vol.46, Pp: 19-35.
Harvey, D. (1989). The Condition Of Postmodernity. Oxford: Blackwell.
Held, D (2000), A Globalizing World? Culture, Economics, Politics, Routledge: Open University Press.
Hirst, P And Thompson,G. (1996). "Globalisation: Ten Frequently Asked Questions And Some Surprising Answers," Soundings, Vol. 4, Autumn 1996, 48.
Hirst, P. And G. Thompson. (1996). Globalization In Question: The International Economy And The Possibilities Of Governance. Cambridge: Polity.
Howard, M. (2002). What`S In A Name? How Fighr Terrorism, Foreign Affairs, 81(1): 8-13.
Hsiao., H.H.L And Wan., P.S. (2007).The Experiences Of Cultural Globalizations In Asia-Pacific, Japanese Journal Of Political Science 8 (3), 361–385
Huntington, S.P. (1991). Democracy`S Third Wave, Journal Of Democracy, Vol.2, Pp: 12-34.
Imai, K. (2002).The Impact Of Globalization On Civil Liberties: Asian Vs Non Asian States, International Journal Of World Peace, Xix(1): 39-65.
Jackman, R.W. (1973). On The Relationship Of Economic Development To Democratic Performance, American Journal Of Political Science, Vol.17, Pp:611-621.
Kausikan, B. (1993). Asia`S Diffeent Standard, Foreign Policy, 32(92), Pp: 24-41.
Keohane, R. O. and Joseph S. Nye, Jr. (2000), 'Introduction', in Joseph S. Nye, Jr. and John D. Donahue (eds), Governance in a Globalizing World, Washington, DC: Brookings Institution Press, pp. 1–44.
Khor, M. (1996). "Globalisation: Implications For Development Theory," Third World Resurgence, No. 74,–21.
Kinnvall, C. (2002a). Analyzing The Global-Local Nexus. In C. Kinnvall & K. Jönsson (Eds.), Globalization And Democratization In Asia: The Construction Of Identity (Pp. 3–18). London: Routledge.
Kinnvall.C. (2004), Globalization And Religious Nationalism: Self Identity, And The Search For Ontological Security, Political Psychology, Vol. 25, No. 5.Pp. 741-766.
Kolodner, E. (1995). The Political Economy Of The Rise And Fall(?) Of Hindu Nationalism. Journal Of Contemporary Asia, 25, 233–260.
Krasner, P. (1976). State Power And The Structure Of International Trade, World Politics, 28.
Kregel, Jan. (1998). ''The Strong Arm Of The IMF.'' Report Of The Jeroe Levy Economic Institute Of Bard College 8 (1), 7–8.
Kull, S. (2001), 'Culture Wars? How Americans And Europeans View Globalization', Brookings Review, Fall, 18–21.
Lieber ., R.J., And Weisberg., R. E. (2002). Globalization, Culture, And Identities In Crisis, International Journal Of Politics, Culture And Society, 16(2): 273-296.

Lipset, S.M. (1959). Some Social Requisites Of Democracy: Economic Development And Political Legitimacy, American Political Science Review, March, Pp: 69-105.
Mazrui, A. (2002). "Interview", Association Of Muslim Social Scientists Bulletin, Spring, 9.
Mele, Christopher (1996). "Globalization, Culture, And Neighborhood Change: Reinventing The Lower East Side Of New York." Urban Affairs Review 32(1), 3–22.
Oppenheim., L.H. (2003). Latin America And The Cultural Consequences And Contradiction, Perspective On Global Development And Technology, Vol.2(1), Pp: 54-76.
Reiser., O. L. And Davies, B. (1944)Planetary Democracy: An Introduction To Scientific Humanism And Applied Semantics, (New York: Creative Age Press, 212, 219.
Rothkopf, d. (1997).In Praise Of Cultural Imperialism?" Foreign Policy, No. 107 :38–53.
Sander, H. (1996). Multilateralism, World Trade, London: Routledge.
Scholte., J. A. (2000). Globalization: A Critical Introduction, (New York: Palgrave, 49.
Sotshangane, N. (2002), What Impact Globalization Has On Cultural Diversity?,Turkish Journal Of International Relations, Vol.1, No.4.
Stiglitz, J. (2002). Globalization's Discontents. The American Prospect, (January), 14.
Taylor, P. J. (2005), 'LeadingWorld Cities: Empirical Evaluations of Urban Nodes in Multiple Networks', Urban Studies, 42(9): 1593–1608.
The Economist (1994), 'Cultural Protectionism: Television Of Babel', 5 February, P. 52.
The Economist (1995), 'French Fantasies', 18 March P. 56.
The Economist (1998), 'Moreover: Culture Wars', 12 September Pp. 97–99.
Theophanous.A. (2011).Ethnic Identity And The Nation-State In The Era Of Globalization: The Case Of Cyprus, Int J Polit Cult Soc
Tiemstra., J.P. (2007).The Social Economics Of Globalization, For Social Economics, 36:143–159.
Tomlinson, J. (1991), Cultural Imperialism: A Critical Introduction, Baltimore: John Hopkins University Press.
UNESCO. 2002. Universal Declaration On Cultural Diversity, Cultural Diversity Series No. 1. Document For The World Summit On Sustainable Development In Johannesburg. Paris: UNESCO.
United Nations (2000), 'Globalization And Its Impact On The Full Enjoyment Of All Human Rights: Preliminary Report Of The Secretary-General', Reference A/55/342, Available Online At Www.Un.Org/ Documents/Ga/Docs/55/A55342.Pdf.
Vaira, M. (2004). Globalization And Higher Education Organizational Change: A Framework For Analysis. Higher Education, 48(4), 483–510.
Waxman, S. (1998), 'What Sells Abroad Influences U.S. Pop Culture', International Herald Tribune, 27 October.
Webber, R. A. (1969). Convergence Or Divergence? The Columbia Journal Of World Business, 4, 75–83.
Yuki, G., & Falbe, C. M. (1990). Influence Tactics In Upward, Downward And Lateral Influence Attempts. The Journal Of Applied Psychology, 75, 132–140.
Zysman, J. (1996). "The Myth Of A 'Global' Economy: Enduring National Foundations And Emerging Regional Realities." New Political Economy 1, July, 157–184.

Alvani, Mehdi (2004). Chaleshhaye modiriyate dolati dar asre jahani shodan, no.9. Modiriyate Tosee.

Wallenstein, Emanoel (2008). Siyasat va Farhang dar Nezame Motahavele Jahani. P. 270.

Turki, Mohammad (2003). Farhange Boumi va Chaleshhaye Jahan.

Davoudi, Ali Asghar (2009). "Jahani shodan va Chaleshhaye Hakemiyate Melli". P. 24 and 25.

Gol Mohammadi, Yahya (2001). "Jahani Shodan va Farhang". P. 47-89

Mir Mohammadi,H. (2002). Jahani Shodan, Abaad va Roykardha. Motaleaate Melli Periodical, Issue 11.

Part 2

Globalization and Social Systems

5

Demistifying Globalization and the State: Preliminary Comments on Re-Commodification, Institutions and Innovation

Hector Cuadra-Montiel
El Colegio de San Luis
Mexico

To Javi and Celia

1. Introduction

It has become commonplace amongst some government officials, business circles, and even academics, to say that social processes are driven by market forces, and that no serious challenge can be posed to those anonymous, yet extremely powerful tendencies. Resistance becomes futile, since we are told that no alternatives exist, and bandwagoning becomes inevitable.[1] However, those economic imperatives, important as they are, do not work independently of, or isolated from, the context in which they become operative. They are embedded in broader social relations and interact with other economic and social agencies and structures. This, in turn, dynamically reshapes the features of the social processes.

Karl Polanyi has famously stated that "... labor, land, and money... must be organized in markets... (which) form part of an absolutely vital part of the economic system. But labor, land and money are obviously *not* commodities; the postulate that anything that is bought and sold must have been produced for sale is emphatically untrue in regard to them... The commodity description of labor, land and money is entirely fictitious. Nevertheless, it is with the help of this fiction that the actual markets for labor, land and money are organized; they are being actually bought and sold on the market; their demand and supply are real magnitudes; and any measures or policies that would inhibit the formation of such markets would ipso facto endanger the self regulation of the system. (Such)… principle according to which no arrangement or behaviour should be allowed to exist that might prevent the actual functioning of the market mechanism on the lines of the commodity fiction." (1944, 72-73).

Fictitious commodities undergo a process of commodification as the first leg of a double movement where the organizing principle of economic liberalism aims at the establishment

---

[1] The phenomena and discourses associated with the first wave of globalization are classic examples of this position. The portrait is one of a homogenising economic force for convergence which brings about irreversible changes. Hay & Marsh, 2000; Held et al, 1999. See also, Dicken, 1998; Held & McGrew, 2000; Hirst & Thompson, 1999; Ohmae, 1996 and 1990; Rodrik, 1997; Scholte, 2000; Strange, 1996; and Weiss, 1998.

of a self-regulating market, while the principle of social protection accompanies in parallel, albeit non-synchronic fashion "...aiming at the conservation of man and nature as well as productive organization... using protective legislation, restrictive associations and other instruments of interventions as its methods" (Polanyi, 1944, 132). It is as part of the double movement that labor, land and money are decommodified.

Post World War II Welfare States have roughly been associated with decommodifaction processes mainly within Western Europe and Anglo-Saxon economies. Likewise, efforts of social protection have been implemented all over the world. However, for most of them, incomplete, segmented and fractured practices of formal social security on one hand, and targeted social protection programs for the informal sector clearly cannot be compared with *The Three Worlds of Welfare Capitalism* Esping-Andersen portrays (1990).

Whenever a person is capable of maintaining a livelihood without reliance on the market, s/he has been decommodified (Esping-Andersen, 1990). However, there is no guarantee that such status will permanently hold. In case of reversal, that is re-entering the market, making use of her/his personal freedom to offer her/his labour power, relying on the market for making a living, such a person has either voluntarily or not, returned to the fictitious commodity status. Thus, a re-commodification process has taken place.

The allegedly retreat of the Welfare State could be associated with a fresh emphasis on a re-commodification agenda and practices where the imperfect, fractured, and flawed social protection and decommodification process in regions such as Latin America, Africa and Asia focuses on dismantling social protection nets, subordinating social needs and priorities after economic fundamentals. It is no secret that the neoliberal preference for outward market orientation carries strong social implications.

The problematic emphasis of policy-makers on re-commodification lies in the denial of its political character and on the neglect of its socially embedded features. Exclusively economic imperatives are unable to provide an integrated account of the processes of globalization and of the complementary role which States and markets play in the economic arena. Furthermore, the process of re-commodification is not limited to the three commodities originally suggested by Polanyi. It has also been suggested that knowledge and information face a similar process of re-commodification (Schiller, 1998; Jessop, 2002). Therefore, knowledge can be added to the list of fictitious commodities too.

Several quite special roles are played by the State, as there is no predetermined transformation from welfare to competition towards a residual form of State as Cerny has suggested (1990). Far from economic determinisms, being a site of strategic selectivity, a sphere of governance, and a locus of public policy and management, the evolution of the State tends to favour the ratification of former trajectories. Insofar as there is a tendency, it is not towards radical change. Rather, policy adaptation and reformism characterize social and political changes, which are in turn reflected in a concern for stability either for economic fundamentals or for political consensus. On the one hand, decommodification practices tend to be associated with patterns of increased protection from markets. Here, for instance, corporatist agencies play a leading role when the implementation of welfare policies is put into practice. On the other hand, the emphasis on re-commodification gives more room for private actors, and tends to be associated with dismantling labour's protection from the market. This latter orientation of governmental affairs is justified in terms of globalization, particularly neoclassical economic orthodoxy and the efficiency of market rules.

Nonetheless, globalization processes are highly political, because actors play a crucial role in shaping and influencing the course of events. However, this is not widely acknowledged.

For instance, according to the neoclassical economic orthodoxy, government failures not only affect optimal economic performance but also increase transaction costs. Therefore, economists trained in this school of thought advocate structural reforms and a minimal State. However, the abandonment of productive and distributive activities to the market is by no means unproblematic. Markets are not failure-free, and this is precisely the reason for government to play an active role, especially when problems of incomplete markets, inefficiencies, imperfect information and market disruptions arise. The aim of an efficient market allocation of resources requires the government to play an active role in the provision of welfare and redistributive policies. By contrast, increased market competition raises incentives and mitigates public failures (Stiglitz, 1989, 1999, and 2002; Chang, 2001).

In addition to material and structural elements, such as those mentioned above, attention is paid to the ideational and agency factors implicated in the evolution of social processes. This chapter also discusses the neoclassical economic ideas and concepts and their influence upon actor´s conduct. Such an antecedent of the globalization idea is prior to the discussion of the problematic emphasis on re-commodification by policy-makers. The next section focuses on the so called 'market friendly' position of the State defended by the World Bank, which is found to be structurally and economically deterministic. This is important, because the World Bank has been one of the main architects of the economic restructuring in several countries throughout the world since the early 1980s. Additionally, in exploring some of the causal mechanisms in the global process of social and political change, an analysis of the relations between the institutional framework and economic agents such as firms is presented. It follows a discussion on how the Schumpeterian notion of 'creative destruction' highlights crises and innovations as fundamental elements which help us in tracing the processes of globalization. The final part of this chapter stresses that the relational character of the exercise of power makes use of causal relations, to continuously build the ever-changing social dynamics and processes. The following section is devoted to the ideational counterpart of the material dimension.

2. Globalization (mis) perceptions: the influence of the neoclassical economic orthodoxy

It has been argued that the causal and constitutive role of ideas in the production of specific material and ideational outcomes is crucial for triggering, without determining, the behaviour and practices of actors. The interaction between ideas and material factors is multi-level and multi-factor, where the former play a casual and constitutive role in the production of material and ideational outcomes (Watson 2000, and 2001). Moreover, there is a growing recognition among scholars of International Political Economy that the elements of ideas are crucial in the social construction of the tangible and intangible contexts and realities in which agencies are situated. In addition, the role of ideas in reducing uncertainty also significantly contributes towards making institutional change possible (Blyth, 2002).

For instance, Blyth presents a sequential set of hypotheses for understanding institutional change under conditions of uncertainty. He presents them in the following order: first, ideas reduce uncertainty during periods of economic crisis; second, once uncertainty is reduced, ideas make collective action and coalition building possible; third, ideas can be used as weapons in the struggle over existing institutions; fourth, after legitimising institutions, ideas function as institutional prints; and fifth, following the institutional construction, ideas make institutional stability possible (2002).

According to him, ideas and interests are not mutually exclusive analytic categories. This is important, since he regards institutional change as an endogenous process which faces a unique situation of uncertainty reducible neither to risk nor to complexity. It is under this unique situation of uncertainty associated with economic crises that agents are unable to anticipate possible outcomes and also to identify their interests in such a situation (Blyth, 2002).

However, important as Blyth's view of endogenous process is, two main problems with his account of institutional change are worth mentioning. The first regards the conditions which trigger changes in institutions. The uniqueness of uncertainty associated with economic crises, he argues, works as an external shock which sets incentives for agents to reconsider the utility of their institutions. But this sort of external incentive cannot be held as the only causal explanation for institutional change. Changes can also be small, incremental, and evolutionary, yet deliver the conditions for the endogenous process which allow for change in the institutions. By emphasizing unique situations which resemble chaos, Blyth stresses the punctuation of the process, albeit at the price of paying less attention to the equally important incremental and evolutionary character of change. The second problem with his perspective lies in his sequentially arranged hypothesis. Suffice it to say that more emphasis should be placed on causal relations than on sequential patterns. The fluid social dynamics alert us to the existence of often over-lapping tendencies and counter-tendencies which would be unaccounted for if we followed a rigid schematized account.

Economic imperatives are socially and discursively constructed by making use of external imposition of limits on what is perceived within the parameters of feasibility. This suggests that it should come as no surprise that such imperatives favour the orientation of certain preferred courses of action and outcomes over others, transforming and mediating external inputs into domestic political priorities (Hay & Rosamond, 2002).[2]

It is important to make clear that ideas are not the only driving force behind political and economic outcomes. Nevertheless, it is equally important to stress that their impact and leverage needs to be analyzed within contextual circumstances specific to certain points of time and space. At the beginning of the 21st century there seems to be an inert and uncritical acceptance by neoclassical economists of ideas and assumptions which have substantial material impacts and social consequences.[3] Some of them are undoubtedly clear exercises of power relations in a way which not only influences governmental and private agendas, but also leads to the shaping of preferences, which in turn influence the context in which agencies are situated. For instance, the rationality of economic actors, perfect competition and symmetric information are recalled in government and private sector circles despite

[2] It is in this sense that the use of discourse and ideas serves to legitimate a range of policies and initiatives which might otherwise be unpalatable and would therefore have faced stronger opposition had there been different circumstances. The recourse of appealing to external constraints has been effectively used for displacing responsibility from accountable and responsible bodies to diffuse structures or unaccountable agencies, such as international priorities and global trends (Hay & Rosamond, 2002).

[3] Associated with Gramsci's explanation and concept of hegemony, the acceptance of a dominant ideology might suffer a twist and turn into beliefs that are appropriated, made their own, taken for granted and rendered simple common sense. Nevertheless, it is important to be aware of this conflation and to clearly draw the conclusion that ideologies do not in and of themselves constitute a form of common sense (Van Dijk, 1998).

overwhelming evidence of the inaccuracy and inconsistency of such assumptions (Stiglitz, 1991). Nevertheless, they are sometimes justified in terms of parsimony which, in turn, implies that the theorist does not regard the assumptions as specific so much as useful. Something similar happens with the omission of social determinants and institutional differences in the abstract neoclassical economic models which have replicated the market homogeneity and policy convergence that the globalization hypothesis takes for granted (Watson, 2003a). In order to be insulated from contradictory evidence, some contemporary policies of welfare retrenchment appeal to ideological justifications, and in so doing they acquire a discursive power of their own.

Within economists' circles the General Equilibrium approach has been appropriated and faced a metamorphosis in which the analytical construct has been used as a framework with an ideological emphasis for the prescription of preferred political actions. For this mathematical neoclassical economics approach is a methodological contribution which takes perfect competition as a precondition for its reconstruction of a pure exchange economy. Despite the caveat that equilibrium is only achieved within the model and cannot be taken out of it, owing to the fact that it is only a constitutive property of the model itself, the prescribed advice has been systematically ignored beyond the academic community and has already spread in less technical and more discursive forms. Therefore, it is necessary to bear in mind that since the General Equilibrium approach is founded on inapplicable assertions, its assumptions should not be treated as realistic ones (Watson, 2003a).

The importance of ideas, and specifically of the assumptions with which economists work has been discussed by the Nobel laureate Milton Friedman in his essay on The Methodology of Positive Economics. There, he argues that positive science as "...a body of systematized knowledge concerning what is..." is different from normative science which focuses on the discussion of criteria of what ought to be.[4] The former is presented as independent of any ethical position, capable of developing predictions about phenomena not yet observed by means of using a set of hypotheses, whereas normative science is said to be always dependent on a positive science (Friedman, 1953).

In this essay, Friedman considers assumptions as short-hand descriptions or presentations of a body of theory which are helpful for testing, the hypothesis by their implications, yet not directly. Although he makes it clear that assumptions offer some convenient means for specifying the conditions under which a theory is expected to be valid, this position is stretched to the limit of arguing how irrelevant it is whether assumptions are descriptively realistic or not. For him, theoretical assumptions are valid if they are used and accepted in a continuous way, and as long as the hypotheses hold for the phenomena they aim to explain (Friedman, 1953). This standpoint on a positive philosophical position needs to be examined in further detail.

The problem of mismatch between theory and practice arises whenever the assumptions of positive economics, which are theoretically presented in a closed system, are then taken out of the context in which they are operative. In the real world it often happens that descriptively unrealistic assumptions are put into practice in open systems. Needless to say, those operations do not at all match the useful approximations in a closed system which Friedman claims. Furthermore, the impact which makes carries intended and unintended consequences. The insulation of the positivist ontological position collides with the practical

[4] Friedman's argument is based on John Neville Keynes' *The Scope and Method of Political Economy*.

prescriptions for real and concrete situations which derive from their initial philosophical and analytical standpoint. The implementation of neoclassical policy advice confronts open systems in reality, which poses a formidable challenge for them to succeed. This explains the important efforts undertaken by some economists such as Stiglitz, either relaxing unrealistic assumptions such as complete markets and perfect information, or the new group of theories which aim, amongst other things, to compensate for the inadequacy of neoclassical economics in the analysis of economic change, the lack of attention paid to institutions and the disregard of the role played by governments in coordinating economic activities (Gilpin, 2001).[5] Moreover, the positivist ontological position defended by Friedman and some other economists has been embraced by international financial organizations whose leverage has been very strong and has had specific consequences in different countries. But before turning to those issues it is important to clarify the differences between the ontological position adopted by neoclassical economics and the critical realist ontological stance adopted here.

3. A critical view on globalization

Hay has claimed that there is a directional dependence between ontology, epistemology and methodology (2002). The former two are philosophical positions, relating the world and knowledge respectively, which cannot be reduced to empirical examples. The latter follows the former two and functions as an analytical strategy and research guide. All theoretical approaches make specific claims and assumptions, either in an implicit or an explicit way, about what is out there to know about the world. Positivism and realism have contrasting perceptions of the nature of the social and political world.[6]

Ontology, as the science or study of being, refers to the claims and assumptions that are made about the world and, more specifically for our purposes, about the nature of social reality. Epistemology is a study of theories of knowledge, which departs from the original (ontological) claims and assumptions, focusing on the ways to gain knowledge. By contrast methodology can be described as the research design, because it tells us how the research proceeds (Blaikie, 1993, 6-7).

Bearing these philosophical distinctions in mind, the ontology of positivism assumes the world to be made of ordered observable events which resemble atoms. It takes into account only observable phenomena, claiming perfect correspondence with reality. According to this position, universal propositions or constant conjunctions can be claimed in its search for the external causes of human behaviour. Positivism does not recognize the existence of unobservable structures at all, because it perceives there to be no dichotomy between appearance and reality. Therefore, it takes the world as real, and considers that there cannot be any mediation by any senses, perceptions, or socially constructed phenomena. The directional dependence of positivism's ontological stance leaves an imprint in its theory of knowledge, allowing its epistemology to affirm that empirical regularities can be given

[5] The group of theories considered include the theory of endogenous growth, the new economic geography and the strategic trade theory (Gilpin, 2001).

[6] Although there are other ontological positions, the nature of this research requires us to concentrate only on positivism and realism. Informed explanations of the different positions in social science can be found in Blaikie's *Approaches to Social Enquiry* (1993). Regarding the scope and methods of economics, see Lawson's *Economics and Reality* (1997).

equal status to scientific laws.[7] By making use of induction, the observations of specific events are taken as starting points for building generalizations which end up as general propositions. These, in turn, are then claimed to provide neutral explanations of the observed phenomena (Blaikie, 1993; Lawson, 1997 and 2003). In other words, the use of direct observations to generate, test and falsify hypotheses about the interactions between the social phenomena is vital for this position, because it is a condition of statements being made about social, political and economic phenomena (Marsh et al., 1999).

In contrast, realist ontology makes distinctions between observations of experiences, events either observed or unobserved, and the processes which generate them. It takes the world as independent of observers, and assumes that as a result of the separation between reality and appearance, social relations are products of material, albeit unobservable, structures of relations. The directional dependence of the realist ontological position makes its epistemology focus merely on the tendencies of events, which makes a sharp contrast with the regularities of positivism. Starting with the observation of often different and contrasting tendencies, realism proposes models and mechanisms to explain the observed phenomena (Blaikie, 1993; Lawson, 1997 and 2003).

The realist ontology makes four primary statements about the nature of the world. Firstly, it contends that there is a clear and neat distinction between the world and all of its parts and components on the one side, and our knowledge about it on the other. In this case, the economic relations of production, distribution and exchange are independent of our knowledge about them and the rest of the world. Secondly, the observation of some structures might not be possible to achieve in a direct way, because their existence has to be inferred. For instance, power interactions are immanent in all social relations, especially at the structural levels of preference and context shaping (Sayer 1992 and 2000; Lawson, 1997 and 2003). Thirdly, the relationship among different elements can be analysed to provide insight into specific cause-effect mechanisms, albeit not necessarily law-like regularities. Objects and social relations are acknowledged to have causal powers and liabilities capable of generating events, where powers might be explained independently of them. Finally, the realist ontological directional dependence leaves a mark on its theory of knowledge, as it argues that structures neither generate nor determine outcomes. Rather, structures offer windows of opportunity and constraints which provide some room for the agencies to manoeuvre. The fact that some of the alternatives appear more feasible to realise does not necessarily mean that there is only one possible course of action, previously given or externally decided and unavoidable (Lawson, 1997 and 2003; Marsh et al., 1999; Sayer, 1992 and 2000; Cuadra-Montiel, 2007a).

Following a directional dependence from the ontology of realism, this interpretative approach features a realist epistemological stance. From the latter, it views knowledge of any kind as a social practice gained mainly through activity and interaction, which is situated in specific contexts and never develops in a vacuum. Since its fallibility and its theory-laden character of observation must be admitted, the plea to adopt a critical approach should come as no surprise. Furthermore, since the production of knowledge is a

[7] For instance, rational choice theory makes strong assumptions about the rationality of individuals, aiming to generate testable and predictive hypotheses. Far from being a universal theory of social behaviour, excessive claims place it dangerously close to the edge of becoming a self-fulfilling prophecy. Reassessing those totalising claims might help and be a useful service to social science analysts (Hay, 2003).

social practice, the explanation and understanding of social phenomena engages the analysts in critical evaluations of society and of our understanding of our own place within society. Therefore, the formulation of informed critiques cannot be avoided (Marsh et al., 1999; Sayer, 1992 and 2000).

Realism is a philosophy of and for the social sciences which draws a distinction between transitive and intransitive dimensions of knowledge (Sayer, 2000).[8] On the one hand, the intransitive dimension comprises objects of science, such as social phenomena or political events. On the other hand, the transitive domain pays attention to theory and discourses, which in turn could also be treated as objects of study themselves. Furthermore, acknowledging that social sciences resemble open systems where social, political and economic phenomena exhibit different degrees of complexity, it is the identification and assessment of connections, rather than of formal associations or regularities, which proves crucial. In so doing, making use of a critical method not merely describes observable, but also unobservable, phenomena, examining necessary and contingent relations, as well as warranted and unwarranted associations (Sayer, 1992; Lawson, 1997 and 2003; Cuadra-Montiel, 2007a). Therefore, the examination of relationships between structures, mechanisms and events is vital for analysing the processes of change; this adds to the importance of paying special attention to the problems of conceptualization and abstraction. For realism, the recognition that social processes are situated within specific spatio-temporal contexts should not be overlooked, as the need for geographical and historical specificity might help to overcome interpretive understandings, and move towards causal explanations, rather than formal regularities of social phenomena (Sayer, 2000; Lawson, 1997 and 2003; Cuadra-Montiel, 2007a).

Crucial ontological distinctions between positive economics on the one hand, and the realism of the hermeneutic perspective on the other, are the distinctions between structure and agency, and the material and ideational factors (Hay 2002). The theoretical perspective adopted in this study has realist epistemological and ontological positions as it pays attention to powers, relations and institutional logics (Jessop, 1990). Suffice it to say that situated agents interpret their structural situations and specific contexts regardless of where they are standing. The decisions and courses of action could affect and modify the context within which the agency is situated, making it impossible to remain unaltered. Additionally, it is argued here that, consistent with the realist ontological position, material and ideational features, observable and unobservable elements, all play a role in the dialectical relations of the social processes, although this happens to different degrees because it has various consequences and impacts within specific spatio-temporal locations.

Intangible factors such as perceptions, discourse, ideology and assumptions are elements which influence the course of actions and the decisions which agencies make when situated in specific circumstances. They are extremely difficult to quantify and measure accurately. However, this is not to say that their existence should be neglected and nor should their causal and constitutive role in social processes. Following Adam Smith's assumption that man has a propensity 'to barter, trade, and exchange one thing for another', the science of economics in its neoclassical form evolved into the study of 'self-adjusting' and 'self-regulating' mechanisms supposedly disembedded from all social relations. By so doing it is

[8] The work of Roy Bhaskar presents and supports the Critical Realist arguments, especially *A Realist Theory of Science* (1975), and *The Possibility of Naturalism* (1979).

ignored the fact that the economic system does not run like all social phenomena, on exclusively economic motives.[9]

It is therefore misleading to follow the reductionist and deterministic neoclassical argument that agencies, either individual or collective, such as States and corporations, are unable to resist, or even to influence, the dictates of impersonal economic forces, allegedly globalization. The use of power is immanent in all social relations and is able to influence the context and the desirability of certain preferences over others. It provides agents with a transformation capacity to favour their aims and objectives, which might either be tangible or intangible.[10] The way in which each capability is used is case-specific and varies in each time and space situation. Markets are embedded in larger social and political systems, where different actors and institutions interact with each other and promote their own agendas. No wonder national governments are among the most important and influential actors not only in the economic realm, but also in broader social and political systems, because markets are inherently political. Thus, as the locus of human interaction, markets are a constitutive part of a broader and more complex, dynamic and ever changing whole, where the social reality cannot and must not be reduced purely to arenas of supply and demand.

Nonetheless, the neoclassical approach to markets often presents the recurrent 'ceteris paribus' caveats, which refer to the consideration that all things being equal in the models makes them work in a static equilibrium scenario. In such scenarios there are no incentives to change any existing situations. Moreover, it places the analysis in a closed system insulated from any contact with a real world situation. Such unrealistic assumptions have considerable impact on the implementation of economic recommendations which many different countries have adopted following the prescriptions of the Bretton Woods institutions. However, before analyzing the World Bank's position on the role of the State, it is necessary to analyse contemporary economic imperatives in the next section.

4. The problematic emphasis on re-commodification

Political interests and economic activities have always been crucial for the all globalization processes. The degree of influence of power relations and the way in which the market is approached also shapes the social processes themselves. Even though economics and political science have been targeting their constituencies from different angles and perspectives, they are not incompatible at all. On the contrary, multidisciplinary approaches can provide insight and substantially enrich the analysis of global social phenomena.

---

[9] Although Adam Smith had a theory of innate rationality which contained ideas about mutual sympathy, rather than personifying the characteristics of 'homo oeconomicus', it was Mill and Bentham who developed the latter concept. Thanks to Matt Watson for clarification of this point.

[10] The pursuit of preferences or self-interest is characteristic of the economic rationality associated with neoclassical economics, and more generally of positivism. Since our perspective is based on a realist ontology and critical realist epistemology, it offers a different account, adopting a method of articulation in its identification of powers immanent in social relations and the causal relations of agencies. Therefore, actors are not perceived as merely rational unitary utility maximizers, but as informed agents situated in contexts. Moreover, this theoretical perspective searches for contingent necessities, presenting the analysis from abstract to concrete and from simple to complex (Jessop, 1990).

Economic activities are social activities per se as Polanyi and Schumpeter, among many other scholars, have shown.[11] For instance, Robert Gilpin has acknowledged that "...despite the growing importance of the market, historical experience indicates that the purpose of economic activities is ultimately determined not only by the markets and the prescriptions of technical economics, but also (either explicity or implicitly) by the norms, values and interests of the social and political systems in which economic activities are embedded..." (2001, 12).

Therefore, neither markets, nor economic activities should be taken out of its own context. Restricting attention to a few 'fundamental' macroeconomic variables omits the social, political and historical aspects which every actor's action or transaction carries within itself.[12] Thus, it is not surprising to find a growing recognition that the goal of sustainable development cannot be achieved without changing current economic policy means and instruments (Chang, 2001).

The problematic emphasis of policy-makers on re-commodification starts from the assumption that economics in general and neoclassical orthodoxy in particular, provides the leading perspectives for the study of social and political phenomena. There are severe problems and inconsistencies with the imposition of allegedly global economic determinism and structuralist explanations. It is not being claimed that economic analysis automatically leads to determinism; rather, that economic analysis alone is no substitute for historical, political and sociological analysis, which situates the phenomena and the actors in specific contexts, crucial for informing their interactions (Lawson, 1997 and 2003). There is no such thing as a market governed exclusively by objective laws and universal principles. Not only is there no incompatibility between market activities and the role of the State, indeed the creation of the former was in itself a political act embedded in the social relation.

Neoclassical economic theory, in so far as it conduces to a false distinction between States and markets, shows clear signs of inconsistency and fallibility. Consider, for instance, one of the main arguments for orientating domestic markets to external competition. It has been argued that greater rates of growth should follow the opening of an economy, due to increases in efficiency in economic activities. However, Rodrik provides compelling evidence that openness does not guarantee economic growth, since there is no straightforward association between trade barrier levels and the long-term growth of Gross Domestic Product (GDP). No indicator of policy towards trade and capital inflows correlates significantly with per capita GDP. Average tariff levels, non-tariff coverage ratios and indexes of capital account liberalization all show a weak correlation between openness and economic growth. Most importantly, the link is contingent on the presence of complementary policies and institutions. It is the investment and macroeconomic policies that remain key in the promotion of economic growth, because the maintenance of macro-

[11] For economics, political science, international relations, sociology, and the social sciences in general, it has been argued, have all the common denominator of Social Theory. This is not the same as saying that there are no clear differences among all of the social sciences. Disciplinary distinctions tend to emphasize theoretical orientations, analytical focus, specific approaches and methods, while the general agenda of the social sciences clearly shows much common ground for all of the disciplines. This should not surprise any specialist, as all social sciences refer to and develop from common sources of Social Theory (cf. Cuadra, 2001; and Lemert, 2004).

[12] The emphasis on the parsimony of the theoretical models stresses their predictive capacity and level of abstraction, although it faces a trade-off between their concreteness and plausibility (Hay, 2002).

economic stability, on the one side, and the investment of an important share of GDP in the provision of welfare and adequate public services on the other, provide adequate conditions for performing economic activities (Rodrik, 1999).

More plausibly, regardless of the degree of openness of the economy, it is economic growth which works as a magnet for the attraction of trade and investment flows. The Bretton Woods institutions' prescriptions for the divestiture of public enterprises in developing countries seized the opportunity to impose detailed neoclassical economic prescriptions. Unfortunately, some of the prescriptions have gone far beyond prudential limits, either on the basis of theoretical support or empirical demonstrations (Rodrik, 1999; and Chang, 2001).

It is no secret that the orientation of economic policies represents a highly political decision. Since there is overwhelming evidence that market discipline empowers financial markets over other constituencies (Ohmae, 1990 and 1996; Strange, 1996), the degree of re-commodification of economic activities is not exempt from difficulties. It is under these circumstances that democratic governance proves increasingly difficult. Unsatisfied social conditions and demands, especially if they are not attended by externally induced disciplines and strategies, may produce unexpected and undesirable social results. Since it is domestic voters who elect their own national governments, the latter must be held accountable to the former. However, the neoclassical economic orthodoxy and discourse point to the increasing importance of foreign investors, fund managers and members of the economic oligarchy for domestic policy makers, taking the responsibility and accountability away from the immediate representatives of the electorate. An important historical lesson which should not be overlooked is that successful economic management must not be induced to converge. There must be enough room for the implementation of economic policies. The domestic focus, design, debate and degree of various issues such as the structure of institutions, the tolerated and permissible extent of inequality and the types of public goods to be provided by the government, are not only a government agenda but a civil society priority. Thus, the government is held responsible for producing outcomes which satisfy the demands and aspirations of the citizens which it represents (Rodrik, 1999).

The succession of economic and financial crises in emerging markets during recent decades has shown strong evidence for not holding the assumption that international markets get things right in all circumstances. The neoclassical economic orthodoxy has modestly made some concessions on its silence on the socially embedded character of the market. For instance, the Washington Consensus of economic reform focused mainly on the role of ten policies aiming to foster growth in the Latin American region after the early 1980s debt crisis. Suffice it to say that the label of this set of policies was intended to reflect what the members of the Washington Congress at that time, the technocrats of the international financial organizations, think tanks, economic agencies of the US government and the Federal Reserve Board regarded as a desirable set of economic policy reforms for the Latin American economies. The reforms emphasized the role of policy instruments, rather than objectives or outcomes. Additionally, there was also recognition that these actors do not always follow their own precepts. The Washington Consensus set of policy instruments featured small budget deficits, redirection of public expenditure, tax reforms, financial liberalization, competitive exchange rates, progressive reduction of trade barriers and tariffs, facilitation of foreign direct investment entry, privatization of public enterprises, deregulation, and the provision of secure property rights (Williamson, 1990).

The Washington Consensus became associated not only with the process of economic restructuring, but also with the ideological agenda of neoliberalism, precluding any concern for distributive policies. Two decades later, characterized by disappointing rates of growth in Latin America, and severe economic crises in many countries, another agenda was launched for the region. Its broadened scope incorporated equity and institutions as core issues. The post Washington Consensus took the completion of first generation reforms, and implementation of crisis-proof mechanisms as necessary conditions for embarking on institutional reforms, and also for improving income distribution and the social agenda. Furthermore, these expanded medium-term objectives were supposed to be complemented at the social and political levels as well (Kuczynski & Williamson, 2003; Birdsall & de la Torre, 2001; Cuadra-Montiel, 2007b).

The myths of 'self-regulating' and 'self-adjusting' markets proved incapable of delivering either economic efficiency or socially equitable growth. Therefore, there is growing recognition that public and private spheres are by no means opposite to each other. The pendulum of the public debate has oscillated between various emphases on markets and government interaction throughout history. Economics, especially in its neoclassical guise, has been an influential social discipline since the last century. Nowadays their economic imperatives are widely portrayed and perceived as the self-induced external mechanisms of recent decades, discursively associated with different phenomena labelled in many different ways, including neoliberalism, Washington Consensus and globalization.[13]

The common denominator of these labels is oriented towards the discourse of powerless agencies incapable not only of opposing the structural determinism of economic imperatives, but the unavailability of options to do anything else than blindly obey whatever the market dictates. It is under these circumstances that the unrealistic assumptions which Friedman (1953), associates with his 'positive' epistemological position can impact upon the open systems in the world from which they were initially isolated as a form of self-induced external enforcement mechanism. Similarly, political science has not been immune from the influence of neoclassical economics. Aiming to emulate the parsimony of this discipline, one of the most significant efforts to import the explanatory power and predictive capacity of the assumptions which distinctively made neoclassical economics important has been rational choice theory. By making use of broad generalizations and simplifications in a similar way to positivist epistemology, rational choice positions itself far away from the complexity of the phenomena which it seeks deductively to analyse.

Unsurprisingly, the assumptions of bounded rationality and utility maximizing actors, on which this theoretical perspective draws, represent one of the main examples of the real impact which ideas can have. It is important to bear in mind one caveat. No quantitative test of any of the economic fundamentals that the neoclassical economic orthodoxy prescribes is provided. On the contrary, what follows is a qualitative analysis of an idea which an international organization has promoted. According to the World Bank, the role which the

[13] The assumptions on which neoclassical economics is based portray a homo oeconomicus who seems to have nothing in common with Aristotle's political animal. However, it is important to stress that it is precisely this lack of contact that is one of the factors which has accentuated an impasse in the dialogue between disciplines. What is needed is a decisive will to open the debate, rather than constraining them with specialists' jargon, since there is no such thing as a uniform model of economic policies and governance.

State should play in economic activities acknowledges rational choice institutionalism as one of the theoretical influences on the basis of which economic policies are prescribed. Those policies in turn, impact upon the material dimension of millions of people throughout the world. There is no intention herein to attempt a global evaluation of the economic advice of the monetary and financial organizations, on the basis of positivist assumptions.
Nonetheless, it is important to highlight the notion of institutions which provide the rules of the game and in turn shape human interaction. By opening up and closing down windows of opportunity, each actor is supposed to take optimal decisions to make him or herself better-off. The structural and deterministic perspective taken by rational choice institutionalism unsurprisingly portrays agencies as powerless to make their own decisions: they can only choose from the given options. According to this perspective, the institutional framework is an important precondition for the performance of an economy, as the analysis of institutional change is pursued from the top structures down to the bottom ones. Furthermore, globalization can only be vertically induced, where organizations are able to modify the institutional framework and to alter the structural setting (North, 1990). It is therefore important to focus on the promotion of an idea by one of the most influential organizations during the post Second World War period. The World Bank has undeniably played a very important role in the dissemination, prescription and introduction of global neoclassical economic orthodoxy prescriptions and advice. They are given to member countries which borrow conditioned resources, and these in turn, either in a direct or in an indirect way, have an impact on the living standards and conditions of the people from the borrowing countries. In many cases, economic resources have been given to developing nations in Latin America, Asia, Africa and Europe. It is, then, to the World Bank's perspective of the State that the following section is devoted.

5. A structural 'market friendly' view of the state

It is not discussed here that the World Bank promotion of its particular State agenda comes before its economic recommendations. Rather, it is argued here that the influence of neoclassical economics and rational choice institutionalism has been decisive in the formulation of the perspective of such international institutions. Economists and staff trained in these schools clearly not only defend but aggressively take for granted, spread and promote the postulates and assumptions on which their economic advice and prescriptions are given. It would not surprise anybody that, based on orthodox approaches such as neoclassical economics and rational choice institutionalism, the 'market friendly' view of the State adopted in some of the World Bank's publications and reports makes explicit its preferences for outwardly oriented market criteria, economic policy convergence and harmonization of best practices.[14] Whenever room is given for heterodox options, the relaxation is never loose enough to pose a real challenge to the 'economics comes first' position. However, as is stressed throughout here, markets do not necessarily set the priorities, nor do they determine some outcomes over others, since they are embedded in broader social contexts, as Schumpeter (1934), Granovetter (1996) and Polanyi (1944) have argued.

[14] There are, nevertheless, some analyses which move away from the orthodoxy. Regarding rational choice institutionalism see mainly, Hall & Taylor, 1996; Hay & Wincott, 1998; and Peters, 1999.

The World Bank's recommendations and structural adjustment programmes have evolved through different phases.[15] The World Bank, as one of the main economic and financial organizations of the post Second World War era, has not been untouched by the specific circumstances in which it and its members are situated.[16] For example, after the oil crises of the 1970s, one of the main concerns of the World Bank for the promotion of sustainable growth in the world economy was the adjustment mechanisms for energy, trade and capital flows. Moreover, general recommendations were based on the distinction between oil importing developing countries, capital-surplus oil exporters and industrial countries. In any case, the emphasis of international policies was orientated towards the improvement of poor countries' gains from trade, assistance for developing countries' energy production and the allocation of aid to the poorest countries (World Bank, 1981). After the debt crisis of the early 1980s and two decades of lost growth and development for a big share of the developing world, the emphasis on macro-economic and micro-economic variables has been 'fine-tuned' between different generations of economic reforms, and a more explicit and intrusive position as regards the economic role of the State has been adopted.

Nowadays international organizations such as the World Bank draw up a list of recommendations and preferences about what the role of the State should and should not be, what its capabilities could allow it to do and what it could not be allowed to do. Interestingly, the recognition of the central role of the State is said to be more that of a "partner, catalyst or facilitator", rather than a major player in its own right (World Bank, 1997). The State, it is argued, has to specifically serve the market, but in a social way. The World Bank proposes a strategy in order to achieve this goal. First, the State needs to match its role to its capability, and second the State needs to have its capabilities raised through reinvigorating public institutions. According to this view, the more capable a State is, the more effective it becomes. The undertaking and promotion of effective collective actions (i.e. infrastructure, the rule of law and public health, among others) represents the State's capability. In addition, it is said to be effective when it satisfies society's demands for these goods and services (World Bank, 1997).

To achieve the first part of the strategy, namely matching the State's role to its capabilities, requires certain mechanisms for choosing what to do and how to do it. Taking into consideration the fact that the socio-political fundamentals include a range of different issues which are case specific, the strategies need to be adjusted accordingly. The fundamentals include the protection of the environment and vulnerable social groups, investment in social services and infrastructure, the maintenance of macroeconomic stability and the overall policy environment, and the establishment of a foundation of law. For the World Bank, getting the State's social and economic fundamentals right, mean providing adequate institutional foundations for markets. Such institutional emphasis is characteristic of the post Washington Consensus. These general considerations need to be evaluated and

---

[15] See the various issues of the *World Development Report*, and Williams, 1999. Particularly useful is Yusuf's *Development Economics Through the Decades*.

[16] An important aspect which needs to be taken into account is that both the role and importance of ideas are contextually specific in time and space. Important developments in economic theory have attempted to tackle some specific problems and theoretical puzzles regarding growth, development, economic cycles, inflation, trade, employment, so on and so forth. Not only are they not automatically triggered, but in some cases it takes several years, even centuries, to bring to maturity the ideas which in turn provide the bases for further theoretical and ideational evolution (Backhouse, 1994 and 2002).

tailored according to the specific circumstances of each individual State. Moreover, attention is paid to the credibility of governments and their way of ensuring the spreading and sharing of the benefits of growth for their populations; for instance, via adequate investment and the provision of education and health (World Bank, 1997).

Taking economic rationality as somehow natural, the World Bank pursues an agenda for implementing reforms at different, albeit complementary, levels. The macro-institutional reforms, such as the structural and sector-specific adjustment programmes, are complemented by other strategies. In addition to the agenda for modifying the social, political and economic role of the State, there are some other specific projects. These include the implementation of micro-level programmes, aiming to teach individuals to think in terms of economic rationality so that they can be then subjected to the discipline of the markets. In short, the construction of economic space and the making of the homo economicus programme target not only governments and institutions, but also the habits and social mores of people (Williams, 1999).

Furthermore, this first part of the strategy goes some steps further. Once they have provided institutional foundations for markets, governments are supposed to ensure that the State does not monopolize the provision of goods and services. According to the World Bank's recommendations, regulatory systems, the privatization of State enterprises and the focus on specific policies are means to avoid a situation in which the State is cast in the role of sole provider. Additionally, the World Bank acknowledges as a crucial element for a capable State the government's political commitment to economic and institutional reforms. The more committed a government is to reforming its macroeconomic policies and institutional structures, the faster and more equitable will be the economic development which it can deliver to its citizenry. The reforms of the State which aim to make it a more effective and capable entity take place not only at the macroeconomic level, where the emphasis has been on the exchange rate, industrial and trade policies, but also at the institutional level, at which they need to deal with regulation, social services, finance and infrastructure (World Bank, 1997).

The second part of the strategy which calls for reinvigorating the institutions of the State matches the institutional emphasis of the post Washington Consensus. The reinvigoration of the institutions of the State aims to stimulate better performance by raising the returns for a more efficient bureaucracy, making sure that the disincentives are always lower and less attractive than the incentives for reinvigorating the institutions of the State. The World Bank's perspective stresses openness, transparency and accountability by offering citizens a voice and partnership; the practice of effective rules and controls, preferably making laws enforceable and backed by an independent judiciary; and the promotion of a competitive environment not only for policy making, but for delivering public goods and services, and within public officials and the bureaucracy (World Bank, 1997).

The fact should be stressed that the World Bank's institutional assessment of the State does not consider it as an agency. Rather, the State is viewed as part of the economic structure, which serves and provides the foundations for markets.[17] And in so doing it reproduces the

---

[17] The phenomena associated with the processes of globalization provide non-deterministic windows of opportunity and constraints for governments to modify their practices together with effective international cooperation, versus rising transnational concerns, such as the promotion of economic stability, the protection of the environment and the aim of making international development assistance

structural and deterministic approach portrayed by neoclassical economics and rational choice institutionalism. The World Bank's market friendly formula aims to achieve faster economic development through two core elements: good policies, on the one hand, and State institutions more capable of putting them into practice, on the other. Depending on the region of the world on which we are concentrating and, specifically, on the characteristics of the specific case study, different agendas are set. For instance, the recommendations for Latin America call for the implementation of democratic practices, and decentralization of power and spending, in addition to reforms of the legal system, civil service and social policies.

In the World Bank's view, the role of the State is crucial for reaching better levels of economic and social development. In advancing this goal, it recommends that the State must never engage itself in this task as a direct provider, but simply as a 'partner, catalyst and facilitator' (World Bank, 1997, 1). The impact of all these sets of ideas is clearly having strong repercussions on the daily lives of millions of people throughout the world. The World Bank's view of the State is a structural perception which reduces the State's raison d'être to a set of mere strategies for effectiveness. It sees effectiveness as the crucial match and interaction between rules and institutions, where the provision of goods and services is the State's most important role. The World Bank argues that the effectiveness of a State's performance is determined by the extent to which markets are able to flourish, and thus the extent to which better living standards can be derived.

What it does not say is that the capacity for change lies in the way in which policies are implemented, and also in the courses of action selected by actors themselves, notably governments. The World Bank does not make any explicit mention that there is a broad range of feasible alternatives, although it accepts that there is no unique model for change. However, for this international organization, the nature and extent of change is reduced to a matter of incentives. According to this argument, the stronger the incentives for throwing out old policies and institutional arrangements, the more likely changes become (World Bank, 1997).

Adopting this perspective, the World Bank views change merely as a structural outcome. There is neither any recognition of the role which agencies play, nor of how vital they are for the provision of contingency in the State's tasks and effectiveness. This should not surprise anybody, since the economic concerns of macroeconomic stability and attraction of investment are perceived to be built upon, and to operate on, a stable social context within a static framework. It is argued that contingency brings uncertainty, which in the eyes of the investors is perceived as an economic disincentive. Nevertheless, the unrealistic assumption that economic transactions and activities take place in static conditions ensures that it is impossible either to reproduce them or even to find them in the real world. The fluid and non-static nature of social processes clearly needs to be taken into account.

The structural deterministic view, not only of the World Bank in particular, but of international organizations in general, promotes inaction, passive behaviour, submission and acceptance of the status quo. The huge potential which actors have for modifying the context in which they live is a cause of concern; therefore, it is deliberately excluded from conservative social, political and economic agendas. Although, in the short-term, policies

more effective, the management of regional crises and the spread and promotion of knowledge (World Bank, 1997).

may induce or select certain strategies over others, in the long-term, change with all its desired and undesired consequences will come. Unsatisfied demands and exclusionary policies can be partially attenuated. However, in circumstances in which they are not corrected, the desire for a radical transformation will build up pressures which are each time more difficult to contain. Regardless of concerns for stability and equilibrium, history teaches us that change always comes in the end.

Consistent with the argument presented herein, it is imperative to explore the links and causal relations between ideas, firms and institutional stability, as all have been instrumental in the orientation of government policies and the social impact of the efforts towards increased re-commodification. In so doing, attention is also paid to the importance of both innovation and crisis which Schumpeter terms 'creative destruction'.

6. Ideas, stability and firms: an institutional link

The role played by institutions clearly has an impact on the contexts and structures agents find themselves in. The spatial and temporal dimensions are especially important in the identification of constituent elements which play a role in the processes of globalization. For, it has been argued, geographical and historical specificity are among the most important features to be taken into account in social, political and economic theory (Sayer, 1992 and 2000; Cuadra-Montiel 2007a).[18] Although the social and political contexts are undoubtedly important, some neoclassical economic analysis and recommendations based on this theoretical perspective tend to de-contextualise the economic phenomena from their specificities of time and space, as it is commonly associated with globalization. Consistent with this position, it is important to mention that, in order to bring those details back into the analysis, some efforts have been made to relax some neoclassical assumptions and present a more rigorous analysis, as are exemplified by the arguments of Stiglitz, some theories of endogenous growth, strategic trade theory and the new economic geography. None of those theories are adopted here. However, there are some common issues showed by their research agenda and the one defended herein.

What is important to stress is how actors, contexts and actions articulate by putting particular emphasis on conceptualization and abstraction. Since an hermeneutic approach is not blind to the geographic and historical contexts in which processes are situated, it acknowledges the spatio-temporal dimensions of the social phenomena, as it does with the analytical distinction between the material and the ideational, as well as that between structure and agency. The notions of institutions affect the windows of opportunity and constraint for all situated economic agents. This is a key issue as it provides a broader perspective than if the analysis had merely focused on quantitative variables. Thus, attention needs to be paid to causal elements and interactions, not merely on statistical regularities.[19]

---

[18] For instance, early 20th century institutionalists argued that taking into account history and the changes which societies display over time is necessary to provide an evolutionary account of the economy. Moreover, it was also argued that the evolution of social structures is a process of natural selection of changing and cumulatively self-reinforcing institutions (Veblen, 1919).

[19] Behaviourism, for instance, reduces the significance of theory to a descriptive record of material regularities. It makes use of inductive logic by applying empirical and statistical methods in its search to discover regular patterns of behaviour which would help it generate probabilistic predictions. Since

Consistent with the emphasis placed on the causal and constitutive role of ideas in globalization processes, a certain pattern of interaction between economic ideas and institutions needs to be taken into account as well. Either in the face of a crisis, or in the narration of one, we are told, institutional stability cannot be promoted without first allowing economic ideas to reduce uncertainty (Blyth, 2002). The proposition that ideas contribute towards the reduction of uncertainty during moments of crisis functions as a preliminary step in the construction of institutions, as they make political coalition and network building possible, which in turn facilitates collective action. Building on these steps and at the same time parallel to these tasks, the dismantling of existing institutions is of use because it justifies a new institutional design. Furthermore, ideas do play a role, not only in building a new set of rules, but also in paving the way for reaching or regaining institutional stability. Once the construction or adaptation and legitimation tasks for a new set of institutions are accomplished facts, stability is made possible to let them provide a framework conducive to the prospering of economic activities (Blyth, 2002). Thus, ideas play a causal and constitutive role in the construction of a stable institutional framework in which situated economic agents such as firms realise their productive endeavours.

Placing more emphasis on institutional change, the way in which the broad pattern of ideas and institutional change follows attempts to regain stable institutions when threatened, discursively or by crisis and instability. Nonetheless, problematizing structural notions of institutional change and focusing on the causal role of ideas is not the same thing as labelling the economic changes in the last quarter of the 20th century 'the second great transformation' as Blyth does. In my humble opinion, a qualitative historical transformation such as that of the 19th century analyzed by Polanyi in his classic work has not taken place in the contemporary period. It is important to recall that the great transformation rested on a few, but crucial, elements: the balance of power system, the international gold standard, the 'self-adjusting' market utopia and the liberal State, where the laws governing the market economy were of the utmost importance (Polanyi, 1944). Even though important economic changes have occurred since then, there is no doubt that the qualitative historical transformations of that time dwarf our times. Rather than claiming a second great transformation, the research agenda must take theoretical tools and methodological criteria to analyse the processes of globalization.

The informal and formal set of rules which actors generally follow, as defended by North, affects the room for agents to manoeuvre, conditioning the latter's interactions. Bearing this in mind, the role institutions play in producing economic and political outcomes is of crucial importance. In particular, regarding the economic sphere, the importance of firms and the ability of institutions to open up or cancel out certain courses of action have been stressed,

behaviourism treats agencies as simple aggregations of individuals and does not rely on theory to inform its observations, it suffers from narrow definitions, albeit compensated by employing rigorous statistical techniques. However, correlations among variables are sometimes confused with causes of the phenomena under scrutiny. This conflation, rare in closed systems, becomes problematic in open social, political and economic systems, where the objects and subjects of study can affect their own contexts. Therefore, the character of the open systems makes it impossible to get a clean observation, where the isolation of variables is vital. For it is one thing to quantify statistical significance between observable variables, and another either to reduce or to leave aside unquantifiable factors such as power and ideas in the analysis (Hay, 2002). What is needed is to analyse the dynamic flows of interaction of situated actors and their context, which continuously reshape the social, political and economic arenas.

among other authors, by Hall and Soskice. In their book *Varieties of Capitalism*, these authors take firms as core economic actors, and portray them as self-interested entities which strategically interact with others. According to this perspective, firms make use of their capacities in a relational way. They orientate their efforts in order to produce, develop and distribute goods and services profitably. In so doing, they also make use of strategic interactions, not only with their peers and counterparts, but also with the institutional set of formal and informal rules. The core competencies or dynamic capabilities which Hall and Soskice consider include a firm's industrial relations, vocational training and education, corporate governance, inter-firm relations and coordination problems in relation with its employees (2001).

From this point of view, structures such as institutions, condition without determining the range of available and feasible strategies for the actors (in this case, corporations). It is the institutional frameworks which provide national economies with comparative advantages in particular activities and products, from where cross-national patterns of specialization emerge, due to the availability of modes of coordination which condition firms' efficiency (Hall & Soskice, 2001). Bringing a loosely Ricardian notion of 'comparative advantage' to their framework, Hall and Soskice argue that nations prosper not by becoming similar, but by building on their institutional differences.[20] Because firms are able to retain the core characteristics of their long-standing strategies, the modification of practices to overcome external shocks allows firms to sustain and recreate their advantage, on the basis of common beliefs and understanding. In other words, there is room for policy diversity, which does not enforce uniformity in policies, practices or strategies. Moreover, Hall and Soskice acknowledge the path-dependent character of institutions when they mention that the institutions of any given economy are inextricably bound up with its particular history (2001).

Appealing at first glance as this 'actor-centred approach' may appear to be (Hall & Soskice, 2001, 6), it is, however, by no means unproblematic. As their analysis is heavily influenced by rational choice institutionalism, it should come as no surprise that some of the latter's deficiencies are also present in the former. The bounded rationality and utility maximizing behaviour of the actors is perceived to be affected by the institutions of the economy. In addition, it is quite evident that Hall and Soskice consider the institutional framework as a precondition for the performance of the economy, similar to rational choice institutionalism. Therefore, this sort of top-down analysis suggests that change can be induced vertically. Even though these authors acknowledge that actors interact with others, they do not make any concession as to the potential for actors to influence, promote and achieve changes.

Furthermore, Watson criticises the use made by Hall and Soskice of the conceptual abstraction of 'comparative advantage' in the face of empirical indicators which do not match the specialization of contemporary trade flows. He argues that the socio- institutional differences of their approach do not correspond to the distinctive patterns of specialization

---

[20] Taking labour and capital as immobile between two countries David Ricardo argued that trade was determined not by the most efficient producer of goods, as Adam Smith had proposed, but by 'comparative advantage' in which the relative efficiency of producers would help expand the market and stimulate growth (Backhouse, 1994). Technicalities aside, Hall and Soskice take principally the pattern of product specialization found across nations and expand the notion to allow them to insert, rather than fitting, the institutional framework into their account of institutional varieties of capitalism.

observed in the real world. His main critique points out fundamental features of the social structure of accumulation are obscured by emphasizing the existence of national models such as the ones which Hall and Soskice employ. Thus, the variety of models is poorly explained, weakening David Ricardo's notions of specialization, trade and comparative advantage (2003b).

There is an additional controversy in Hall and Soskice's work besides the strong traces of deterministic structural logic and the loose adaptation of the Ricardian notion of comparative advantage. This is the paradoxical reductionism of two broad types of market economies. The liberal model, which they associate with Anglo-Saxon countries, is juxtaposed with the coordinated model, associated with European countries and Japan. According to Hall and Soskice's analysis, the main feature of the Anglo-Saxon liberal economies is the competitive market arrangements set for firms. By contrast, in the European and Japanese coordinated economies, as well as the market mechanism, firms depend more heavily on non-market relationships to coordinate the orientation of their activities. Even though those authors hint that their typology could not fit many national cases, no efforts are undertaken to provide a more balanced and less schematized account of national systems of political economy. Clearly, there are certainly more varieties of capitalism, to use Hall and Soskice's term, than the ones which they identify. If institutions matter to the efficiency with which not only goods but also services can be produced, it follows then that we need to consider the conditions for domestic policies which aim especially at promoting endogenous growth. This makes innovation one of the crucial dimensions of economic success. A discussion of innovation in the following section is needed for a further analysis of institutions, firms and innovation to provide a different pattern of economic relations from those presented by Hall and Soskice.

7. The 'creative destruction' of crises and innovation

Innovation has been identified as one of the most important dimensions of economic success. Hall and Soskice point to one of the important elements of the distinctiveness of Anglo-Saxon economies, its tendency towards radical innovation, whereby not only production processes, but also goods, services and technology sectors are equipped with better capacities. By contrast, the coordinated market economies tend to have a more incremental model of innovation, providing continuous but small scale improvements (2001). From their analysis emerge patterns of specialization in economic activities and products which could be interpreted as responses to institutional frameworks. Therefore, the importance of innovation creates market niches and incentives for increased levels of efficiency, both of which are praised in the re-commodification dynamics which characterize contemporary economic activities. It follows firms are revealed as important units of analysis, because they are economic agents situated within an institutional framework. Thus, the analysis of economic agencies such as firms might help to provide insight into causal and endogenous mechanisms.

The academic literature on economic development takes technological issues such as innovation and transfer as crucial elements which may help national economies to develop. Besides technological developments, innovation can also be identified in social, political and economic affairs, although it is not as widely acknowledged and praised there as in its impact of technology. Limited space and analytical scope does not allow us to discuss the different contributions in this field since the post World War II era onwards.[21] Suffice it to say, however, that there seems to be some common ground based on two important authors. The first one is John Maynard Keynes, whose recommendations that the State should play a role in economic development, along with the caveat against market failures, gained considerable political influence in the post World War II period. Since this time, analysis of the economic role of the State, imperfect markets and asymmetric information has been expanded by Stiglitz. The other influential author whose ideas about innovation and economic development have had considerable impact is Joseph A. Schumpeter, whose publications have also influenced economics, political economy, economic sociology and political science.

Innovation in economic activities was regarded by Schumpeter as a core part of the economic process. These, in turn, were never isolated from, or independent of all the social processes (1934). As open systems work, he held that social facts are never purely or exclusively economic. Like Polanyi, Schumpeter does not consider land and labour as commodities. There are, however, important differences in their accounts. In the latter's perspective, the economic exchanges between labour and land continually renew the stream of economic life, as do consumption goods as well. Money is regarded as a technical instrument which functions as an intermediate link, facilitating the circulation of commodities (Schumpeter, 1934). It is the commodification of land and labour in the first leg of the expansion of the markets, operating alongside the protection to society and nature associated with the 'double movement', which distinguishes Polanyi's contributions (1944).

Situated within a broader social realm, the economic dynamics feature circular flow processes, development processes and crises, which prevent development from following an undisturbed course. The business cycle was described as having different stages. Those are i) a situation of boom which creates out of itself dynamics and which, when they end, gives way to a crisis; ii) the crisis may turn into depression which might be followed by a temporary absence of development, leading to a new equilibrium; iii) the fact that this is an underemployment equilibrium may trigger the reorganization of production which precedes another boom stage (Schumpeter, 1934).

Schumpeter argued that cyclical fluctuations are as important as economic stability, because they foster the continual emergence of new economic and social forms. Overall, this has the effect of improving economic well-being (1934). In order to achieve economic development, he maintained that changes in economic life alter and displace states of equilibrium. In his perspective, changes in economic life would be more likely to appear in the supply-side of activities of industrial production and commercial life, rather than as demand-driven phenomena of consumer wants. He went on to say that changes in economic life require new combinations in materials and forces which make productive economic activities. The innovative combinations draw necessary means of production from former combinations. Innovation, therefore, becomes a core component for the introduction of new goods, new

[21] Development economics has been associated among others, with the work of Raúl Prebisch, Gunnar Myrdal, Alexander Gerschenkron, Paul Rosenstein-Rodan, as well as analysis and reports from the United Nations Conference on Trade and Development and the Economic Commission on Latin America and the Caribbean. Albert O. Hirschman, Moses Abramovitz, Paul M. Romer, Amartya Sen and Paul R. Krugman have also made important contributions. Placing more emphasis on structural adjustment, the International Monetary Fund and World Bank programmes and recommendations have been put into practice, leaving no continent untouched.

methods of production, the opening of new markets, or carrying out the new organization of any industry (Schumpeter, 1934).

Innovations and crises combine in a process of 'creative destruction'. If crises do not permanently obstruct economic and social processes, it is in the emergence of new economic and social forms where social and economic sectors rise and fall, that innovation plays a pivotal role. For Schumpeter, the process of 'creative destruction' is regarded as an evolutionary form of economic change. As the label suggests, it incessantly revolutionizes the economic structure from within, destroying the old and creating the new. The 'creative destruction' brought by innovation and crises might translate in the economic sphere into increased levels of competitiveness as one participant finds that the latter factor command a decisive cost or quality advantage. This, in turn, strikes at the foundation of other firms (Schumpeter, 1954).

The fundamental impulse towards novelty in consumer goods and services, methods of production, forms of transportation, market shares and niches, industrial organization and management reduces the long-term scope and importance of established economic entities. To introduce new goods, services, processes and technologies, a revised and updated economic and industrial reorganization is required. This may bear little relation to the neoclassical economic orthodoxy of perfect competition. Even though new methods of production, technology or commodities do not per se confer monopolistic tendencies, those positions are often approximated. Furthermore, imperfect competition affecting market prices and economic output is situated within an institutional pattern, which in turn also creates conditions for another institutional framework (Schumpeter, 1954). Therefore, the crises and innovations which characterize the processes of 'creative destruction' decisively impact upon and make the institutional frameworks follow a similar or equivalent dynamic pattern of renovation, as they also need to adapt themselves to the ongoing changes and processes in a dialectical fashion. While crises, as mechanisms of change, provide windows of opportunity which are appropriate for a macro and meso level of analysis, innovation is better dissected at the micro and meso levels of analysis.

8. Final remarks

Since it is virtually impossible to control for all of the interactions among variables which affect global complex social and economic systems, efforts have been orientated towards revealing the contribution of causal processes of re-commodification linked phenomena. The dynamic nature and fluid interactions which characterize this orientation is undoubtedly fertile ground for contingency and indeterminate tendencies and countertendencies.

Attention was devoted to an exploration of some of the causal relations which might be found in the contemporary orientation of economic activities. Those activities are not performed in a vacuum, isolated from the world outside. They are embedded in a broader social spectrum. They are part of an inclusive social universe and, therefore, need to be analysed and dissected with these conditions and characteristics in mind. Thus, the ever-changing social dynamics do not allow us to make universal claims.

Rather than following a uniform pattern, the exercise of power makes use of a broad range and variety of causal relations which move in different directions and affect, to different degrees, actors and structures alike. The suggested causal relations were analyzed in order to highlight the interactions between structures and agencies, as well as the interactions between material and ideational factors. Foucault stressed that power is attributed to strategic situations in all social relations (1976, 1977 and 1978). As such, its immanency in all social interactions makes use of a range of mechanisms, such as the ones suggested here, in a non law-like regular form, to continuously build perpetually moving social dynamics and processes i.e. globalization. The relational character of the exercise of power provides actors with the endogenous capacity to trigger, produce, and bring about changes which affect them, as well as the contexts in which they are situated. Moreover, the omnipresence of power interactions is not alien to economic activities as the 'invisible hand' of market forces might suggest. On the contrary, it is articulated and integrated in all and every phase of the re-commodification process. Markets are highly political, so are their transactions and activities, and especially so are the frameworks and actors which operate and interact there.

If power is the core factor triggering globalization, it operates through a variety of otherwise intangible causal relations, such as the ideational and institutional, which the situated actors in context systematically transform. Power has neither an a priori essence, nor a privileged origin. The strategies through which it is relationally exercised from innumerable points never move uniformly in the same direction, or aim for the same goals. Furthermore, power relations are uneasy and unpredictable phenomena. These open-ended and indeterminate features are the ones to analyze. Exercises of power can be deciphered by tracing agencies' strategies and causal relations. Yet, the account is never conclusive. Nonetheless, no theoretical models or analytical strategies should be blamed for this, because contingency and open-endedness are the wealth, never the misery, of all social sciences.

Praising this wealth, it was emphasized the contemporary outward orientation of domestic markets to external competition. Here, rates of growth, contrary to conventional wisdom, are reported to show weak law-like regularities or correlations with the degree of openness of an economy. Markets are socially and politically embedded. They are by no means neutral or independent of the context in which actors interact. The consideration of social factors other than merely economic variables reflects the highly political character of the markets and the implementation of economic policies. The socio-political context could not be left aside, nor could stability be taken for granted, since the social character of the market provides enough room for different orientations of policies, actors' roles to be played and diversity in the implementation of strategies.

According to the analysis undertaken, the World Bank perspective on the economic and political role of the State was found deterministic and structuralist. Since, it has been contended that it is within globalization processes that agencies themselves have the capacity to internally decide which course of action to take. They are, however, situated in circumstances not necessarily of their own choosing, leaving the door ajar for contingency and indeterminacy. Emphasis is placed on the role played by agencies and on their interactions and capabilities as well. This perspective, as shown above, is not shared by the World Bank, as it emphasises a top-down view, with the perception of change as a structural outcome.

It was herein considered the interaction between firms as economic agents and institutional structures as a useful approach for the analysis of innovation. The relevance of this task lies in the fact that innovation has been identified as a core component in the economic performances and development of the State. A vital element of the expansion and strengthening of productive economic activities is novelty in the production of goods and services, channels of distribution, management and market shares and niches. As such, it highlights its association with the 'creative destruction' which, together with crises, helps to propel the onward march of economic cycles. The aim was to provide a theoretically informed and empirically grounded analysis of the overlapping, irregular and contingent convergence of global tendencies and countertendencies in play, where agents undeniably take a decisive role.

9. Acknowledgments

The argument presented herein owes an infinite debt of gratitude to Colin Hay, Matthew Watson, Magnus Ryner and Adam Morton. Their ever generous and critical insights greatly improved the original argument. Remaining errors are all my own responsibility. Mexico's Consejo Nacional de Ciencia y Teconologia CONACYT, provided research funding.

10. References

Backhouse, R. (2002). The Ordinary Business of Life: A History of Economics from the Ancient World to the Twenty-First Century, Princeton, Princeton, USA.

Backhouse, R. (1994). Economists and the Economy: The Evolution of Economic Ideas, Second edition. Transaction Publishers, New Brunswick, USA.

Birdsall, N. & de la Torre, A. (2001). Washington Contentious: Economic Policies for Social Equity in Latin America, Carnegie Endowment for International Peace and the Inter-American Dialogue, Washington DC, USA.

Blaikie, N. (1993). Approaches to Social Enquiry, Polity Press, Cambridge, UK.

Blyth, M. (2002). Great Transformations: Economic Ideas and Institutional Change in the Twentieth Century, Cambridge University Press, Cambridge, UK.

Cerny, P. (1990). The Changing Architecture of Politics: Structure, Agency, and the Future of the State, Sage Publications, London, UK.

Chang, H. (ed.) (2001). Joseph Stiglitz and the World Bank: The Rebel Within, Wimbledon Publishing Company, London, UK.

Cuadra, H. (2001). Las Ciencias Sociales frente al Siglo XXI, Nuevas Agendas de Investigación y Docencia: las Relaciones Internacionales. Revista Mexicana de Ciencias Políticas y Sociales, Vol. XLIV, No. 181, (Enero-Abril), pp. 95-113.

Cuadra-Montiel, H. (2007a). Critical Realism and the Strategic-Relational Approach: Comments on a Non-Typical KWNS-SWPR Experience. Journal of Critical Realism, Vol. 6, No. 1, pp. 87-113.

Cuadra-Montiel, H. (2007b). Incompleteness of Post-Washington Consensus: A Critique of Macroeconomic and Institutional Reforms. International Studies, Vol. 44, No. 2, pp. 103-122.

Dicken, P. (1998). Global Shift: Transforming the World Economy, Third Edition. Paul Chapman Publishing Ltd, London, UK.

Esping-Andersen, G. (1990). The Three Worlds of Welfare Capitalism, Polity Press, Cambridge, UK.

Foucault, M. (1978/1990). The History of Sexuality. Vol. 1: An Introduction, (Translated by Robert Hurley). Vintage Books, New York, USA.

Foucault, M. (1977). Discipline and Punish: The Birth of the Prison, Penguin Books, London, UK.

Foucault, M. (1976). 'Two Lectures' in Kelly, Michael. (ed.) 1994. Critique and Power: Recasting the Foucault / Habermas Debate, The MIT Press, Cambridge, USA.

Friedman, M. (1953). The Methodology of Positive Economics. In Essays in Positive Economics, The University of Chicago Press, Chicago, USA.

Gilpin, R. (2001). Global Political Economy: Understanding the International Economic Order, Princeton University Press, Princeton, USA.

Granovetter, M. (1996). Economic Action and Social Structure: The Problem of Embeddedness. In Swedberg, R. (ed.) Economic Sociology, Edward Elgar, Cheltenham, UK.
Hall, P. & Soskice, D. (eds.) (2001). Varieties of Capitalism: The Institutional Foundations of Comparative Advantage, Oxford University Press, Oxford, UK.
Hall, P. & Taylor, R. (1996). Political Science and the Three New Institutionalisms. Political Studies, Vol. XLIV, pp. 936-957.
Hay, C. (2003). 'Be Careful What You Wish For: Rationality, Self-fulfilling Prophecies and the Status of Economic Analogies in Contemporary Political Science' Paper presented at the London School of Economics. February 2003.
Hay, C. (2002). Political Analysis: A Critical Introduction. Palgrave, Basingstoke, UK.
Hay, C. & Rosamond, B. (2002). Globalization, European Integration and the Discursive Construction of Economic Imperatives. Journal of European Public Policy, Vol. 9, No. 2, (April), pp. 147-167.
Hay, C. & Wincott, D. (1998). Structure, Agency and Historical Institutionalism. Political Studies, Vol. 46, No. 5, pp. 951-957.
Hay, C. & Marsh, D. (eds.) (2000). Demystifying Globalization, Macmillan / St Martins Press in association with POLSIS. London, UK.
Held, D. & McGrew, A. (eds.) (2000). The Global Transformations Reader: An Introduction to the Globalization Debate, Polity Press, Cambridge, UK.
Held, D. et al. (1999). Global Transformations: Politics, Economics and Culture, Polity Press, Cambridge, UK.
Hirst, P. & Thompson, G. (1999). Globalization in Question: The International Economy and the Possibilities of Governance, Second edition. Polity Press, Cambridge, UK.
Kuczynski, P. & Williamson, J. (eds.) (2003). After the Washington Consensus: Restarting Growth and Reform in Latin America, Institute for International Economics, Washington DC, USA.
Jessop, B. (2002). The Future of the Capitalist State, Polity Press, Cambridge, UK.
Jessop, B. (1990). State Theory: Putting the Capitalist State in its Place, Polity Press, Cambridge, UK.
Lawson, T. (2003). Reorienting Economics, Routledge, London, UK.
Lawson, T. (1997). Economics and Reality, Routledge, London, UK.
Lemert, C. (ed.) (2004). Social Theory: The Multicultural and Classic Readings, Third edition. Westview Press, Oxford, UK.
Marsh, D. et al. (1999). Postwar British Politics in Perspective, Polity Press, Cambridge, UK.
North, D. (1990). Institutions, Institutional Change and Economic Performance, Cambridge University Press, Cambridge, UK.
Ohmae, K. (1996). End of the Nation State: the Rise of Regional Economies, Special overseas edition. Harper Collins, London, UK.
Ohmae, K. (1990). The Borderless World: Power and Strategy in the Interlinked Economy, Collins, London, UK.
Peters, G. (1999). Institutional Theory in Political Science: The 'New Institutionalism', Pinter Publishers, London, UK.
Polanyi, K. (1944/1957). The Great Transformation: The Political and Economic Origins of our Time, Beacon Press, Boston, USA.
Rodrik, D. (1999). The New Global Economy and Developing Countries: Making Openness Work, Overseas Developing Council, Washington DC, USA.
Rodrik, D. (1997). Has Globalization Gone Too Far?, Institute for International Economics, Washington DC, USA.

Sayer, A. (2000). Realism and Social Science, Sage Publications, London, UK.

Sayer, A. (1992). Method in Social Science: A Realist Approach, Second edition. Routledge, London, UK.

Schiller, D. (1998). How to Think About Information. In V. Mosco, and J. Wasko (eds.) The Political Economy of Information. Madison, USA.

Scholte, J. (2000). Globalisation: A Critical Introduction, Macmillan, London, UK.

Schumpeter, J. (1954/1974). Capitalism, Socialism and Democracy, Fourth edition. London: Unwin University Books.

Schumpeter, J. (1934/1951). The Theory of Economic Development: An Inquiry into Profits, Capital, Credit, Interest, and the Business Cycle, Harvard University Press, Cambridge, USA.

Stiglitz, J. (2002). Globalization and its Discontents, Allen Lane, London, UK.

Stiglitz, J. (1999). Quis Custodiet Ipsos Custodes? Challenge, Vol. 42, No. 6, (November-December), pp. 26-67.

Stiglitz, J. (1991). Another Century of Economic Science. The Economic Journal, Vol. 101, No. 404, pp. 134-141.

Stiglitz, J. (1989). On the Economic Role of the State. In Stiglitz, J. et al. The Economic Role of the State, Heertje A.(ed.) Basil Blackwell in association with Bank Insinger de Beaufort N.V., Cambridge, USA.

Strange, S. (1996). The Retreat of the State: The Diffusion of Power in the World Economy, Cambridge University Press, Cambridge, UK.

Van Dijk, T. (1998). Common Sense. In Ideology: A Multidisciplinary Approach, Sage Publications, London, UK.

Veblen, T. (1919). Why is Economics not an Evolutionary Science? In The Place of Science in Modern Civilization and Other Essays, B.W. Huebsch, New York, USA.

Watson, M. (2003a). Constructing and Contesting Orthodoxies: General Equilibrium Economics and the Political Discourse of Globalization. Paper presented to the Annual Conference of the International Studies Association. Portland, Oregon, USA, February 2003.

Watson, M. (2003b). Ricardian Political Economy and the 'Varieties of Capitalism' Approach: Specialization, Trade and Comparative Institutional Advantage. Comparative European Politics, Vol. 1, No. 2, pp. 227-240.

Watson, M. (2001). International Capital Mobility in an Era of Globalisation: Adding a Political Dimension to the 'Feldstein-Horioka Puzzle. Politics, Vol. 21, No. 2, pp. 81-92.

Watson, M. (2000). The Political Discourse of Globalisation: Globalising Tendencies as Self-Induced External Enforcement Mechanisms, PhD Thesis. POLSIS, School of Social Sciences. The University of Birmingham, Birmingham, UK.

Weiss, L. (1998). The Myth of the Powerless State: Governing the Economy in a Global Era, Polity Press, Cambridge, UK.

Williams, D. (1999). Constructing the Economic Space. The World Bank and the Making of the Homo Oeconomicus. Millenium: Journal of International Studies, Vol. 28, No. 1, pp. 79-99.

Williamson, J. (1990). What Washington Means by Policy Reform. In Williamson, J. (ed.) Latin American Adjustment: How Much Has Happened?, Institute for International Economics, Washington DC, USA.

World Bank. (1997). World Development Report 1997: The State in a Changing World, The World Bank, and Oxford University Press, Washington DC, USA.

World Bank. (1981). World Development Report 1981, The World Bank, Washington DC, USA.

6

Media Globalization and the Debate on Multiculturality

Josu Amezaga-Albizu
Department of Audiovisual Communication and Advertisement;
University of the Basque Country, UPV/EHU
The Basque Country

1. Introduction

When in the mid-1980s, Joshua Meyrowitz proposed the concept of 'placeless cultures' to draw attention to the consequences of the transmission of information becoming freed from spatial limits thanks to the electronic media (Meyrowitz, 1985), he was pointing to a key aspect for understanding the globalization of the following decades. Following situationist postulates, Meyrowitz said that our social behavior is based on the definition we make of the situation, which in its turn is based on the information we receive about it. In this way, when the electronic media modify the relationship between the transmission of information and physical space, they are also affecting the relation between the latter and culture, giving rise to those cultures that do not depend on the physical and social setting that surrounds them.

This idea, which is increasingly relevant in my opinion, is interesting for us to be able to gain a better understanding of the globalization of communications, understood for now as the diffusion of the media and their content at the planetary level. And it also helps us to see how it is affecting not only our societies, but even our way of understanding them. It is not in vain that sociology has developed historically on the basis of a national scheme, according to which the very term society is defined on the basis of a territory, delimited by a state and constituted as a nation (Robins, 2006). That is how we speak of North American society, Indian society or Arab society, usually in order to refer to the structures and populations resident in a determinate and delimited physical space.

In those countries where history, economy and political power have given rise to the existence of a state with a great implantation in the society and a strong system of communications media, the tendency of the latter has been historically to reproduce an idea of the nation as a culturally homogeneous society. This has been the most habitual manner, at least in those states that have had more opportunities to be successful as such, in order to manage cultural diversity with the aim of building the political community; the management of multiculturality is a question that has accompanied the modern nation-state from its origins. That is due to the need that states have had of building a nation around themselves, that is, a political community that would share a feeling of belonging so the sate would appear as a socially legitimate power (Letamendia, 2000). To the extent that the community of culture has traditionally been one of the most important bases for collective identity, the construction of the nation thus had need of a national culture, that is, a cultural basis common to that community. In this way, anything that might represent a risk for the cultural unity of the nation was considered as a threat. This was very well expressed in the midst of the French Revolution by the Committee of Public Safety, which, in 1794, affirmed that

'Federalism and superstition speak low Breton; emigration and hatred of the Republic speak German; counter-revolution speaks Italian and fanaticism speaks Basque. Let us break these instruments of injury and error. We have a duty to our fellow-citizens, we must strengthen the Republic and ensure that the language in which the declaration of the Rights of Man is written is spoken throughout its territory.' (Barère-de-Vieuzac, 1794).

Following this declaration, the decision was taken to send teachers of the French language to all the schools of the territory where French was not the habitual language.

That is how cultural exclusion is found to be at the basis of the formation of the political community. But this exclusion, as Robins has rightly indicated, does not refer exclusively to those considered to be minorities affected by the hegemony of the state; it also directly affects those considered to be foreigners: immigrants fundamentally. Starting from this need to unify the nation culturally, and with respect to immigrants, different policies have been developed to deal with diversity. Thus we can basically speak of three models or ways of dealing with this question (Castles, 1995).In the first place, there is the model of exclusion, in which immigrants are treated as a group separated from the political community and therefore from the rights that this involves; one example of this would be the German policy with respect to immigration of Kurdish or Turkish origin. In the second place, we have the policy of assimilation, which makes an effort to integrate culturally, or acculturate, those who are different, in order to achieve the homogenization of the nation; the model here would be the French one with respect to immigrants proceeding from the former colonies. And in the third place, the pluralist model, where what is sought is to build a political community that is compatible with a certain level of cultural diversity, an example found in some of the principal Anglophone countries. This latter model is the one that least affects the nation as a cultural unit, although it is necessary to point out that even in its main variant, multiculturalism, a minimum common denominator has been considered indispensable for the existence of the political community itself, with this denominator normally being the language; this would be the case in Quebec, for example (Kymlicka, 2001).

While, as we have noted, since the creation of modern states the school has been one of the big paths of cultural unification, the mass media have been the greatest instrument in that undertaking. Starting from the printed press of the eighteenth and nineteenth centuries, with its importance in the formation of national public spheres, up to the audiovisual media like the radio, cinema and television, which broadened those public spheres and constructed cultural spaces, the media have without doubt been the greatest element of cohesion of national societies, in so far as they are privileged agents of civil society (Castells, 2009b).Things being that way, we must now ask ourselves about the manner in which the delocalization of communication, that '*no sense of place*' of which Meyrowitz speaks, might be affecting the construction of cultural or political communities, formerly more closely linked to the territory.

2. From cultural imperialism to globalization, via cultural exception

Concern about the unifying pressure of the media and efforts to adopt measures in this field to defend communities excluded in the formation of nations is an old phenomenon in many communities of this type. The attempts by national minorities to provide themselves with mass media of their own, or in their language, are a good example in this respect. Nonetheless, this concern took on a new dimension in the 1970s, with the debate on the New World Information and Communication Order (NWICO). Thus, in an atmosphere enriched by the processes of decolonization in Africa and Asia and the national liberation movements in numerous regions of the world, it became patently necessary to confront in a different way what was by then a tangible fact, that is: the spread at a world scale of cultural models and communication agents that, proceeding from the richer countries - and especially the United States - were increasingly penetrating the rest of the societies. This penetration prevented the less wealthy (developing or underdeveloped, according to the terminology of the time) countries from attending to their own cultural and communicative needs, by which means they became dependent countries in these fields (MacBride, 1985). Similarly, cultural homogenization was perceived as a growing threat for the great majority of the peoples and cultures of the world.

The concept that would best describe that state of affairs was to be, in the 1970s, that of cultural imperialism:

'*The concept of cultural imperialism today best describes the sum of the processes by which a society is brought into the modern world system and how its dominating stratum is attracted, pressured, forced, and sometimes bribed into shaping social institutions to correspond to, or even promote, the values and structures of the dominating centre of the system. The public media are the foremost example of operating enterprises that are used in the penetrative process. For penetration on a significant scale the media themselves must be captured by the dominating/penetrating power. This occurs largely through the commercialization of broadcasting*' (Schiller, 1976, p. 10).

This penetration of the communicative and cultural models proceeding from a few countries was increasingly perceived as a threat not only in the less wealthy societies, but also in those that had, apparently, enjoyed a good status as a nation and had even been protagonists of cultural homogenization towards their interior. This fact is clearly observable in the negotiations that, almost a decade after the debate on the NWICO, gave rise in 1995 to the World Trade Organization, one of the international agents that has most contributed to globalization. Thus, in a context in which the state, as a major player in the cultural field, had already lost much of its effective power facing the private cultural industry, the former demanded for themselves the right to 'cultural exception': that is, the right to exclude cultural and communicative products from the free flow of goods at the planetary level. This right was, in 2005, to be ratified by the United Nations Educational, Scientific and Cultural Organization (UNESCO, 2005), and was to be claimed by states that feared that the liberalization of the communication and cultural market would end up by weakening their project of cultural unification around the nation.

However, this more or less orderly debate about the pre-eminence of the media and cultural industries of a few countries over other communities, whether these were national minorities (the debate on peripheral nationalism), developing countries (debate on the NWICO) or non-Anglophone rich countries (cultural exception), was deeply transformed with the advance of globalization. Not in vain, John Tomlinson points out, is imperialism followed by globalization. And one of the characteristics of the latter, in relation to communication, culture and the nation-state, is precisely that far from being a more or less orderly process, where a few powers impose their cultural models on the rest, it is a much more complex process in which even the formerly dominant powers find themselves affected. To the point, Tomlinson indicates, that '*the effects of globalization are to weaken the cultural coherence of all individual nation-states, including the economically powerful ones - the "imperialist powers" of a previous era*' (Tomlinson, 1991, p. 175).

Nowadays there is abundant data in support of Tomlinson's analysis. If the French revolutionaries of the late eighteenth century considered the existence of regions of the state where French barely had any presence to be an obstacle to national unity, how should one today evaluate the fact that the number of people in the United States who use a language other than English in their homes rose from 11% in 1980 to 20% in 2007 (USA Census, 2010)? Or that the tendency amongst the immigrants of this country to maintain their domestic language is growing (Siegel, Martin, & Bruno, 2000)? Similar figures for Europe are not available, but partial works on the presence of languages of the immigration in the metropolis of the old continent (Baker & Eversley, 2000) or on the level of family transmission of these languages (Extra & Yagmur, 2004) suggest similar conclusions. We do have data available for Australia, where the 2006 census showed that 22% of the population spoke languages other than English at home, against 17% in 1991.

In addition, reactions to the changes taking place as a result of globalization in countries that appeared to have achieved a certain level of stability as national communities appear to indicate that globalization is indeed affecting their cultural coherence. The creation in France of a Ministry of National Identity and Immigration; the fact that a growing number of countries of the European Union, 23 over 27, require that immigrants should know the official language to obtain rights such as residence, family regrouping or nationality[1]; or the debate over whether some cultural groups really can form part of the national community (Sartori, 2000), are all elements that seem to confirm the same idea.

3. Television and transnational communication spaces

The coming of globalization as a set of disordered and undirected processes does not in any way mean the disappearance of the previous stages, at least with respect to the cultural predominance of certain hegemonic agents. Thus, we can observe that barely half a dozen companies possess the greater part of the communications market at the world level. These companies are besides concentrated in a few countries, such as the USA (Time-Warner, Disney, Viacom and News Corporation), Japan (Sony) and Germany (Bertelsmann) (Thussu, 2006, p. 99).

Nonetheless, at the same time as we can observe that domination, which confirms many of the concerns that had been expounded from the approach of cultural imperialism, other tendencies are also tangible that, as Tomlinson said, show the disordered character of globalization. Television is a good example of the coexistence of the cultural power of certain big actors at both the planetary level and the local level with other new agents. With their presence, these new agents are undermining the near exclusiveness with which the former had been acting in their national territories until very recently, and by which means they had imposed their cultural models and created their own public spheres. To put this graphically and in figures, we can say that at the same time as over one thousand television broadcasts are directed, via satellite and in English, from the Anglophone countries (fundamentally the USA) towards areas of the planet where that language is not official, a similar number of broadcasts is directed towards the USA in languages other than English

[1] Sources: Extramiana (Extramiana 2008) and our own account.

(Amezaga, 2007). Economic potential is the driving force in both cases, in the former that of the big television companies seeking to widen their markets in different areas of the globe, and in the latter that of immigrants who have acceded to the standard of living of the receiver country.

Turning our attention towards the latter case, we must consider the economic importance of immigrants in rich countries as one of the principal underlying factors in the development of satellite television in the world. In this respect, John Sinclair speaks of geolinguistic regions to refer to communication spaces that are dispersed in physical space but united by language, thanks to satellite television broadcasts (Sinclair, Jacka, & Cunningham, 1996). These spaces are considered in many cases as genuine niches where broadcasters who broadcast in that language beyond the frontiers of their state are seeking markets, given the significant economic potential that immigrants represent for many countries (Karim, 1998). We must bear in mind that while the number of immigrants[2] at the global level has risen from 150 to 214 million in the last decade (United Nations, 2008), the volume of remittances that they have sent to their countries of origin has grown from $132 billion to $414 billion in the same period. Besides, three quarters of this sum has been directed towards developing countries, which today represents an income three times higher than international development aid as a whole (International Organization for Migration, 2010).

This interest in attracting the remittances and investments of immigrants who have achieved a greater economic capacity in other countries, in converting them into consumers of goods and services generated in their countries of origin, or in using them as a bridgehead for expanding the economies of the latter, is joined to other interests of a geopolitical, cultural or even religious type. The result is that diasporas and immigrants have become a significant target for broadcasters, both private and public, of their countries of origin.

That is how the mass media of the diaspora are also becoming globalized. Indeed, an historical analysis would show us the importance that the media, first printed, then audiovisual, and today online, have had for diasporas, both for the relationship of their members amongst themselves, and for the relationship with the country of origin or reference. And, to the extent that the media have overcome geographical distance, the tendency seems to be towards a strengthening of the relationship with the countries of origin.

Thus, Jean Chalaby distinguishes amongst three types of media for immigrants (Chalaby, 2009). In the first place, there are the *local migrant media*, basically those created for the immigrant community. This would be the case, for example, of the numerous newspapers that circulated amongst the different immigrant groups in the USA in the nineteenth century. Nowadays, printed media of such characteristics continue to be published in many of the receiver countries. Another example of these local media would be those programs, on both radio and television, which were set up by the public powers of the receiver societies and are directed towards the immigrant population in their territory, fundamentally with the aim of integration, and that underwent a big growth until the 1980s. A second type is that of the *transnational migrant media*, made up of the radio and television broadcasts from the countries of origin towards the diasporas. This model expanded rapidly from the mid-1980s onwards, thanks to the development of satellite television. Behind these

---

[2] Following the terminology of the reports on migrations of the United Nations, we understand an immigrant here to be a person who lives in a country different from the one they were born in.

broadcasts were the interests, already referred to, of both private companies and public organizations, to maintain contact with immigrants and their descendants. Besides, the rise of these broadcasts resulted in a reconsideration of local programs, especially those directed by receiver states with the aim of integrating immigrants, and in some case even led to the abandonment of this type of program, which were at a clear disadvantage facing the competition of programs proceeding from the exterior.

Nowadays, to continue with Chalaby, we find ourselves in a new phase, which he calls the stage of the *trans-local migrant media*. The main characteristic of this phase is that the immigrants can access not only the broadcasts specifically realized for them, but also the everyday content of the media of their countries of origin. This is due both to the growth of the offer of satellite television (giving access to broadcasts originally emitted in those countries) and to the possibilities offered by Internet, thanks to which anybody can read the newspaper, listen to the radio or - increasingly - watch the television of his/her country of origin or reference. We have thus moved from transnational broadcasts to transnational audiences.

Having reached this point, we can raise the following question: how is access to the media of their places of origin or reference by the immigrant populations affecting multiculturality?

Besides dealing with this question, it will be useful to make an estimate of the real dimension of the media for immigrants and diasporas. This estimate will give us an idea of the real importance that this aspect of globalization could hold. To this end we will concentrate on satellite television, as one of the indicators of those dimensions. In 2004, I made a count of the distribution at the world level of satellite television broadcasts according to the language of those broadcasts, the area of the planet to which they were directed and their encrypted or Free To Air (FTA) character (which normally indicates a diffusion that is more centered on national markets, or more directed towards transnational audiences). In that count I found that English was clearly dominant amongst the almost 80 languages that had by then acceded to satellite television, with over 40% of the broadcasts. It was followed by Spanish with 11% (Amezaga, 2007). However, a detailed analysis of these broadcasts showed that the great majority of the broadcasts in these two languages were directed, through encrypted pay-to-view broadcasts, to national markets, fundamentally the USA. On the contrary, broadcasts in languages that have significant numbers of speakers amongst the immigrant populations around the globe, such as Chinese, Arabic or Turkish, for example, show a clear tendency to be broadcast on FTA signals; that is, to be broadcast to wider regions of the planet, since their reception is not conditioned by the existence of a national market which limits the geographical field in which that signal can be decoded - through payment systems.

Another interesting fact emerging from that count was that in the USA more than 90% of the population that speaks a language other than English in their home had access to satellite broadcasts in their language. I am obviously speaking here of the possibility of accessing signals, not their real use. This is a result of the already mentioned phenomenon of the importance of the United States television market for broadcasters seeking audiences in their language in rich countries as well. A similar count to the foregoing one, this time carried out in Australia in 2006, showed a comparable panorama.

We do not have homogeneous figures available on the number of speakers of languages of the immigration in Europe and other parts of the world. However, a more recent count shows a significant increase in the number of broadcasts directed to the groups of immigrants in the old continent. Table 1 offers the main data of that count.

Language	Encrypt	FTA	Total	Language	Encrypt	FTA	Total
English	1.474	535	2.009	Latvian	12	1	13
Arabic	164	800	964	Azerbaijan	1	11	12
German	326	275	601	Estonian	10	1	11
French	396	144	540	Macedonian	-	10	10
Italian	240	226	466	Luxemburgese	-	9	9
Turkish	195	237	432	Tamil	6	2	8
Spanish	252	131	383	Pashto	3	5	8
Romanian	255	67	322	Korean	1	5	6
Hungarian	260	12	272	Japanese	4	2	6
Polish	222	27	249	Sinhala	-	6	6
Russian	153	87	240	Bengali	2	4	6
Portuguese	136	41	177	Philippine	5	-	5
Swedish	139	6	145	Malayalam	2	3	5
Bulgarian	77	42	119	Armenian	1	4	5
Czech	100	11	111	Georgian	2	3	5
Norwegian	103	3	106	Galician	1	3	4
Dutch	77	13	90	Punjabi	3	-	3
Serbo-Croatian	69	20	89	Hebrew	3	-	3
Danish	79	1	80	Gujarati	3	-	3
Greek	50	19	69	Breton	3	-	3
Ukrainian	18	44	62	Maltese	3	-	3
Finnish	56	1	57	Thai	-	2	2
Albanian	47	8	55	Icelandic	2		2
Hindi	39	12	51	Belarusian	-	2	2
Farsi	1	44	45	Welsh	-	2	2
Slovak	33	10	43	Basque	-	2	2
Chinese	12	13	25	Kazakh	-	2	2
Kurdish	1	22	23	Vietnamese	-	1	1
Croatian	17	5	22	Uzbek	-	1	1
Urdu	14	5	19	Somali	-	1	1
Slovenian	11	7	18	Nepali	-	1	1
Lithuanian	14	1	15	Amharic	-	1	1
Catalan	7	8	15	Frisian	-	1	1
Bosnian	8	5	13	Gaelic	-	1	1

Table 1. Satellite Television Signals in the European Union (2008)[3]

[3] Source: Prepared by the author based on the data of Lyngsat (Lyngsat, 2003), Satco (Satco, 2002), King Of Sat (KingOfSat, 2008) and other minor sources. It should be pointed out that television signals were

As can be seen from the table, the presence of broadcasts in languages lacking any official recognition and that are not covered by the European Charter for Regional or Minority Languages is frankly significant. Even more significant is the tendency towards concentration in national markets of the official languages of Europe to remain steady or even increase, facing the greater openness in the diffusion of the non-official languages, those of a large part of the immigrant populations in the continent. Thus, while English once again appears as the main language of the broadcasts in total numbers, if we attend to open broadcasts (Free To Air, or FTA), Arabic is the language that appears in the first place. That is due to the combination of two overlapping factors: the fact that many of the broadcasts mainly directed towards the countries of North Africa reach a large part of Europe in non-crypted form; and the presence of numerous broadcasts that are specifically aimed beyond the northern shore of the Mediterranean.

On the other hand, if we compare these figures with those of 2004, we can highlight the fact that while the number of satellite broadcasts in official languages of Europe has grown by 33%, the number of broadcasts in non-official languages has increased by 72%, which shows the importance of this type of broadcasts in the development of this global range medium.

We do not have audience figures available for these broadcasts at the European level. The growing evolution of the offer, or the fact that in the European Union there are more than 30 million people proceeding from non-member states (Eurostat, 2010), leads us to suppose that they certainly have a considerable projection. Audience studies carried out in the USA strengthen this opinion. Thus, a recent survey amongst the Latin population of this country, showed a significant use of the media in Spanish (Nielsen, 2010). According to the same survey, amongst the population that mainly speaks Spanish in their home, this language surpassed English when it came to watching television. On the other hand, Spanish is also a habitually used language in the consumption of radio, the printed press and Internet. The fact that a third of those who speak Spanish in their homes never watch television in English is notable.

I am aware that the number of languages which have acceded to satellite television, about 80, is certainly limited in comparison with the number of languages estimated for the whole planet, between 3,500 and 7,000, depending on the source. It continues to be a small figure even if we compare it with the 389 that, according to the Ethnologue database, have more than a million speakers (Grimes, 1992). And it is highly significant that amongst those that have not yet acceded to this medium, there are 30 that have more than 10 million inhabitants, basically in Africa, although also in Asia and America. However, if we consider not only satellite television but also the presence of languages on Internet (whether in written or audiovisual formats), there is a clearly observable tendency of languages having access to this medium that, until now, had not had any mass media of their own. Given the technical difficulty of combing the net in search of languages, we do not yet have precise data on the number of languages present in the digital setting. However, a recent report of the intergovernmental agency *International Telecommunication Union* (International Telecommunication Union-ITU, 2010) estimated that there were 500 languages that, technically, can now accede to this setting thanks to the codification of their systems of writing or *scripts*. The question of the content that can be accessed in each of these languages

counted, not channels. The same channel can be broadcast on several satellites, or even in different packets of the same satellite, thus generating different signals.

is obviously a different matter (the number of languages that have entries in Wikipedia is nearly 300). On the other hand, it should be recalled that, in a world where three out of four people do not have Internet access, the presence of a language on Internet does not mean access to the net by all of its speakers. However, such access is much more habitual amongst emigrants due to both the increase in their spending power and the observed tendency of a high use of telecommunications by these populations. All of this strengthens the idea that the great majority of the over 200 million immigrants (especially those who have settled in the richer countries) can access, through satellite technology and/or the net, communication spaces that go beyond national borders. That is, in my opinion, one of the aspects of media globalization that must be analyzed, in so far as it could hold significant implications for the way of understanding societies and nations in the near future.

4. Multiculturalism, multiple identities and restructuring of the public spheres

When speaking about how this aspect of globalization, that is, the shaping of transnational communication spaces, can affect the ways of understanding and constructing national societies, it becomes necessary to distinguish amongst at least three different levels: the cultural level, the level of identity, and the level of the public sphere.

With respect to the cultural level, it can be pointed out that the societies of the age of globalization appear to be increasingly similar to each other. The great cultural and economic flows at the planetary level mean that the ways of life and cultural models proceeding from the richer countries are spreading to the rest[4]; and the fact is, as I have pointed out above, globalization does not replace the previous stage of cultural imperialism, but is added onto it. On the other hand, those societies - especially in the cities - appear increasingly diverse in their interior, due to the flows of migration and information, as I have indicated. While, as we have seen, cultural homogenization was, in the majority of the cases of strong nation-states, a condition for the creation of the political community or the nation, is it possible nowadays to construct that community on the same foundations?

At this point, the debate on multiculturalism arises as a way of organizing societies on the basis of different cultural communities. The solemn declaration by the German prime minister Angela Merkel, announcing the failure of multiculturalism in a country with an Islamic population of 4 million (The Guardian, 2010), or the revolts by the descendants (children and grandchildren) of immigrants of Maghrebi origin in France during the autumn of 2005 seem to indicate that two of the main models for the management of cultural diversity within nations (that of exclusion and that of integration) are being placed in doubt. The academic debate is also open, with works like those of G. Sartori that put into question the possibility of constructing a national community on a multicultural basis (Sartori, 2000). Thus, this author wonders whether a democratic society, based on a series of shared values (values that imply the acceptance of certain principles of equality, rights and obligations), can accept groups within it whose culture does not include those values. That, obviously, leads him to reject policies of multiculturalism that promote the reproduction of those 'other cultures' inside the receiver societies. And those 'other cultures' are, in the

[4] This tendency is not free of contradictions either. As Manuel Castells indicates, in the age of globalization there is also taking place, by way of reaction, an increase in religious fundamentalism - not only Islamic but also Christian and other types, which in its turn entails great cultural implications (Castells 2009).

present context of international tension, principally those identified with Islam. The question here resides in the fact that nowadays the reproduction of those other cultures does not depend so much on the policy developed by each state in its territory, since, as we have seen, the transnational communication spaces are realities that surpass the capacity of action of those states. It is therefore not so much a question of discussing how states should act in the face of diversity (multiculturalism or pluralism, promotion or negation), but of rethinking the nation itself on the basis of that evident reality. That is the line that authors like Kymlicka propose, in defending the possibility of certain minimum foundations on which to construct nations while maintaining cultural diversity (Kymlicka, 2001).

On the level of identity, too often consumption of the media of their countries of origin by immigrants or their descendants has been confused with identification with a national community external to the host society. Moreover, if this analysis is made from the classical perspective that national identities are by definition exclusive with respect to each other, we obtain the equation that recourse to the media of the diaspora is associated with a lack of integration in the country where one lives. Thus, Christiansen points out how the consumption of news proceeding from so-called 'countries of origin' by immigrants, or even by their descendants, appears linked, on numerous occasions, to a concern about the lack of integration of the latter in the host society. This lack of integration would, besides, be closely related to the fact that immigrants prefer to have recourse to the media of those countries rather than those of the receiver society (Christiansen, 2004, p. 187) For her part, Caglar points to the debate and controversy that, both in the public and academic spheres, is taking place around the possible negative impact that access to the mass media proceeding from Turkey might have on immigrants from that country in Germany (Caglar, 2004).

Nonetheless, we should not confuse identity with culture, nor think of identity in an exclusive way. Culture is no more than one of the foundations on which collective identity has been based historically, but nothing leads one to think that it will continue to be so in the future, or that it will not be constructed on other equally solid foundations. On the other hand, in a complex world like the one we live in, identity is becoming less structurally determined and is increasingly the product of our own decision (Melucci, 1989); and it is increasingly less exclusive and more shared (Robins, 2006). A. Askoy, in a work on young Turkish-speaking immigrants in the United Kingdom, shows how following the 9-11 attacks the dominant political scheme put their loyalty to the test, obliging them to choose between 'us' and 'them'(Aksoy, 2006). And how their answer consisted in developing a type of 'transnational sensibility', which challenges that scheme and opens up the perspective of a new way of understanding identity and loyalty towards the community in which they lived, as well as towards other communities with which family, historical, cultural, religious or linguistic relations are maintained. In this way, there is a break with the idea that identity is what leads immigrants to consume certain media: it was precisely the ambivalence of this population, with access to media in different languages and the pragmatic use made of them, which made it possible to construct that transnational sensibility and to overcome a dichotomy whose imposition was being attempted.

Finally, the level of the construction of transnational public spheres is another important aspect of media globalization. I will here make use of the concept of the public sphere as it is analyzed by J. Habermas (Habermas, 1962). Thus, the bourgeois public sphere, based at the end of the eighteenth and early nineteenth centuries on limited communication spaces such as Parisian salons or London coffee-shops, and later on the broader spaces built by the media, was the place where discussion of public affairs took place and a political subject was generated that gave rise to the modern state. In my opinion, there is no room for doubt that this public sphere, which later became a space for the construction of identities, is to be found at the base of civil society with a national foundation. Nowadays, the question resides in determining whether the globalization of the mass media is permitting the construction of new public spheres, this time going beyond the nation state.

The evidence seems to confirm this. To cite a few cases, M. Milikowski studies how access to Turkish-language media by immigrants in Europe, far from contributing to the formation of ghettos, is generating a model of de-ethnicization of Turkish culture. Indeed, the culture that accompanied the immigrants in their journey towards the host societies was transmitted in an almost static way to the new generations born in the diaspora. Access by these new generations to the Turkish commercial television channels, however, has enabled them to bring those cultural models up to date and to keep their transformation in step with transformations taking place in the country of origin, with the result that in a certain way they are being de-ethnicized (Milikowski, 2000). I found a similar process in a work on the Basque diaspora in Latin America (Amezaga, 2006). Access to satellite television by the descendants of Basques in the continent was producing what we understand as a displacement of the object and, therefore, of the subject. Displacement of the object because the Basque Country, thanks to the daily consumption of news about what was happening there, ceased to be something related to the past and became part of the present: the subject of conversation in the meeting centers of the diaspora ceased to be 'what the country was for our grandparents' to become 'what is happening now'. And displacement of the subject, because while the only role that one can have with respect to the past is that of its transmission, the subject who situates him/herself facing the present has the option of taking part in it; and in this way contributing to the future of the country of origin, as in fact many members of the diaspora try to do through different activities: as a lobby, through political participation, economic investment, the creation of networks, etc.

Another case in which the construction of transnational public spheres can be observed is provided by P. Mandaville (Mandaville, 2001). Observing the use that Islamic immigrants make of the new information technologies, he finds that these are used, amongst other purposes, for reinterpreting and updating the practice of Islam. Living in non-Islamic contexts, these immigrants find themselves needing an interpretation that enables them to combine their religious practice with the concrete conditions of the place where they live, which leads them to use IT (CD-Rom, Internet, etc.) to that end. In this way, far from traditionalist readings, new readings are made of Islamic texts and practices. This takes place, besides, in a communication space where those who live in the diaspora coincide with those who inhabit the country that exports emigrants, a space in which the former are more active in the use of the new technologies both through need and through opportunity.

Finally, mention must be made of the contribution that the new social networks based on Internet (the so-called web 2.0) are making to the construction of transnational public spheres, with consequences not only for the rich countries that receive immigrants but also for the rest. Although we are dealing recent facts that require greater analysis, the social movements talking place at the start of 2011 in North Africa suggest a great importance of these networks in some social mobilizations. The development of that dimension of the net, which is at the basis of what Castells calls 'mass self-communication' (Castells, 2009a) and is characterized by the generation of content by multiple users, does no more than multiply the effect of disorder brought by globalization.

5. Conclusions

The history of the construction of the national states has been the history of the creation and reproduction of a political community, the nation, based on a shared identity. That identity has been based on different elements, depending on the socio-historical and geographical context of each case: culture, religion, ideology, political structures, territory, etc. The mass media, like other actors such as the educational system for example, have played a leading role in the construction of that shared identity: on the one hand, as agents for the reproduction of certain elements around which this identity is structured, as is the case of language, culture, etc.; on the other, as a basis for the creation of the public sphere, the privileged place for the development of civil society, understood as the bridge mediating between political power and the individual. This public sphere is where the nation is constituted as a subject formed by people who share certain values and a will to live together in society. I thus understand the public sphere in the Habermasian sense indicated previously.

The importance of these spaces of communication in the formation of the national communities has meant that the states have historically been very jealous in their creation and maintenance. Policies have thus been developed to secure those spaces, in both the first modern nation states that emerged in Europe and America, and those created more recently; in both the most powerful and the most dependent in terms of communication. That importance can also be observed in the positions defending their own communication spaces in the case of those states that perceived their communicative and cultural sovereignty to be under threat. From state control of audiovisual media to the protectionist policies of the GATT negotiations, there are numerous examples of this jealousy.

The globalization of the media, coinciding in time with other factors, is placing those communication spaces in question. We must not lose sight of the fact that globalization is taking place in a context in which other elements are appearing, to a large extent related to the globalising processes themselves, such as: the development of new and powerful communications technologies, which are making possible a formerly unknown flow of information to any part of the planet, together with a unification of formats under digitization; the flows of population, goods and capital, which are facilitating situations of contact amongst cultures and public spheres that had been relatively isolated until now; or the loss of power of the states facing the industries in the field of communication and culture, which interferes with their possibilities for action and regulation in maintaining their national spaces. All of this is giving rise to the generation of new communication spaces, based more on telecommunications and networks than on physical proximity and adscription to a national territory.

B. Anderson said, in a formulation that has enjoyed considerable success in the sociology of identities, that nations are imagined communities; that is to say, communities in which we do not directly know the majority of the members, but we know of their existence and we identify with them (Anderson, 1983). The media are leading mediators in this identification, to the extent that it is through them that we can see that community formed of unknown people represented. That is why this author, together with many others, attributes such importance both to the access of people to literacy in vernacular languages and to what he calls printing press capitalism, as some of the determinant elements of the birth of nationalism. This importance of the media for the nation is the hypothesis underlying a large part of the research on transnationalism and globalization of the media.

Even taking into account the criticisms levelled at the excessive use of Anderson's concept of imagined communities, there should be no doubt, in my opinion, about the fact that the globalization of the media is going to affect the very concept of the nation. Especially when other factors are added to the possibility of access to transnational media spaces, such as the flow of goods and capital at the planetary level, the greater facility for direct personal relations through space (Internet, telephone), greater mobility of the population, etc. All of this obliges us to think about how our societies are going to evolve in the near future.

The separation between physical space and the transmission of information is conceivably taking us towards the placeless cultures of Meyrowitz; which would result in an increase of cultural diversity within each national society. This leads us to reflect on how we can build a political community on the basis of cultural diversity. The proposals on multiculturalism as a form of managing diversity can contribute elements to the debate. On the other hand, we should flee from the temptation of identifying the presence of diverse communication spaces with the disintegration of common loyalties and identities. In this respect significance is acquired by the fear - especially present when an attempt is made to analyse the uses of the Net by some immigrant collectives in the rich countries - that immersion in communication spaces other than the national one occasions disaffection with the host society. Instead we should think that, in a world traversed by great North-South and East-West tensions, the possibilities of access to the media of other places should be seen as a rupture of the monopoly of communication and culture, which until now had been cloistered within the national space. Seen in this light, the globalization of the media represents an advance in plurality, similar to that brought in its time by the freedom of the press - with all of its limitations, which Lenin pointed out.

That does not mean that we can consider globalization as an element that democratises the media. I have already pointed out that this phase does not annul the previous phase of big agents that are hegemonic at the world level. But the appearance of new agents with a planetary presence, and the facility with which any medium, no matter how small, is available in any corner of the globe thanks to the Net, widens the possibilities for democratic debate and for the creation of new public spheres.

This will not only affect the way in which the rich societies will have to face their processes of national construction in the future. It is also affecting the societies of origin of the emigrants, which see how the latter become, thanks to global communication, points of contact between different cultures and public spheres. Similarly, these changes must also affect the emergent states (those that have recently obtained their independence), those states that attempted to follow the model of the nineteenth century European nation-state after the processes of decolonization, and even national minorities that, when demanding their rights, saw in that model a course to be imitated in order to satisfy their desires for independence. All of them must confront the need to combine differentiated communication spaces with common political structures, at least while the latter continue to be linked to the territory. Nor should this be something unmovable, although, at present, it would appear to be difficult to articulate some type of virtual state above physical space. Indeed, if we consider, from a very long term historical perspective, the extent to which changes in the systems of communication (birth of writing, development of the printing press, implantation of the press, spread of audiovisual media and of the cultural industry in general, etc.) affected the form of constructing both the old societies and the present-day nation states, we can begin to imagine how the current changes in communication (convergence between globalization of the media and technological development, together with other factors) are going to affect our world. I myself do not hold many certainties about what the near future will be like, but I have little doubt that it will be very different from what we know.

6. Acknowledgments

I wish to thank the members of the Nor Research Group, in which I take part at the University of the Basque Country, for their help and engagement in the project we are carrying out on minority languages, media and globalization: K. Agirre, E. Arana, P. Azpillaga, M. Gonzalez-Abrisketa, eta B. Narbaiza. This paper was also made possible by the support of the Basque Government, who granted our research group for a three years period (project reference IT438-10). Likewise I would like to express my gratitude to the Centre for Cultural Policy Research, University of Glasgow, and specially its Director P. Schlesinger, for having accepted me as a Visitor Fellow during the time I was working in this paper.

7. References

Aksoy, A. (2006). Transnational Virtues and Cool Loyalties: Responses of Turkish-Speaking Migrants in London to September 11. *Journal of Ethnic & Migration Studies*, Vol. 32, No. 6, pp. 923-946.

Amezaga, J. (2007). Geolinguistic Regions and Diasporas in the Age of Satellite Television. *International Communication Gazette*, Vol. 69 No. 3, pp. 239-261.

Amezaga, J. (2006). New Uses for Old Needs in the Diaspora: Watching Basque Television in Latin America. *The Journal of International Communication*, Vol. 2 No. 12, pp. 52-69.

Anderson, B. R. O. G. (1983). *Imagined communities: reflections on the origin and spread of nationalism*. Verso, London.

Baker, P., & Eversley, J. (2000). *Multilingual capital: The languages of London's schoolchildren and their relevance to economic, social and educational policies*. Battlebridge Publications, London,

Barère-de-Vieuzac, B. (1794). *Rapport du Comité de salut public sur les idiomes*. Paris. Date of access 2010. Retrieved from http://www.tlfq.ulaval.ca/axl/francophonie/barere-rapport.htm

Caglar, A. (2004). Mediascapes, advertisement industries and cosmopolitan transformations: German Turks in Germany. *New German Critique*, No. 92, pp. 39-61.

Castells, M. (2009a). *Communication Power*. Oxford University Press, USA.

Castells, M. (2009b). *The Power of Identity: The Information Age: Economy, Society, and Culture Volume II* (2. ed.). Wiley-Blackwell, UK.

Castles, S. (1995). How nation-states respond to immigration and ethnic diversity. *Journal of Ethnic and Migration Studies*, Vol. 21 No. 3, pp. 293-308.

Chalaby, J. K. (2009). Diversity within homogeneity: Migrant television in a transnational media order. Presented at the *Migration, Languages and Television Seminar*, CCPR, Glasgow, January 2009.

Christiansen, C. (2004). News Media Consumption among Immigrants in Europe: The Relevance of Diaspora. *Ethnicities*, Vol. 4 No. 2, pp. 185-207.

Eurostat. (2010). Eurostat. Retrieved March 3, 2011, from http://epp.eurostat.ec.europa.eu/portal/page/portal/eurostat/home/

Extra, G., & Yagmur, K. (2004). *Urban Multilingualism in Europe. Immigrant minority languages at home and school.* Multilingual Matters Limited, Clevedon.

Grimes, B. (1992). *Ethnologue: Languages of the World, 12th edition.* Dallas, Texas: Summer Institute of Linguistics. Date of access 2010. Retrieved from http://www.ethnologue.com/print.asp

Habermas, J. (1962). *The Structural Transformation of the Public Sphere: An Inquiry into a Category of Bourgeois Society* (1991. ed.). The MIT Press.

International Organization for Migration, O. (2010). Executive Summary: World Migration Report 2010 - The Future of Migration: Building Capacities for Change. Date of access 2010. Retrieved from http://publications.iom.int/bookstore/index.php?main_page=product_info&cPath=37&products_id=665

International Telecommunication Union-ITU. (2010). World Telecommunication/ICT Development Report 2010: Monitoring the WSIS targets. Date of access 2010. Retrieved from http://www.itu.int/pub/D-IND-WTDR-2010/en

Karim, K. (1998). From Ethnic Media to Global Media: Transnational Communication Networks Among Diasporic Communities. Date of access 2004. Retrieved from http://www.transcomm.ox.ac.uk

KingOfSat. (2008). Anuario y Zapping Satélite Europeo. Date of access 2008. Retrieved from http://es.kingofsat.net/

Kymlicka, W. (2001). *Politics in the Vernacular: Nationalism, Multiculturalism, and Citizenship.* Oxford University Press, New York.

Letamendia, F. (2000). *Game of Mirrors: Centre-Periphery National Conflicts.* Aldershot, Ashgate.

Lyngsat. (2003). Lyngsat. Date of access 2008. Retrieved from http://www.lyngsat.com.

MacBride, S. (1985). *Many Voices, One World: Communication and Society, Today and Tomorrow* (Abridged Ed.). UNESCO, New York.

Mandaville, P. (2001). Reimagining Islam in Diaspora: The Politics of Mediated Community. *International Communication Gazette: International Journal for Communication Studies,* Vol. 63 No. 2-3, pp. 169-186.

Melucci, A. (1989). *Nomads of the present. Social movements and individual needs in contemporary society.* Hutchinson Radius, London.

Meyrowitz, J. (1985). *No sense of place. The impact of electronic media on social behavior.* Oxford University Press, New York

Milikowski, M. (2000). Exploring a model of de-Ethnicization. *European Journal of Communication,* Vol. 15 No. 4, pp. 443-468.

Nielsen. (2010). *A Snapshot of Hispanic Media Usage in the U.S.* New York: Nielsen. Date of access 2011. Retrieved from http://www.nielsen.com/us/en/insights/reports-downloads/2010/snapshot-of-hispanic-media-usage-in-us.html?status=success

Robins, K. (2006). *The Challenge of Transcultural Diversities Cultural Policy And Cultural Diversity.* Council of Europe. Strasbourg.

Sartori, G. (2000). *Pluralismo Multiculturalismo E Estranei.* Rizzoli, Milano.

Satco. (2002). SATCODX Satellite Control Center. Date of access 2008. Retrieved from http://www.satcodx.com

Schiller, H. I. (1976). *Communication and Cultural Domination.* M.E. Sharpe, New York.

Siegel, P., Martin, E., & Bruno, R. (2000). Language Use and Linguistic Isolation: Historical Data and Methodological Issues. *Presented at the FCSM Statistical Policy Seminar, Bethesda*: US Census Bureau. Date of access 2010. Retrieved from http://www.census.gov/hhes/socdemo/language/data/census/li-final.pdf

Sinclair, J., Jacka, E., & Cunningham, S. (1996). *New patterns in global television: peripheral vision*. Oxford University Press, New York.

The Guardian. (2010, October 17). Angela Merkel: German multiculturalism has 'utterly failed'. London. Date of access 2010. Retrieved from http://www.guardian.co.uk/world/2010/oct/17/angela-merkel-german-multiculturalism-failed

Thussu, D. (2006). *International Communication: Continuity and Change*. Bloomsbury USA.

Tomlinson, J. (1991). *Cultural imperialism. A critical introduction*. The Johns Hopskins University Press, Baltimore.

UNESCO. (2005). *Convention on the Protection and Promotion of the Diversity of Cultural Expressions*. Paris. Date of access 2010. Retrieved from http://portal.unesco.org/en/ev.php-URL_ID=31038&URL_DO=DO_TOPIC&URL_SECTION=201.html

United Nations. (2008). International Migrant Stock: The 2008 Revision Population Database. Date of access 2011. Retrieved from http://esa.un.org/migration/

USA Census. (2010). 2010 Census. Date of access 2011. Retrieved from http://2010.census.gov/2010census/

7

Explaining Global Media: A Discourse Approach

Ulrika Olausson
Örebro University
Sweden

1. Introduction

That communication technologies in general and the media in particular are essential ingredients in the process of globalization has long been a commonly accepted assumption in the social sciences (Thompson, 1995). The deterritorialized nature of new communication technology generated early idealistic ideas about the emergence of a "global village" (McLuhan, 1964), and in response to the rapidly increasing complexity of global communication infrastructures, theories about the rise of a "network society" (Castells, 1996) followed. Satellite technology has enabled the simultaneous distribution of news across nation-state borders, and transnational[1] media networks such as CNN have "become emblematic of a world in which place and time mean less and less" (Hjarvard, 2001: 18). Transnational news services are believed to offer new styles and formats for journalistic practices, contributing to the loosening up of national identities, and arguments about an emerging "global public sphere" have been pursued (e.g. Volkmer, 2003). Thus, the media are allegedly key elements of the compression of time and space, one of the salient features of globalization (Harvey, 1989), and are viewed as both products of and significant contributors to the fluidity of globalization (Chalaby, 2003).

However, these notions about the media's pertinent role in globalization processes have also been fiercely challenged by quite a few media scholars, who instead emphasize the continuing stability and centrality of the nation-state paradigm. National propaganda is often present in transnational media as well, not least in CNN, as are stereotypical and negative depictions of the "others" (Hafez, 2009; Thussu, 2003). Given the existence of obstacles such as language barriers and the "digital divide," which separates the "haves" from the "have nots" with regard not only to communication technology itself, but also to the skills necessary for using it, there are no real signs of a media network with the ability to constitute a global public sphere (Hafez, 2007). Severe scepticism concerning the notion of global media has also been expressed by scholars within the political economy tradition who claim that global media are in fact better described as Western or American media, and only contribute to maintaining Western dominance (e.g. Herman & McChesney, 1997). Some authors are critical of the very idea of globalization, of the way the concept has developed

[1] The term "transnational" is here used to describe events, technology, processes, connections, etc. which transcend nation-state borders but do not necessarily encompass the entire globe (Hannerz, 1996).

and been used in the social sciences (e.g. Calhoun, 2007; Sparks 2007a, 2007b). Thus, within the field of global media studies there is an ongoing conflict between the "globalists," proponents of the fluidity argument, and the "sceptics," who pursue the stability argument (Cottle 2009: 30f).

Nonetheless, these two positions - their obviously conflicting views notwithstanding - have in common one fundamental and largely taken-for-granted assumption about global media: global media are interpreted as media networks or technology whose nature is global (or at least transnational) in terms of geographic reach. I would propose, however, that having global reach is not a necessary condition of global media. From a discourse theoretical perspective, an emergent trajectory of the research field (Cottle, 2009), "global" is instead understood as a discursive feature. From this point of view it could be argued that global media cannot be reduced to transnational media networks; a global discourse might develop in any kind of media, be it local, national, or transnational, as well as in any kind of media content - local, domestic, or foreign (Berglez, 2008; Olausson, 2010). Any medium might, in fact, be labeled "global" if it provides its audiences with a global interpretative framework. Thus, *the argument put forward in this chapter is that the view on global media as transnational media networks and technology needs to be supplemented with a discourse theoretical approach, which also includes national media and takes the very knowledge production of the global into consideration.*

I will develop this position first by examining the arguments of the line of research that equates global media with transnational media networks, including its contradictory arguments about the ability of these networks to contribute to or be part of globalization processes. Following this, the discourse perspective will be introduced and exemplified with some empirical examples from a study on the emergence of a transnational (European) identity in national news reporting on global climate change (Olausson, 2010). The chapter ends with a discussion in which the discourse theoretical approach is put in relation to broader issues of cultural and political transformation, conclusions are drawn about the media's relationship to globalization processes, and suggestions are made for an integral explanation of global media.

By necessity, the two perspectives on global media are outlined here with rather broad strokes and the presentation might be somewhat lacking in detail and precision. This is the price to be paid when trying to squeeze the complexity of a research field into rather rigid "boxes." Nonetheless, this categorization will hopefully elucidate the argument that the established understanding of global media as media of transnational reach needs to be complemented with a discourse approach that also includes national media if we want to achieve an integral explanation of global media.

2. Global media as transnational media networks

Cross-border communication technologies such as the internet, mobile phones, and satellites have contributed to the deterritorialization of space over the last decades, and transnational media networks and news services such as CNN, BBC World News, FoxNews, and Al-Jazeera have entered and transformed the media landscape. In a dialectic fashion, these media are believed both to constitute and to be constituted by globalization, transforming understandings of time and space (Chalaby, 2003; Thompson, 1995). Due to their deterritorialized nature, diverse audiences, and independence of any national loyalties, arguments about their ability to loosen up distinctions between domestic and foreign have been pursued:

"The cross-border coverage of transnational television networks, their multinational audience and international production operations tear apart the relationship between place and television and challenge the traditional relationship between broadcasting and the nation-state." (Chalaby, 2003: 457)

Global broadcasting corporations not only provide people with a better understanding of global politics (Chalaby, 2003), they also offer new journalistic styles and formats able to transgress the nation-state outlook and, in a dialectic relationship with national news angles, give rise to new horizons for political identity and citizenship (Volkmer, 2003). Accordingly, transnational media have been attributed the potential to constitute a global, or at least a transnational, public sphere (Chalaby, 2003; Volkmer, 2003).

The idea that transnational media networks are able to move beyond the nation-state paradigm has, however, not escaped criticism. Hafez (2007) argues that there is not enough empirical evidence of a media system that could accurately be described as "global" in the sense of enhancing the possibilities of a global public sphere. On the contrary, the majority of empirical evidence points in the direction of reinforced stability of the nation-state paradigm. Information and news may be transnational in character, but the media in fact still are, to a considerable extent, local and national phenomena. In times of war, Western propaganda is also present in transnational media, as are polarizing perspectives of "us" and "them" and stereotypical depictions of the "other" (Hafez, 2007; Thussu, 2003):

"Today's international exchanges of images and information, it seems, are no guarantee for global intertextuality in news, for growing awareness of 'the other's' stories and perspectives, and for an increased complexity of world views in the mass media and beyond." (Hafez, 2009: 329)

Even though CNN, as the topical case in point, under regular circumstances does contribute various "global" perspectives and viewpoints, it is extremely sensitive to American patriotism and displays bias in times of military conflicts in which the US is involved, such as the 2003 Iraq war (Hafez, 2009). Not even the communication technology most associated with cross-border communication, the internet, has according to Hafez (2007) proved to fulfil this expectation. Most people use this technology locally - to communicate with people in their nearby surroundings - not to engage in cultural interaction across nation-state borders. Furthermore the necessary technological means are far from being globally diffused; "no electricity, no internet," as was pointed out by Sparks (2007b: 152). The nation-state paradigm is, according to this view, as powerful as ever before and has, in several respects, even gained in importance. Hafez (2007) illustratively labels this viewpoint in the field of global media studies "the myth of media globalization," and Sparks (2007a) dismisses the entire theoretical framework of globalization arguing that current developments are better explained as part of the continuing capitalist and imperialist expansion (cf. Nohrstedt & Ottosen, 2001).

The scepticism surrounding global media is far from new. The well-established field of international communication, based on the political economy tradition, has a long history of persistently arguing that global media are in fact best described as Western (or American) media, at most of global scope (e.g. Herman & McChesney, 1997; Schiller, 1993). The central argument of these scholars is that escalating media conglomeration has led to a notable Western (American) bias both in terms of ownership and with regard to the distribution of media products. The media achieve their global characteristics as a result of purchases made by a small number of Western-, predominantly US-based multinational media giants, who distribute their products - permeated with neoliberal values and Western lifestyles - all over the globe. Even the "glocalization" that takes place when cultural products are tailored to fit a specific local market is viewed as a commercial strategy and as such nothing more than yet another sign of cultural imperialism (Sparks, 2007b). The rise of competing non-western media networks such as Al-Jazeera notwithstanding, the westernizing tendencies of global media have not been eliminated since the power of western, and particularly US-dominated media networks such as CNN, is not only restricted to their own large-scale activities; they set the agenda also for other networks (Thussu, 2003).

Thus, claims about cultural imperialism and cultural homogenization have been made, and warnings have been issued about the democratic dangers that surface when it is no longer possible to hold media institutions accountable to political regulation at the nation-state level. The prospects for democracy do not seem any brighter if we add the argument that active citizens, due to the commercial logic of global media, over time transform into pure consumers in Western-dominated markets (e.g. Herman & Chomsky, 1988; Herman & McChesney, 1997). The consequences of the ravages of seemingly global media, it is alleged, are harmful both to indigenous cultures and to democracy. In this fashion global media counteract rather than promote a global public sphere, and contribute to the maintenance and stability of Western (US) dominance.

In this research tradition, media conglomeration, concentration, and commercialization have functioned as the analytical point of departure - restricting the interest to the shape and structure of transnational media institutions - and claims about media effects have been made without much analytical attention being paid to the actual reception and use among locally situated audiences. As a counterbalance to this macro-perspective, the research field of cultural studies has instead focused on the micro-dimension of global media (e.g. Barker, 1999; Crane 2002; Tomlinson, 1999). Instead of viewing the impacts of global media as a one-way process that completely erases local cultures, scholars within this research tradition emphasize processes of cultural "creolization" (Hannerz, 1996) or "hybridization," i.e. the creation of completely new cultural expressions in the encounter between different cultural forms:

"Most forms of culture in the world today are, to varying extents, *hybrid cultures* in which different values, beliefs and practices have become deeply entwined." (Thompson, 1995: 170, emphasis in original)

The idea of the "active audience," quite capable of negotiating and opposing media information, has been a guiding principle in cultural studies. Suggestions have even been made (though not uncontested) that the opportunities to "pick and choose" cultural forms due to the rapid development of communication technologies and the creative hybridization that follows, will most likely lead to new and improved conditions for global dialogue (Lull, 2007). Thus, cultural studies have to a considerable extent problematized the idea of the homogenizing effects of global media and questioned the cultural imperialism thesis of the international communication field.

The perspectives accounted for above are fairly well established in the research field of global media. The main arguments of international communication and of cultural studies respectively are frequently discussed in the literature (e.g. Rantanen, 2005), as are the "globalist" and the "sceptic" perspectives (e.g. Cottle, 2009). Despite their conflicting opinions when it comes to the media's relation to globalization, the "globalists" and the "sceptics" share at least one basic viewpoint on global media, namely that the proper objects of study first and foremost are those media whose global nature is defined in terms of geographic reach. The discourse perspective that will now be discussed takes a somewhat different stance towards this assumption.

3. Global media as global discourse

The discourse approach to global media proposed here does not direct specific attention to the geographic reach of the media, but focuses primarily on the very *epistemology of the global* (Berglez, 2008). As pointed out by Cottle (2009: 28) in his discussion of the principle paradigms structuring the field of global media studies, it is necessary to go beyond the paradigms of "global dominance" and "global public sphere," since these approaches to global media fail to explain how issues such as crises of different kinds are mediated and constituted in practice and how they, through their formation in the news media, achieve their "global" characteristics:

"Global crises are principally constituted *epistemologically* as 'global crises' through the news media where most of us get to know about them and where they are visualized, narrativized, publicly defended and sometimes challenged and contested." (Cottle, 2009: 165, emphasis in original)

Admittedly, local or national crises, such as 9/11, the 2010 flooding in Haiti, or the 2011 Egyptian revolution, need the connectivity that a cross-border communication infrastructure provides in order to become known, more or less simultaneously, to people around the globe. But, to achieve their global features - to become *global* crises, involving people and generating action across the world - they are entirely dependent on discursive constructions of them as such.

Extending this line of argument, when studying the production of knowledge about the global it is necessary to acknowledge national media as equally important objects of study as any media of transnational reach. As Robertson (2008) argues, the issue of media globalization is an empirical question, and the assumption of most authors that global broadcasters are, or at least should be, more inclined to produce global outlooks than national broadcasters, must be empirically demonstrated rather than axiomatically asserted. In the debate on global media, however, national media, which doubtlessly still are the media that most people turn to, are most often dismissed as not significant knowledge producers concerning the global due to their inclination to depict the world according to nation-state logic (Altmeppen, 2010; Hafez, 2007, 2009). This logic saturates much of their contents, not least in the form of what Billig (1995) terms "banal nationalism," a national mode of reporting which makes the world orbit around the nation-state, and in terms of taken-for-granted conceptions of the world as constituted by self-governing national "islands" rather than being a complex transnational network (Berglez & Olausson, 2011). In national media the domestic and foreign worlds are, by tradition, separated, and the nation-state becomes disconnected from the rest of the world (Berglez, 2007). At best, relations between the domestic and foreign are constructed through the domestication of foreign events, i.e. by the addition of a national angle to the story from "outside" in order to make it more relevant to the national audience as it is perceived (Clausen, 2004; Gurevitch et al., 1991; Riegert, 1998).

This tendency of national media to reproduce and maintain nation-state discourse and identity must of course be acknowledged. However, the national outlook should not be viewed as totally precluding other, transnational or global outlooks on the world. As suggested by Volkmer (2003), national media are to an increasing extent influenced by transnational media style and formats. Furthermore, and even more importantly, due to the globalization of risks such as climate change, and conflicts such as transnational terrorism or the Global War on Terror (as labeled by George W. Bush), national discourse is constantly (and perhaps to an increasing extent) challenged by transnational or global discourses that strive for the hegemonic position (Laclau & Mouffe, 1985). It is thus not a question of *either* national *or* global discourse but *both-and*, with national and local views functioning in interaction with transnational or global outlooks (Beck, 2006).

In a similar fashion, Hjarvard (2001) suggests that the possible emergence of a global public sphere should be viewed in terms of *both-and*; the transnational communicative space that has come into existence through the development of transnational media should be seen as a supplement to national public spheres. The globalizing tendencies of politics, economics, and culture have put the national public sphere under constant pressure, as has the increasing connectivity with other national public spheres. This will ultimately lead to what Hjarvard labels a "global reflexivity," since fewer and fewer topics can be dealt with without including information from "outside." In this way, national public spheres will gradually become deterritorialized through the "increased presence of global *connections* within the national framework" (Hjarvard 2001: 24, emphasis added). Like Hjarvard, Cottle (2009) emphasizes the media's ability to provide…

"…a transnational and global perspective on a problem that both migrates across and transcends national frames of reference or explanation, exposing international *interconnections*, contextualizing motives and exploring both the scope of the problem and its human consequences." (Cottle 2009: 100, emphasis added)

The issue of whether or not the media are capable of displaying global or transnational connections is pivotal to the discourse approach to global media suggested here. Global discourse in the news media is, as argued by Berglez (2008), characterized by the depiction of connections - including antagonistic ones - between people, processes, events, and phenomena at the local, national, transnational, and global levels. This focus on interconnections between various geopolitical scales makes the global news style quite different from the traditional foreign news style, which primarily reports from one nation to another without displaying any connections between the two (Berglez, 2008). If a global discourse is present, the most local (in terms of geography) of all media might be labeled "global" (in terms of discourse), providing a global interpretative framework by linking national and transnational identities or positioning a local event in a global context or vice versa.

Thus, the decisive criterion of global media, from a discourse theoretical perspective, is the ability to display complex and often subtle connections between various geopolitical scales. These relations do not have to be of the "objective" or realist kind to be acknowledged as building blocks of a global discourse. More precisely, a global discourse does not have to comprise "real" relations of causality, motives, and interconnections, for instance that it is the carbon dioxide emissions of the First World that is the cause of the extreme droughts in the Third World. The connections displayed in media discourse could also be of a purely constructivist nature, i.e. be the "creations" of media logic itself. The inherent characteristics of news media, such as their preference for dramatic and emotionally charged reporting (perhaps occasionally also supplemented with the journalist's deliberate intent to incite action among citizens) sometimes lead to the emergence of a global discourse that involves interconnections between people across vast distances.

A telling example of this kind of global discourse, building on pure constructivist connections, is the "globalization of emotions" (Cottle, 2009: 99) that the media have engaged in over the last decades in relation to human suffering caused by wars or natural disasters. As noted by Nohrstedt (2009, cf. Shaw, 1996), there has been an increasing tendency in the news media to display the "true face" of war, i.e. the casualties and human suffering it causes, something which could be viewed as an invitation to audiences around the world to unite in compassionate responses. In her seminal work on "the spectatorship of suffering" Chouliararki (2006: 24) discusses on the one hand how the various routines of the media, such as almost endless repetition, in all probability create distance between the audience and the distant sufferers, and on the other hand how the media are capable also of establishing an "imaginary 'we' that brings all spectators together in the act of watching." With the purpose of exploring how distant suffering is depicted in television news, and building on Boltanski's (1999) theories on the topic, she distinguishes between the following three different modes of representation, each of which invites the viewers to respond to the suffering observed on the television screen in a specific way: empathy, denunciation, and contemplation. Another example, which builds on the theories of Boltanski (1999), is Robertson's (2008) exploration of the news reporting on the 2004 Asian tsunami. In searching for a global, or cosmopolitan, outlook deriving from compassion for and empathy with the sufferers, she examines five nationally-based European broadcasters and compares them with three European channels broadcasting to global audiences. Interestingly enough, the results show that a global discourse, in terms of constructions of "togetherness," could be found on all the channels. It was far from the case that transnational broadcasters contribute more global outlooks than the national channels; in one case a transnational broadcaster even provided a less global outlook - a finding which indisputably strengthens the argument of including national media when exploring global discourse.

As Cottle (2009) points out, media research has been focused on examining how news content "positions" the audience in relation to distant suffering; there has been a lack of empirical studies that show how the "discourse of global compassion" (Höijer, 2004) in the news media actually is received and handled by the audience. Höijer (2004), however, has demonstrated that the emotionally charged portrayal of human suffering in the news tends to trigger a variety of complex responses among the audience, and her findings challenge the notion of a pronounced compassion fatigue among people in general (Moeller, 1999). Audience research has also shown that the news reporting on distant suffering has the potential to trigger transnational identification with distant sufferers, if not for more than a moment (Olausson, 2005; Olausson & Höijer, 2010). These processes of identification are characterized by the empathetic capacity for "feeling oneself in one's fellow man" (Boltanski, 1999: 92).

The global discourse built on compassion in the news media is composed - not always but in many cases - of pure constructivist connections. There are no "real" relations between the sufferers and the spectators beyond those "created" in news discourse, which highlights the constitutive role of the media in the process of globalization. Global media are not only the products of a globalized economy and technology, or the intermediaries of pre-existing events, processes, or connections already shaped by globalization, but are to a considerable extent also contributors to the expansion of transnational identifications and connections (cf. Volkmer, 2008a).

Thus, events or processes in various parts of the world, be they natural disasters, environmental hazards or wars, take global shape not only, or even primarily, in terms of worldwide impacts or as effects of the technological reach of transnational media, but also, and most essentially in this context, in terms of their formation in the news media where people, places, and objects are linked more closely together (cf. Cottle, 2009). This discursive demonstration or "creation" of transnational connections takes place not least in national media, their inclination to apply national angles and reinforce national identity notwithstanding.

When arguing in favor of the inclusion of national media in the search for a global discourse, it is necessary to address the question of "methodological nationalism," raised by Beck (2006). Not only the media but also social research has been criticized as being caught in a nation-state logic in ways that do not correspond to the globalizing trends of late-modern society. However, the determining cause of methodological nationalism is not the study of national media per se; this fallacy rather comes into existence when the analysis is conducted through a national lens, and this could be the case whether the object of study is national or transnational in character. Or, to put it differently, when examined through a "national prism" both national and transnational media might take on national features, just as both national and transnational media might assume global features when examined through a "transnational prism" (Cottle 2009: 168). Indeed, the nation-state logic still permeates national news media but with a discourse theoretical approach and the analytical application of a "transnational prism" it is possible to detect at least embryonic forms of transnational or global connections also in national media, a suggestion that will be empirically illustrated below.

3.1 The question of a European public sphere and identity

Much research on the possible emergence of a European public sphere and a European identity has been carried out over the last years. Volkmer (2008b: 231), as an example of an "optimistic" view on this, argues that advances in satellite technology have created, if not a public sphere in the traditional sense, at least "a platform for new, interesting flows of trans-European communication." However, there are also quite a few voices that are less hopeful regarding the possibility of a European public sphere. Sparks (2007a, 2007b) concludes that despite the development of supra-national political bodies such as the EU, there is as yet no sign of a corresponding media system; most media remain confined within the borders of the nation-state. This is commonly used by authors in the field as an argument against the possible development of a European public sphere: since there is no functioning European media system, the prospects of a European public sphere are rather discouraging. And, additionally, since the national realm has considerable power as *the* point of reference for the making of identity, the chances of creating a common European "us" are minute. The only viable way to enhance political interest at the EU-level among citizens and to instill a sense of European belonging is for national news media to present news about the political institutions of the EU: EU policy-making, EU-level actors, EU politics, etc. The more frequently EU topics appear in various national media, the better the breeding-ground for a sense of community and for the development of "Europeanized national public spheres," it has been argued. Accordingly, EU topics in national media have been measured quantitatively - the more the EU topics, the more the transnationalization, or Europeanization, of national news media, it has been assumed (e.g. D'Haenens, 2005; De Vreese, 2007; Koopmans & Erbe, 2004; Machill et al., 2006).

I would argue, first, that the sheer presence of EU topics in national news media does not automatically lead to the emergence of a transnational discourse. Following the argumentation above, in order for EU topics in national media to contribute transnational outlooks and not traditional "foreign" ones, they have to be, in one way or another, discursively *connected* to local and/or national conditions. These connections should not be interpreted in terms of mere domestications of EU topics (what will happen with Swedish moist snuff when the EU legislates against it?), which rather reproduce national outlooks (Sweden *and* the EU), but through the discursive *intermingling* of EU and national horizons, for instance the forging of a common European "us," as in the example presented below

(Sweden *in* the EU). Secondly, it is not only EU news in national media (whether intertwined with national horizons or not), that might contribute to a sense of EU belonging. Instead, such topics tend to impose themselves on national media from above as "Europeanization projects" (Lauristin, 2007). I would suggest that the everyday reporting of events or phenomena of transnational scope is just as relevant an object of study since such events, due to their borderless character, have the potential to trigger discursive transformation. According to Beck (2006), it is transnationalized threats and the suffering they cause that by necessity pave the way for a global outlook, since traditional dichotomies such as internal and external, national and international, and us and them lose their validity when confronted with these kinds of dangers (cf. Nohrstedt, 2010); a new cosmopolitanism becomes essential in order to survive in "world risk society" (Beck, 2009). The transnationalization of risks and crises such as climate change, terrorism, and financial crises pushes even national media - slowly and unsteadily perhaps, and most likely not at the same pace everywhere, yet nevertheless - in the direction of transnational modes of reporting. These transnational outlooks could well be in embryonic stages, not entirely explicit in nature, but instead common-sensical and "banal" in the words of Billig (1995), and deeply embedded and naturalized in the everyday language of news. This means that they are difficult to capture empirically without the aid of sensitive discourse analytical tools (Olausson, 2010; cf. Berglez & Olausson, 2011).

Some authors (e.g. Schlesinger, 2008) dismiss the entire notion of a European identity and argue that there are too many obstacles, such as the lack of a common language, history, and worldview, for such an identity to evolve. However, it is not very productive to cling to this "cultural" conception of identity, which can only lead to the discouraging conclusion that a European identity is a rather unachievable project. Instead, identity could be treated in a more modest way which does not demand cultural homogeneity; from such a perspective, identity concerns the *identification with a political "us,"* in relation to some given events, phenomena, or issues more than others (Mouffe, 1995, 2005). Thus, European identity could simply be treated as, in the words of Habermas and Derrida (2003: 293), "a feeling of common political belonging" as is illustrated by the empirical example presented next.

Elsewhere (Olausson, 2010), I have shown how the embryo of a European political identity is being forged in Swedish news reporting on climate change. In the construction of this transnational outlook, the discursive transcendence of national identity is pivotal and occurs when the national and the transnational become so closely entwined that they merge into a common "us." Admittedly, this study also confirms the common conclusion of media research that national identity holds a hegemonic position in national news media. In this case, it is constantly reproduced through, for instance, elements of national self-glorification such as "*If any country can manage this, Sweden can,*" and "*Sweden is one of the countries that have succeeded best.*" The national outlook is also nourished through domestications of the climate issue, for example when maps of Sweden recurrently fade in and out between images of flooded areas and other alleged consequences of the changing climate on the television screen.

However, it is also evident that the national mode of reporting does not entirely preclude the emergence of transnational outlooks. As a matter of fact, it seems as if national identity functions as a necessary anchoring mechanism in the construction of a common European "us" which momentarily dissolves the distinction between the national and the transnational. Sweden and the EU are on the one hand mentioned in the news reporting as two separate entities, but on the other hand they are also closely tied to each other in the sense of their all being part of the group of "climate heroes." In contrast to the "climate villain," the USA, "we," the EU, take climate change seriously and make earnest efforts to mitigate it, the message reads. The quotation from the broadsheet Dagens Nyheter "*Perhaps it is not unknown to us in Sweden and Europe that greenhouse gas emissions cause great changes in the world climate*" implies how national identity is transcended and incorporated into a European identity, how a common "us" is established.

Thus, the already established and naturalized national outlook becomes a means to introduce a transnational counterpart, which is not yet an integral part of everyday thinking and discourse. In the news program, Rapport, produced by the Swedish public service broadcaster, SVT, a sense of European community in relation to the climate issue takes shape through an intriguing blend of national and transnational identity positions. In the initial phrase of the reporter's statement a "we" that transcends the national and includes the European sphere is constructed: "*Exactly the way we do things within the EU…*" However, when the reporter continues, this European "we" becomes integrated within the national: "*…says our Swedish Minister for the Environment,*" with "our" here referring to the national community.

The purpose of these brief empirical examples of the construction of a European political identity is to demonstrate that national and transnational outlooks are not engaged in discursive struggles where the destruction of one or the other is the inevitable outcome (Laclau & Mouffe, 1985). As Sparks (2007a: 150) suggests, the local, national, and global exist alongside each other in news discourse and tensions do arise between them, but "the evidence does not support the contention that one is being undermined by the other two." I would even go so far as to claim that they in fact are highly *dependent* on each other: in order for less established transnational outlooks to become naturalized and integrated in everyday thinking and discourse, they need to become anchored within the familiar and established national horizon (Olausson & Höijer, 2010). Thus, there is reason to suppose that national and transnational discourses work interactively and that they mutually (re)construct each other (cf. Delanty, 2000; Olausson, 2007).

4. Conclusion

In this chapter, I have put forth the argument that the research field of global media needs to acknowledge not only the trans-boundary nature of media technology but to a greater extent the very knowledge production of the global that takes place not least in national media. When the given assumptions about what exactly the "global" in "global media" refers to are changed from being a matter of geographic reach to becoming a discursive feature, then it is possible to discover transnational and even global "embryos" in several as yet relatively unexplored media contexts, as has been shown (cf. Berglez, 2008).

As noted by Volkmer (2003), there is still a remarkable focus on the cultural impact of new communication technologies in the sociological debate on globalization. Cultural transformation has also been a dominating issue, not least in the disagreements between the fields of international communication and cultural studies over the cultural imperialism thesis. Hafez (2007) for his part, regards absence of cultural transformation generated by cross-border communication as a sign that a truly global media does not exist. Before there is reason to talk about global media it must be clarified "whether receiving cultures are changed by transmitting cultures in the process of cross-border communication through the Internet, satellite broadcasting, international broadcasting or through media imports and exports" (Hafez, 2007: 14). Thus, it seems that without the evidence of cultural transformation generated by cross-border communication, the notion of global media remains utopian.

It is true that the discourse perspective on global media, as proposed here, says little about cross-border communication and cultural transformation, but it does not totally exclude these aspects. In particular, this holds true if we go beyond the traditional technology platforms of the news media - newspapers, radio, and television - and widen the focus of research to include web-based forms of news reporting. The digital versions of newspapers, for instance, offer links to other websites around the world, hyperlinks which enable user interaction, etc. The digitalization of (national) news allows, to a greater extent than previous technologies, for cross-border communication and perhaps also cultural transformation (Berglez, 2011; Heinrich, 2008). But, what is deemed even more important here is *political* transformation - how the nation-state logic of political identity loosens up, is transgressed, and transforms into transnational political identities in certain contexts, as in the example above of the discursive construction of EU-identity in relation to climate change. I would argue that the discourse perspective contributes knowledge of a fundamental ingredient, both in a global public sphere and in what Berglez (forthcoming) describes as a global political culture, namely how and under what circumstances the media - national or transnational - provide their audiences with a global interpretative framework capable of including politically relevant interconnections between various geopolitical scales (cf. Volkmer, 2003).

A central aspect of this line of reasoning is the idea of late modernity being characterized by contingency in every respect, which means that everything that exists right now could take quite a different form in another situation and context (Mouffe, 1995). The contingent character of today implies that it is not reasonable to expect the media, be they national or transnational, to produce global knowledge all the time - the reporting on certain objects or phenomena, such as global risks, is probably more inclined to assume global characteristics than the reporting on local events such as a traffic accident. But it is also true that the media do not reproduce the nation-state logic throughout their reporting. And the same goes for the media audience; our national identity positions are, in all probability, activated in relation to quite a few of the events and phenomena reported in the media, but in certain cases and under certain circumstances, possibly in relation to distant suffering or global risks such as climate change, we accept global outlooks provided by the media and take on transnational identities, if not for more than a brief moment (e.g. Olausson, 2007, forthcoming). The national and global, as shown, are not mutually exclusive, but reinforce and reconstruct one another. Thus, it is rather unproductive to understand the media as contributing to *either* the stability of the nation-state *or* the fluidity of globalization, since they most likely contribute to *both* of these conditions depending on context and circumstances, and in a dialectic fashion. Stability and fluidity are two sides of the same coin.

The discourse approach to global media studies, for which I argue in the present chapter, is certainly not the perspective that provides us with the only "correct" version of reality. However, this perspective is currently somewhat obscured by the dominant view on global media as consisting of transnational media networks and technologies, and there is reason to draw attention to the discursive aspect of global media, which is something qualitatively different from technological reach. Nonetheless, I would like to bring this chapter to a close by emphasizing the fruitfulness of there being a variety of theoretical perspectives that pose different kinds of questions about global media and together enrich the research field. Considering their, in all essentials, complementary nature, the diversity of theoretical perspectives and approaches is indispensable for an integral explanation of global media.

5. References

Altmeppen, K-D. (2010). The Gradual Disappearance of Foreign News in German Television: Is there a Future for Global, International, World or Foreign News?, *Journalism Studies*, Vol.11, No.4, pp. 567–576.

Barker, C. (1999). *Television, Globalization and Cultural Identities*, Open University Press, Buckingham, United Kingdom.

Beck, U. (1992). *Risk Society: Towards a New Modernity*. Sage, London, United Kingdom.

Beck, U. (2006). *Cosmopolitan Vision*. Polity Press, Cambridge, United Kingdom.

Beck, U. (2009). *World at Risk*. Polity Press, Cambridge, United Kingdom.

Berglez, P. (2007). For a Transnational Journalistic Mode of Writing, In B. Höijer (ed.), *Ideological Horizons in the Media and among Citizens: Theoretical and Methodological Approaches*. pp. 147–161, Nordicom, Gothenburg, Sweden.

Berglez, P. (2008). What is Global Journalism? Theoretical and Empirical Conceptualisations, *Journalism Studies*, Vol.9, No.6, pp. 845–858.

Berglez, P. (2011). Global Journalism: An Emerging News Style and Outline for a Training Programme, In B. Franklin & D. Mensing (eds), *Journalism Education, Training and Employment*. pp. 143–154. Sage, London, United Kingdom.

Berglez, P. (forthcoming). *Global Journalism: Theory and Practice*, New York: Peter Lang Publishing.

Berglez, P. & Olausson, U. (2011). Intentional and Unintentional Transnationalism: Two Political Identities Repressed by National Identity in the News Media, *National Identities*, Vol.13, No.1, pp. 35–49.

Billig, M. (1995). *Banal Nationalism*, Sage, London, United Kingdom.

Boltanski, L. (1999). *Distant Suffering: Morality, Media and Politics*. Cambridge University Press, Cambridge, United Kingdom.

Boyd-Barrett, O. & Rantanen, T. (eds) (1998). *The Globalization of News*. Sage, London, United Kingdom.

Calhoun, C. (2007). *Nations Matter: Culture, History, and the Cosmopolitan Dream*, Routledge, New York, USA.

Castells, M. (1996). *The Rise of the Network Society, The Information Age: Economy, Society and Culture Vol. I*, Blackwell, Cambridge, MA; Oxford, United Kingdom.

Chalaby, J. (2003). Television for a New Global Order: Transnational Television Networks and the Formation of Global Systems. *Gazette*, Vol.65, No.6, pp. 457–472.

Chouliararki, L. (2006). *The Spectatorship of Suffering*, Sage, London, United Kingdom.

Clausen, L. (2004). Localizing the Global: "Domestication" Processes in International News Production, *Media, Culture and Society*, Vol.26, No.1, pp. 25–44.

Cottle, S. (2009). *Global Crisis Reporting: Journalism in the Global Age*, Open University Press, Maidenhead, Berkshire, United Kingdom.

Crane, D. (2002). Culture and Globalization: Theoretical Models and Emerging trends, In D. Crane, N. Kawashima & K. Kawasaki (eds), *Global Culture: Media, Arts, Policy and Globalization*, Routledge, New York, USA.

De Vreese, C. H. (2007). The EU as a Public Sphere, *Living Rev. Euro. Gov.*, Vol.2, No.3. Available at: www.livingreviews.org/lreg-2007-3.

Delanty, G. (2000). *Citizenship in a Global Age*. Open University Press, Buckingham, United Kingdom.

D'Haenens, L. (2005). Euro-vision: The Portrayal of Europe in the Quality Press. *Gazette*, Vol.67, No.5, pp. 419–440.

Gurevitch, M., Levy, M. & Roeh, I. (1991). The Global Newsroom: Convergences and Diversities in the Globalisation of News, In P. Dahlgren & C. Sparks (eds), *Communication and Citizenship: Journalism and the Public Sphere in the New Media Age,* pp. 195–216, Routledge, London, United Kingdom.

Habermas J. & Derrida J. (2003). February 15, or what Binds Europeans Together: A Plea for a Common Foreign Policy, Beginning in the Core of Europe. *Constellations,* Vol.10, No.3, pp. 291–297.

Hafez, K. (2007). *The Myth of Media Globalization.* Polity Press, Cambridge, United Kingdom.

Hafez, K. (2009). Let's Improve "Global Journalism"! *Journalism,* Vol.10, No.3, pp. 329–331.

Hannerz, U. (1996). *Transnational Connections: Culture, People, Places,* Routledge, London, United Kingdom.

Harvey, D. (1989). *The Condition of Postmodernity,* Basil Blackwell, Oxford, United Kingdom.

Heinrich, A. (2008). Network Journalism: Moving Towards a Global Journalism Culture. Paper presented at the RIPE conference, Mainz, October 9–11.

Herman, E. & Chomsky, N. (1988). *Manufactoring Consent,* Pantheon Books, New York, USA.

Herman, E. & McChesney, R. (1997). *The Global Media: The New Missionaries of Corporate Capitalism,* Cassell, London, United Kingdom.

Hjarvard, S. (2001). News Media and the Globalization of the Public Sphere, In S. Hjarvard (ed.), *News in a Globalized Society,* pp. 17–39, Nordicom, Gothenburg, Sweden.

Höijer, B. (2004). The Discourse of Global Compassion: The Audience and Media Reporting on Human Suffering, *Media, Culture & Society,* Vol.26, No.4, pp. 513–531.

Koopmans, R. & Erbe, J. (2004). Towards a European Public Sphere? Vertical and Horizontal Dimensions of Europeanized Political Communication, *Innovation,* Vol.17, No.2, pp. 98–118.

Laclau, E. & Mouffe, C. (1985). *Hegemony and Socialist Strategy: Towards a Radical Democratic Politics.* Verso, London, United Kingdom.

Lauristin, M. (2007). The European Public Sphere and the Social Imaginary of the "New Europe", *European Journal of Communication,* Vol.22, No.4, pp. 397–412.

Lull, J. (2007). *Culture-On-Demand: Communication in a Crisis World,* Blackwell Publishing Ltd., London, United Kingdom.

Machill, M., Beiler, M., & Fisher, C. (2006). Europe-topics in Europe's Media: The Debate about the European Public Sphere: A meta analysis of Media Content Analyses, *European Journal of Communication,* Vol.21, No.1, pp. 57–88.

McLuhan, M. (1964). *Understanding Media: The Extensions of Man,* McGraw Hill, New York, USA.

Moeller, S. D. (1999). *Compassion Fatigue. How the Media Sell Disease, Famine, War and Death.* Routledge, London, United Kingdom.

Morley, D. (2000). *Home Territories: Media, Mobility and Identity.* Routledge, London, United Kingdom.

Mouffe, C. (1995). Democratic Politics and the Question of Identity, In J. Rajchman (ed.), *The Identity in Question,* pp. 33–46,Routledge, New York, USA.

Mouffe, C. (2005). *On the Political.* Routledge, New York, USA.

Nohrstedt, S. A. (2009). New War Journalism: Trends and Challenges. *Nordicom Review,* Vol.30, No.1, pp. 35–112.

Nohrstedt, S. A. (ed.) (2010). *Communicating Risks: Towards the Threat Society?* Nordicom, Gothenburg, Sweden.

Nohrstedt, S. A. (2001). Summary and Conclusion. Globalization and the Gulf Conflict 1990–2000: Challenges for War Journalism in the New World Order, In S. A. Nohrstedt &

R. Ottosen (eds), *Journalism and the New World Order: Gulf War, National News Discourses and Globalization.* Nordicom, Gothenburg, Sweden.

Olausson, U. (2005). *Medborgarskap och globalisering: Den diskursiva konstruktionen av politisk identitet* (Citizenship and Globalization: The Discursive Construction of Political Identity), Dissertation, Örebro Studies in Media and Communication 3, Örebro, Sweden.

Olausson, U. (2007). The Ideoogical Horizons of Citizenship: National Media as Discursive Bridge, In B. Höijer (ed.), *Ideological Horizons in Media and Citizen Discourses: Theoretical and Methodological Approaches.* pp. 51-72, Nordicom, Gothenburg, Sweden.

Olausson, U. (2010). Towards a European Identity? The News Media and the Case of Climate Change. *European Journal of Communication,* Vol.25, No.2, pp. 138–152.

Olausson, U. (forthcoming). "We're the Ones to Blame": Citizens' Representations of Climate Change and the Role of the Media.

Olausson, U. & Höijer, B. (2010). The Role of the Media in the Transformation of Citizens' Social Representations of Suffering, In M. Chaib, B. Danermark & S. Selander (eds), *Education, Professionalization and Social Representations: On the Transformation of Social Knowledge,* pp. 200–217, Routledge, London, United Kingdom.

Rantanen, T. (2005). *The Media and Globalization,* Sage, London, United Kingdom.

Riegert, K. (1998). *"Nationalising" Foreign Conflict,* University of Stockholm, Stockholm, Sweden.

Robertson, A. (2008). Cosmopolitanization and Real Time Tragedy: Television News Coverage of the Asian Tsunami. *New Global Studies,* Vol.2, No.2, Article 3.

Schiller, H. I. (1993). Transnational Media: Creating Consumers Worldwide, *International Affairs,* Vol.47, No.1.

Schlesinger, P. (2008). The Babel of Europe?: An Essay on Networks and Communicative Spaces, In A. F. Mathew (ed.), *Some Essays on Post-Modernism, Globalization & The Media.* pp. 13–34, MICA, Ahmedabad, India.

Shaw, M. (1996). *Civil Society and Media in Global Crises: Representing Distant Violence,* Pinter, London, United Kingdom.

Sparks, C. (2007a). *Globalization, Development and the Mass Media,* Sage, London, United Kingdom.

Sparks, C. (2007b). What's Wrong with Globalization? *Global Media and Communication,* Vol.3, No.2, pp. 133–155.

Thompson, J. B. (1995). *The Media and Modernity,* Polity Press, Cambridge, United Kingdom.

Thussu, D. K. (2000). *International Communication: Continuity and Change,* Arnold, London, United Kingdom.

Thussu, D. K. (2003). Live TV and Bloodless Deaths: War, Infotainment and 24/7 News, In D. K. Thussu and D. Freedman (eds), *War and the Media: Reporting Conflict 24/7,* Sage, London, United Kingdom.

Tomlinson, J. (1999). *Globalization and Culture,* Polity Press, Cambridge, United Kingdom.

Volkmer, I. (2003). The Global Network Society and the Global Public Sphere. *Development,* Vol.46, No.1, pp. 9–16.

Volkmer, I. (2008a). Conflict-related Media Events and Cultures of Proximity. *Media, War & Conflict,* Vol.1, No.1, pp. 90–98.

Volkmer, I. (2008b). Satellite Cultures in Europe: Between National Spheres and a Globalized Space. *Global Media and Communication,* Vol.4, No.3, pp. 231–244.

8

Cultural Globalization and Transnational Flows of Things American

Mel van Elteren
Tilburg University
The Netherlands

1. Introduction

It has been argued that there is an emerging "global culture," which is heavily American in origin, structures, and contents. While it is certainly not the only player in the global cultural arena, America's transnationalizing culture is expected to remain the most dominant one in the foreseeable future (Berger, 2002: 2-3). This chapter takes a fresh look at today's cultural globalization and explores the various interconnections and underlying dynamics, focusing more particularly on its American and Americanized components. Needless to say, the emerging global culture actually consists of a plurality of global cultures. In various cultural domains globalizing tendencies occur, which neither all run parallel nor all show the same tempo; there have been lively debates on the cultures of globalization in the plural. Nevertheless, for the sake of convenience the single term "global culture" will be used here too; it refers first of all to the prevailing forms that originate as yet mostly from the West, although we do find reverse cultural flows from the East as well.

Classifying countries into different subsections of the globe is a tricky and inexact business, since there is a high level of interpenetration and cultural exchange between countries as this chapter will illustrate too. One should be wary of Western centrism or a more specific Euro- or America-centrism, as manifested in forms of Orientalism especially (which have their Eastern counterparts of Occidentalism). The terms "West" and "East" are used only as a rough indication and should certainly not be reified. What is meant by the two terms changes both in historical time and geographical space; there are many mixed forms, and behind each of both labels all kinds of subdivisions are hidden.[1]

[1] The same holds true for the distinction between "North" and "South," although it has become the primary one to approach global inequality today (Nederveen Pieterse, 2004: 107-119). It might be interesting to look more specifically at transnational cultural flows along these lines. The use of the terms "First," "Second" and "Third World" has become problematic, especially after the demise of communism in Eastern Europe and the former Soviet Union. The terms "developed" or "advanced" societies versus "less developed" or "developing societies" have drawbacks too, because of increased differentiation between the rich and poor countries -- and differing degrees of industrialization and capitalist globalization between countries -- of Asia, Africa, Latin America, and the Middle East (Cohen & Kennedy, 2000: 10; Sklair, 2002: 13). One must also be cognizant that "Asia" is a geo-historical construct rooted in a Euro-centric view of the world, and each country in Asia is different in terms of its relationship with Europe and the U.S. (and other parts of the West). Furthermore, many Asian countries have a continuing legacy of cultural and intellectual connections with former colonizers such as Great

2. The dialectical interplays of globalization

More generally, leading cultural theorists on globalization emphasize "deterritorialization" as one of the major driving forces in the modern world (Appadurai, 1996). It is not a new process, of course; local cultures have long been influenced - and even shaped - by outside forces, and, historically, have become detached from their local anchorings under capitalism. The current phase of globalization differs from the past because of the dramatically increased transnational movement of material foods, images, and people, which leads to new mixtures of culture or hybridization. Transnational capitalism's division of labor and free trade produce multivariegated fusions, blurred borders, cultural "homelessness" as well as cosmopolitanism. Its worldwide infrastructure of airports, malls, computer terminals, chain restaurants, and other "nonplaces" erase distinct space and history, whereas its basic means of communication, the Internet, is even more radically deterritorialized (Tomlinson, 1999: 108-120). Cultural goods with indefinite origins abound; what appears to be traditional, on closer inspection is invented, and what seems to be homogeneous, is hybrid. "American" and various other "nationally" made products often entail design and engineering ideas, parts, and labor from many nations, which makes it hard to specify a country of origin.

The major dynamics involved in cultural globalization can be summarized in terms of the following dualities and related dialectical interplays:

- *Universalization versus particularization*. Whereas globalization universalizes certain aspects of modern social life (e.g., the nation-state, production and management processes, consumer trends etc.), it simultaneously encourages particularization by relativizing both "locale" and "place" so that endeavors to articulate uniqueness or difference are stimulated.
- *Homogenization versus differentiation*. Globalization tends to bring about a certain sameness to the surface appearance and institutions of modern social life across the globe. On the other hand, it also entails the incorporation and re-articulation of the global in relation to local circumstances.
- *Integration versus fragmentation*. Whereas globalization leads to new forms of global, regional and transnational communities or organizations that unite people across geographic boundaries, it also divides and fragments communities, both within and across nation-state boundaries. For example, ethnic and racial divisions are more articulated as the "others" become more proximate.
- *Centralization versus decentralization*. Globalization facilitates an increasing concentration of power, knowledge, information, capital etc. (embodied by various transnational political organizations and corporations), but it also generates a powerful decentralizing dynamic as local entities, communities and groups attempt to obtain more power over the forces that influence their situation and further development.
- *Juxtaposition versus syncretization*. Globalization brings about the coexistence of different cultures, ways of life, and social practices. This reinforces boundaries and articulates sociocultural differences and prejudices, but simultaneously creates shared cultural identities and social spaces, in which an intermingling of ideas, knowledge, values, lifestyles and so on takes place (McGrew, 1992: 42-43).

Britain, France, and the Netherlands, while they are inevitably influenced by the presence of the United States in this entire region as a superpower particularly since World War II (Notoji, 2002: 105).

One overarching feature needs to be highlighted here: The emerging global culture brings along transnationally shared discourses encompassing sets of common structures and categories that organize differences. This means that the various cultures of the world are becoming different in uniform ways, which amounts to the emergence of "structures of common difference" (Wilk, 1995). This term refers to a new global hegemony, that is a hegemony of structure, not of content. The new global cultural system promotes difference, but selects the dimensions of difference, thereby celebrating particular kinds of diversity, while submerging, deflating or suppressing others.

In order to get a good intellectual grip on cultural globalization we need to broaden our perspective. The key to understanding today's globalization as a whole is to conceptualize it as a product of particularly the third technological revolution and the global restructuring of modern capitalism in which economic, technological, political, and cultural features are intertwined. This means that we should avoid both technological and economic determinism and all other one-sided perspectives on globalization in favor of a view that sees globalization as a highly complex, contradictory, and thus ambiguous set of institutions and social relations, as well as one involving flows of goods, services, ideas, technologies, practices, cultural forms and people. As Douglas Kellner puts it, "The transmutations of technology and capital work together to create a new globalized and interconnected world. A technological revolution involving the creation of a computerized network of communication, transportation, and exchange is the presupposition of a globalized economy, along with the extension of a world capitalist market system that is absorbing ever more areas of the world and spheres of production, exchange, and consumption into its orbit" (Kellner, 2002: 287).

The dynamics of globalization are very unevenly distributed around the globe, between regions and between different strata of the population within regions. A significant factor is the unequal geographic power distribution of globalization. How individuals experience and respond to the forces of globalization is, to a great extent, a consequence of their economic, social, and geographic positions in the world. Globalization is predicated on a complex interconnection between capitalism and democracy and "haves" and "have-nots" that involves both positive and negative features and both empowers and disempowers individuals and groups, undermining and yet at the same time creating potential for new democratic projects of all kind. Globalization imposed from above can be contested and reconfigured from below (Steger, 2002: 145-147). This is not to suggest that one form is per definition "bad" and the other "good" from a social-emancipatory vantage point. Global forces from above may very well advance democratization and the spread of human rights in various areas of the world, while globalization from below may promote special interests or reactionary goals (for example, in the case of transnational right-wing movements, extreme fundamentalist-religious groups or terrorist networks).

Thus, globalization exists of fundamental transformations in the world economy, politics, and culture, which entail contradictions and ambiguities, that is, both progressive and emancipatory features *and* oppressive and negative attributes. Such internal conflicts and tensions are more generally characteristic of modernity, which can be framed in two separate discourses, one of liberation and another of "disciplinization." Each discourse emphasizes only one side of the double-edged sword of modernity, that is, its fundamental internal tension between an emphasis on human autonomy and the restrictive controls inherent in the institutional realization of modern life (Wagner, 1994: 40-41). Contrary to modernization theorists of the 1950s and 1960s who tended to attach merely positive values of progress to such processes, classical theorists of modernity recognized that the modern world was ambiguous in its capacity to deliver human happiness and fulfillment. Modernity, in particular the scientific rationality and the liberal-democratic political projects associated with the Enlightenment, delivered emancipation from many forms of domination. But modernity also entailed costs, new forms of cultural pathology that classical theorists have tried to capture through concepts like "alienation" (Marx), "anomie" (Durkheim), the "iron encasement" of instrumental reason (Weber). Each of these views recognized that one form of domination had been replaced by another – they differed in their precise analysis of the source of this domination (Tomlinson, 1991: 142-144).

To the extent that this heritage of classical sociology acknowledges the discontents at the core of modernity (as well as its historical changes) it still has its merits as a living tradition for analyses of modern life today (Turner, 1999). But in trying to develop a more up-to-date approach, we must account for the existence of multiple modernities, that is, a number of different sites and forms of modernity, including those outside the West (Featherstone et al., 1995). Western patterns of modernity are not the only "genuine" modernities, even though they have historical precedence and continue to be a major reference point for the others (Eisenstadt, 2000: 2-3). Processes of modernity may be globally alike to the extent that they all entail the demolishing of the old order to make room for the new. But the values, norms, and cultural forms and practices that result from these processes, the way in which they are interpreted, and even the driving forces behind them, may differ from one cultural context to the other (Therborn, 1995).

3. Reconfiguration of the state and capitalist globalization

In his book *Culture in the Age of Three Worlds* (2004) the historian Michael Denning sees the fall of the Berlin Wall in November 1989 as the symbolic moment when the current era of globalization can be said properly to begin, with the "corporate states" of the Cold War being superseded by the "beginnings of a transnational cross-fertilization" as peoples, capital and commodities began to flow more freely across frontiers. Denning stipulates that area studies (such as American Studies) in the traditional sense fitted well with the period between 1945 and 1989 when the world was conventionally divided into discrete, partitioned spaces: the capitalist First World, the communist Second World, and the decolonizing Third World. But as an intellectual enterprise, area studies made much less sense after interventions of the International Monetary Fund and the flourishing of "postnational" economies had destabilized government forms on both sides of the political spectrum, thereby undermining the legitimacy of national authorities and forcing their territorial autonomy to be repositioned within a global system (Denning, 2004: 24, 9, 2-4, 46). Thus Denning, a protagonist of a transnationalized American Studies, seems to have joined the chorus of "hyperglobalist" thinkers of globalization, who contend that transnational capitalism, international governance, and hybrid global culture have effectively put a halt to the modern nation-state.

This position is open to question, however. The increasing importance of transnational corporations and other non-state actors and agencies notwithstanding, many states have survived intact and a number of new ones have been founded. The available evidence points to the sustained importance of the nation-state as a political and economic entity, and this certainly holds true for the United States. On balance, nation-states are not withering, but rather undergoing a transformation in their structures and processes, which implies the modification of their institutional forms and their policies by transnational forces (Cohen &

Kennedy, 2000: 89-93). These changes are a pre-condition for further globalization *and* a consequence of it. But this reconfiguration is to some extent a question of deliberate choice. The rapid expansion of global economic activity since the 1980s is first of all a result of political decisions made by governments to lift the international restrictions on capital as part of a more general adoption of neoliberal policies. Once these decisions were implemented, the technology came into its own, and accelerated the speed of communication and calculations that helped bring the movement of money to an extraordinary level. The implication is that nation and territory do still make a difference - even in a globalized context. These conventional political units remain as yet important, operating either in the form of modern nation-states or "global cities" where global processes carried by corporate complexes and supporting specialized services (financing, accounting, information processing etc.) actually take place. The latter strategic places are embedded in national territories and therefore stay, at least partly, within the judicial orbit of various state-centered regulatory systems.

In the ongoing process of capitalist transnationalization, corporate geography has been reconfigured into a new system of worldwide time-space connections, but they are neither hardly decentered nor fully integrated, retaining a hierarchical structure and uneven distribution. Like other business organizations, transnational corporations (TNCs) are certainly not "placeless" or "derritorialized entities." The reason is that hypermobility of capital and time-space compression of corporate globalization need to be actively produced and this requires vast concentrations of material and not so mobile facilities and infrastructures. Most TNCs still have their headquarters in the richest developed countries, that usually provide the best overall socioeconomic, political, and legal bases for their operations, and where their owners and managers reside.

Yet, the growing importance of electronic space in the global economy, and the accompanying "virtualization" of economic activities do raise questions of control in the global economy that not only go beyond the state but also beyond current notions of non-state-centered systems of coordination. Private digital networks bring along forms of power that differ from the more widely distributed power associated with public digital networks. Major examples are wholesale financial markets, corporate intra-nets, and corporate networks bringing together borrowers and lenders in a private domain rather than the public domain of stock markets. The vastly expanded global capital market that emerged in the 1980s has the structural power and organizational connections with national economies to make its requirements felt in national economic policymaking. In providing some of the norms for national economic policymaking the operational logic of the capital market exerts an influence that goes far beyond the financial sector. However, the supranational electronic market space, which partly operates outside any government's exclusive jurisdiction, is only one of the spaces for finance. There is also the embeddedness of global finance in the environments of actual financial centers, places where national laws continue to be operative, although these often entail greatly modified laws (Sassen, 2006: 336-338, 382).

4. Disseminators of globalizing American culture

For a good understanding of globalizing American culture outside its country of origin it is necessary to examine the local appropriations in relation to the projections of American powers (hard and soft; military, economic, political, social and cultural) in the international arena. This entails a *theoretical* middle ground between the cultural transmission model, which if taken to its extreme amounts to a crude version of "cultural imperialism," and the assimilationist view, which can exaggerate the capacity of local recipients to creatively appropriate things American (Kuisel, 2000: 209). Yet it does not imply that the actual process of globalizing American culture is necessarily always located in a neat middle position between American projections of power and domestication of "traveling American culture" by locals across the world responding to its various manifestations. In other cases this process may tilt towards being "imperial" or the very opposite, complete incorporation into the local culture.

While popular culture, mass media, and cultural industries have high visibility and receive much attention in this context, significant components of America's global reach that concern economic policies and international politics and security are underexposed or ignored. The latter are, to a degree, "cultural" too, but less overtly so, and not as visible in everyday life (Nederveen Pieterse, 2004: 80-81). Important American cultural influences are implicated in U.S.-style capitalist globalization and the corporate cultures, business, management and labor practices associated with it, along with economic, cultural and political development policies for developing countries, as well as academic and professional cultures and so forth. It must also be recognized that intercultural influence does not by definition run parallel with international political and economical relationships. A local society may demonstrate complex hybridizations in its indigenous production and reproduction of culture vis-à-vis a globalizing world, while as a nation it becomes voluntarily or involuntarily more implicated in U.S. projections of economic, military, social and political power (Bell & Bell, 1993: 199).

For the time being, the United States maintains a strong position in many of the domains that matter most in the current era of globalization. Examples include the standards and rules governing the Internet and other international communication networks; securities law and practice; and international legal, accounting, and management practices. Much of the information revolution originated in the United States and a large part of the content of global information networks is manufactured there, giving globalization a U.S. face (Nye, 2002: 79, 81). Various technologies and technological devices that propel current globalization have been largely invented and originally popularized in the United States. Eminent examples are: Automated Teller Machines (ATMs); the newly structured money market and financialization of capitalism taken to a new extreme; "flexible manufacturing" and "just-in-time" production; franchising and McDonaldization; airfreight and containerized freight along with the use of bar codes, the Global Positioning System (GPs) and advanced logistics; computing and the associated search habits and preferences fostered by prevailing software (Marling, 2006: 144-193). These technologies entail important *cultural structures* that both enable and constrain people's everyday behaviors around the world and are all involved in enhanced time-space compression.

An influential religious movement that carries cultural globalizing from the West is evangelical Protestantism, particularly in its Pentecostal version. In the past fifty years or so U.S. "new-style," fundamentalist Protestantism (as distinct from "old-style," separatist fundamentalism) has made major inroads in large areas of East and Southeast Asia, in the Pacific islands, in sub-Saharan Africa, and most dramatically in Latin America. In many of these places new fundamentalist Protestant ministries from the United States - mostly neo-Pentecostalist and evangelist strains - have been holding crusades in which they disseminated their versions of the Gospel. They often combined these with a belief system such as "prosperity theology" that is very much in tune with U.S.-style capitalist culture, and the emerging global culture of consumption and consumer gratification. This "business" of exporting the American gospel of success, wealth and prosperity has significantly expanded since the early 1980s when Christian fundamentalism became a more dynamic social and political movement in America. It has turned into one of the most significant cultural influences from the United States (Brouwer et al., 1996; Corten & Marshall-Fratani, 2001).

The American face of much of today's globalization is partly a result of the prevailing world orientation among American globalizers. By the turn of the new millennium, a major study among senior managers and chief executives of U.S.-based transnational firms and nongovernmental organizations, all global leaders in their respective fields, revealed strong American ethnocentrism. These leaders proved to share a "market idiom" that equates neoliberal deregulation with "human progress and enlightenment" and resistance to the process as thick-skinned irrationality. The executives claimed to be totally objective and neutral about their views on globalization, and seemed oblivious to the fact that their American background might limit their vision. The attitudes of these "parochial cosmopolitans," as Hunter and Yates call them, evolve from a pattern of large-scale physical mobility along with a strong tendency of remaining in a protective "sociocultural bubble" through similar physical localities, means of traveling, lodging and leisure and entertainment all across the world, which precludes them from serious engagements with the local cultures that they influence. When they visit other countries, they stay in U.S.-style hotels, health clubs, restaurants, office buildings and so forth, and associate almost exclusively with like-minded Western-educated professionals who are conversant in English, thereby sidestepping the necessity of learning foreign languages. Their way of working also shields them from serious doubts about their activities because of insufficient feedback from locals and others. There were notable exceptions, however, among people employed by international nongovernmental organizations that focused on environmental protection, human rights, emergency humanitarian relief, and the like. These individuals tended to have more face-to-face interaction with local populations and organizations at the grassroots (Hunter & Yates, 2002: 332-336).

Of course, living and working in a particular sociocultural bubble is not an exclusively American practice, as corporate business managers and professionals from many other countries move around in the same insulated transnational world. And members of international professional organizations as well as professionals and politicians allied with organizations like the European Union, the Association of Southeast Asian Nations, the Arab League or the United Nations may have their own sociocultural bubbles. Nonetheless, because, for the time being, Americans predominate among the movers and shakers of current globalization, they continue to play a central role in setting the agenda and general tone of today's globalization.

This leads us to one other important issue. The Western culture that is conveyed through globalization has a conflict-laden heterogeneity that is carried along too. This certainly applies to the American or Americanized components of this globalizing culture, given America's diversity. It means that criticisms of the dominant American way of life (and specific parts thereof) by, among others, American anti-capitalists, environmentalists, feminists, concerned journalists, intellectuals, and politicians are spread abroad as well. American culture wars and identity politics have been exported as part and parcel of the globalization process. Clashes between "pro-life" and "pro-choice" protagonists around the abortion issue have been taken to the global level by American agencies. This is the major point of contention. But the American culture wars are also being fought on foreign ground around broader issues surrounding sexuality, the family, and education by progressive and conservative special interest groups. These have established offices and staffs around the world to lobby foreign governments and international organizations on behalf of their respective causes. All of this concerns more generally Western culture wars transposed to the global level, but the discourses and practices of the agencies concerned are as yet strongly modeled after American exemplars; these agencies may even merely be global extensions of American organization movements and other institutions. The language that these globalizers and their foreign contacts use is English (usually its American version) and the vocabularies of their "global speak" derive from the social sciences, and the idioms of human rights, the market, and multiculturalism as these have first of all developed in the United States. This also means that initially American discourses obtain a broader, transnational character (Hunter & Yates, 2002: 326, 337-341).

Thus, the global spread of the ideology of "universal human rights" has great potential for ideological and judicial support to oppressed individuals across the world. But one must be aware that at times the United States and other Western countries have used (and still use today) "human rights" selectively as a political instrument to advance their own interests in their meddlings in other countries' affairs. America's defense of human rights also tends to exclude rights of individuals in the economic sphere, that is, regarding social security and conditions of work and standards of living (Johnson, 2000: 166-167).

The emerging global culture is most visibly manifest in the domain of mass-popular culture. Needless to say, however, most forms of European-originated "high culture" (classical music, opera, ballet, sculpture, paintings and literature) have always operated on an international scale. Modernist art in post-World War II America was internationalist from the start as well. European émigrés who were fleeing from Nazism and World War II brought the impulses of European modernist art to the United States. It was from the creative synergy of European-born painters and U.S.-bred talent that a dynamic cultural scene emerged, which would generate a series of art works that drew worldwide acclaim. In the 1940s and 1950s, the abstract expressionist painters created the first internationally significant U.S. art and turned New York into the center of the modern art world (Best & Kellner, 1997: 167-170). In recent decades, one can witness a restructuring of older patterns and transnational flows of high culture (especially concert hall music). This development results from the usage of global communication technologies, cross-media marketing and distribution techniques by globalizing cultural industries, as well as the increased transnational significance of the culture of performance and attendant celebrity cults originating in the United States.

The postmodern shift in the arts (and its intricate mixtures of "high" and "low" culture) has helped to generate the new global culture of postmodern forms in a variety of aesthetic fields (ranging from architecture, painting, and literature to multimedia art), media, computer, and consumer culture traveling across the globe with high speed (Best & Kellner, 1997: 188-189). Postmodernist forms of global culture often have an American imprint, because of the global outreach of U.S. art worlds and cultural industries, and the undeniable fact that postmodernism is preeminently American. As Malcolm Bradbury pointed out, the United States has been the site of both the Americanization of modernity – the condition that resulted from processes of modernization - and the Americanization of modernism - the iconoclastic, anti-traditionalist movement in the arts that took of in late-nineteenth century Europe. These two forms of Americanization have merged into one within the crucible of postmodern culture in America during the late twentieth century (Bradbury, 1995: 463).

U.S.-based or U.S.-owned TNCs have contributed much to the global dissemination of forms of "superculture" (Bigsby, 1975) driven by the further development of globalizing capitalism and worldwide spread of the culture-ideology of consumerism (Sklair, 2002: 108-111). This globalizing popular culture is to some degree detached from its American roots, but on the other hand it still continues to be fed with new inputs from the changing U.S. cultural repertoire continuously hybridizing with other cultural sources. One should also realize that the manifest cultural content is not all-important. The *forms* of commercial popular culture, the genres and social relationships established through cinema, television, the Internet or otherwise, may have a more decisive influence. For example, the mediation of formal politics by the spectacular modes of television news and current affairs programs (and the rise of infotainment) originating in the United States has radically altered local politics in many places of the world. One may label such changes as part of more general processes of modernization rather than "Americanization." Yet it cannot be denied that the genres and programs concerned express material forces and cultural practices that grew (and still grow) out of the social and media history of the United States (Bell & Bell, 1993: 187). More generally, there was a price in terms of quality to be paid in the commercialization of the local television systems in Europe and similar systems elsewhere through the adoption of the American "way of television." This implied a deficit especially with regard to innovation, risk-taking, minority appeal, cultural authority and non-commercial values. On the one hand, the proliferation of TV channels allowed by new digital technologies enabled the development of niche markets. On the other hand, however, commercial pressures, whether driven by the quest for greater advertising or subscription revenue (largely achieved, although not exclusively, through high circulations and audience ratings) tended to induce producers to opt for the tried and tested formula and to routinize their formats or schedules rather than take creative risks (McQuail, 1996: 115-116).

The 1990s saw a huge explosion of U.S. mergers in industry as a whole, which was reflected in the cultural industries. In the early twenty-first century a small group of corporations were obvious leaders in terms of the revenues they gained from global cultural-industry markets. This also included the growing influence of U.S.-corporate style conglomerates in the cultural industries not located in America, such as at that time the French-based company Vivendi and the German-based company Bertelsmann. The names and organizational structures of these companies change regularly, as further mergers, acquisitions and sell-offs take place or are suspended by regulatory agencies. In September 2004 the seven biggest cultural-industry businesses, in descending order of 2003-2004 revenue based on company reports, were Time Warner (formerly AOL Time Warner, New York), Vivendi Universal (Paris/New York), Walt Disney (Burbank, CA), Viacom (New York), Bertelsmann (Gütersloh, Germany), News Corporation (Melbourne, New York). Below these mega-corporations there was a second tier of regional corporations consisting of 43 companies, which were, apart from one Latin American company (Televisa, Mexico) and one Australian company (PBL), all based in either North America (21 companies, including three Canadian), Europe (ten companies, including five

British) or Japan (nine companies (Variety, 2004). Overall, U.S.-based companies remain powerful in the production of a wide variety of popular cultural forms. In the past few decades intellectual property has become of major significance – that is, the cultural industries increasingly operate around the ownership rights of films, TV programs, songs, brands. This enables them to circulate characters, icons, and narratives across many different media, and deploy intensive cross-promotion (Hesmondhalgh, 2002: 135-137, 143).

However, one must not overlook the co-implication of non-American investors in all of this. Ironically, French companies have been major investors in Hollywood since the 1980s. The management of conglomerates in the French film industry no longer felt obliged to defend those established values of high culture so long espoused by their intellectual compatriots. Whatever their underlying rationale may have been, companies like Canal+ and Chargeurs had no scruples about investing in Hollywood, while at the same time the majority of French producers and policymakers were engaged in a strenuous battle to prevent American movies from flowing unimpeded onto Europe's cinema and television screens (Puttnam, 1998: 261). (Indeed, French intellectuals led the 1993 GATT battle over Europe's need for "culture exception" to free-trade laws in film and television. In addition to a ticket surcharge, the French government spent up to $400 million in giving financial support of French-made films.) The restructuring of Hollywood went so far that by 2000 it was largely a place where deals were done, where studios, as Warner Brothers' vice-president Richard Fox said, were just "distributors, banks, and owners of intellectual copyrights, contracting out creative and production activities in others." The profits landed in bank accounts across the world, and the U.S. audience no longer determined what was made (Marling, 2006: 37-38). But this did not mean basic changes in cultural content. Even after this far-reaching transnationalization of economic ownership of the American film industry, most movies associated with "Hollywood" continued to have features characteristic of the various genres concerned.

At the turn of the new millennium, Americanizing forces were expected to remain strong in popular culture in the foreseeable future (Rosendorf, 2000: 110-123). However, certain American cultural media contents have become less popular around the world. Foreign sales of American TV programs have declined, as locals increasingly preferred locally produced shows. This has much to do with the cultural specificity in television drama which does not simply transfer well to all foreign cultures. There has to be a "narrative fit" between program and viewer, as research has shown regarding a large international sample of U.S. television programs shown abroad. Export programming appeared to take hold only in cultural niches of narrative compatibility (Frau-Meigs, 1996). In 2001, among the 60 countries in a worldwide survey 71 percent of their top 10 programs were locally produced. The worldwide television market is growing, but America is becoming less dominant in it. By 2002 Latin America evidenced as much Mexican and Spanish programming as American, while Asian and African stations mixed British and French shows with U.S imports. Indian, Egyptian, and Mexican soap operas undercut the price of U.S. syndications and exploited growing diasporic language markets. Then Mexico and Brazil had even become the world's top exporters of television drama.

By 1990 Mexico's Televisa was the largest producer of syndicated export programming in the world; it also purchased *telenovas* (local versions of soap operas) produced in other countries. By 2004, Brazil's Globo corporation was as big an exporter as Televisa, its sales covering 130 countries. (However, the latter companies have extensive ties to and joint ventures with American media companies, as well as with Wall Street investment banks. They are also primary instigators and beneficiaries of the expansion of the U.S.-dominated global media market in Latin America.) Syria has become a major exporter of television dramas to the Arabic world. China, potentially the largest cable TV market in the world, proved to be hard to penetrate by Fox, Time Warner and other big program providers. By 2002 the rate of cable growth in China had slowed to 3 percent per year, and Time Warner's access was restricted to diplomatic enclaves in the north and to the southern development zones near Hong Kong, where Cantonese is spoken. (Only 50 million Chinese speak Cantonese, however, while 874 million speak Mandarin.) Disney experiences heavy competition from Japanese, Philippine, and Taiwanese producers for the 40 percent market left for cartoons, as Chinese law requires that 60 percent of all cartoons on the air be made in China (McChesney, 2000: 107; Mann, 2003: 105; Marling, 2006: 42-43, 47).

The U.S. share of the worldwide web has also declined, from a half to a third during the 1990s. In 2002, 32 percent of Internet sites were American, 28 percent European and 26 percent Asian. And the non-English content of the Internet was growing very fast, which could be gauged, among other things, by the growth in registration of new domain names. By 2001 the U.S. accounted for only 40 percent of new domain names. Great Britain and German were second and third, each with about 10 percent, followed by Canada, South Korea, and the Netherlands. The total number of domains attributable to English-speaking nations declined from 74 percent in 1998 to 59 percent in 2001. By 2006, 605 million people could access the Internet - 183 million of them lived in the United States or Canada, but the rate growth had slowed there. Equally large numbers of Internet users lived both in Europe (191 million) and the Asian Pacific region (187 million), while there were more than 33 million users in Latin American and over 6 million in Africa (Mann, 2003: 105; Marling, 2006: 63-64).

In recent years we have seen the rise of new forms of popular culture invented, produced, and marketed in Europe, Australia or Japan which are then turned into global phenomena. Intriguingly, this takes place according to the former principles of Americanization, including those of the United States. Exemplary cases are local programs that feature "reality television" such as real-life police pursuit originating in Australia, the Netherlands, and Britain, and the popular TV show "Big Brother" from the Netherlands (Marling, 2006: 41). Even more interesting in this regard are the children's games Pokémon (short for pocket monsters) and its digitalized versions Digimon from Japan, which are transculturations of Walt Disney's Donald Duck figures and the global commerce connected with it. Donald Duck figures, which originated as popular culture in the United States and reemerged as major components of Euro-Disney in Paris and Disneyworld in Tokyo, have returned to the United States as transformed, and "perhaps grotesquely modified," products of Americanization. This transcultural traffic has been called "Americanization in reverse," which appears to be "the latest example of an Americanized world in which the world recycles Americanization and sells it back to America" (Hornung, 2002: 114). Clearly the dissemination is not a one-way process, and American popular culture undergoes changes as well through these foreign influences.

5. Globalizing cultural influences from outside the Western world

Next to the abovementioned globalizing forces first of all coming from the West (including cultural flows from the South, Latin America, to the North), one can notice the rise of cultural movements with a global outreach that originate outside the Western world but impinge on the latter. In this context one should not forget the influence of Japanese and East Asian forms of capitalism and the associated business practices (Nederveen Pieterse, 2004: 38, 144-146). A specific example is the Japanese management vogue from the late 1970s, which lasted until the economic difficulties in Asia in the 1990s, when this influence began to wane. Western business elites and policy circles were bent on trying to emulate Japanese industrial policy and management techniques, which was partly an "Americanization in reverse" to American industries, however.

A large part of the globalizing cultural influence from outside the Western world concerns religion. A world religion such as Islam involves diverse cultural movements. For example, the Taliban and warlords in Afghanistan and al Qaeda's wider Islamicist movement, along with the Islamic regimes in Iran and Sudan, are all "anti-modern" in their own ways (which does not exclude using modern technologies and media). But Islamic movements in Turkey and elsewhere in the Muslim world (e.g., Indonesia, Egypt, and Morocco) do not reject modernity and seek to construct a modern society that participates economically and politically in the global system and are driven by a self-consciously Islamic culture. Other examples of influential religious movements on a global scale can be found in India, for example the Sai Baba movement (which is strongly supernaturalistic, and opposed to a modern scientific worldview) with many centers in Europe and North America, and Hare Krishna, a more visible case of an Indian cultural export. Successful in this regard as well have been a number of Buddhist movements, such as Soka Gakkai hailing from Japan and the Tzu-Chi Foundation in Taiwan with branches in forty countries. Last but not least, there is New Age culture, not conveyed by organized religious movements, but arguably the most important cultural influence coming from Asia into the West, which has affected the beliefs and behaviors of millions of people in America and Europe. This can be traced to creative reinterpretations of Hindu, Buddhist, indigenous American, and other non-Western traditions that have been going on for more than a century (Berger, 2002: 12-14). But it must be noted that in quite a few instances these processes of "Easternization" have been filtered through American and European intermediaries before impinging on other parts of the Western world.

Another interesting example of reverse cultural flows to the West is the dissemination of traditional Asian medicines, health and fitness practices and approaches to mental health. These have become popular among substantial sections of the middle classes in Europe and North America. A similar cultural influx has occurred in the case of the martial arts such as karate, judo, t'ai kwando and kung fu (Cohen & Kennedy, 2000: 243). There is also the phenomenon of "world music" under which label music from non-Western cultures has become subsumed in recent decades in the West. Transnationally operating record companies have forced an immense variety of globally available music styles into categories like "folk music," "world music," and "indigenous music," which is an eminent example of "structures of common difference" mentioned earlier. The music ranges from ethnomusicologists' recordings of relatively authentic indigenous music to music that has adopted a Western format of popular culture, to musicians that draw on diverse influences to create synthetic world music - not unlike the way in which "California" fusion cuisine is created (Hall et al., 2003: 161). However, the local producers and musicians concerned - many living and working in developing countries - tend to have little control over the categorization of their music. And Western consumers largely determine the criteria for "authenticity" and quality. In order to gain recognition and compete on the world market, these musicians are obliged to adapt their products to the established categories and expectations (Breidenbach & Zukrigl, 2001: 116). Consequently, structural molds such as these tend to be biased towards a Western, predominantly Anglo-American staple that expresses the global hegemonic position of the metropolitan centers concerned.

6. Local engagements with U.S.-inflected cultural globalization

The study of cultural globalization as it impinges on local settings should always imply appropriate contextualization and localization. Context is to be understood here as a multidimensional, time- and place-bound phenomenon that includes the political-economic and technological contexts and the geographic dimension, place or location of the process; the relational dimensions, such as the social positioning of the recipients; as well as the temporal dimensions, such as historical memory (particularly of earlier globalizing influences, including alleged or real American influences in the past) and the juxtaposition of historical experience and interpretation of the people concerned. Social positioning refers to dissimilarities in gender, class, race, ethnicity, ideological, and other subject characteristics that lead to different ways in which locals respond to the cultural globalization they are facing or actively involved in. For our interest in this chapter, one should try to locate and "weigh" America's part appropriately amidst the various influences that are part of transnational flows reaching local cultures. For pragmatic reasons, empirical studies of "Americanization" often block other cross-national transfers. This may, if not cautiously done, lead to myopia in that important influences from other countries, broader cultural-geographic areas or regional subglobalizations are downplayed or even ignored.

Some forms of globalizing culture allow for more selective borrowing and creative appropriation than others. Mass-popular culture as part of consumer culture appears to be most open to active reception. For people looking for signs and symbols of a lifestyle, U.S. popular culture – especially as metamorphosed into "superculture" – has presented itself as one big "self service store" - everywhere present and with almost unlimited choice and opportunities, offering an iconography that remains open to all kinds or readings (Hebdige, 1988: 74). By contrast, the opportunities for opposition, "creative appropriation," "subversion," and "resistance" by local recipients abroad appear to be much smaller with regard to cultural components of U.S. economic policies and international politics and security (Strinati, 1992: 53). The latter-day version of this "superculture" continues to provide a cultural repertoire from which people across the world borrow freely in creating their own, sometimes highly idiosyncratic versions of "things American" as they assimilate these into their everyday life-worlds. Here an intriguing process has been at work regarding local appropriations of globalizing U.S. culture. Thorough socialization into mass-mediated American culture during the formative years of people growing up in a society located firmly within the U.S. cultural orbit (such as many countries in postwar Western Europe, for example) tends to lead to an ambiguous position and attendant 'double consciousness,' which entails a strong reflexivity in dealing with U.S popular culture because of being both an outsider and an insider to American culture. The responses of students in discussions about this subject in media and culture courses recently given in the Netherlands, showed diverse patterns that demonstrate the complexities of Americanization abroad, ranging from what can be seen as an interpretation in terms of U.S. imperialism on the one hand and full incorporation into the local culture on the other. And, like among previous generations, enjoyment of American popular culture could very well coincide with criticism of U.S. politics (Kooijman, 2011).

It has been argued that in contradistinction to the cultural values underlying various civilizations, which are likely to spread less easily to other cultures, consumption of mass-popular culture tends to be superficial in the sense that it does not deeply affect people's beliefs, values, or behavior. But against this it should be noted that the influx of globalizing popular culture can have a crucial impact locally. It all depends on time and circumstances, which are both critical to the meanings and effects of the cultural objects in question. In this context Peter Berger has suggested a distinction between "sacramental" and "non-sacramental" cultural consumption. The former is at stake when the adoption of a Western practice amounts to an embrace of Western culture in a deeply meaningful - sacred - way. For example, some consumption of the globalizing popular culture, such as eating a burger - especially when it takes place under the golden icon of a McDonald's restaurant - is a visible sign of the real or imagined participation in global modernity with an American face. But much consumption of Western culture takes place on a routine basis - sometimes a burger is just a burger, and thus a non-sacramental act (Berger, 2002: 7) Which type of consumption prevails cannot be decided a priori but only on the basis of empirical research of the case in question.

There are both tensions and convergences between the different sectors of today's cultural globalization. On an abstract level, in terms of conventional modernization theory, they have one theme in common, that is "individuation": "all sectors of the emerging global culture enhance the independence of the individual over against tradition and collectivity." Individuation is understood here as "a social and psychological process…manifested in the behavior and consciousness of people regardless of the ideas they may hold about this" (Berger, 2002: 9).This means that individuation as an empirical phenomenon should not be conflated with "individualism" as an ideology (although the two are frequently linked in everyday practice). Peter Berger is correct in stating that this insight helps explain the broad appeal of the new global culture. I would argue, however, that the appeal value concerns foremost a transculturally shared structure of feelings among people taking part in the dominant form of Western modernity. It does not pertain to those groups of people (even whole cultures) who are not, or to a much lesser degree, committed to this type of modernity. Their members may not feel attracted to or even be repulsed by particular elements of the new global culture (such as the excesses of possessive individualism and consumer culture, for example) as they take part in one of the other modernities there are. Capitalist modernity, especially in its neoliberal mold, uproots many people and leaves them "homeless" and feeling powerless.

Other forms of modernization may be less threatening to ordinary people in this regard, even though these modalities all experience the ongoing influence of neoliberal globalization to a lesser or greater degree as well. These alternatives include forms of social market capitalism in continental Europe, state-assisted capitalisms in East and Southeast Asia, capitalisms embedded in specific variants of Islamic culture as, for example in Anatolia, Turkey, as well as state-led (post)industrialization and mobilization of the masses in various Latin American countries with newly emerged forms of left-wing populism and socialism (Nederveen Pieterse, 2004: 143-144, Robinson, 2008). The question remains how much leeway there is for the articulation of these alternative modernities within the emerging global culture.

The challenges that the new global culture poses to the societies it impinges upon evoke a variety of responses occurring on a scale between acceptance and rejection, with in-between positions of coexistence and synthesis. In addition there is a wider variety of reactions by the target societies, including those initiated by governments. There are cases of *unreserved acceptance* as occurs among members of a global network of ambitious young people in business and the professions whose members speak fluent English and dress and act alike, at work and at play, and up to a point think alike (a yuppie-like transnational group) (Berger, 2002: 3-4). Acceptance may also lead to *cultural imitation*, especially when the "real thing" is not easily accessible or available (or too expensive) to locals in the periphery. Local culture creators may, upon being exposed to foreign culture, attempt to create imitations of it for local consumption. Imitations may range from "copycat" versions of the original to the appropriation of certain techniques or methods (Lewis , 1996: 272).)

But at the other extreme there are attempts at *militant rejection*, be it from the standpoint of religion or nationalism. Some states, like North Korea and Afghanistan when it was ruled by the Taliban, have tried to hermetically close its territory and people off from alien cultural influences. There are also relatively less totalitarian forms of rejection, typically practiced by governments trying to balance global economic participation with resistance against Western globalizing culture – China is the most important contemporary example of this. Its course toward economic neoliberalization on which the Chinese Communist Party embarked in the late 1970s has led to ruthless "free market reforms" along with measures that seek either to deny entry into the country of Western cultural imports or to "harmlessly" incorporate those into the existing social, political, and cultural conditions through national gatekeeping policies (especially restrictive legislation, censorship and control of access to particular websites on the Internet).

There are many cultures that seek to resist intermingling with others by *creating new certainties*. One manifestation is the creation of new states defined on the basis of a single ethno-nationality. The new states that emerged from the collapse of the Soviet Union and the disintegration of Yugoslavia provide abundant examples of am extreme tendency to homogenize the nation, based on the seriously flawed notion of an "essential" national identity. In the worst-case scenario the drive for ethnic territorialism leads to ethnic cleansing and even systematic attempts at genocide. Other groups have resisted cultural globalization through a purist reaffirmation of one's religion or ethnicity. This new insistence on ethnic and religious difference has created serious dilemmas for established nation-states, which have shown a large variation in the extent to which they are open to newcomers or, by contrast, demand cultural and social adjustment on the part of immigrants and residents. There is also a tendency among some national governments to recognize sub-national claims for devolution or regional autonomy, as has occurred to a varying degree in Britain, Spain and elsewhere (Cohen & Kennedy, 2000: 355-356).

Then there are the cases *in-between acceptance and rejection*. Almost everywhere one finds instances of *localization*, in which the global culture is accepted but with significant modifications. This has happened, for example, with the incorporation of McDonald's in East Asian countries. One important element was that the contract with customers had to be modified in order to allow for lingering: housewives relaxing in the restaurant after shopping or other errands and schoolchildren before going home. From the perspective of globalization theory, McDonaldization is subject to the forces of pluralism indeed. When McDonaldized models are imported they are always undergoing indigenous adaptation (Watson, 1997). These models can develop locally in a process of *emulation* and a

McDonaldized model can be employed for a variety of purposes, with different products, organization, and effects. On the other hand, however, one should not exaggerate the heterogeneity of McDonaldized systems in diverse local settings, thereby downplaying their cultural power as a major force of a homogenizing globalization predicated on Western corporate logic and business systems (Kellner, 1999).

The cultural localizations can be more far-reaching. For example, Buddhist movements in Taiwan have adopted the organizational forms of American Protestantism to propagate their non-American, non-Western religious message. These newly revitalized Buddhist groups have taken on a worldly approach through their involvements in social welfare and medical services, education, publishing books, and environmentalism, which has drastically transformed the way in which religion has been practiced in Taiwan for centuries. A local religious philosopher has interpreted this as a "renewal" of a lost tradition, that is, when the dynastic emperors espoused Chinese Buddhism, it too made direct contributions to society (Hsiao, 2002: 62-64). However, another way to look at it is that not only Taiwan Buddhists' practices but also their belief systems have become "Americanized" by incorporating U.S.-style Protestant denominationalism and emulating the Western Christian tradition by building colleges and universities and establishing the institutional form of the foundation to promote culture, welfare, and reform causes.

One can also argue, as William Marling does with regard to U.S.-originated technologies, that, through various localizations, the "ways of doing things" or "use habits" that Americans have pioneered are becoming the ways that millions of people elsewhere do things. From ATMs and container ports to airfreight and bar codes, technologies and technological devices pioneered in the United States have been adopted by other societies, which are now going into competition with and sometimes surpassing the United States. Marling correctly emphasizes that local adaptations of U.S.-originated technology are often locally superior, which sets limits to the advance of certain Americanisms, such as the drive-through ATM or burger joint. The logistical systems that deliver products and services – financial services, container shipping, airfreight, computing – will move toward standards, such as technological efficiency and economies of scale. These enable flows of goods and services across cultures. To the extent that logistical systems can, they accommodate to local cultures. For example, the language interfaces of ATMs can be local (incorporating languages locally in use), but their logistical systems will be global. The cultural "local" with its folkways (associated with language, communicative distance, food, modes of land use, habitation patterns, work habits, attitudes toward race and ethnicity etc.) endures, although its interplay with the "global" has increased, leading to further disembedding of cultures.

Sharing logistical expertise with Americans, nations like India and China are likely to be drawn closer to the United States in some ways, as they adopt practices like franchising or just-in-time manufacturing but customize them to their use. On the other hand, however, Americans still remain far ahead in the domain of logistical invention as demonstrated by the highly sophisticated level of systems integration by a company like UPS. Other Anglo-American practices, such as using the money market, allow people elsewhere in the world to invest in money market funds as well, which reduces the advantage Americans initially have had in accumulating (including the risk of losing) wealth this way (Marling, 2006: 191, 203-204). It is also true that across the world standardization in production and delivery systems and in the associated management practices of corporate businesses takes place. This is not the same as a complete leveling out of national cultural differences and homogenization of products. Most products or practices must also be adapted to the tastes and cultural preferences of the local market.

Strictly speaking, however, there is nothing uniquely American about standardization, commercialization, automation, computerization, digitalization and the like. As early as the nineteenth century, but increasingly after World War II, many Europeans and other observers overseas thought things to be American that are merely characteristics of a modern technological age, which has flourished first and most visibly in the United States. But, "it could be argued that the typically American contributions to science and technology have been mostly concerned with the 'conquest' of distance and time" (Wagnleiter, 1993: 78). They have therefore been of particular relevance for the ongoing processes of enhanced globalization.

Global influences also can bring about a *revitalization of indigenous cultural forms*. This may lead to identification with, and stronger articulation of, the local culture; it involves the retention and creation of local cultural artifacts and forms vis-à-vis the incoming global culture in order to resist the loss of cultural identity that total assimilation may bring. Thus the inroad of Western-based fast food chains in India, Japan, and Turkey has led to the development of fast food outlets for traditional foods, and the invasion of Western fashions in Japan has fostered the development of an indigenous fashion industry marked by distinctively Japanese aesthetics (Aoki, 2002; Chase, 1994; Srinivas, 2002). The latter cultural practices have partly shaded over into processes of cultural invention, "folklorization" and "fabricated" and "staged authenticity." Entrepreneurs, in attempting to sell "authenticity," can and do invent cultural artifacts, which they attribute to local cultures and sell to outsiders as symbolic of that culture. Many tourist art objects, souvenirs, and "ritual" performances are of this sort (Lewis, 1996: 272-273).

A local response to the globalizing culture in question may entail a more *conscious cultural opposition*, whereby local culture is used to challenge or oppose (part of) it. This can take, for example, the form of an "indigenous literature movement," in which writers search for an indigenous literary identity in a deliberate rejection of modernism/postmodernism in Western literature. Such a movement can be extended to include other cultural fields like music, the performing arts, and films, as occurred in Taiwan in the 1970s and 1980s (Hsiao, 2002: 61). It is against globalizing capitalism's modernity that sometimes at the local level an older form of modernity is put forward in which the older emancipatory idea of a national project and a national culture reemerges as an oppositional value. For example, in recent years several Asian civilizations reasserted the role that a nationalist project may play through the oppositional power of a national literature (as in South Korea) or a national art and cinema, with India as the prototypical example. Thus, Fredric Jameson argues, "alongside a multiple and postmodern postcoloniality, there also exist a modernist one, for which the 'liberation' brought by Americanization and American mass culture and consumption can also be experienced as a threat and a force of disintegration of traditions from which new and alternative possibilities might otherwise have been expected to emerge" (Jameson, 1998: xv).

Localization may also shade over to another response, *hybridization*, which refers to the deliberate effort to synthesize foreign and native cultural traits. An eminent example is the development of an overseas Chinese business culture from Taiwan, combining the most modern business techniques with traditional Chinese personalism extending to employer-employee relations with an emphasis on family-like harmony, unity, loyalty and emotional commitment, and a strongly family-orientated private life of managers. Thus a defining feature of Taiwanese businesses is a strong paternalistic organizational culture. Yet in the business cultures of the locally active multinational companies as well as in many of the local companies operating in world markets some fusion of American, European, Japanese, and Taiwanese-Chinese management styles has emerged.

Now that mainland China has become more integrated into the global economy, similar hybridizations can be observed, as in the notion of the "Confucian merchant" which means that many of these elites combine the use of modern business and management practices with a traditional mentality and lifestyle regarding gender relationships, the education of children, and interpersonal relationships. In both cases the hybridization does not involve an intermixing of diverse capitalisms. The first case builds upon the coexistence (or juxtaposition) of the Taiwanese family business model with globalized Fordism from the United States and Toyotism from Japan (Hsiao, 2002: 51-54). The second case includes the state-led capitalism of this newly industrialized, communist state in which the key to business success is special connections to key persons who are in charge of relevant government agencies and determine the policies and regulations in question (Yan, 2002: 21-24).

Other interesting cases are the multiple syncretisms between Christianity and traditional religions in the African indigenous churches (Bernstein, 2002: 227-230) and between popular Catholicism, African collective memories, and indigenous (Indian) religions in Latin America (Ortiz, 2000: 250). In the case of mass-popular culture, hybridization sometimes evolves further away from the Western-originated cultural input. For example, the films produced by India's thriving popular commercial film industry "Bollywood" do not simply imitate Hollywood's genres. Rather they are anchored in the diverse cultures and centered on issues of Indian society (Tyrell, 1999).

Needless to say, the concept of hybridity is problematic in so far as it suggests the mixing of completely separate and homogeneous cultural spheres or identities, while the anthropological and historical records show that all cultures are hybrid. In fact, contemporary accelerated globalization entails the hybridization of hybrid cultures. The concept is acceptable, though, "as a device to capture cultural change by way of a strategic cut or temporary stabilization of cultural categories" (Barker, 2000: 203). But hybridization has another side which makes it even more complex, as Nederveen Pieterse points out. Consider examples like the following, referring to a general tendency, of which many more could be given: "Mexican schoolgirls dressed in Greek togas dancing in the style of Isadora Duncan ... reflects transnational bourgeois class affinities, mirroring themselves in classical European culture. Chinese tacos and Irish bagels reflect ethnic crossover in employment patterns in the American fast food sector. Asian rap refers to cross-cultural convergence in popular youth culture" (Nederveen Pieterse, 1995: 50). Paradoxically, what appears from one perspective as hybridization here can, from another angle be interpreted in terms of transnational affinities in sensibility or attitude. In other words, the other side of cultural hybridity is transcultural convergence in cases such as these.

One should also recognize that in hybridization itself power inequities are involved: "Relations of power and hegemony are inscribed and reproduced within hybridity for wherever we look closely enough we find the traces of asymmetry in culture, place, descent. Hence hybridity raises the question of the terms of the mixture, the conditions of mixing and mélange. At the same time it's important to note the ways in which hegemony is not merely reproduced but refigured in the process of hybridization" (Nederveen Pieterse, 1995: 57). For our purpose the basic issue is the existence, in varying degrees, of a "U.S.-accented cultural hybridity" in various places across the world (Antonio & Bonanno, 2000: 55-56).

With regard to the dissemination of American culture abroad the anthropological literature abounds with interesting examples of creative appropriation of imported consumer goods, as well as the impact of modern means of communication and transportation in facilitating the continued interaction and identification of migrants from developing countries in America with their societies and cultures of origin. The cultural complexities of the hybridization process that can be at issue here are well illustrated by the following elaborate example borrowed from a case study of Haitian transnational migration (Richman, 1992). In order to finance the lavish feasts that their gods - the *lwa* of *vodun* - occasionally demand from them, Haitian peasants have become almost exclusively dependent on remittances from their family members who migrated to North America. This is possible, because these migrants, despite their residence in New York, Miami or Toronto, retain membership in bilateral descent groups. These social entities, known as *eritaj*, comprise ancestors as well as living kin, and membership includes not only the right of inheritance of family land, but also the obligation to serve the *lwa* associated with this corporate unit and the susceptibility to the influence of these gods. Stephan Palmié has summarized the sociocultural processes that are relevant in this context:

"Nowadays, the *lwa* not only traverse enormous distances to look after their children up north, they also shrewdly play on kinship-ties: for if neglected they tend to punish not the offenders, but their descendants. This fact, as well as others... necessitates that the migrant (usually, of course, a younger member of a descent group) participate in the ceremonial life of the *eritaj* to insure his or her own health and productivity – if only by contributing the funds to maintain the *lwa* contented. Here, modern media help translate such absentee ownership of communal rites into transnational practice: cassette tapes of ritual *chants de pwen* and, most recently, even videotaped *sèvis lwa* circulate between migrant and home communities – thus initiating a new channel of communication between men and gods. At the same time, just as money from abroad economically vertebrated the ritual system, so have the gods themselves adapted to new consumption patterns: many of them, most prominently the 'African' *lwa blan,* have evolved a taste for foreign products. While the more rustic and dangerous creole *zandò lwa* are fed the coarse staples and 'unsophisticated' beverages the peasants themselves consume, some of the *lwa blan* apparently crave and demand imported stuff: while raw native rum will do for Ti Jean, Erzili wants American soft drinks or Champagne" (Palmié, 1993: 289-290).

This can be interpreted as an instance in which the "periphery" quite successfully incorporates consumer goods from the "core." It is not the American center that contaminates and undermines a formerly autonomous peripheral world. It is Haiti that "creolizes" an American world of consumer goods. Even the African gods in question are subjected to the magical workings of commodity fetishism. Yet they "work its magic" in their own favor by re-transforming commodities into social relationships, which proves the vitality of a "genuinely" Haitian culture. We may wonder, however, to what extent power inequities between the metropolitan and peripheral cultures are reproduced in the cultural mix in question. It also needs to be added that this focus on some peculiar aspects of *vodun* leaves out the socioeconomic context of this transnational subculture, which makes living hard for both the Caribbean labor migrants in the North-American metropoles (where they face radical discrimination too) and their peasant kinfolk in Haiti. It also ignores the implications of U.S. foreign policy with regard to the plight of Haiti's people at home and abroad.

More generally, in studying processes of hybridization we cannot leave it at that and marvel at the variety of voices and representations in creolizing cultural forms and expressions: "The challenge rather lies in empirically charting the flow not only of meaning, but power, through culturally complex fields; in investigating the coalescence or dissipation of aggregates of symbolic matter over time - not as a free play of forms or texts, but as struggles and politics mediated by the agency of interested actors and collectivities" (Palmié, 1993: 296).

It is possible to differentiate hybridization analytically from *indigenization,* which is at stake when the cultural imports are incorporated into the indigenous culture to such an extent that they have become fully "naturalized," that is, turned into taken-for-granted, integral components of the local culture, and are no longer recognized as of foreign origin. Ever since the Meiji Restoration, Japan has been a highly successful pioneer of this type of response (Tomlinson, 1991: 92-93). Examples in several domains (architecture, designs, customs and lifestyle, language, etc.) indicate that in borrowing things from foreign sources the Japanese tend to adopt the forms and often the rituals of these imports without being concerned with the significance of the "orginal." In this process of appropriation they give new meaning to the borrowed element - a signification that is often incompatible with that of the original - or else they manage to drain it of meaning and symbolism, thereby turning the cultural import into empty form or ritual (Bognar, 2000: 63). In this connection several observers have signaled an all-pervasive "subversion of Americanization" in Japan's encounters with America, which would set severe limits to any transformation of Japanese culture in the American mold (Delanty, 2003).

7. Conclusion

Cultural globalization is an integral part of broader processes of globalization driven by transnationalizing corporate capitalism, for the time being foremost in the American mold. It is a complex amalgam of both homogenizing forces of sameness and uniformity *and* heterogeneity, difference, and hybridity. It is also a contradictory mixture of tendencies that foster democratization and others that go in the opposite direction. Globalization is a contested terrain with opposing forces attempting to use its institutions, technologies, media, forms and practices for their own purposes. On the one hand, globalization entails a process of standardization in which mass-cultural forms circulate around the world, creating sameness and homogeneity. On the other hand, globalizing culture makes possible unique localizations and developments everywhere. Each local setting involves its own appropriation and reworking of global products and symbols, thus encouraging difference, otherness, diversity, and variety, and possibly evoking resistance and democratic self-determination against forms of global domination and subordination. Furthermore, cultural globalization is not only driven by Western/American cultural influences; it also moves in the opposite direction as we noted earlier with regard to forms of capitalism, religion, and health practices coming from the East. When hybridizations from outside the West are sufficiently coherent and vigorous as a cultural movement, they may manifest themselves as alternative globalizations, sometimes based on alternative conceptions of modernity, other than those in the West (Gaonkar, 1999). In this light, we can envision in the long run increasingly competing civilizational efforts to dominate globalization, notably from the West (and particular parts of it), Islam, India and China, whereby U.S.-style modernity recedes to the background as America's global powers wane.

8. References

Antonio, R. J. & Bonanno, A. (2000). A New Global Capitalism? From "Americanism and Fordism" to "Americanization-Globalization", *American Studies* 41 (2/3): 33-77.

Aoki, Tamotsu (2002). Aspects of Globalization in Japan, *in* P.L. Berger & S.P. Huntington (Eds.), *Many Globalizations,* pp. 68-88.

Appadurai, A. (1996). *Modernity at Large,* University of Minnesota Press, Minneapolis.

Barker, C. (2000). *Cultural Studies: Theory and Practice,* Sage, London.

Bell, P. & Bell R. (1993). *Implicated: The United States in Australia,* Oxford University Press, Oxford.

Berger, P.L. (2002). Introduction, *in* P.L. Berger & S.P. Huntington (Eds.), *Many Globalizations,* pp. 1-16.

Berger, P.L. & Huntington, S.P. (Eds.). *Many Globalizations: Cultural Diversity in the Contemporary World,* Oxford University Press, Oxford.

Bernstein, A. (2002). Globalization, Culture, and Development: Can South Africa Be More Than an Offshoot of the West?, *in* P.L. Berger & S.P. Huntington (Eds.), *Many Globalizations,* pp. 185-249.

Best, S. & Kellner, D. (1997). *The Postmodern Turn,* The Guilford Press, New York.

Bigsby, C.W.E. (1975). Europe, America and the Cultural Debate, *in* C.W.E. Bigsby (Ed.), *Superculture: American Popular Culture and Europe,* Bowling Green University Press, Bowling Green, OH, pp. 1-27.

Bognar, B. (2000). Surface above All? American Influence of Japanese Urban Space, *in* H. Fehrenbach & U.G. Poiger (Eds.), *Transactions, Transgressions, Transformations,* Berghahn, New York, pp. 45-78.

Bradbury, M. 1995). *Dangerous Pilgrimages: Trans-Atlantic Mythologies and the Novel,* Penguin, Harmondsworth.

Breidenbach, J. & Zukrigl, I. (2002). Up and Down the Music World: An Anthropology of Globalization, *in* A. Gebesmair & A. Smudits (Eds.), *Global Repertoires: Popular Music Within and Beyond the Transnational Music Industry,* Ashgate, Aldershot, pp. 105-117.

Brouwer, S., Gifford, P. & Rose, S.D. (1996). *Exporting the American Gospel: Global Christian Fundamentalism,* Routledge, New York.

Chase, H. (1994). The *Meyhane* or the McDonald's? Changes in Eating Habits and the Evolution of Fast Food in Istanbul, *in* S. Zubaida &. R. Tapper (Eds.), *Culinary Cultures of the Middle East,* I.B. Tauris, London, pp. 73-86.

Cohen, R. & Kennedy, P. (2000). *Global Sociology,* Macmillan, London.

Corten, A. & Marshall-Fratani, R. (Eds.). *Between Babel and Pentecost: Transnational Pentecostalism in Africa and Latin America,* Indiana University Press, Bloomington, IN.

Delanty, G. (2003). Consumption, Modernity and Japanese Cultural Identity: The Limits of Americanization?, *in* U. Beck, N. Sznaider & W. Winter (Eds.), *Global America: The Cultural Consequences of Globalization,* Liverpool University Press, Liverpool, pp. 114-133.

Denning, M. (2004). *Culture in the Age of Three Worlds,* Verso, London.

Eisenstadt, S.N. (2000). Multiple Modernities, *Daedalus,* 129 (1): 1-30.

Featherstone, M., Lash, S. & Robertson, R. (Eds.) (1995). *Global Modernities,* Sage, London.

Frau-Meigs, D. (1996). The Cultural Impact of American Television Fiction in Europe. Transfer of Imaginary Worlds or Cultural Compatibility? Unpublished paper presented at the European American Studies Association, Warsaw, Poland, March 21-24, 1996.

Gaonkar, D. P. (1999). On Alternative Modernities, *Public Culture*, 11 (1): 1-18.

Hall, J.R., Neitz, M.J. & Battani, M. (2003). *Sociology on Culture*, Routledge, London.

Hebdige, D. (1988). *Hiding in the Light: On Images and Things*, Routledge, London.

Hesmondhalgh, D. (2002). *The Cultural Industries*. Sage, London.

Hornung, A. (2002). Contribution to Debate on "Transculturations: American Studies in a Globalizing World – the Globalizing World in American Studies," *Amerikastudien/American Studies*, 47 (1): 110-114.

Hsiao, Hsin-Huang, M. (2002). Coexistence and Synthesis: Cultural Globalization and Localization in Contemporary Taiwan, *in* P.L. Berger & S.P. Huntington (Eds.), *Many Globalizations*, pp. 48-67.

Hunter, J.D. & Yates, J. (2002). In the Vanguard of Globalization: The World of American Globalizers, *in* P.L. Berger & S.P. Huntington (Eds.), *Many Globalizations*, pp. 323-357.

Jameson, F. (1998). Preface, *in* F. Jameson & M. Miyoshi (Eds.), *The Cultures of Globalization*, Duke University Press, Durham, NC, pp. xi-xvii.

Johnson, Ch. (2000). *Blowback: The Costs and Consequences of American Empire*. Henry Holt and Company, New York.

Kellner, D. (1999). Theorizing McDonaldization: A Multiperspectivist Approach, *in* B. Smart (Ed.), *Resisting McDonaldization*, Sage, London, pp. 186-206.

Kellner, D. (2002). Theorizing Globalization, *Sociological Theory*, 20 (3): 285-305.

Kooijman, J. (2011). Americans We Never Were: Teaching American Popular Culture in the Netherlands, *Journal of American Culture*, 34 (1):16-25.

Kuisel, R.F. (2000). The French Cinema and Hollywood: A Case Study of Americanization, *in* H. Fehrenbach & U.G. Poiger (Eds.), *Transactions, Transgressions, Transformations*, Berghahn, New York, pp. 208-223.

Lewis, G.H. (1996). The Somersaults of Monkeys: Diffusion of Culture and Meaning Across the Pacific Rim, *Journal of Popular Culture*, 31 (1): 263-276.

McChesney, R.W. (2000). *Rich Media Poor Democracy: Communication Politics in Dubious Times*, The New Press, New York.

McGrew, A. (1992). A Global Society?, *in* S. Hall, D. Held & T. McGrew (Eds.), *Modernity and Its Futures*, Polity Press, Cambridge, pp. 61-102.

McQuail, D. (1996). Transatlantic TV Flow: Another Look at Cultural Cost-Accounting, *in* A. van Hemel, H. Mommaas & C. Smithuijsen (Eds.), *Trading Culture: GATT, European Cultural Policies and the Transatlantic Market*, Boekman Foundation, Amsterdam, pp. 111-125.

Mann, M. (2003). *Incoherent Empire*, Verso, London.

Marling, W. H. (2006). *How "American" Is Globalization?*, The Johns Hopkins University Press, Baltimore, MD.

Nederveen Pieterse, J. (1995). Globalization as Hybridization, *in* M. Featherstone, S. Lash & R. Robertson (Eds.), *Global Modernities*, Sage, London, pp. 45-68.

Nederveen Pieterse, J. (2004). *Globalization or Empire?*, Routledge, New York.
Notoji, M. (2002). Contribution to Debate on "Transculturations: American Studies in a Globalizing World – the Globalizing World in American Studies, *Amerikastudien/American Studies*, 47 (1): 107-108.
Nye, J.S., Jr. (2002). *The Paradox of American Power: Why the World's Only Superpower Can't Go It Alone*, Oxford University Press, Oxford.
Ortiz, R. (2000). From Incomplete Modernity to World Modernity, *Daedalus*, 129 (1): 249-260.
Palmié, S. (1993). Conceptualising Cultural Flow: Perspectives on Globalisation, *in* R. Kroes, R.W. Rydell & D.F.J. Bosscher (Eds.), *Cultural Transmissions and Receptions. American Mass Culture in Europe*, VU University Press, Amsterdam, pp. 271-301.
Puttnam, D. (1998). *Movies and Money*, Knopf, New York.
Richman, K. (1992). *They Will Remember Me in The House: The Pwen of Haitian Transnational Migration*. Unpublished Ph.D. dissertation, University of Virginia, Charlottesville, VA.
Robinson, W.I. (2008). *Latin America and Global Capitalism*, The Johns Hopkins University Press, Baltimore, MD.
Rosendorf, N.M. (2000). Social and Cultural Globalization: Concepts, History, and America's Role, *in* J.S. Nye, Jr. & J.D. Donahue (Eds.), *Governance in a Globalizing World*, Brookings Institution Press, Washington, DC, pp. 109-134.
Sassen, S. (2006). *Territory, Authority, Rights: From Medieval to Global Assemblages*, Princeton University Press, Princeton, NJ.
Sklair, L. (2002). *Globalization: Capitalism and its Alternatives*, Oxford University Press, Oxford.
Srinivas, T. (2002). "A Tryst with Destiny": The Indian Case of Cultural Globalization, *in* P.L. Berger & S.P. Huntington (Eds.), *Many Globalizations*, pp. 89-116.
Steger, M.B. (2002). *Globalism: The New Market Ideology*, Rowman & Littlefield, Lanham, MD.
Strinati, D. (1992). The Taste of America: Americanization and Popular Culture in Britain, *in* D. Strinati & S. Wagge (Eds.), *Come on Down: Popular Media Culture in Post-War Britain*, Routledge, London, pp. 46-81
Therborn, G. (1995). Routes to/through Modernity, *in* M. Featherstone, S. Lash & R. Robertson (Eds.), *Global Modernities*, Sage, London, pp. 124-139.
Tomlinson, J. (1991). *Cultural Imperialism: A Critical Introduction*, Pinter Publishers, London.
Tomlinson, J. (1999). *Globalization and Culture*, Polity Press, Cambridge.
Turner, B.S. (1999). *Classical Sociology*, Sage, London.
Tyrell, H. (1999). Bollywood versus Hollywood: Battle of Dream Factories, *in* T. Skelton & T. Allen (Eds.), *Culture and Social Change*, Routledge, London, pp. 260-273.
Variety (2004). Variety's Global 50, *Variety*, September 13, 2004. June 6, 2006, Available from <https://www.high.beam.com/library>.
Wagner, P. (1994). *A Sociology of Modernity: Liberty and Discipline*, Routledge, London.
Wagnleiter, R. (1993). Propagating the American Dream: Cultural Policies as Means of Integration, *in* R. P. Horwitz (Ed.), *Exporting America*, Garland Publishing, Inc., New York.

Watson, J. (Ed.) (1997). *Golden Arches East: McDonald's in East Asia,* Stanford University Press, Palo Alto, CA.

Wilk, R. (1995). The Local and the Global in the Political Economy of Beauty: From Miss Belize to Miss World, *Review of International Political Economy,* 2 (1): 117-134.

Yan, Y. (2002). Managed Globalization: State Power and Cultural Transition in China, *in* P.L. Berger & S.P. Huntington (Eds.), *Many Globalizations,* pp. 19-47.

9

Recognition of Real-World Activities from Environmental Sound Cues to Create Life-Log

Mostafa Al Masum Shaikh, Keikichi Hirose and Mitsuru Ishizuka
Dept. of Information and Communication Engineering,
The University of Tokyo, Tokyo,
Japan

1. Introduction

There are several studies that collect and store life-log for personal memory. This chapter explains about a system that can create someone's life-log in an inexpensive way to share daily life events with family, friends or care-givers through simple text messaging with a notion to remote monitoring of someone's wellbeing. In the developed world where people are usually busier than ever, ambient communications through mobile media or the Internet based communication can provide rich social connections to their loving ones ubiquitously whom they care about by sharing awareness information in a passive way. For users who wish to have a persistent existence through ambient communication – to let someone else to know about their daily activity – new technology is needed. Research that aims to simulate virtual living or logging daily events, while challenging and promising, is currently rare. Only very recently the detection of real-world activities has been attempted by processing multiple sensors data along with inference logic for real-world activities. Detecting or inferring human activity using such simple sensor data is often inaccurate, insufficient and expensive. Therefore, this chapter discusses a technology, an inexpensive alternative to other sensors (e.g., accelerometers, proximity sensors etc.) based approaches, to infer human activity from environmental sound cues and common-sense knowledgebase of everyday objects and concepts. A system prototype to log daily events to infer activities in 'as you go' manner from environmental sound cues is explained with a few case studies. The input of the system is the patterns of sounds that are usually produced from activities (e.g., toilet flushing), occurring environmentally (e.g., road sounds) or due to interaction with the objects (e.g., cooking utensils clattering). A robust signal processing processes the input sound signal and Hidden Markov Model (HMM) classifiers are developed to detect pre-determined sound contexts. Based on the detected sounds and along with the common-sense knowledge regarding human activity, object interaction, ontology of human life (e.g., living pattern of a single old man, or an old couple) and temporal information (e.g., morning, noon etc.) inference engine is employed to detect the activity and the surrounding environment of the person. Preliminary results are encouraging with the accuracy rate for outdoor and indoor related sound categories for activities being above 67% and 61% respectively.

2. Environmental sound cues and life-log

Although speech is the most informative acoustic event, but environmental sounds are also useful to process because those can provide useful information regarding context of the environment. In a given environment human-activity can be reflected by a variety of acoustic events, either produced naturally or by the human body or by the objects manipulated or interacted. For example: Jingling sound of cooking utensils (like cooking pan, spoon, knife etc.) may lead to infer someone's cooking activity, likewise vehicle passing sound may lead to infer that someone is on the road, etc. Many sources of information for sensing the environment as well as activity are available (Chen et al., 2005; Philipose et al., 2004; Temko and Nadeu, 2005). In this chapter, we consider two objectives namely, sound-based context awareness, where the decision is based merely on the available acoustic information at the surrounding environment of the user and automatic life-logging, where the detected sound context infers an activity to be logged along with temporal information.
Acoustic Event Detection (AED) is a recent sub-area of computational auditory scene analysis (Wang and Brown, 2006) that deals with the first objective. AED processes acoustic signals and converts those into symbolic descriptions corresponding to a listener's perception of the different sound events that are present in the signals and their sources.
Life-log is a chronological list of activities performed by the user with respect to time. Such a list might indicate the user's well-being or abnormality according to the consideration of the person's self assessment or by someone else who cares about the person (e.g., relatives or care-givers). Therefore we apply the concept of AED to perform automatic generation of life-log. This life-log can be transmitted autonomously as a simple text message to someone else with the notion of ambient communication.

Life logs include people's activities performed in specific locations at a specific time and it can be collected from various sources. We envisage that with the proliferation of computing power of hand held devices (HHD), availability of the Internet connectivity and improvements in communication technologies ambient communication will find a universal place at our daily life and allow us to realize virtual living through ambient social communication. Let's consider the following scenario of a globalized family.

Scenario 1: Rahman family (Mr. and Mrs. Rahman) lives in Khulna, one of the metropolitan cities of Bangladesh. They have three sons living overseas, one in Texas, another in Ottawa and the youngest one in Bonn of Germany. Both Mr. and Mrs. Rahman are now at their age of over 50 and Mr. Rahman had a massive heart operation last year. Mrs. Rahman is also ailing from several sicknesses like diabetics, high blood pressure, etc. The three sons are always worried regarding the well being of their parents and consequently they often talk to their parents over the phones to know their whereabouts. Though calling to Khulna, Bangladesh from USA, Canada, and Germany is relatively cheaper now-a-days than before, but having a phone conversation with their parents is not always possible due to various reasons, for example, due to inconvenience in time differences (e.g., when it is 10 am in Khulna it is 11:00 pm in Texas, 12:00 am in Ottawa and 6:00 am in Bonn) that is, when the sons have convenient time to call, their parents are usually sleeping or resting. But they are often worried to know at least how their parents are doing everyday. Therefore, let's imagine that Rahman family has internet connectivity at their home and installed an inexpensive system capable of doing the followings. The system makes automatic life-logging of daily activities by detecting and recognizing sound cues from their surrounding environments and sends email message(s) to their sons reporting their daily life-sketch. In this case, an example email message containing life log for a particular day, as follows, might be very relieving to the sons. *"Your parents woke up at 7:30 am today and they had breakfast around 8:15 in the morning. They watched TV several times in the day. Went out of home for two times and walked in the roads and parks. They took lunch and dinner at around 2 PM and 8 PM. Your mother went to toilet for 5 times and father went to toilet 6 times in a day. They had communicated with each other or other people by talking. It seems they are doing fine."*

In this chapter, we describe a listening test made to facilitate the direct comparison of the system's performance to that of human subjects. A forced choice test with identical test samples and reference classes for the subjects and the system is used. The second main concern in this chapter is to evaluate how acceptable the automatic generation of life-log is. Since we are dealing with a highly varying acoustic material where practically any imaginable sounds can occur, we have limited our scope in terms of location and the activities to recognize at a particular location. It is most likely that the acoustic models we are using are not able to sufficiently model the observation statistics. Therefore, we propose using discriminative training instead of conventional maximum likelihood training.

The chapter is organized as follows: Section 3 reviews the background studies related to this research. Our approach, in terms of system architecture and description of the system components is explained in Section 4. Section 5 discusses about several development challenges and our response towards those. Section 6 explains the experimental setup, the results obtained by the detection and classification system as well as user evaluations. Conclusions are presented in Section 7.

3. Background

A number of researchers have investigated to infer activities of daily living (ADL). Mihailidis et al. (2001) have successfully used cameras and a bracelet to infer hand washing. Wan (1999) used radio-frequency-identification (RFID) tags functionally as contact switches to infer when users took medication. The system discussed in (Barger et al., 2002) used contact switches, temperature switches, and pressure sensors to infer meal preparation. Tran et al. (2001) used cameras to infer meal preparation. Glascock and Kutzik (2000) used motion and contact sensors, combined with a custom-built medication pad, to get rough inference on meal preparation, toileting, taking medication, and up-and-around transference. A custom wearable computer with accelerometers, temperature sensors, and conductivity sensors to infer activity level is used in (Korhonen et al., 2003). Mozer (1998) used 13 sensors to infer home energy use, focusing on the heating-use activity. Motion detectors to infer rough location were used in (Campo and Chan, 2002). Several sensors like motion sensors, pressure pads, door latch sensors, and toilet flush sensors to infer behavior are reported in the system described in (Guralnik and Haigh, 2002). Chen et al. (2005) have described monitoring bathroom activities based on sound. The system (Philipose et al., 2004) utilized RFID tags to detect objects and thereby inference of activities is done from the interaction with the detected objects. The research on MIT's *house_n* project (MIT house_n, 2008) places a single type of object-based adhesive sensor in structurally unmodified homes and sensor readings are later analyzed for various applications—kitchen design, context sampling, and potentially ADL monitoring. All of these systems have a commonality that they perform high-level inference from low-level by coarse sensor data reporting and analyses. Some have added special pieces of hardware to help performance improvement, but progress toward accurate ADL detection has nevertheless been slow. Only a few researchers have reported the results of any preliminary user testing (Mihailidis et al., 2001; Glascock and Kutzik, 2000; Campo and Chan, 2002; Guralnik and Haigh, 2002). The level of inference using sensors has often been limited, for example, reporting only that a person entered the living room and spent time there. Moreover, as an example, research aiming to detect hand washing or tooth brushing have had nearly no synergy, each using its own set of idiosyncratic sensors and algorithms on those sensors. Furthermore a home deployment kit designed to support all these ADLs would be a mass of incompatible and non-communicative widgets. Our approach instead focuses on a general inference engine and infers activities from the sound cues that are likely to be produced either naturally or from the interactions with objects. Thus we can use our system for a broader range of ADLs.

The idea of a "life-log" or a personal digital archive is a notion that can be traced back at least 60 years (Bush, 1945). Since then a variety of modern projects have spawned such as the *Remembrance Agent* (Rhodes and Starner, 1996), *the Familiar* (Clarkson and Pentland, 1999; Clarkson et al., 2001), *myLifeBits* (Gemmell et al, 2002), *Memories for Life* (Fitzgibbon and Reiter, 2003) and *What Was I Thinking* (Vemuri and Bender, 2004). In (Blum et al., 2006) the authors evaluate the user's context in real time and then use variables like current location, activity, and social interaction to predict moments of interest. Audio and video recordings using a wearable device can then be triggered specifically at those times, resulting in more interest per recording. Some previous examples of this approach are the Familiar and *iSensed* systems (Clarkson and Pentland, 1999; Clarkson et al., 2001; Blum et al., 2006) which structure multimedia on the fly; the *eyeBlog* system (Dickie et al., 2004) which records video each time eye contact is established; and the *SenseCam* (Gemmell et al, 2004), which records images and sound whenever there's a significant change in the user's environment or the user's movement. Life log includes people's experiences which are collected from various sensors and stored in mass storage device. It is used to support user's memory and satisfy user's needs for personal information. If he wants to inform other people of his experience, he can easily share his experience with them by means of providing his life log.

To collect life log (e.g., GPS based location, SMS, call, charging, MP3, photos taken, images viewed, and weather information, etc) smart phones (e.g., iPhone 3G) are usually used. Smart phone is a mobile device that includes color LCD screen, mass storage, large memory, and communicative function by using Wi-Fi, Bluetooth, and infrared. It also has a variety of softwares like scheduler, address book, media player, and e-book. Raento et al., (2005) developed a framework for collecting contexts from smart phone which collects GSM Cell ID, Bluetooth, GPS data, phone data, SMS data, and media information that are transmitted to the server. The contexts could be provided for other contents as additional information. Panu *et al.* collect log data from mobile devices, and extracts features by pre-processing the log data (Panu et al., 2003). The mobile device uses GPS log, microphone, temperature, moisture, and light sensor. *MyLifeBits* Project is one of the implementations of personal record database system (Gemmell et al, 2002). Personal information is collected by PC, *SenseCam* and so on, and stored in database server with relationships among personal information. However, user faces difficulties to explore and search contents because of large amount of personal data. KeyGraph-based mobile contents management system was suggested to manage user's information in mobile device, which extracted important information using KeyGraph algorithm and provided searching or exploring contents (Kim et al., 2007). The problem of the system is using only log data. If analysis and inference of the data was added to the system, it would give better performance.

Our work differs from others in three key ways. First, we utilize environmental sounds cues to infer the interactions with objects or environment instead of sensor or camera data. Thus we can identify a large set of objects like spoons, toothbrushes, plates etc. Second, due to simple use of portable microphone to capture environmental sound we can also infer outdoor environments like on the road, in a park, in a train station etc., that previous research was limited to perform. Thirdly, our model is easy to incorporate new a set of activities for further needs by just adding more appropriately annotated sound clips and re-training the HMM based recognizer.

4. Our approach

Our approach to log daily events employs the technique to detect activities of daily living (e.g., laughing, talking, traveling, cooking, sleeping, etc.) and situational aspects of the person (e.g., inside a train, at a park, at home, at school, etc.). The system infers human-activity from environmental and object-interaction related sound cues as well as common-sense knowledge. Initially, with a view to creating a sound corpus of environmental sounds, 114 types of acoustic sounds are collected that are usually produced during object interaction (e.g., cooking pan jingling sound while cooking) or by the environment itself (e.g., bus/car passing sound while on a road) or by a deliberate action of a person (e.g., laughing, speaking). This sound corpus serves the purpose to train the system to infer a person's activity and one's surroundings with the help of common-sense knowledge. For example, for a sound-clip recorded from the environment at a particular time if the system identifies cooking pan's jingling and chopping-board's sound as consecutive cues and the system's local time indicates evening then from common-sense database the system infers this activity as 'cooking' for the input.

4.1 System architecture

The top-level pipelined architecture of the system is portrayed by Figure 1. Due to the rapid development and popularity of Hand Held Devices (HHD), HHD (e.g., portable computer or smart phone) has been considered as an implementation medium to deploy this application as an "always on" type system. The application pays heed to the environment to capture environmental sound continually with due intervals (in this case 10 seconds) and thereafter that recorded sound-clips are be processed. According to Figure 1, a sound-clip resulted from the listening of the environment, is passed through a robust signal processing and sound cues are detected by the trained HMM classifiers. HMM classifiers are trained using the collected sound corpus. Based on the detected sound cues and common-sense knowledge regarding human activity, object interaction, ontology of human life (e.g., daily life of a student, or a salary man etc.) and temporal information (e.g., morning, noon etc.) are applied to infer the activity and the surrounding environment of the person. This information is then stored in the log of activities as English sentences.

4.2 Description of system components

In this section the system components are described briefly.

4.2.1 Sound corpus

The patterns of sounds arising from activities occurring naturally or due to interaction with the objects are obviously a function of a many environmental variables like size and layout

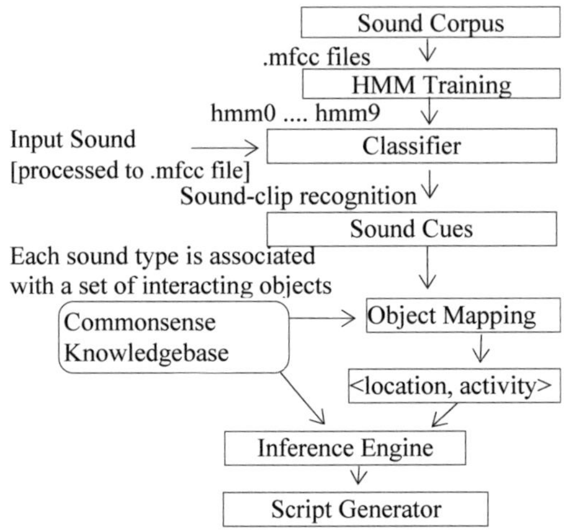

Fig. 1. The System's Architecture

or the indoor environment, material of the floors and walls, type of objects (e.g., electrical or mechanical) and persistent ambient noise present in the environment etc. In is essential to install this system to the same culture and environment from where sound samples are acquired and proper training of the system is made. It is analogous to the practice adopted for speech recognition whereby the system is individually trained on each user for speaker dependent recognition because such environmental sounds may vary in different cultures and places. Therefore the sample sounds we have collected are from the different places of Tokyo city and Tokyo University. For clear audio-temporal delineation during system training, the sound capture for each activity of interest was carried out separately. A number of male and female subjects were used to collect the sounds of interest; each subject would typically go into the particular situation as depicted in Table I with the sound recording device and the generated sounds are recorded. We used the digital sound recorder of SANYO (model number: ICR-PS380RM) and signals were recorded as Stereo, 44.1 KHz, .wav formatted files. It is important to note that in the generation of these sounds, associated 'background' sounds such as the ambient noise, rubbing of feet, friction with cloths, undressing, application of soap, etc., are being simultaneously recorded. The

Location	Activities
Living Room	Listening Music, Watching TV, Talking, Sitting Idle, Cleaning (e.g., by vacuum-cleaning)
Work Place	Sitting idle, Working with PC, Drinking
Kitchen	Cleaning, Drinking, Eating, Cooking
Toilet	Washing, Urinating, Flushing out
Gym	Exercising
Train Station	Waiting for Train
Inside Train	Traveling by Train
Public Place	Shopping, Traveling on Road
On the Road	Traveling on Road

Table 1. List of locations and activities of our interest

variability in the captured sounds of the each activity provides realistic input for system training, and increases the robustness and predictive power of the resultant classifier. Some sounds (e.g., water falling, vacuum cleaning machine sounds etc.) are generally loud and fairly consistent. There are samples that needed to sufficiently train the classification model due to a high degree of variability even for the same individual. For example, hands washing, drinking, eating, typing related sounds exhibited a high degree of variability. This required us to collect many more samples for such kind of activities related sounds to capture the diversity of the sounds. According to the location and activities of our interest mentioned in Table I, we have collected 114 types of sounds. Each of the sound types has 15 samples of varying length from 10 second to 25 seconds.
The typical waveforms and energy spectrum of the water related sounds of three different actions are shown in Fig. 2. As can be seen, the water splashing on hand or face (frame 1), toilet flushing (frame 2), shower water (frame 3), the sounds as depicted in the waveforms and spectrum have distinct patterns, different durations, energy spectrum and amplitudes.

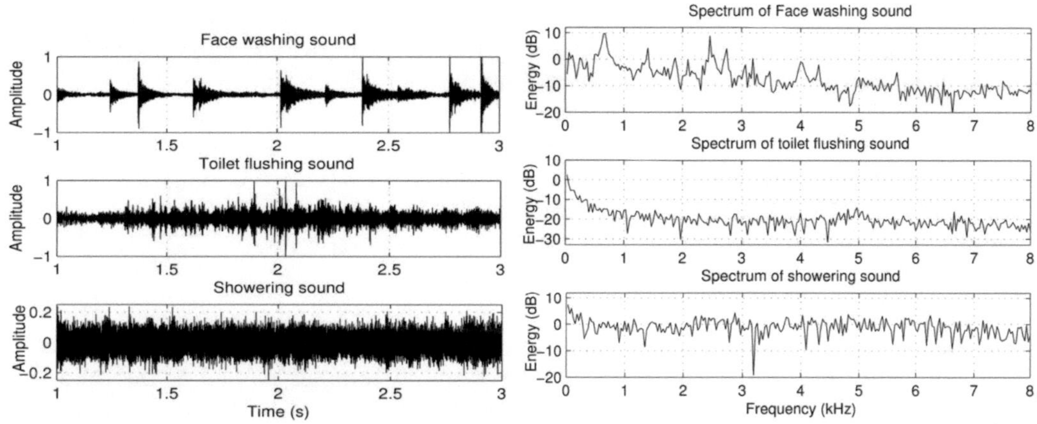

Fig. 2. Waveforms of different water related sound types

4.2.2 HMM training

An accurate and robust sound classifier is critical to the overall performance of the system. There are however many classifier approaches in the literature, e.g., those based on Hidden Markov Models (HMMs), Artificial Neural Networks (ANN), Dynamic Time Warping (DTW), Gaussian Mixture Models (GMM), etc. From these options, we have chosen an approach based on HMM as the model has a proven track record for many sound classification applications (Cowling, 2004; Okuno et al., 2004; Rabiner and Juang, 1993). Another advantage is that it can be easily implemented using the HMM Tool Kit (HTK) (Young, 1995), which is an open source Toolkit available on the Internet. It is also notifying that HTK was originally designed for speech recognition, which means we need to adapt the approach when applying it for environmental sounds of our interest.
Each sound file, corresponding to a sample of a sound type, was processed in frames pre-emphasized and windowed by a Hamming window (25 ms) with an overlap of 50%. A feature vector consisting of a 39-order MFCC characterized each frame. We modeled each sound using a left-to-right forty-state continuous-density HMM without state skipping.

Each HMM state was composed of two Gaussian mixture components. After a model initialization stage was done, all the HMM models were trained in eight iterative cycles.

4.2.3 Classifier

It was obvious that simple frequency characterization would not be robust enough to produce good classification results. To find representative features, previous study (Cowling, 2004) carried out an extensive comparative study on various transformation schemes, including the Fourier Transform (FT), Homomorphic Cepstral Coefficients (HCC), Short Time Fourier Transform (STFT), Fast Wavelet Transform (FWT), Continuous Wavelet Transform (CWT) and Mel-Frequency Cepstral Coefficient (MFCC). It was concluded that MFCC might be the best transformation for non-speech environmental sound recognition. A similar opinion was also articulated in (Okuno et al., 2004; Eronen et al., 2003). These finding provide the essential motivation for us to use MFCC in extracting features for environmental sound classification.

For classification, continuous HMM recognition is used. The grammar used is as follows: (<alarm_clock | ambulance | body_spray | chop_board | cycle_bell | dish_cleaning | egg_fry | face_wash | female_cough | toilet_flush | food_eating | gargle | hair_dry | in_open_air_train | insect_semi | in_shower | in_subway_train | in_train_station | liquid_stir | lunch_time_cafe | male_cough | male_male_Speak | male_sniff | meeting_talk | microwave_oven | paper_flip | phone_vibration | plate_clutter | plate_knife | silence | pan_spoon | tap_water | tooth_brush | train_enter_leave | tv_watching | urination | vacuum_cleaner | vehicle_pass | water_basin | water_sink>), which means that there is no predefined sequence for all the activities and each activity may be repeated at time at any sequence.

4.2.4 Sound cues

The present system deals with 114 types of sounds that are grouped into 40 sound cues to infer 17 kinds of activities. For example, we have sound samples named as the following types, "eating soba", "food munching", "belching", "spoon plate friction", which are grouped into one sound cue called "food_eating". Similarly, the sound samples named as, "news on TV", "talk-show on TV", "baseball game on TV", "football game on TV" are grouped into "tv_watching" sound cue. By such grouping of the samples into a particular sound cue, we mean that the group of samples is used to train the classifier to recognize that particular sound cue. In this manner the present system is limited to 40 sound cues.

4.2.5 Object mapping

Each of the sound cue is annotated with a list of objects considering that those objects are conceptually connected or related to that particular sound cue. For example, Table 2 provides a set of sound cues along with the associated list of objects pertaining to the corresponding sound cue. After the classifier has detected an input sound sample to a particular sound cue, the "object mapping" module returns a list of associated object that are mapped to that particular sound cue. This list of object resolved from the sound cues are given to the common-sense knowledge module to facilitate activity inference.

4.2.6 Commonsense knowledgebase

Once the system gets the list of objects pertaining to the recognized sound cues, it calculates the probability of each object involved to the activities of our interest. For example, the

Sound Cue	Mapped Objects
vehicle_pass	road, bus, car, cycle, wind, people
toilet_flush	water, toilet, toilet-flush
in_shower	bathroom, shower, towel, water, body-wash
in_open_air_train	train, journey, people, announcement
food_eating	soba, noodle, people, chop stick, soup, rice, plate, cutleries, food, kitchen, restaurant
TV_watching	TV, game, living room, news
train_enter_leave	people, train, announcement, station
water_basin	restroom, water basin, wash, hand soap
water_sink	kitchen, sink, water, dish washer

Table 2. Sample list of sound classes and mapped objects

activity "eating" usually involves objects like food, plate, people and water. Requiring humans to specify the probabilities of involvement would be time consuming and difficult. Instead, an automatic approached is developed so that the system determines the probabilities by utilizing a technique adopted from Semantic Orientation (SO) (Hatzivassiloglou and McKeown, 1997; Grefenstette et al., 2004), employing NEAR search operator of AltaVista's web search result. The technique is described briefly as follows:

List of objects, $O = \{O_1, O_2, \ldots O_K\}$ (K=63)

List of locations, $L = \{L_1, L_2, \ldots L_M\}$ (M=9)

List of activities, $A = \{A_1, A_2, \ldots A_N\}$ (N=17)

Each location is represented by a set of English synonym words. $WL_i = \{W_1, W_2, \ldots, W_P\}$. For example, L_1= "kitchen" and it is represented by, $W_{kitchen}$ = {"kitchen", "cookhouse", "canteen", "cuisine"}

$SA(O_i\,|\,L_j)$ = Semantic Associative value representing the object O_i to be associated with location L_j

$SA(O_i\,|\,A_j)$ = Semantic Associative value representing the object O_i to be associated with activity A_j

The formulae to get the *SA* values are indicated by Equation 1 and 2.

$$SA(O_i \mid L_j) = \log_2\left(\frac{\prod_{W \in WL_j} hits(O_i \text{ NEAR } W)}{\prod_{W \in WL_j} \log_2(hits(W))}\right) \tag{1}$$

$$SA(O_i \mid A_j) = \log_2\left(\frac{hits(O_i \text{ NEAR } A_j)}{\log_2(hits(A_j))}\right) \tag{2}$$

The obtained values support the concept that if an activity name and location co-occurs often with some object name in human discourse, then the activity will likely involve the object in the physical world. An excerpt from the list of SA values is provided in Figure 3.

Our approach is in the spirit of such manner while we use these obtained values as commonsense knowledgebase to assign a semantic associative value to the object pertaining to a sound sample as a model of relatedness in human activity. Thus, for example, if the system detects that the sound samples represent frying, saucepan, water sink, water, and

Object/Concept	Living Room	Work Place	Kitchen	Toilet	Gym	Inside Train	Train Station	Public Place	On Road	Max	Main Location
alarm	13.4523	10.9779	15.6387	14.3182	13.5427	13.6354	12.5480	14.7602	26.5531	26.5531	On Road
ambulance	10.6623	9.8535	10.3223	10.4926	9.0773	13.2013	11.7684	13.9239	28.2662	28.2662	On Road
announcement	14.3604	11.1248	16.0972	9.2678	10.5512	13.8032	26.1961	17.9592	12.9867	26.1961	Train Station
basin	12.7283	5.9383	16.1699	28.9758	8.7026	11.7622	10.0058	13.9179	16.5886	28.9758	Toilet
bicycle	12.0660	11.0806	13.8415	12.0582	13.3464	15.3610	13.5217	15.2338	32.6992	32.6992	On Road
blender machine	11.8717	3.0209	13.9110	9.2424	9.4124	8.9493	5.4949	7.5778	8.4731	13.9110	Kitchen
boiling	9.5302	6.1547	24.4261	9.4636	6.5960	9.6467	6.4360	11.0327	20.3290	24.4261	Kitchen
bottle	13.0488	9.5051	26.6152	14.2667	13.1362	14.0160	11.7199	13.2167	19.7792	26.6152	Kitchen
bowl	13.7426	9.8700	17.8777	14.2508	12.7417	13.9041	11.0942	14.3702	16.6401	17.8777	Kitchen
bus	14.2397	12.9289	14.6048	13.9183	14.3850	20.2331	19.0066	17.8408	35.9963	35.9963	On Road
car	17.1100	14.6828	18.1602	16.0323	16.8431	20.0676	18.1988	18.4553	39.7680	39.7680	On Road
cash register	12.1217	9.9955	11.9475	9.4562	9.6013	11.4610	9.5857	25.1415	17.6097	25.1415	Public Place
CD player	25.6021	9.1017	16.1107	12.8777	12.4728	12.5130	10.2689	13.8115	15.8466	25.6021	Living Room
chopping board	8.5498	3.8075	14.2755	7.0313	4.6498	9.3692	8.6712	11.5121	7.8466	14.2755	Kitchen
computer	16.3240	31.8790	17.5224	14.1969	15.2711	16.4552	13.8168	17.9183	23.2398	31.8790	Work Place
computer keyboard	12.3061	18.7801	10.6458	2.6458	10.2165	11.9073	9.1364	11.6065	14.6086	18.7801	Work Place
computer mouse	13.2372	23.1333	14.8366	9.0008	9.6654	11.8587	9.7082	10.4672	13.3829	23.1333	Work Place
cracking	10.6623	9.0055	11.8475	9.3253	8.5748	10.3801	8.2313	12.0505	13.3048	13.3048	On Road
drawer	12.9415	7.9088	22.7453	11.3453	9.7799	12.5932	9.0008	10.9119	12.3491	22.7453	Kitchen
dumbbell	3.7768	0.3912	5.6062	2.7826	13.1475	8.9878	4.0432	4.0513	7.5435	13.1475	Gym
electric train	11.7125	9.1475	11.3674	12.0942	10.6748	21.0071	25.2866	19.5850	20.0099	25.2866	Train Station
electric train door	12.4523	5.1316	13.4495	11.7333	9.6903	20.9529	16.2980	13.1332	12.5128	20.9529	Inside Train
escalator	6.2726	4.2041	8.3290	8.1634	7.7694	12.6316	12.1842	22.2830	15.5998	22.2830	Public Place
exhaust fan	10.6772	5.5149	19.1245	11.4133	6.1127	9.4541	6.4716	10.2535	9.2111	19.1245	Kitchen
female voice	12.8120	10.0351	12.0059	10.2803	9.3277	12.6765	11.5340	14.7703	13.0861	14.7703	Public Place
flush	11.4644	8.6960	14.3849	23.2391	9.1508	10.6882	8.9278	12.9179	17.8435	23.2391	Toilet
free weights	9.9000	5.6122	11.2942	8.2078	21.1491	13.4281	9.2604	11.1668	12.1073	21.1491	Gym
frying	8.6380	2.7667	16.6655	7.0626	4.5181	9.4947	4.3209	8.8550	11.5229	16.6655	Kitchen
gas	17.6590	13.1532	21.5666	15.1191	13.2346	15.7500	14.0495	17.6987	19.1024	21.5666	Kitchen
glass mug	16.3417	12.7021	30.9630	15.6146	13.5848	15.0419	13.2498	15.1203	26.0057	30.9630	Kitchen
hot drink	13.3394	9.5398	25.4527	13.7928	12.0367	12.9505	11.4037	14.1870	20.6605	25.4527	Kitchen

Fig. 3. Semantic Associative (SA) values for objects and locations of our interest

chopping board from consecutive input samples the commonsense knowledge usually infers a cooking activity located in kitchen.

Moreover we have also considered another kind of knowledge namely, ontology of daily-life that contains usual routines of peoples of different roles in terms of their presence at specific locations at specific time. In this initial prototyping three types of users are considered and based on empirical study the ontology of daily life (listed in Table 3) of each type of user is considered along with common sense knowledge base to perform legitimate inference. For example, if the system detects a sound cue related to eating activity during BN (before noon) time frame on a weekday and if the user is a service-holder, it doesn't log the event because the user is not happened to be present in a kitchen around that time. We also plan to provide the flexibility to personalize such ontology of daily life on the basis of each respective user.

Role	Weekday							Weekend						
	EM	M	BN	AN	E	N	LN	EM	M	BN	AN	E	N	LN
Graduate Student	H	H, T	H, U, K,T, R, Tr	U, G, T, P	H, U, R, Tr, K, T, G, P	H, U, R, Tr, K, T, P	H, K, T	H	H, T	H, K,T, R, Tr	G, T, P	H, R, Tr, K, T, G, P	H, R, Tr, K, T, P	H, K, T
Service-Holder	H	H, K, T, R, Tr	O, T	O, T	O, T, H, R, Tr, P	H, P, R, Tr, T	H	H	H, K, T	H, T, P, R, Tr	H, T, P, R, Tr, G	H, T, R, Tr, P	H, P, R, Tr, T	H
Elderly People	H, T	H, T, R, K	H, T, R, Tr, P	H, T, R, Tr, P	H, T, R, Tr, K, P	H	H,T	H, T	H, T, R, K	H, T, R, Tr, P	H, T, R, Tr, P	H, T, R, Tr, K, P	H	H,T

H: Home; O: Office; U: University; K: Kitchen; T: Toilet; G: Gym; R: Road; Tr: Train; P: Public place EM: Early Morning [03:00 – 05:00], M: Morning [05:00 – 8:00], BN: Before Noon [8:00 – 12:00], AN: After Noon [12:00 – 17:00], E: Evening [17:00 – 20:00], N: Night [20:00 – 01:00], LN: Late Night [01:00 – 03:00]

Table 3. An example of Ontology of daily life

4.2.7 Inference engine
The system continuously listens to the environment but it records sounds for ten seconds with an interval of ten seconds pause between two recordings. Thus for a minute the system gets three sound clips of equal length (i.e., ten seconds) that serves as the input to the classifier to get three sound cues in one minute. After that the object-mapping module provides a list of objects pertaining to the recognized sound cues. In this manner, the system produces a list of objects at every minute. The inference engine works by considering the list of objects that are prepared in every three minutes of time. This list of objects is then consulted with the involvement probabilities of activities stored in the commonsense knowledge base. An example of inference process is described in the sub-section "A Schematic Solution".

4.2.8 Script generator
At a preset specific time (e.g., midnight of each day) the whole day's activities are summarized and a daily report is automatically generated and archived at a database for further references. This report typically contains a consolidation of the frequency of occurrences of major activities of interest. A series of pre-prepared words are used and intelligently strung together to form simple sentences that conform to the basic rules of English grammar. An example of this is given as following:

Daily Report of Mr. Rahman's Activity, December 12, 2008

Mr. Rahman woke up at 8:20 am in the morning. He went to bathroom then. He had his breakfast at 9:38 am. He spent most of his time in living room. He watched TV. He had lunch at 2:13 PM. He talked with people. He went out and walked by the roads during evening. He didn't take shower today. At night he talked with someone.

The generated script is then automatically emailed to preset email address. The archival of these daily reports may enable a caregiver or a doctor to review records very quickly and in the process, build a detailed understanding of the subject's daily behavioral/activity patterns.

4.3 A schematic solution
The system continuously listens to the environment and captures sound regularly at 10 seconds of interval for 10 seconds of duration. Each captured sound-clip is sent to a computer wirelessly where the clip is processed. Thus for a three-minute interval the system gets nine sound clips. These nine sound clips are considered to infer an activity at that moment. Each sound clip is processed by a HMM classifier that outputs a particular sound cue. Each sound cue actually represents some real-word objects out of which interaction the sound maybe produced. For example, Let's assume that the system received nine sound clips to process and the HMM classified those nine clips into the following five unique sound cues: "chop_board", "pan_spoon", "water_sink", "plate_clutter", and "plate_knife". These five classes of sounds are pre-mapped to the objects as following,
"chop_board" → {knife, chop-board, onion, meat, people}
"pan_spoon" → {cooking-pan, spoon, stirrer, people}
"water_sink" → {water-sink, water, dish-washer}

"plate_clutter" → {cup-board, plate, glass, saucepan, people}
"plate_knife" → {plate, knife, spoon, people}
The list of interacting objects is consulted with the Semantic Associative (SA) value of the activities and locations stored in the commonsense knowledgebase. From this example, the unique list of objects obtained from the sound cues, U= {chop-board, cooking-pan, cup-board, dish-washer, glass, knife, meat, onion, people, plate, saucepan, spoon, water-sink, water, stirrer}. In this case, the objects yield a maximum SA value of having a relationship with "cooking" activity in "kitchen" location and the near candidates are "eating", "drinking tea/coffee" as activities. From the ontology of daily life the system finds that it is likely to have "cooking" activity at the concerned time (i.e., Table 3). Therefore, the activity inference engine considers this event as a legitimate event and logs it by either animating this event on a virtual world or generating a text message. This schematic solution is depicted in Figure 4.

5. Development challenges

In order to develop this system we have the following challenges and concerns:

5.1 Environmental sound corpus and features

For simplicity our collected sound corpus is limited to sound cues related to certain genres like, cooking, bathroom activity, human physiological action, outdoor, home, etc. Since the recognition rate is the only performance measure of such system, it is hard to judge how suitable the selected feature is. To solve this problem, it is essential to analyze the feature itself, and measure how good the feature itself is. It is concluded that MFCC may be the best transformation for non-speech environmental sound recognition (Okuno et al., 2004). This finding provides the essential motivation for us to use MFCC in extracting features for environmental sound classification.

5.2 Computing power of iPhone or Hand Held Devices

The computing potentials of HHDs are increasing in a rapid manner with respect to memory and incorporation of full-fledged operating system but they are still inferior to personal computer comparing to the speed of data processing. Running of the core signal-processing task requires high-end computing and therefore the processing should be done by means of external devices connected to the HHDs through the Bluetooth or wireless data transmission. Therefore in this case a light process to capture environmental sounds after some intervals will be running on the HHDs to be transmitted wirelessly to a server for activity detection.

5.3 Privacy and social issues

To manage their exposure, users should be able to disconnect from the virtual worlds at any time or be able to interrupt the sound capturing of their activities. The actual representation of users in the virtual world may be disclosed according to pre-configured user policies or users list. Additional privacy issues are related to the collection of environmental data by means of people carrying devices to different places and data collected about them. We consider important privacy and security challenges related to people-centric sensing (Mihailidis et al., 2001; Wan 1999; Barger et al., 2002).

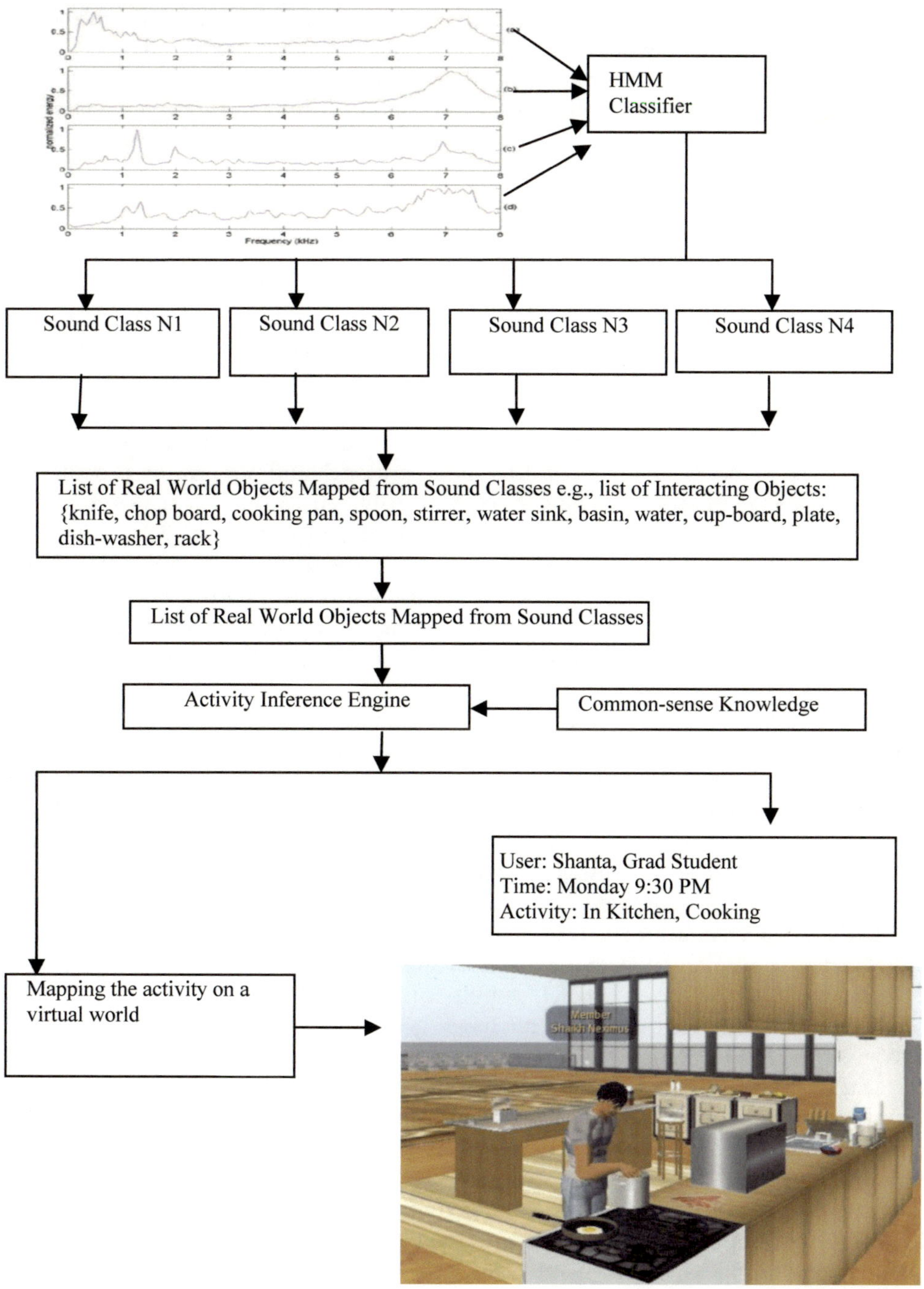

Fig. 4. An schematic solution of our approach

5.4 Scalability of the solution

Our default approach is to run activity recognition algorithms on the mobile HHDs to decrease communication costs and also to reduce the computational burden on the server. However, we recognize that signal processing based classification algorithms may be too computationally intensive for present HHDs and propose to run the classifier on a back-end server in this case. This may be particularly appropriate during the training phase of a classification model.

6. Experiment results and discussion

The purpose is to test the performance of the system in recognizing the major activities of our interest. The system was trained and tested to recognize the following 17 activities: Listening Music, Watching TV, Talking, Sitting Idle, Cleaning, Sitting idle, Working with PC, Drinking, Eating, Cooking, Washing, Urinating, Exercising, Waiting for Train, Traveling by Train, Shopping, Traveling on Road. As explained earlier, the sound samples recording for each activity was carried out separately. For example, for Listening Music, each subject played a piece of music of his/her choice, with this repeated a number of times for the same individual. The other subjects followed the same protocol and the entire process was repeated for developing the sound corpus for each activity being tested. It is also noted that we have various kinds of sounds (i.e., different sound-clip types) that are grouped together to represent one particular activity. The training data set was formed utilizing a 'leave-one-out' strategy. That is, all the samples would be used for their corresponding models' training except those included in the signal under testing. Hence, each time the models were trained respectively to ensure that the samples in the testing signal were not included in the training data set.

Since each sound clip resolves to a set of objects pertaining to the recognized sound class which is then considered to infer activity and location related to that sound class, we developed perceptual testing methodology to evaluate the system's performance on continuous sound streams of various sound events to infer location and activity. 420 test signals were created, each of which contained a mixture of three sound clips of respective 114 sound types. Since these 420 test signals are the representative sound clues for the 40 sound classes to infer 17 activities, we grouped these 420 test signals into 17 groups according to their expected affinity to a particular activity and location. Ten human (i.e., five male, five female) judges were engaged to listen to the test signals and judge an input signal to infer the activity from the given list of 17 activities (i.e., forced choice judgment) as well as the possible location of that activity from the list of given nine locations of our choice. Each judge was given all the 17 groups of signals to listen and assess. The number of test signals in a group varied from 3 to 6 and each test signal was the result of three concatenated sound clips of same sound type. Therefore a judge had to listen each test signal to infer the location and activity that the given signal seemed most likely to be associated with. In the same way the signals were given to the system to process. For the system the entire group of signals was given at a time to output one location and activity for each group. Since human judges judged each signal individually, in order to compare the result with the system, a generalization on the human assessment was done. The generalization was done in the following manner. A group of signals had at lest more than 3 signals and each of the signals was assigned a location and activity label by the judges. Thus a group of signals obtained a list of locations and activities. We counted the frequencies of location and activity labels for each group assigned by each judge and took the maximum of the respective labels to finally assign the two types of labels (i.e., activity and location) for the group of signals. For each type of label, if more than one labels obtained equal frequency the random choice of the labels are considered. Thus we considered the judges' labels and system's inference with respect to the expected labels for the 17 groups of signals. Recognition results for activity and location are presented in Figure 5 and 6 respectively.

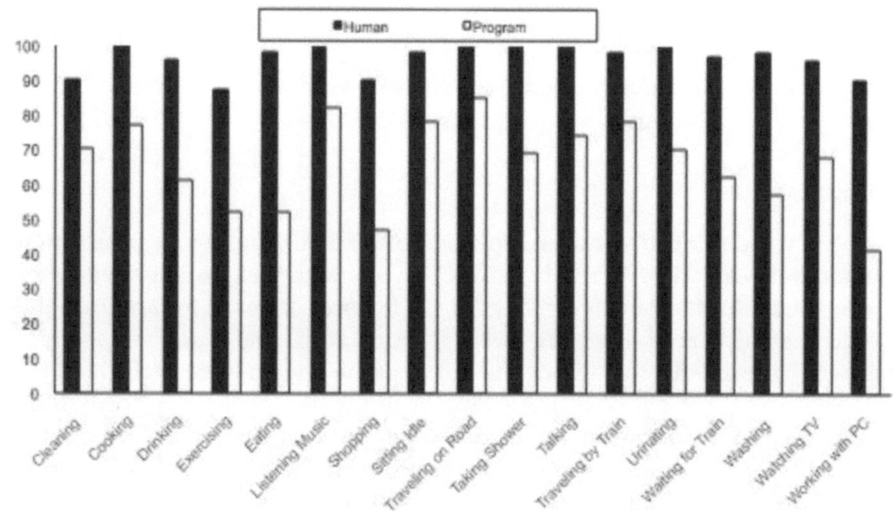

Fig. 5. Comparisons of recognition rates for 17 activities of our interest with respect to human judges

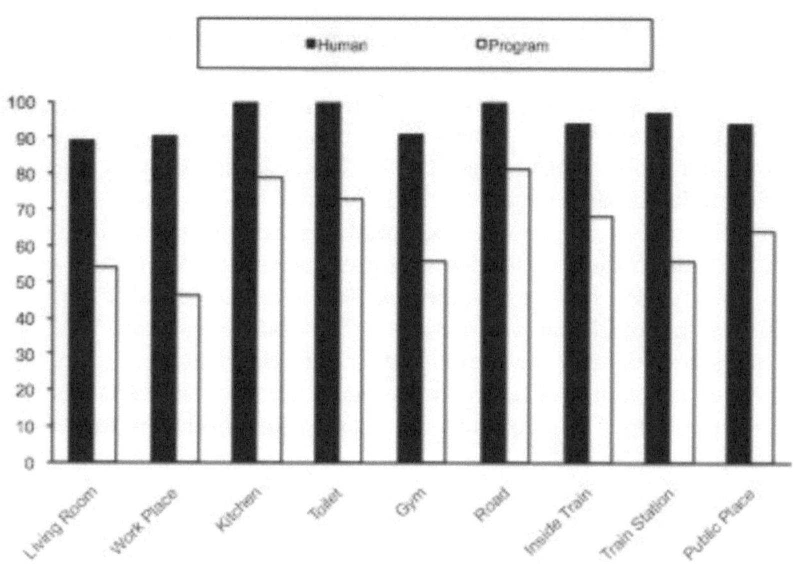

Fig. 6. Comparisons of recognition rates for 9 locations of our interest with respect to human judges

The recognition accuracy for activity and location is encouraging with most being above than 66% and 64% respectively. From Figure 5 and 6, we notice that humans are skillful in recognizing the activity and location from sounds (i.e., for humans' the average recognition accuracy of activity and location is 96% and 95% respectively). It is also evident that the system receives the highest accuracy (i.e., 85% and 81% respectively) to detect "traveling on road" activity and "road" location respectively, which is a great achievement and pioneer effort in this research that no previous research attempted to infer outdoor activities with sound cues. The correct classification of sounds related to activity "working with pc" and location "work place" were found to be very challenging due to the sounds' shortness in duration and weakness in strength, hence the increased frequency for them to be wrongly classified as 'silence' type sound class.

7. Conclusion

In this chapter, we described a novel acoustic indoor and outdoor activities monitoring system that automatically detects and classifies 17 major activities usually occur at daily life. Carefully designed HMM parameters using MFCC features are used for accurate and robust sound based activity and location classification with the help of commonsense knowledgebase. Experiments to validate the utility of the system were performed firstly in a constrained setting as a proof-of-concept and in future we plan to perform actual trials involving peoples in the normal course of their daily lives to carry the device running our application that listens to the environment and automatically logs the daily event based on the mentioned approach. Preliminary results are encouraging with the accuracy rate for outdoor and indoor sound categories for activities being above 67% and 61% respectively. We sincerely believe that the system contributes towards increased understanding of personal behavioral problems that significantly is a concern to caregivers or loving ones of elderly people. Besides further improving the recognition accuracy, we plan to enhance the capability of the system to identify different types of human vocalization, which provides useful information pertaining to the mental wellbeing of the subject. We also believe that integrating sensors into the system will also enable acquire better understanding of human activities. The enhanced system will be shortly tested in a full-blown trial on the most needy elderly peoples residing alone within the cities of Tokyo evaluating its suitability as a benevolent behavior understanding system carried by them.

This type of application may have another potential use. Software like Google Earth and Microsoft Virtual Earth map the real world with great accuracy in terms of geographical locations and local features. We believe that the next step is to enable a user to represent real world activities in this kind of virtual world whereby personal avatars will be able to reflect what the real persons are doing in the real world by inferring activities from sound cues. This type of application is a source of fun for young generation while it has lots of potential regarding virtual shopping mall in e-commerce context, easy monitoring for elderly people for the caregivers etc.

8. References

Chen, J; Kam, A. H., Zhang, J., Liu, N., and Shue, L. (2005). Bathroom Activity Monitoring Based on Sound, Proc. 3rd Int'l Conf, PERVASIVE 2005, Munich, Germany, LNCS 3468/2005, pp. 47-61.

Philipose, M ; Fishkin, K. P., Perkowitz, M., Patterson, D. J., Fox, D., Kautz, H., & HahnelInferring, D. (2004). Activities from Interactions with Objects. *IEEE Pervasive Computing*, Vol. 3, No. 4, pp. 50-57.

Temko, A. & Nadeu, C. (2005). Classification of meeting-room acoustic events with Support Vector Machines and Confusion-based Clustering. Proc. ICASSP'05, pp. 505-508.

Wang, D. & Brown, G. (2006). *Computational Auditory Scene Analysis: Principles, Algorithms and Applications.* Wiley-IEEE Press

Mihailidis, A. ; Fernie, G. & Barbenel, J.C. (2001). The Use of Artificial Intelligence in the Design of an Intelligent Cognitive Orthosis for People with Dementia. *Assistive Technology*, Vol. 13, No. 1, pp. 23–39.

Wan, D. (1999). Magic Medicine Cabinet: A Situated Portal for Consumer Healthcare. Proc. 1st Int'l Symp. Handheld and Ubiquitous Computing (HUC 99), LNCS 1707, Springer-Verlag, pp. 352–355.

Barger, T. ; Alwan, M., Kell, S., Turner, B., Wood, S., Naidu, A. (2002). Objective remote assessment of activities of daily living: Analysis of meal preparation patterns. Poster presentation, Medical Automation Research Center, University of Virginia Health System.

Tran, Q. ; Truong, K., & Mynatt, E. (2001). Cook's Collage: Recovering from Interruptions. demo at 3rd Int'l Conf. Ubiquitous Computing (Ubi-Comp 2001).

Glascock, A. & Kutzik, D. (2000). Behavioral Telemedicine: A New Approach to the Continuous Nonintrusive Monitoring of Activities of Daily Living. *Journal of Telemedicine.* Vol. 6, No. 1, pp. 33–44.

Korhonen, I. ; Paavilainen, P. & Särelä, A. (2003). Application of Ubiquitous Computing Technologies for Support of Independent Living of the Elderly in Real Life Settings. Proc. UbiHealth 2003: 2nd Int'l Workshop Ubiquitous Computing for Pervasive Healthcare Applications.

Mozer, M. (1998). The Neural Network House: An Environment That Adapts to Its Inhabitants. Proc. AAAI Spring Symposium. Intelligent Environments, tech. report SS-98-02, AAAI Press, pp. 110–114.

Campo, E. & Chan, M. (2002). Detecting Abnormal Behavior by Real-Time Monitoring of Patients. Proc. AAAI Workshop Automation as Caregiver, AAAI Press, pp. 8–12.

Guralnik, V. & Haigh, K. (2002). Learning Models of Human Behaviour with Sequential Patterns. Proc. AAAI Workshop Automation as Caregiver, AAAI Press, pp. 24–30.

house_n Project, http://architecture.mit.edu/house_n

Bush, V. (1945). As we may think, *Atlantic Monthly*, 1945

Rhodes, B. & Starner, T. (1996). Remembrance Agent: A Continuously Running Automated Information Retrieval System. Proc. 1st Int'l Conf. Practical App. of Intelligent Agents and Multi-Agent Technology, pp. 487-495.

Clarkson, B. & Pentland, A. (1999). Unsupervised Clustering of Ambulatory Audio and Video. Proc. IEEE Int'l Conf. Acoustics, Speech, and Signal Processing, IEEE CS Press, Vol. 6, pp. 3037-3040.

Clarkson, B. ; Mase, K. & Pentland, A. (2001). The Familiar: A Living Diary and Companion. Proc. ACM Conf. Computer–Human Interaction, ACM Press, pp. 271-272.

Gemmell, J ; Bell, G., Lueder, R., Drucker, S. & Wong, C. (2002). MyLifeBits: Fulfilling the Memex Vision. Proc. ACM Multimedia, ACM Press, pp. 235-238.

Fitzgibbon, A. & Reiter, E. (2003). 'Memories for Life': Managing Information over a Human Lifetime. UK Computing Research Committee Grand Challenge proposal.

Vemuri, S. & Bender, W. (2004). Next-Generation Personal Memory Aids. *BT Technology Journal*, Vol. 22, No. 4, pp. 125-138.

Blum, M. ; Pentland, A. & Troster, G. (2006). InSense: Internet-Based Life Logging. , Vol. 13, No. 4, pp.40-48.

Dickie, C. ; Vertegaal, R., Fono, D., Sohn, C., Chen, D., Cheng, D., Shell, J.S. & Aoudeh, O. (2004). Augmenting and sharing memory with eyeBlog. Proc. 1st ACM Workshop on Continuous Archival and Retrieval of Personal Experiences, ACM Press.

Gemmell, J. ; Williams, L., Wood, K., Lueder, R. & Bell, G. (2004). Passive Capture and Ensuing Issues for a Personal Lifetime Store. Proc. Continuous Archival and Retrieval of Personal Experiences, ACM Press.

Raento, M. ; Oulasvirta, A., Petit, R. & Toivonen, H. (2005). ContextPhone: A Prototyping Platform for Context-aware Mobile Applications. *IEEE Pervasive Computing*, vol 4, no 2, pp. 51–59.

Panu, K.; Jani, M., Juha, K., Heikki, K. & Esko-Juhani, M. (2003). ContextPhone: Managing Context Information in Mobile Devices. *IEEE Pervasive Computing*, vol 2, no 3, pp. 42–51.

Kim, K.; Jung, M. & Cho, S. (2007). KeyGraph-based chance discovery for mobile contents management system Source. Int'l Journal of Knowledge-based and Intelligent Engineering Systems archive, vol 11, no 5, pp.313-320.

Cowling, M. (2004). Non-Speech Environmental Sound Recognition System for Autonomous Surveillance, Ph.D. Thesis, Griffith University, Gold Coast Campus.

Okuno, H.G.; Ogata, T., Komatani, K. & Nakadai, K. (2004). Computational Auditory Scene Analysis and Its Application to Robot Audition. International Conference on Informatics Research for Development of Knowledge Society Infrastructure (ICKS), pp. 73–80

Eronen, A.; Tuomi, J., Klapuri, A., Fagerlund, S., Sorsa, T., Lorho, G. & Huopaniemi, J. (2003). Audio-based Context Awareness-Acoustic Modeling and Perceptual Evaluation. Proc. IEEE International Conference on Acoustics, Speech, and Signal Processing (ICASSP '03), vol. 5, pp. 529-532.

Rabiner, L. R. & Juang, B.H. (1993). Fundamentals of Speech Recognition, PTR Prentice-Hall Inc, New Jersey.

Young, S. (1995). The HTK Book, User Manual, Cambridge University Engineering Department.

Hatzivassiloglou, V. & McKeown, K. R. (1997). Predicting the Semantic Orientation of Adjectives. In 35th annual meeting on ACL, pp.174-181.

Grefenstette, G. ; Qu, Y. Evans, D. & Shanahan, J. (2004). Validating the Coverage of Lexical Resources for Affect Analysis and Automatically Classifying New Words along Semantic Axes. In Computing Attitude and Affect in Text: Theory and Applications, eds. J. Shanahan, Y. Qu, and J. Wiebe, 93-107. The Information Retrieval Series Vol. 20, Netherlands: Springer Verlag.

Part 3

Globalization and Natural Systems

10

Biodiversity, Ecosystem and Commodities in Amazonia

Peter Mann de Toledo[1], Ima Célia Guimarães Vieira[2], Gilberto Câmara[1], Roberto Araújo[1], Andrea Coelho[3] and Sergio Gomes[3]
[1]*Instituto Nacional de Pesquisas Espaciais*
[2]*Museu Paraense Emilio Goeldi*
[3]*Instituto de Desenvolvimento Econômico, Social e Ambiental do Pará*
Brazil

1. Introduction

The Amazonian Region has undergone constant pressure from human activities in the past 100 years, with dramatic changes in the landscapes caused by significant impacts on a great number of rainforest biotic communities. Historical data show that the last pulse of expansion of the forest, which initiated 4-5,000 years ago (Burnham & Johnson, 2004; Bush & Silman, 2007), has been permanently halted due to intensification of land use and occupation along the southern ecological contact zone between the forest and savanna ecosystems. Such a pristine environment, in similar scale and richness as witnessed by the first Europeans who arrived in South America and wrestled the land from the Native South Americans, can no longer be preserved or even restored to its original state. Almost twenty percent of the primeval Amazon tropical forest has been altered or destroyed in Brazil, the country that encompasses most of this diverse biome.

An important portion of this original information is now preserved in maps, natural history and anthropology books and scientific collections (Moran & Ostrom, 2009). Such documentation showing different pathways from these past 500 years is crucial to understand and learn from experiences of success and failure. Resiliency, adaptation and modification of a tropical environment rich in biodiversity have shaped a dynamic biome that shifted in magnitude and intensity in the past decades due to human activity (Joels & Camara, 2001; Buckeridge, 2008). Understanding these successive events is one of the most important challenges facing the modern scientific community. Accurate information on science and technology can potentially improve the future management of a complex tropical environment.

The current trend of environmental awareness as reflected in the conservation, ecological services, global change and sustainable activities at odds with economic growth and tensions caused by social injustice in tropical regions have placed Amazonia under a worldwide spotlight in terms of collective consciousness for nature preservation. To reduce human impact and simultaneously preserve indigenous and other traditional cultures have been top priorities in the agendas of most Non Governmental Organizations. The level of scientific publications on different aspects of biological diversity in Brazilian Amazonia has been constantly improving. Similarly, public and private institutions are experiencing new and more thorough forms of partnership, with mutually complementary agendas, joining forces toward common goals in multidisciplinary approaches. Such actions and institutional strategies are closing the knowledge gap on the measuring of the impact of deforestation on species ecology and habitat losses, as it has been perceived that natural landscapes are being destroyed much faster than one could possibly understand the functioning of such ecosystems and organisms (Stuart et. al. 2010).

With population growth at current rates, more land for agriculture and energy supply will be demanded. In this context, a new trend of pressure wave on the Amazonian forest has initiated. The high potential for hydroelectric power and the availability of extensive areas for food and biofuel production are additional threats to conservation efforts. A globalized world and the current Amazonian economic strength exerts increasing demands for productive terrains, increasing the tension on deforestation and land use.

In this chapter we will address the dynamics of human occupation of Amazon biome, present the problems and perspectives of the main commodities in Para state and discuss the mechanism of Reducing Emission from Forest Deforestation and Degradation (REDD) and the challenges for solving the infrastructure/biological conservation duality in Amazonia.

2. The Amazonian biome and the patterns of human occupation

Throughout the new Anthropocene Era, the ever-diminishing pristine habitats, arranged into isolated sets of natural landscapes around the globe, are changing at a speedy rate due to an unplanned pressure on natural resources in the form of aggressive, non-sustainable actions of land use and conversion into croplands. The Amazonian Region, together with the African Continent, is regarded as one of the few remaining lands appropriate for agricultural expansion in the tropics. An increase in human population, the expansion of most Third World economies taking whole populations out of poverty levels, and technological improvement of food production will maintain such an ongoing pressure trend. The awareness of such a menace to natural habitats is instigating the scientific community to engage in transdisciplinary programs in order to ensure developmental actions that are in conformity with the sustainable use of natural resources.

The Amazonian Region holds the largest tropical forest in the planet, with a very high number of biological species and increasing numbers in all biodiversity categories. Such diversity, in scale and complexity, receives worldwide attention vis-à-vis conservation efforts and scientific interest. The total area of the Amazon basin is of nearly 6.7 million square kilometers, including parts of Bolivia, Brazil, Colombia, Ecuador, French Guiana, Peru, Surinam and Venezuela. Amazonia is dominated by dense humid tropical forests, but also contains exclusive habitats such as lowland forests, seasonally flooded areas ('várzeas' and 'igapós'), open areas, marshes, bamboo-dominated vegetations, mountain forests and palm forests. The entire region encompasses an area 50% as larger as the 27 European countries. Not only Amazonia houses half of the preserved tropical forests of the world, it also includes the latter's largest freshwater basin. The Amazon River, the main river system in this region, discharges into the Atlantic Ocean a water volume equivalent to 15% of the total freshwater flowing into the oceans worldwide.

The natural history of Amazonia has been shaped and controlled by alternating dynamic phases with more stable environmental conditions, remodeling its landscapes since the Miocene age. Despite an overall comparatively less intensive change in climatic regimes if compared to other regions of the world, especially during more recent glacial periods with drier climates, those differences were subtle enough to induce new local and regional conditions that may have been an important driver in modifying terrestrial biotic communities through time. Pulses of expansion and retraction of forests mixed with savanna-like habitats have been extensively recorded in the region throughout its geological history, as were alterations in river patterns and strong tectonic activity. Altogether, such ecological conditions and evolutionary pressure played an important role in forming the present pattern of spatial species distribution and endemism, resulting in a rich biota unevenly distributed over an extensive geographical area. Nevertheless, forests appear to have been the dominant landscape during most of the Recent period, especially in the last 7 thousand years. Consequently, the Amazonian biota comprises both ancient and recent species. There have been eight areas of endemism identified by means of the distribution patterns of avian communities and some groups of terrestrial plants, to wit: Belém, Napo, Guiana,Tapajós, Imeri, Inambari, Xingu and Rondônia (Silva et al., 2005).

Scientists have estimated that, despite the ongoing extinction crises, there are between 111 million and 3.6 billion species living in the planet. But only 1.7 million of those have been known and described by science. According to Mittermeier et al., (2005), there are 17 megadiverse countries, harboring disproportionally large fauna e flora in their territories, and Brazil is singled out as the largest of them all. Considering species already described and the potential numbers of those groups yet to be known, Brazil may account for 13% of the world's biota -- some 1.8 million species. Despite the large number of lifeforms described for the country - 13,000 species of fungi, 60,000 plant species, 136,000 animal species - Brazilian biodiversity is still in need to be properly accounted for. In Amazonia, 40,000 plant species are known at the present, 75% of them endemic. And at least 430 mammals, 1,300 birds, 400 amphibians and 3,000 fish species are known by taxonomic names (Instituto de Pesquisa Econômica Aplicada [IPEA], 2011). Ongoing research using newly-developed techniques of DNA sequencing may even increase these numbers by distinguishing between cryptic species, and many biological inventories are currently under way. On the other hand, according to the International Union for the Conservation of Nature [IUCN], the planet is undergoing a human-induced wave of extinction, threatening a significant number of animal and plant species.

In the past hundred years, land use in Amazonia has changed with respect to six major activities: mineral and forest exploitation, extensive rangeland for cattle, infrastructure projects for hydroelectric power plants, roads, colonization projects and, more recently, production of agricultural commodities (Araújo & Lená, 2010).

Grounded on a developmentalist model, the Federal Government has induced a process of opening the frontier land that is distinct from prior similar processes, and characterized by an extensive and predatory use of natural resources, as represented in Table 1.

The Modern phase (1960-1980) is characterized by the dominance of a developmentalist ideology, implemented by an authoritarian State that did not hesitated in using bureaucratic strategies in order to regulate illegal practices of land tenure expropriation, in favor of a few large economic groups and companies.

Currently, there seems to be a trend of convergence among several of the productive and developmental sectors, both public and private, as well as some segments of the social and environmental fields, in the need to transform environmental assets into goods, resulting in a new panacea aiming at an ideally "developed" Amazonia (Araújo & Lená, 2010). This rationale would be centered on the carbon trade of the biomass held by the forests, and, at a

DEVELOPMENT PHASES	DEMOGRAPHY	ECONOMY	MODES OF SOCIAL AND POLITICAL PARTICIPATION	ROLE OF THE STATE	NATURAL ESOURCES
1) **Colonial Model**	Genocide, Western acculturation of indigenous populations, import of exotic populations	Exploitation of nature goods, first commercial plantations (for example, cocoa trees)	Slavery, forced labor, working in religious missions and military recruitment	Military conquest and confirmation of territorial dominance	No restriction in regional ecosystem exploitation
2) **Debt peonage system**	Demographic hecatomb (19th Century) and considerable extra-regional demographic immigration	Hegemony of rubber economy, private activities, barter system	Immobilization of work force, exclusion from the market and no political engagement	Weak State intervention	Unrestricted and broad exploitation of regional ecosystem without restoration of Forest cover
3) **Developmentalism**	Highly considerable extra-regional immigration, public and private settlements	Governmental investment in infrastructure and subsidies to large enterprises from the private sector. Beginning of wage remuneration	Authoritarian inclusion in developmental projects, exclusion of local populations	Authoritarian State	Massive destruction of the natural capital and substitution by exotic cultivations
4) **Socio-environmental model**	Intra-regional demographic recomposition, spatial differentiation	Diversification of investment sources and descentralization of projects and policies	Collaborative and participatory model	Regulatory State/Third sector (networks, associativism, participation of the private sector	Giving value for biodiversity and creating sustainable agricultural systems
5) **Commoditization of environmental assets**	Intra-regional demographic recomposition, spatial differentiation	Land tenure market, agribusiness, financing of private initiatives	Model of administration of public forest for timber exploitation, legal environmental clauses	Alliance of State and market towards environmental protection	Monetary valuation of environmental services/ REDD

Table 1. Phases of development in the Amazonian Region (modified from Araújo & Lena, 2010).

more general level, on the logic of the ecological services in a worldwide global change situation (Diaz et al., 2009). According to that reasoning, if one establishes market values to ecosystems or parts of them, it would lead to more effective environmental protection, by bringing changes in land use patterns and/or by financing rural developments of small land owners or traditional communities - ultimately giving value to and conserving natural habitats. Such an hegemonic view of the international environmentalist community is having strong repercussions in Brazil, despite criticism from scientists and economists.

The different phases represented in Table 1 should not be seen as successive events, but partially overlapping, mutually interacting and even being recycled in different times and places in distinct portions of Amazonia. In this matter, it is important to adopt a critical view not only with respect to development and its many expressions (infrastructure, public financing programs for the expansion of cattle ranches and extensive soybean plantations, etc.), but also in regards to the actual logic of the social-environmental reasoning of the ecological market.

3. Forest conversion and degradation in Amazonia and its insertion in the global context

Global rates of deforestation have accelerated in the past decades, as shown recently by an international survey on the status of forest cover in the world. FAO reports that an average of 13 x 10^6 hectares of forest was converted annually in the last decade. In the tropics, a massive conversion of closed forests and arboreal savannas into rangeland has been the main operative causes of pressure on exclusive forest-dwelling species (Dirzo & Raven, 2003). In fact, the great majority of threats to species classified as vulnerable or endangered, according to the IUCN 'red lists', are related to the conversion of natural habitats by agricultural projects, mainly in large tropical countries of emergent economies, such as Brazil (Green et al., 2005).

With 35% of the world's primary forest cover, Brazil has a key role in the conservation of forest organisms, as well as in maintaining the ecological services produced by such ecosystems (Stuart et al., 2010). The great majority of these services are not accounted for by conventional metrics of market economies, their importance being underestimated by urban consumers. Due to this, Brazil, as a large forest owner, also presents high rates of total forest cover, even if compared to other frontiers elsewhere in the globe. For instance, an aggregated deforestation average rate in Brazil in the past two decades (1990-2010: 2.8 X 10^6 hectare/year) is well over the average rate registered in this same period in Indonesia, the country with the second greatest tropical forest. Most of the forest conversion and degradation in Amazonia were concentrated in regions with fertile soils and easy access to seasonally dry forest areas (Laurance et al 2002, Peres et al 2010), locally known as the Arc of Deforestation (Figure 1).

In a similar pace with the expansion of the largest areas of croplands for agribusiness, the second cycle of cattle production in Brazil induced the transformation of 80% of deforested areas into pasture, an area effectively occupied today by extensive ranches (Smeraldi & May, 2008). In Amazonia alone, this area corresponds to an expansion of 57 million hectares of pastures to accommodate 80 million heads of cattle (Instituto Brasileiro de Geografia e Estatística [IBGE], 2006). Most of this beef production is to meet domestic and international demands, in a context of constant rising prices of agricultural commodities. Agribusiness has been very successful - due to the expansion of the production area by means of converting natural habitats in illegally owned public lands - and claims to provide for worldwide needs for food. Economic growth in Asia has dramatically changed the demand for agricultural products from Latin America: exporting biomass goods for China alone have increased nine-fold in the past decade (from US$ 4.6 billion in 2000 to US$ 41.,3 billion in 2009). Soybean exports from Brazil to China also increased between 1995 and 2009, much at the expense of the destruction of 528,000 km^2 of Amazonian primary forests and savannas (Gallagher & Porzecanski, 2010).

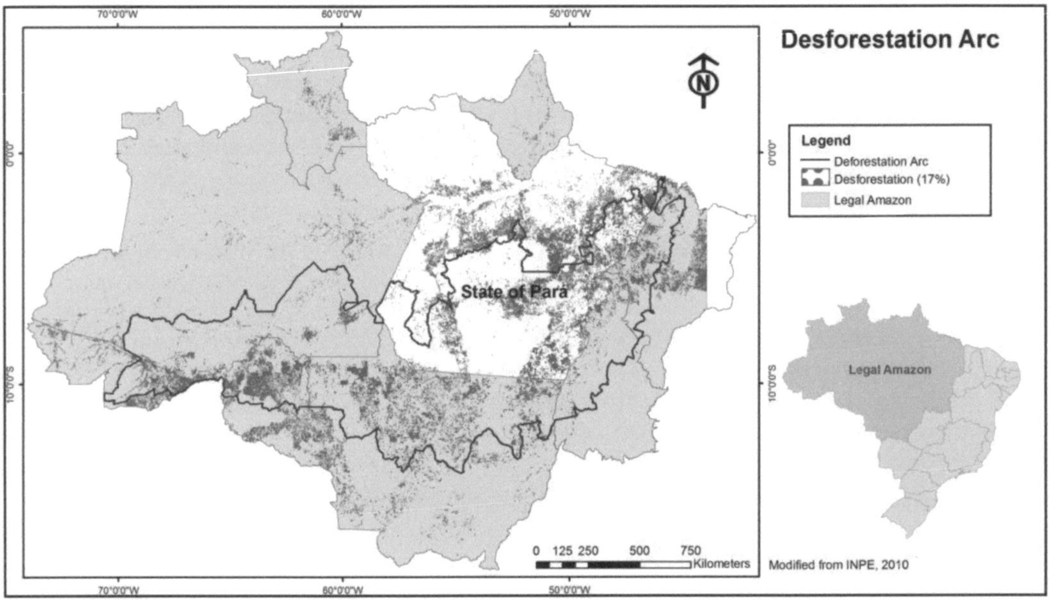

Source: PRODES/Instituto Nacional de Pesquisas Espaciais [INPE], 2010.

Fig. 1. Map of Amazonian deforestation.

Another threat to the impact of natural landscapes and ecosystems in the tropics is the ongoing expansion of the cultivation of plant species with potential for biofuel production Scharlemann & Laurance (2008). Presently Brazil is considered a leader in the production of environmentally clean fuels, such as ethanol, due to the large and country-wide industrial production framework of sugarcane derivatives, with considerable help from fiscal incentives and other subsidies for rural production. Almost 95% of the total area for biofuels in South America is planted in Brazilian territory. Since 2004, sugarcane plantation area has expanded 50%, and expected to double with new areas by 2018 (Sparovek, 2009). More recently, Brazil implemented a National Biodiesel Plan, and in Amazonia, the cultivation of oil palm has quickly grown. A drastic increase in palm trees cultivation is expected for the region.

The accelerated deforestation rate observed in the past 30 years has led to record high levels of landscape degradation and natural habitat destruction (Pereira et al., 2010). However, scientists have not yet been yet been able to fully correlate local loss of biodiversity with land conversion processes, and further elaborate regional comparisons, since different land use occupation patterns show distinct impacts on local ecological processes (Peres et al 2006).

Figure 2 shows that the different components of a human-induced landscape in Eastern Amazonia, established according to its floristic diversity, should maintain a collectivity of species characteristic of the total area they occupy. For instance, the younger secondary forests may contribute with a smaller percentage to the total diversity level, due to its relatively smaller area of distribution. The preserved primary forests, despite their smaller area in the landscape, contribute at a considerably higher rate to the total floristic diversity, due to its higher specie density/area relationship.

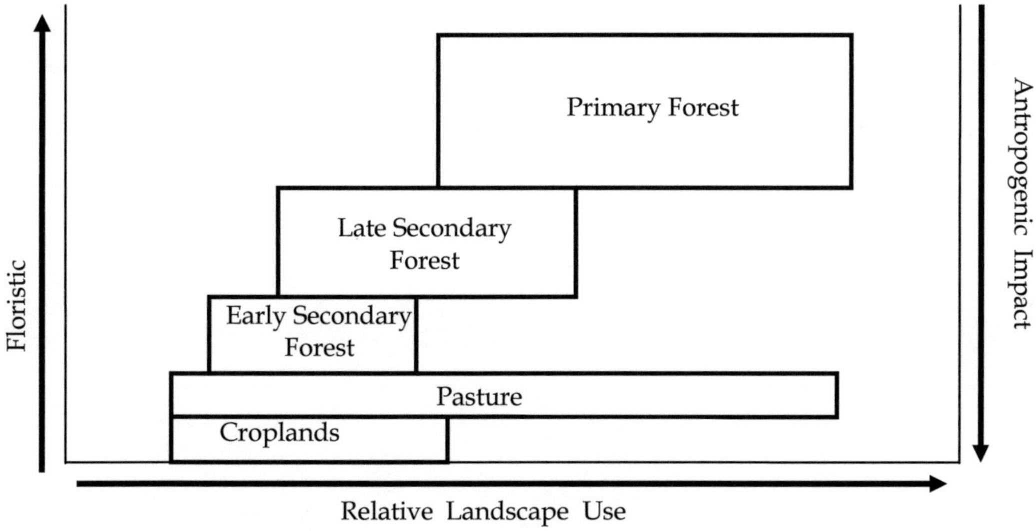

Fig. 2. Elements of human-made landscape in Eastern Amazonia as a function of the floristic diversity and relative landscape use (after Dirzo et al. 2009)

In the face of the dramatic rates of forest conversion in areas used for agricultural activities, (Vieira et al., 2008) it is important to maintain the heterogeneity of the landscape, including well-preserved areas of both primary and secondary forests. However, there is no scientific agreement on the ideal level of floristic biodiversity of each category to adequately maintain the ecological services so as to congregate production and conservation actions in a specific territory. Moreover, additional knowledge on biogeochemical interactions is needed, as is also necessary to maintain genetic diversity and other ecological processes for the equilibrium of the system (Mooney et al., 2009).

4. Commodities in the Amazonian region: the State of Pará as a case study

Brazil occupies a prominent place in the production of commodities crucial to the international markets, such as soybean, beef, corn, coffee beans and others (Martinelli et al., 2010). In this view, the Amazonian Region plays an important role in its potential as a frontier in expansion for the agribusiness sector. Due to recent debates related to environmental issues and mitigation actions to reduce global changes problems, Brazil has been undergoing strong international pressure to adopt procedures to bring social justice and even economic growth without further destruction of forested areas.

Due to its geographical characteristics and accessibility by roads, the State of Pará has always been a port of entry for expanding agricultural activities, one of the main causes of deforestation, particularly in the area known as Arc of Deforestation. Levels of forest cleaning have reached a total of 245,035 km^2 in 2009, equivalent to 19% of the State territory and 33% of the total deforested area in Brazil in that year.

The main productive activities in the state are cattle, timber exploitation, grain plantation and, more recently, cultivation of oil palm. This last culture calls the attention due to the rapid land tenure and demographic pattern changes that follow such an economic activity (Figure 3).

Cattle ranching is singled out as the main cause for deforestation in Amazonia, and has been noted to contribute little to diminish social disparities in the region, despite some significant gains in terms of scale in the agricultural sector (Margullis, 2003). The State of Pará holds the second largest cattle herd in the Amazonian Region, second only to the State of Mato Grosso at a national level, with a herd of 16,856,561 heads of cattle in 2009. In 1990, the number of heads was 6,182,090, indicating a significant growth of 173% in the past two decades.

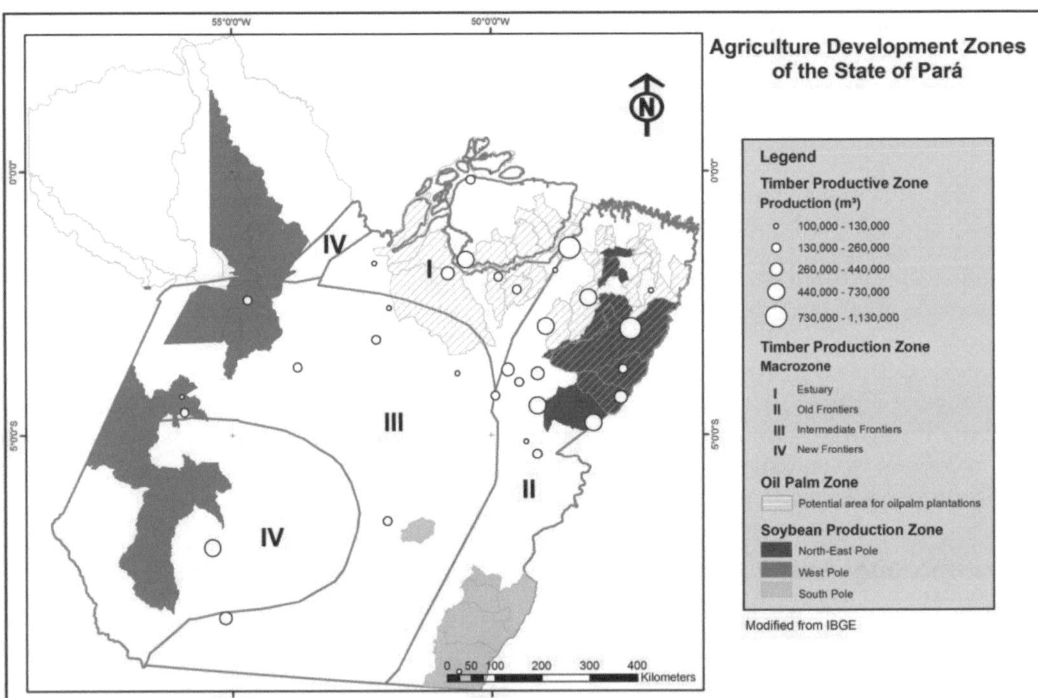

Fig. 3. Timber and agriculture development zones in the state of Pará, Brazil.

The expansion of soybean plantations in the State of Pará was forwarded by the conversion of small family-owned ranches into aggregated agricultural lands, and by turning pasture into grain cultures. At the base of the land tenure structure, such an initiative has induced a new arrangement of productive territories, promoting the substitution of several small properties into a large sole-owned plantation (Guilhoto et al., 2006). Several reasons can be identified for the shift of a great number of rural entrepreneurs who took interest in expanding their activities from Mato Grosso into Pará: attractive international prices for soybean, good agricultural conditions and lower prices for land in the new State, and government incentive programs. With some previous experience and self-owned capital to cover crop costs and infrastructure investment, the newcomers the transformed land use patterns into a more intensive, technology-based productive areas.

This regional land use pattern led to the appearance of an array of export-driven facilities and infrastructure, helping the flow of soybean through the Amazon river. This is exemplified by the construction of the international Cargill grain port in the city of Santarém, with an investment of US$20,000,000 and the capability to commercialize 800,000 tons of grains a year, with a storage capacity of 60,000 tons. In the same wave of investments, a new port near the State capital city of Belém is being constructed for the trading of soy, corn and sugar cane products. Following this trend, the conclusion of the dikes of the Tucuruí Dam, the second largest hydroelectric power plant dam in Brazil, leads one to expect this new port near Belém will become the largest fluvial export complex in the world, with an waterway extension of 2,5 thousand kilometers in the Tocantins-Araguaia river systems.

Concern for social problems in the wake of high deforestation rates induced by soybean plantations have caused a series of articulated campaigns by NGOs, the Catholic Church and rural workers syndicates, with serious accusations of violent land expropriation by locals at the service of large companies or individuals. Disparities in the process of land appropriation, involving different actors with a multitude of interests, are one of the main causes of social conflicts in Amazonia - a social paradox, if one considers the continental extension of the region and the extremely low index of demographic occupation. Public manifestations against the presence of soybean crops in Amazonia escalated into an international level, with the establishment of a 'moratorium on soy' originated in areas of tropical deforestation. In this particular case, international soy trade companies such as Cargill, Bunge, Dreyfuss and the Brazilian Maggi agreed in 2006 not to purchase and trade products coming from newly deforested areas in Amazonia. In 2008, the Brazilian Ministry of the Environment extended the moratorium until 2010, the Federal Government being responsible for coordinating the productive units, and putting NGOs in charge of monitoring compliance to the rules. Such environmental and social awareness led to the increase of certified crops in terms of sustainability and social benefits.

Palm oil has received special attention due to the edaphic and climatic adaptations of the plant in the northeastern portion of the State of Pará. Technical studies have shown that this particular oil is suitable as biofuel, and also as a substitute for trans fat in the food industry. Brazil has a potential of 232 million hectares of land for oil palm cultivation. The Amazonian Region is better adapted for such crops: the state of Pará answers for 80% of the production of the country, and is currently using 8,000 hectares of land, with a potential of 4-5 million hectares.

Brazil is also one of the main world producers of tropical timber. Processed wood production in 2009 reached 291 million m^3, and Brazil contributed with 25 million m^3, about 3% of the total amount exported worldwide, rounding up an income of 695 million dollars

(3.5%). The Brazilian share in the global market of plywood in 2009 was 4% of the total production. As plywood has a wide range of uses (construction, furniture, house utensils, etc.), its market value is higher and the exported volume claimed an income of US$635 million.
Between 2000 and 2009, the Brazilian share of the total amount of sawed timber in the world remained around 11%; there was nevertheless a sharp reduction in the past two years, with a decrease in 6 percent points in 2008 and 2009. This downward trend began in 2005, when the federal government started checking on illegal timber extraction, using a complex and efficient satellite system in Amazonia.
The distribution of international participation in tropical wood forest products reveals that Brazil still has an important role as a supplier of unprocessed material, while value aggregation in this economic chain occurs in developed countries of Europe, North America and Asia. Top-ranking importers of tropical sawn timber are the US, China, Japan, Italy and UK (Table 2). They consume altogether 40 million m^3. A current decrease in the Brazilian production of timber is related to the growth rate of China.

Country	Rank	Imported volume (thousands of m^3)	Country	Rank	Import value (thousands of US$)
US	1	15,671.19	US	1	3,236,649.27
China	2	7,039.92	Japan	2	2,360,697.14
Japan	3	6,508.95	China	3	1,891,849.20
Italy	4	6,400.00	Italy	4	1,876,209.22
UK	5	5,070.00	UK	5	1,714,667.89

Source: International Tropical Timber Organization (ITTO)

Table 2. Ranking of the main importers, in quantity and value, of sawn timber from tropical forests, 2009.

Expectations are of a growth in the market of tropical wood in the next coming years, with a simultaneous increase of pressure from environmental institutions demanding certified products and more efficient ground and remote sensing monitoring systems.

3. REDD (Reducing Emissions from Deforestation and Forest Degradation): Solution or problem?

In the center of the ongoing debate to assign value to forest conservation and green economy, a worldwide movement of carbon trade by reducing GHGs through the reduction of avoided forest deforestation and degradation has been discussed. However, there are concerns from some authors that this approach may not be fully applicable to avoid tropical deforestation -- specifically in the Brazilian Amazonia, where most of the natural tropical forests of the world are located.

The first point to be considered is the lack of data and reliable measurements, an issue that must be fully mastered before bringing this idea to a market economy (Kintisch, 2007). . The first problem with REDD is the lack of reliable data to provide information on tropical deforestation. An associated problem is the lack of capability in developing nations to provide accurate and verifiable measurements.

Since 1988, the Brazilian National Institute for Space Research (INPE) has conducted annual surveys of deforestation in the Brazilian Legal Amazonia, an area of about 5 million km^2 which, until the 1950s, included 4 million km^2 of tropical forests. INPE maps deforestation using LANDSAT-class images (30m resolution) and performs wall-to-wall measurements. The latest data produced by INPE used 330 images from the LANDSAT, CBERS and DMS systems, fully covering Amazonia. The results are detailed digital maps showing both the extent and the location of deforestation.

However, Brazil is currently the exception. There are no comparable maps being produced elsewhere. Thus, current estimates for other countries are based on unreliable methods, such as sampling, or on low-resolution satellite data, such as MODIS 250m resolution images. The difference is substantial. For example, FAO estimates that 31,000 km^2 of tropical forest was cut yearly in Brazil from 2000 to 2005, on average. By contrast, INPE's data gives an average of 21,500 km^2 for the same period. Furthermore, the average for the entire Brazilian territory for the period 2005-2008 is 14,300 km^2, which is half of FAO's estimate.

Despite the problems with FAO's and other data sources, many researchers use such unreliable and outdated data as their source of information for assessing current global deforestation. IPCC AR4 estimated that deforestation accounts for between 10% and 20% of global GHG emissions. However, despite the proven unreliability of FAO's and other data, the uppermost value of the IPCC AR4 report (20%) has been quoted widely in other governmental and multilateral reports and is being used in the current climate negotiations. For example, the recent G8 declaration in L'Aquila stated that "deforestation accounts for approximately 20% of annual CO2 emissions": no uncertainties, no error bars.

A major effort is needed to solve the problem of unreliable measures. First, data from remote sensing satellites needs to be available for all the world's tropical forests (Grainger, 2008). Based on INPE's experience, such data must at least be obtained from LANDSAT-class satellites (30m resolution, multispectral bands). The only continent for which such data are currently available is Latin America. Data are lacking for Africa, Southeast Asia, and Australasia. Data for India do exist but is not openly available. Furthermore, it will take at least three to five years before the data gap problem is solved.

Also, most tropical forest nations currently lack the skills to provide detailed and reliable estimates of land change. Moreover, to allow independent verification, data, methods, and maps must be made openly available on the Web. This poses a double problem for developing nations: capacity building and governance. How many governments would allow their national institutes to publish data that might be damaging to their own short-term interests?

It could well take over a decade for a reliable system for monitoring tropical deforestation worldwide to be built. Building such as system would be a pre-requisite for REDD. This would demand a significant upfront investment from developed nations without any short-term carbon credit benefits to them.

A second, and most important issue, is the correct definition of avoided deforestation. This concept is central to the REDD proposal. Yet this concept is misleading. Since there are many possible interpretations, one idea is to use the *maximum acceptable level* of deforestation for a tropical nation. Should the country reach a rate of deforestation lower than the cap (in a cap-and-trade scheme), it could trade the avoided emissions.

Take the case of Brazil. What is the *maximum acceptable level* of deforestation for Brazil? A direct attempt to answer this question could make use of historical rates. Given these rates, some proposals take a five-year moving average as the initial cap. This average is then reduced progressively as a target for the future deforestation.

There must be a concerted action by governments and markets for deforestation to slow down. The recent experience on Brazil shows what is possible. By a combination of market pressure and law enforcement, Brazil managed to reduce deforestation from 27,000 km^2 in 2005 to 13,000 km^2 in 2008. During the same period, the price of soybean increased from US$250 per metric ton to US$500 per metric ton. The price of beef oscillated from US$1.1 per pound to US$1.3 per pound. Thus, the decrease in deforestation is not correlated to commodity prices.

However, the rate of deforestation in Brazil remains high. The current five-year average should not be taken as a 'cap', below which Brazil would earn tradable carbon credits. The main reason is the stabilization of agricultural expansion and the current prevalence of cattle raising and timber extraction as the main drivers of deforestation. As a result, the economic value extracted from the land is much smaller than in the 1990s.

The three main areas of occupation in Amazonia are the States of Pará, Rondônia and Mato Grosso. In each State, there are different driving forces for deforestation (Aragao et al, 2008). A large part of the deforestation during the 1990s was associated with agricultural expansion. From 1990 to 2005, 110,000 km^2 were deforested in Mato Grosso, in the southern part of Amazonia. Such deforestation was associated to a large migration from farmers from the south of Brazil (States of Paraná, Santa Catarina and Rio Grande do Sul). This resulted in a large expansion of the soybean producing area and contributed to Brazil's exports. In 2008, Brazil produced 58 million tons of soybean; Mato Grosso accounted for 15 million tons (25% of total). The other states in Amazonia have no significant contribution to the production of grains.

Agricultural expansion has slowed down since 2000, due to four reasons: (a) a slowdown in migration from the South; (b) a relative stabilization of the production area, with emphasis on improved productivity; (c) newly available areas were found to have unfavorable soil conditions and worse connections to markets; and (d) the international market pressure for avoiding further deforestation. From 1970 to 1980, Mato Grosso's population almost doubled from roughly 600,000 to 1,130,000 people. From 1980 to 1990, it increased to 2,000,000 people. Growth was smaller in the next decade, reaching 2,500,000 people in 2000. Less migrants means less pressure for new land. Furthermore, Greenpeace and ABIOVE (Brazilian Association for Vegetable Oil) have signed an agreement in 2006 (the "Soy Moratorium"), whereby the soybean exporters have pledged not to deforest any more land. The "Soy Moratorium" has been renewed in 2007 and 2008.

In short, the current levels of deforestation in Amazonia are too high and too unsustainable to be considered as a *maximum acceptable level* below which Brazil could get tradable carbon credits. Therefore, Brazil would need to achieve significant gains in fighting deforestation before it could reach an annual rate that could be considered 'acceptable'.

Other problems central to this issue, concerning the final destination of the money resulting from carbon credits to be negotiated from the REDD system, and the potential problem of distorting markets, also have to be addressed in detail. Considering that large-scale deforestation are associated with expected economic returns, market forces could provide an effective alternative to REDD.

6. Global markets, local challenges

A renewed vision of nature as a source of well-being, and how such a limited resource can affect humans lives, has given the Amazon forest an strategic value in the new frontier of natural capital (United Nations Environment Programme-UNEP, 2010), bringing the region to the center stage of distinct and diverse interests, as well as of conflicting demands. This view needs to be dealt with for the better and efficient use of the Amazonian natural heritage to the benefit of local and global societies. In an apparent paradox, international interests in the use of the Amazonian natural capital is in conflict with the predominant Brazilian national view of a mobilization in order to oversee Amazonia as a vast space for sustainable businesses, which would strengthen regional development-related actions.

The predominant environmental policy since the 1980s to the beginning of the third millennium has given signs of trouble in fully confronting the new globalization agenda. Its major, most evident result was the demarcation of record-size tropical land territories for preservation and/or sustainable, and as protected lands for indigenous territories and biological conservation units, corresponding to 20% of the regional Amazonian territory in Brazil. However, there is a common agreement that protected areas are not sufficient to refrain further deforestation or to induce economic growth under a globalized world perspective. Protection actions have not been able to contain the expansion of newly productive lands to respond for global demands for food and energy, as well as to meet the growing demand of local communities in the region. Therefore a new standard of regional development is needed.

At a global level, conflicts of interest in the use of natural assets of Amazonia can be associated to three different market categories:

The market of proteins represented by soybean and beef, dominated by big agribusiness industries and owners of extensive ranchland. The growing international demand stimulates the exporting of soybean and cattle, which encompasses huge extensions of cerrado in the soy-beef belt that extends from Bolivia to the States of Bahia and Piauí in Brazil. Such a pressure reinvigorates the mobility and expansion of that economic land belt into forested areas, enhancing land tenure conflicts in the southern fringes of the Amazonian Biome. In this case, two types of land use and predominant action upon territories are put into conflict, with technological and logistic disparities between them: the large companies and land owners against local and traditional communities. Despite the high mobilization and volume in economic transactions, agribusiness in the long run does not seem as either a sustainable or a social solution for the entire region. In the future, this market should be confined to the exploration of areas of cerrado and currently deforested regions, without further destruction of the remaining primary and old secondary forests.

The market of natural goods, characterized by the financial interests of large multinational banks, such as BIRD and BID, which strive to organize it. It is the case of the Clean Air market, which is the more advanced in the discussions of the Kyoto Protocol, and the mechanism of clean development. More recently the REDD mechanism brought into play the Market of Life, with the intention to organize everlasting meetings under the Biodiversity Convention protocol. A third case is the Market of Water, which, under global regulation, is being taken by different multilateral agencies as well.

A third important market component is represented by the problems facing environmental issues related to oil production and energy, with the intensification of conventional ways of production - hydroelectric power, oil and gas - as well as of the bioenergy paradigm that expands greatly in the Brazilian territory, including the eastern Amazonian Region.

In a more regional view, there are growing demands for better social and economic conditions of the 20 million inhabitants of Amazonia. Intense transformations have occurred in the societies locally in the past decades, transforming the region with a coherent internal consistency expressed by social demands and aspirations. State-level governments, international cooperation and, especially, organized civil societies have transformed the region and gave it a heavier weight in the political arena. Demands for better living conditions and development requirements cannot be ignored in regional and national development projects.

At a national level, this conflict of interests seems to immobilize the Federal Government, which proves unable to define a consistent, long-term regional agenda for Amazonia. The main task is to confront globalized demands of prosperity and, at the same time, try to solve crucial social problems. Despite recent public policies that tried to stop deforestation through costly command and control programs, sustainable development was not simultaneously encouraged, and in practice there were few effective results.

It is also important to notice the mismatch between the magnitude of the potential of resources with the restricted number of entrepreneurs, which translates in low levels of regional production. In other words, business opportunities are waiting for bold and competent businessmen to fulfill the potential for prosperity in the region. Among the various protein and the natural goods markets, great opportunities exist in the valuation of forest ecosystems. Such unexploited assets hold the most strategic potential in the millennium for a sustainable exploitation of biodiversity, water, tourism, etc.

The bioenergy trend opens clear opportunities for countries to optimize their energy matrix, where Brazil, due to its geographical extension and tropical situation, has the potential to become one of the largest exporters of energy in the world.

7. Conclusions

The Amazonian Region can contribute to the dynamic trends of use and management of resources in the tropical world. The great challenge, however, is to produce social justice and economic profits to be shared with most of the population without destroying further natural ecosystems.

In this case some challenges should be put up front in order to promote the development of the region. One prerequisite is to make economic growth compatible with social inclusion, minimizing the destruction of natural habitats. We can suggest three strategic actions in this regard:

1. To invest in science, technology and innovation. The destruction of the forest will only be halted if there is some economic value that may compete with agribusiness, unsustainable timber exploitation and cattle ranching;

2. To have a customized, long-term regional development policy program as a prerequisite for Governmental strategy, to reduce intraregional disparities and adjust development agendas coined with potentials and challenges of each region;
3. To strengthen institutional agendas, decoding regional society demands into Government actions. It is in this segment where the institutional strategy of governance and accountability for development and economic actions will be established;

On the other hand, while environmental conservation and economic development are often thought to be at odds, Brazil's approach strives to merge the two in Amazonia. The rise of new commodities in Brazilian Amazonia is particularly relevant for understanding Brazil's current economic success, with growth at a record 9% in the first quarter of 2010. Although Legal Amazonia contributes with less than 10% of the national GDP, new industries and emerging markets involving payments for ecosystem services hold the potential to sway billions of dollars of wealth to the nation because of Amazonian resources. These important attributes are tempered by social unrest and often extreme inequalities in the region, which keep a significant portion of the population living with high rates of agrarian conflict and rural poverty. It is fair to hope that today's "green commodities boom" in Amazonia will not be destined to repeat the same unfortunate conjunctures of environmental losses and social conflicts that have tarnished the history of the region.

We defend that, to better organize the economic trends demanding more productive land, sustainability programs on managed territories (see sustainable territory *sensu* Vieira et al, 2005) may be important so as to minimize impacts and to optimize actions on conservation. The scientific framework of a sustainable territory, based on a multidisciplinary program with transdisciplinary actions, is a solid approach for combining conservation and economic production in rural areas of Amazonia. Its basic premise is that the combination of scientific information and the best practices of land use and conservation can yield customized solutions for rural production areas. The scope and scale of activities, as well as the economic features of the farmers, are diverse and change through time. Despite such features, recent studies have established which activities might yield better ecological services and help enhancing the quality of life in rural populations. Therefore, linking scientists with public interests is an important part of the equation of sustainability in the Amazonian Region.

8. References

Aragao, L.; Malhi, Y.; Barbier, N.; Lima, A.; Shimabukuro, Y.; Anderson, L.; Saatchi, S. (2008) Interactions between rainfall, deforestation and fires during recent years in the Brazilian Amazonia. *Philosophical Transactions*, vol. 363, 1779-1785. ISSN 0962-8436

Araújo, R. & Lená, P. (2010). Da Predação à Sustentabilidade na Amazônia: A Difícil Metamorfose. In: *Desenvolvimento Sustentável e Sociedades na Amazônia*, R. Araújo & P. Lená, (Eds.), 13-53, Editora Museu Goeldi, ISBN 978-85-61377-46-5 , Belém-Pará, Brazil.

Buckeridge, M.S. (2008). Biologia e Mudanças Climáticas no Brasil. Editora RIMA, São Carlos, Brasil. 295 p. ISBN 9788576561439

Burnham, R.J & Johnson, K.R. (2004). South American palaeobotany and the origins of neotropical rainforests. *Philosophical Transactions of Royal Society of London. B vol. 359 no. 1450 1595-1610* ISSN 1471-2970

Bush, M.B.; Silman, M.R. 2007. Amazonian exploitation revisited: ecological asymmetry and the policy pendulum *Front Ecol Environ* 5(9): 457–465.ISSN 1540-9295

Diaz, S.; Hector, A. & Wardle, D.A. (2009) Biodiversity in forest carbon sequestration initiavies: not just a side benefit. *Current Opinion in Environmental Sustainability*, No.1, pp. 55-60, ISSN 1877-3435

Dirzo, R..& Raven, P. (2003). Global state of biodiversity and loss. *Annual Review of Environment and Resources*. Vol. 28, pp. 137-167. ISSN 1441-9335

Dirzo, R.; Aguirre, A. & López, J.C. (2008). Diversidad florística de las selvas húmedas en paisajes antropizados. *Investigación Ambiental*. No. 1, pp. 17-22

Grainger, A. (2008) Difficulties in tracking the long-term global trend in tropical forest area. Proceedings of the National Academy of Sciences, Vol. 105 pp 818. ISSN *0027-8424*

Green, R. E.; Cornell,S.J.; Scharlemann, J.P. & Balmford, A. (2005). Farming and the fate of wild nature. *Science* Vol.307. Pp. 550-555. ISSN 1095-9203

Gallagher, K.P. and R. Porzecanski. (2010). *The Dragon in the Room: China and the Future of Latin American Industrialization*. Stanford University Press, California. ISBN 9780804775-98-4

Guilhoto J. J. M.; Silveira, F. G.; Ichiara, S. M.; Azzoni, C. R. (2006) A importância do agronegócio familiar no Brasil. *Revista de Economia e Sociologia Rur*al, Vol 44, No. 3, pp. 355-383, ISSN 0103-2003

Instituto Brasileiro de Geografia e Estatística- IBGE (2006). Censo Agropecuário. Available from www.ibge.gov.br

Instituto nacional de Pesquisas Espaciais - INPE (2010). PRODES. Available from www.inpe.br

Instituto de Pesquisas Econômicas Aplicadas - IPEA (2011). Sustentabilidade Ambiental no Brasil: biodiversidade, economia e bem-estar humano. *Comunicados do IPEA*, No.78, Série Eixos do Desenvolvimento Brasileiro. Available from www.ipea.gov.br

ITTO. *International Tropical Timber Organization (ITTO)*. Available from: www.itto.int

Joels, L. C. & Câmara, G. (2001) Modelos e cenários para a Amazônia: o papel da ciência. *Parcerias Estratégicas*, Vol. 12, pp. 129-134. ISSN 1413-9375

Kintisch, E. (2007). Carbon Emissions: Improved Monitoring of Rainforests Helps Pierce Haze of Deforestation. Science, Vol. 316, pp.536-537. ISSN 1095-9203

Laurance, W.F.; Albernaz, A.K.M;, Schroth, G.; Fearnside, P.M.; Bergen, S.; Venticinque, E.M. & da Costa, C. (2002). Predictors of deforestation in the Brazilian Amazon.. *Journal of Biogeography* . Vol.29, pp. 1365-2699. ISSN: 0305-0270

Margullis, S. (2003). *Causas do desmatamento na Amazonia Brasileira*. ISBN: 85-88192-10-1 Avaiable from www.bancomundial.org.br

Martinelli, L. A.; Naylor, R.; Vitousek, P. M. & Moutinho, P. (2010). Agriculture in Brasil: impacts, costs, and opportunities for a sustainable future. *Current Opinion in Environmental Sustainability*. Vol. 2, pp. 1-8. ISSN 1877-3435

Mittemeir, R.A; Fonseca, G. A.B. da; Rylands, A.B. & Brandon, K. (2005). A Brief History of Biodiversity Conservation in Brazil. *Conservation Biology*, Vol. 19, No. 3, (June 2005), pp. 601–607. 2010 ISSN ISSN 0888-8892

Mooney, H.; Larigauderie, A.; Cesario, M.; Elmquist, T.; Hoegh-Guldberg, O.; Lavorel, S.; Mace, M. G.; Palmer, M.; Scholes, R. & Yahara, T. (2009). Biodiversity, climate change, and ecosystem services. *Current opinion in Environmental Sustainability*, No. 1, pp.46-54, ISSN 1877-3435

Moran, E.F. & Ostrom, E. (2009. Ecossistemas florestais. Interação Homem-Ambiente. EDUSP editora, São Paulo. 543 p. ISBN 9788531411342

Pereira, H. M.; Leadley, P.W.; Proença, V.; Alkemade, R.; Scharlemann, J. P.W.; Fernandez-Manjarrés, J.F.; Araujo, M.B.; balvanera, P.; Biggs, R.; Cheung. W.W.L.; Chini, L.; Cooper, H.D.; Mace, G.M.; Oberdorff, T.; Revenga, C.; Rodrigues, P.; Scholes, R.J.; Sumaila, U. R. & Walpole, M. (2010). Scenarios for Global Biodiversity in the 21st Century. *Science*, Vol. 330, pp.1095-9203, ISSN 1095-9203

Peres, C.A.; Barlow, J. & Laurance, W. (2006). Detecting anthropogenic disturbance in tropical forests. *Trends in Ecology and Evolution*. Vol. 21, pp. 227-229. ISSN: 0169-5347

Peres, C.A.; Gardner, T.A.; Barlow, J.; Jansen, J.; Michalski, F.; Lees, A.C.; Vieira, I.C.G.; Moreira, F.M.D.; & Feeley, K.. (2010). Biodiversity conservation in human-modified Amazonian forest landscapes. *Biological Conservation*, pp. 2314-2327, ISSN *0006-3207*

Silva, J. M. C.; Rylands, A. B. ; Fonseca, GAB. (2005) The fate of the Amazonian areas of endemism. *Conservation Biology*, Vol. 19, No. 3, pp. 689-694. ISSN 0888-8892

Scharlemann, J.P.W. & Laurance, W.F. (2008) How green are biofuels? *Science* Vol, 319, pp. 43-44, ISSN 1095-9203

Smeraldi, R. and P. May. 2008. O Reino do Gado: Uma Nova Fase na Pecuarização da Amazônia Brasileira. Amigos da Terra, Brasília.
Avaiable from www.amigosdaterra.org.br

Sparovek, G. 2009. Environmental, land-use and economic implications of Brazilian sugarcane expansion 1996-2006 Mitigation and Adaptation Strategies for Global Change, 14: 285-298 ISSN 1381-2386

Stuart, N.S.; E.O. Wilson; J.A.McNelly; R.A. Mittermeier; and J.P. Rodriguez. (2010). The barometer of life. *Science*, Vol.328, p.177, ISSN 1095-9203

Stuart, H.; Butchart, M.; Walpole, M.; Collen, B.; van Strien, A.; Scharlemann, J. P.W.; Almond, R. E. A.; Baillie, J.E.M.; Bombard, B.; Brown, C.; Bruno, J.; Carpenter, K.E.; Carr, G.M.; Chanson, J.; Chenery, A.M.; Csirke J.; Davidson, N.C.; Dentener, F.; Foster, M.; Galli, A.; Galloway, J.N.; Genovesi, P.; Gregory, R.D.; Hockings, M.; Kapos, V.; Lamarque, J-F.; Leverington, F.; Loh, J.; McGeoch, M.A.; McRae, L.; Minasyan, A.; Morcillo, M. H.; Oldfield, T. E.E.; Pauly, D.; Quader, S.; Revenga, C.; Sauer, J.R.; Skolnik, B.; Spear, D.; Stanwell-Smith, D.; Stuart, S.N.; Symes, A.; Tierney, M.; Tyrrell, T.D.;Vié, J-C. & Watson, R. (2010). Global Biodiversity: Indicators of Recent Declines. *Science*,, Vol. 328, pp. 1164-1168 ISNN 1095-9203

Tallis, H. & Kareiva, P. (2005). Ecosystem services. *Current Biology*. Vol.15, PP. R746-758. ISSN: *0960-9822*

UNEP. (2010). TEEB report. Avaiable from www.unep.org

Vieira, I.C.G.; Silva, J.M.C. da; Toledo, P. M. (2005). Estratégias para Evitar a Perda de Biodiversidade na Amazônia. *Estudos Avançados*, USP, Vol. 19, No.54, pp. 153-164. ISSN 0103-4014 UNEP. (2010). TEEB report. Avaiable from www.unep.org

Vieira, I.C.G.; Toledo, P. M; Silva, J.M.C. da & Higuchi , H.. (2008) Deforestamention and Threats to the Biodiversity of Amazonia. *Brazilian Journal of Biology Vol.* 68, pp. 631-637. ISSN 1519-6984

11

Globalization: Ecological Consequences of Global-Scale Connectivity in People, Resources, and Information

Debra P.C. Peters
Jornada Basin Long Term Ecological Research Program and U.S. Department of Agriculture – Agricultural Research Service, Las Cruces, New Mexico USA

1. Introduction

Globalization is a phenomenon affecting all facets of the Earth System. Within the context of ecological systems, it is becoming increasingly apparent that global connectivity among terrestrial systems, the atmosphere, and oceans is driving many ecological dynamics at finer scales and pushing thresholds of change (Fagre et al., 2009; MEA, 2005; Rial et al., 2004). For example, increasing atmospheric CO_2 and other greenhouse gases are increasing temperature and modifying precipitation regimes with short- and long-term impacts on ecological systems (IPCC, 2007). Changes in climate also have secondary effects by influencing disturbance regimes, such as changing the intensity of North American hurricanes that link to rainfall patterns in Africa (Emanual, 2005; Trenberth, 2005). Climate also interacts with terrestrial systems to alter wildfire regimes and to connect large areas within a continent as well as connecting locations globally through particulates in the atmosphere (Allen 2007; Dale et al., 2001; Kitzberger et al., 2007). Massive dust storms driven by hot and dry weather interacting with human activities can connect continents, such as dust storms in Asia that deposit dust particles in North America (Jaffe et al., 2003). Glacier melt in polar regions is increasing sea level globally with consequences for near-shore and inland ecosystems (Hopkinson et al., 2008). Movement of humans through improved transportation is leading to spread of pests and pathogens with ecological consequences for agricultural crops (Perrings et al., 2010). Long-distance movement of invasive plants and animals is often facilitated by human activities (Crowl et al., 2008).

In addition, fine-scale ecological dynamics can propagate spatially to influence broad spatial extents with feedbacks to global drivers (Peters et al., 2004a). Dust storms in Asia are initiated as cultivated marginal lands in dry years that become connected by wind and water. Erosion and deposition of soil, nutrients, and dust particles occur locally, but also propagate to regions and continents (Field et al., 2010). As the dry conditions continue, large dust storms can develop with transport of materials eventually to North America. Similar intra- and inter-continental dynamics have been observed historically with the Dust Bowl in the central U.S. (Peters et al., 2006a), in the southwestern US (Neff et al., 2008), and in Antarctica (McConnell et al., 2007), and are occurring in the deserts of Africa and Asia to contribute to most of the global mineral aerosol load (Tanaka & Chiba, 2006).

Because global change drivers, including climate, landuse, and movement of the biota, as well as ecosystem dynamics are changing nonlinearly through time for many locations, it is critical that connections across different aspects of the Earth System be examined to improve both understanding and prediction of future ecological dynamics (Peters et al., 2008). A better understanding is needed about these various drivers, how they are changing in response to globalization, and what are the consequences to ecological dynamics and ecosystem services globally. This chapter addresses two objectives. The first objective is to describe three classes of events that emerge from a common, integrated framework; each class has different characteristics that connect ecological systems at fine to broad scales with consequences for globalization. Examples are provided to illustrate how various global change drivers can influence and interact with heterogeneity in land surface properties of vegetation and soil pattern to either synchronize, attenuate or amplify impacts of drivers on ecological systems. The second objective is to describe approaches to deal with global change impacts when locations may be connected at multiple scales.

2. Integrated framework to link local to global scales

Recently, a conceptual framework was developed to understand and predict broad-scale ecosystem dynamics. This framework is based on connectivity in material and information flow that links multiple scales of observation, from local sites within landscapes to regions and continents (Peters et al., 2008). The basic premise of the framework is that both the climate system and human activities operate across multiple spatial and temporal scales to influence and be influenced by ecological systems (Fig. 1). The term "driver" refers to atmospheric or Earth-surface processes and human activities that affect ecological systems. This definition allows for interactions among drivers as well as feedback mechanisms between drivers and responses.

Patterns in drivers occur across a range of scales. For example, the drivers influencing rainfall and temperature occur mainly at three scales: (1) global circulation patterns, which influence long-term climatic averages, (2) subcontinental to continental-scale phenomena driven by patterns such as the El Niño-Southern Oscillation (ENSO), and (3) meso-scale patterns as weather interacting with local and regional topography. Other drivers also exhibit multi-scale patterns, such as connectivity within and among major river systems that leads to variable patterns in land use, human settlement, invasive species, and nutrient distribution. Although human activities occur at multiple scales, local scale impacts increasingly drive ecosystem dynamics and land change at broader, regional scales (Luck et al., 2001, Dietz et al., 2007). Interactions among climate, human populations, and disturbance agents have both ecological and socio-economic consequences (Yates et al., 2002).

Thus, connectivity across scales results from broad-scale drivers (climate and people) interacting with finer-scale patterns and processes that redistribute materials within and among linked terrestrial and aquatic systems (Fig. 1) (Peters et al., 2008). Climate and human activities interact with patterns and processes at multiple, finer scales (blue arrows). These drivers can influence broad-scale patterns directly, and these constraints may act to overwhelm heterogeneity and processes at meso-scales, and at fine scales of local sites. Broad-scale drivers can also impact broad-scale patterns indirectly through their interactions with disturbances, including the spread of invasive species or fire. Connectivity via the transfer of materials occurs both at the meso-scale and at fine scales within sites where terrestrial and aquatic systems are connected. Transport vectors (e.g., wind, water, animals, people) move materials and resources (e.g., dust, soil, water, energy, nutrients, propagules, diseases, chemical constituents) within and among terrestrial and aquatic systems across a range of spatial and temporal scales (Fig. 1 red arrows). Changes in the drivers and pattern-process relationships through time and across space can alter ecosystem dynamics within particular locations (Fig 1; black arrows), and can change dynamics across locations and large regions (Allen, 2007).

3. Classes of driver impacts on ecological dynamics

Although this framework shares some similarities with hierarchical systems where broad-scale drivers constrain fine-scale patterns, and fine-scale patterns provide the mechanistic understanding for broad-scale patterns (Allen & Starr, 1982), the focus here is understanding and predicting the conditions when broad-scale drivers overwhelm fine-scale variability, and the conditions when fine-scale processes propagate nonlinearly to influence broad spatial extents. I define and illustrate three classes of events that connect ecological systems globally, and can be explained using this overarching framework. These cases differ in: (1) initial properties of the driver, (2) change in ecological response, and (3) the explanatory variables for the response. These differences are summarized in Table 1, and detailed below.

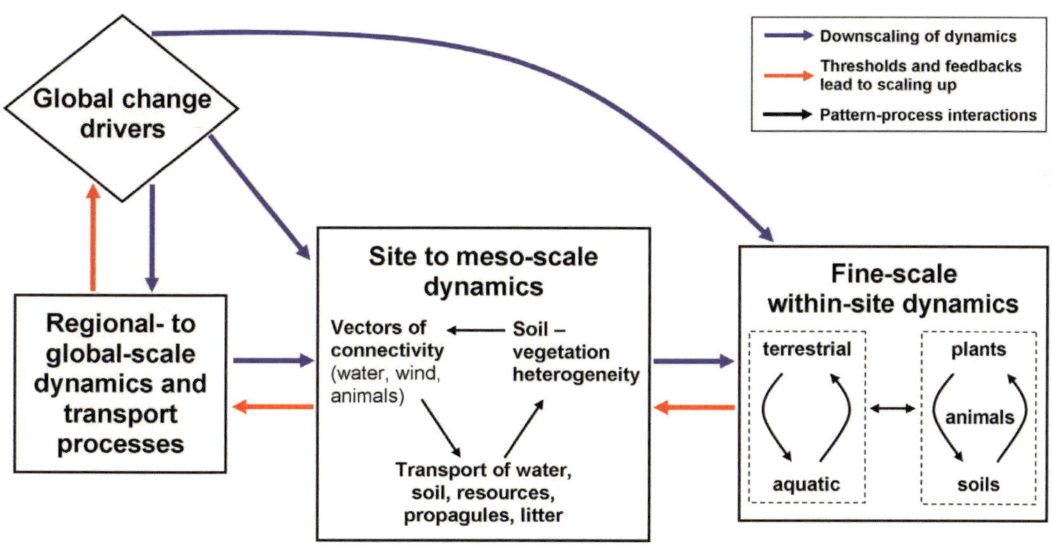

Fig. 1. Conceptual framework to link spatial and temporal scales to result in continental-scale patterns and dynamics leading to globalization with consequences to ecological dynamics at finer scales. Both downscaling of global change drivers to finer scales (blue arrows) and upscaling of ecological dynamics to regional and continental scales (red arrows) are shown. Adapted from Peters et al. (2008).

Class of event	Initial conditions of driver			Spatial extent of ecological impact through time	Explanatory variables for magnitude of ecological impact	
	Intensity	Spatial extent	Duration		Initially	Through time
Synchronization	Low	Meso- to global scale	Years to decades	No directional change: varies with driver and event	Driver intensity	Driver intensity
Attenuation	Very high	Local- to meso-scale	Sub-daily to months	Rapid increase followed by gradual asymptote	Physical properties of event - Initial driver intensity - Distance to impacted system at onset	Physical properties of event Ecological properties
Amplification	Low to moderate	Local	Sub-daily to decades	Increases non-linearly with thresholds	Ecological processes and properties (dominant processes change through time and space)	Ecological processes and properties Spatial extent of impact increases through time Land-atmosphere feedbacks

Table 1. Three classes of globalization events determined by ecological responses that result from interactions between drivers and ecosystems.

3.1 Synchronization of ecological responses across scales

The first case occurs when a driver of low intensity over a large spatial extent for a long period of time overwhelms fine-scale heterogeneity in landscape structure of vegetation, soils, topography, and degree of urbanization (Fig. 2). These drivers, also called press disturbances (Bender et al., 1984), can occur for years to decades or centuries. Impacts of the event tend to be related to the intensity or magnitude of the driver. The less well-known or appreciated feature of this class of events is that the driver acts to synchronize ecological dynamics over a large spatial extent. An example is provided by global circulation patterns interacting with sub-continental to continental-scale phenomena to generate regional to continental-scale drought. The most intense, widespread, long-term drought in recent US history occurred in the 1930s (Fig. 3). Long-term climate data combined with average on-site conditions have been used to characterize this drought within the longer-term record using the Palmer Drought Severity Index (PDSI). The PDSI is calculated based on precipitation and temperature data, as well as the local Available Water Content (AWC) of the soil (Palmer, 1965). Data starting in 1895 for nine locations from different ecosystems and locations across the US show the variability in PDSI through time (Fig. 3) (data from http://www.cpc.ncep.noaa.gov/; excerpted from Peters et al., 2011). Although all locations had at least one drought year (negative PDSI), the extended sequence of dry years was more pronounced in the western and central parts of the country. It is expected that this synchronicity in climate drivers had large impacts on ecosystem dynamics over the same time period, although comparable multi-site data across the country for this historical period do not exist. However, it is known that synchronicity in ecosystem dynamics occurred at the regional scale during this drought. A number of research sites were monitored for vegetation change in the central Great Plains during the 1930s, and the results showed high losses in grass recovery throughout the region (Albertson & Weaver, 1942; Weaver & Albertson, 1940). Recent studies show that plant production can be synchronized at the landscape scale during long-term drought, but these same locations act independent from each other during individual dry or wet years as well as during a period of multiple wet years (Peters et al., submitted). These results suggest that broad-scale drivers can have different influences on connectivity and ecological dynamics depending on changes in magnitude and duration of the driver.

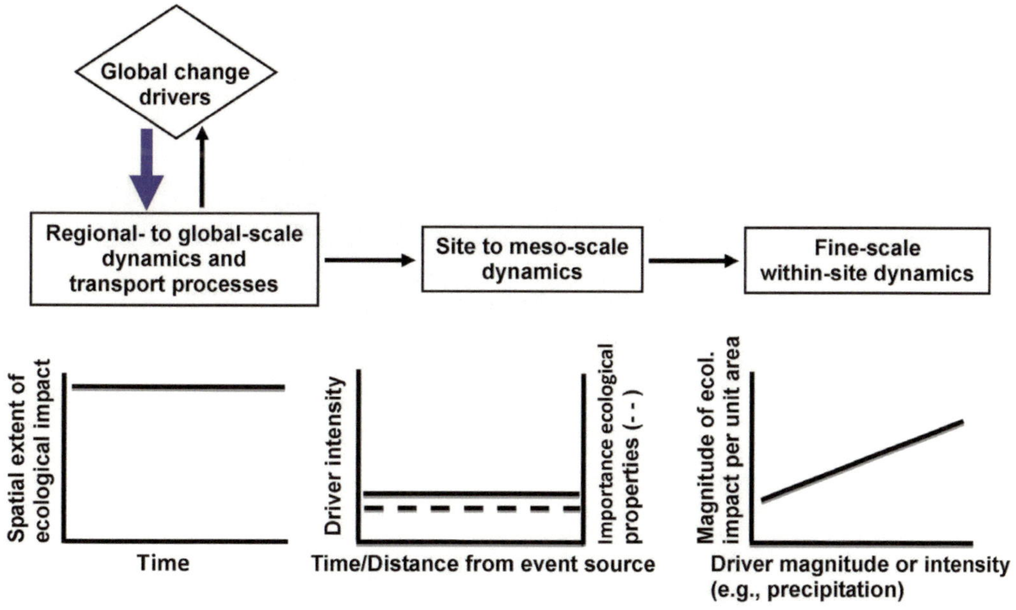

Fig. 2. Synchronization occurs when a driver of low intensity over a large spatial extent for a long period of time (thick blue line) overwhelms fine-scale heterogeneity in landscape structure of vegetation, soils, topography, and degree of urbanization to result in similar impacts. These drivers, also called press disturbances, can occur for years to decades or centuries. Impacts of the event tend to be linearly related to the intensity or magnitude of the driver. Driver intensity and importance of ecological properties are not related to the time since the event or distance from the event source.

Other examples of spatial synchronization in magnitude of drivers include higher human population density in the eastern US causing higher total sulfur dioxide and nitrogen oxide emissions compared to the West (Driscoll et al., 2011). Emissions of sulfur dioxide are the result of coal-fired electric utilities in the east (Dennis et al., 2007). Emissions of nitrogen oxides result from electric utilities and transportation sources in the east whereas ammonia emissions are higher in the west due to agricultural activities (Driscoll et al., 2003). These patterns in emissions are reflected in continental-scale patterns in atmospheric deposition. For example, nitrogen in precipitation is higher in the east compared to the northwest (Fig. 4a,b). The largest decreases in atmospheric deposition of nitrogen in the past several decades has occurred in the east (Fig. 4c, d) as a result of the Clean Air Act and greater reductions in fossil fuel emissions at that broad scale (Peters et al., 2011). Studies of effects of broad-scale synchronicity in deposition of nutrients limiting to plants and animals are needed to determine if ecological responses are also synchronized or if they are dependent on fine-scale heterogeneity in other drivers and ecological patterns and processes.

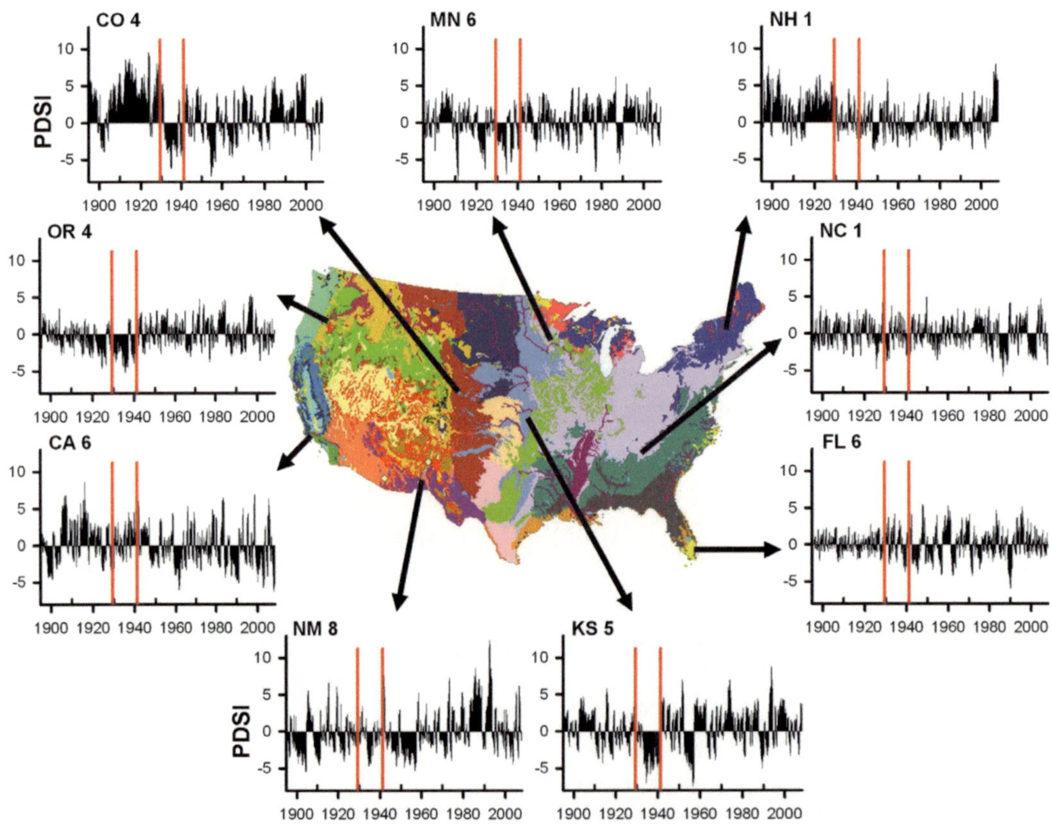

Fig. 3. Palmer Drought Severity Index (PDSI) through time from 1895 to 2008 for nine sites selected to cover the continental US and to represent major ecosystem types (background colors). Synchronicity in climate drivers across the West (excluding California) and Midwest is shown by negative values during the drought of the 1930s (between red lines).

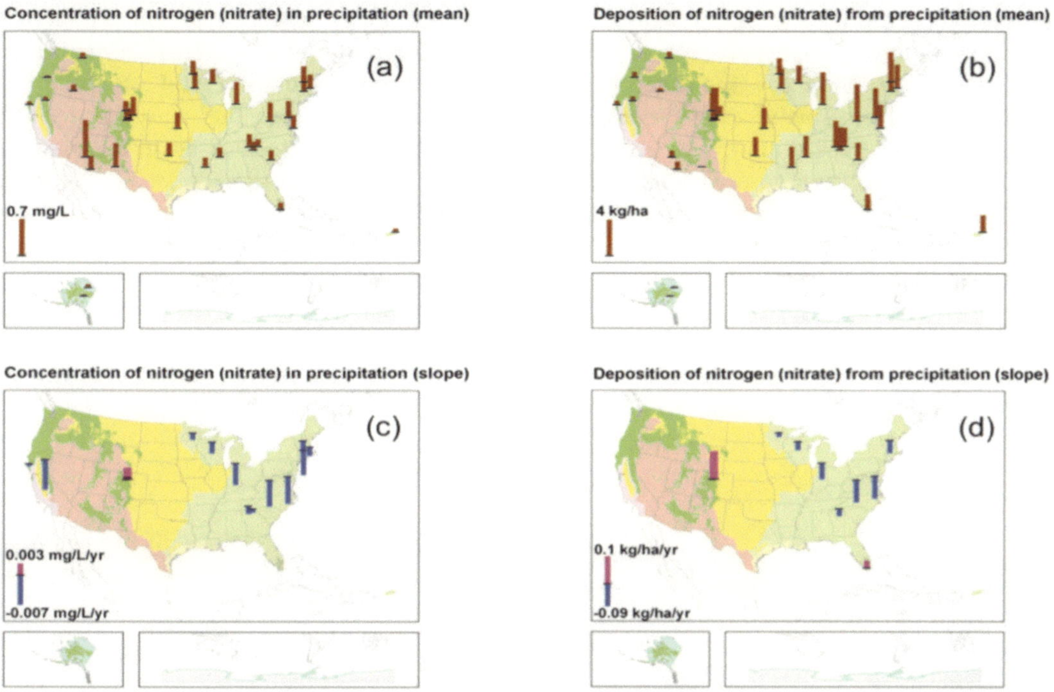

Fig. 4. Atmospheric deposition of nitrogen in precipitation as (a) and (c) volume weighted concentration (mg/L) and (b) and (d) wet deposition (kg/ha). Top panels are long-term averages. Bottom panels are slopes of regressions through time where positive values are pink and negative values are blue. Original data from http://nadp.sws.uiuc.edu/. Synthesized data from http://www.ecotrends.info. Figure from Peters et al. (2011).

3.2 Attenuation of ecological responses across scales

The second case occurs when a very high intensity driver occurs over a relatively short time period (days to weeks) to initially impact a large area (Fig. 5). Through time, these broad-scale "pulse" events (Bender et al., 1984) can propagate globally. However, the rate of spread slows down and dissipates over time with an attenuation in intensity of impacts. Fine-scale heterogeneity in landscape structure becomes increasingly important to the ecological response as the intensity of the driver decreases in time and space. The interaction between a driver and fine-scale ecological and transport processes results in no relationship between driver intensity or magnitude and ecological impact.

Examples of broad-scale pulses that propagate spatially, but lose intensity include tsunamis and volcanoes. In both examples, a high intensity event occurs within short time period of days to weeks over a fairly large area that then propagates spatially, often to impact global systems. The tsunami in December 2004 resulted from a 9.0 magnitude earthquake that influenced a large area under the Indian Ocean (Fig. 6a). An extremely high intensity wave and the following successive waves were spread globally within 44 hours (Fig. 6b). The rate of spread decreased through time and space (Merrifield et al., 2005) such that the severity of impact was negatively related to distance from the source of the event. Closer locations to the earthquake were devastated by the impact of the wave regardless of land- or seascape structure. As distance from the source increased, impact decreased and structures in the form of vegetation, buildings, marshes, forests, and geologic formations were more effective at minimizing the impact to both ecological and human-dominated systems (Fernando & McCulley, 2005). Similarly, the Icelandic volcano of 2010 spewed an ash cloud over much of the Northern Hemisphere within several weeks (Fig. 6c). This dense cloud closed European air space and affected air travel globally. Ecological effects of volcanic eruptions can be indirect as a result of interactions across scales. For example, sulfur dioxide in the ash from the 1991 eruption of Mount Pinatubo in the Philippines combined with water vapor in the upper atmosphere to reflect sunlight back to the atmosphere, and decrease in air surface temperatures globally 0.4 to 0.5°C for several years. Effects of multi-year temperature decreases and atmospheric inputs to ecological systems are unknown and not well-recognized as to their potential importance because these are rare events. However, the propagation of these impacts and their high intensity with pulses of material inputs need to be examined within the broader context of global change drivers interacting across scales.

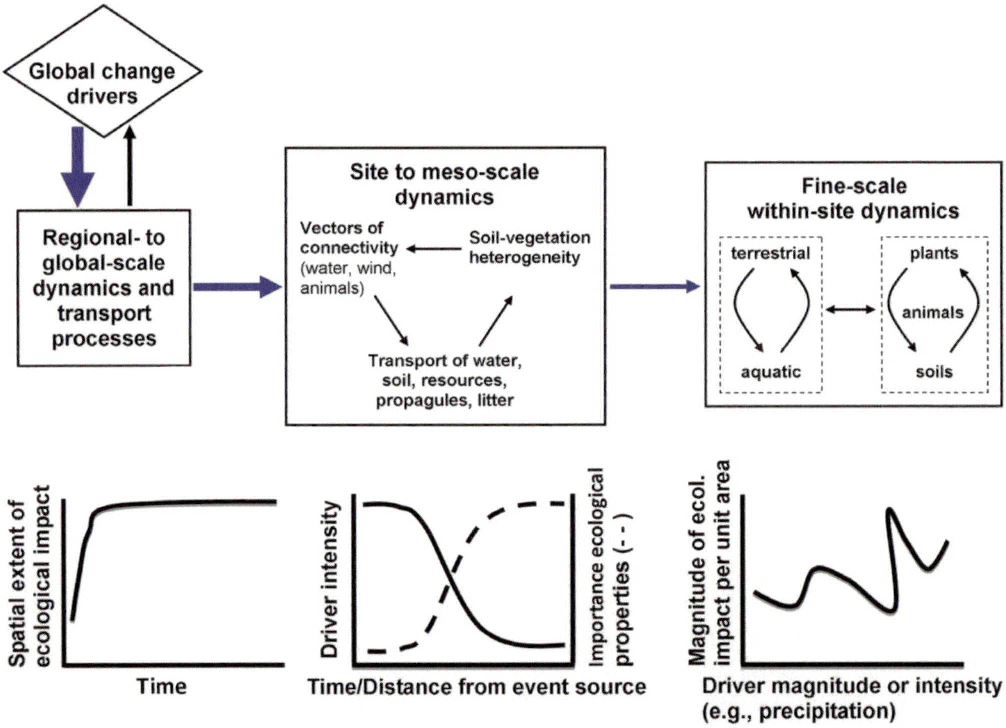

Fig. 5. Attenuation occurs when a very high intensity driver occurs over a relatively short time period (days to weeks) over a large area (thick blue line). Through time, these broad-scale "pulse" events dissipate and attenuate spatially. Fine-scale heterogeneity in landscape structure becomes increasingly important to the ecological response as the intensity of the driver decreases in time and space. Magnitude of impact is not linearly related to driver characteristics.

3.3 Amplification of ecological responses across scales

In the third case, low intensity drivers over a small spatial extent interact with properties of the ecological system to modify pattern-process relationships through time and space (Fig.

7). The result is that ecological responses propagate non-linearly to affect a broad spatial extent as a result of transport processes at multiple scales. The dominant process changes through time to result in threshold dynamics and qualitatively different kinds and rates of change than were involved in the initial interaction (Peters et al., 2004a). The rate of propagation of fine-scale changes to broader spatial scales depends on the spatial configuration, connectivity, and flows within and among fine- to meso-scale units, the interaction of these patterns with broad-scale drivers, and feedbacks among these elements across scales (Okin et al., 2009). The thresholds indicate that distinct exogenous processes or endogenous positive feedbacks are governing rates of change. This framework based on spatial nonlinearities complements antecedent concepts about the rate and spatial pattern of change by relating fine-scale processes to drivers and feedbacks at broader extents.

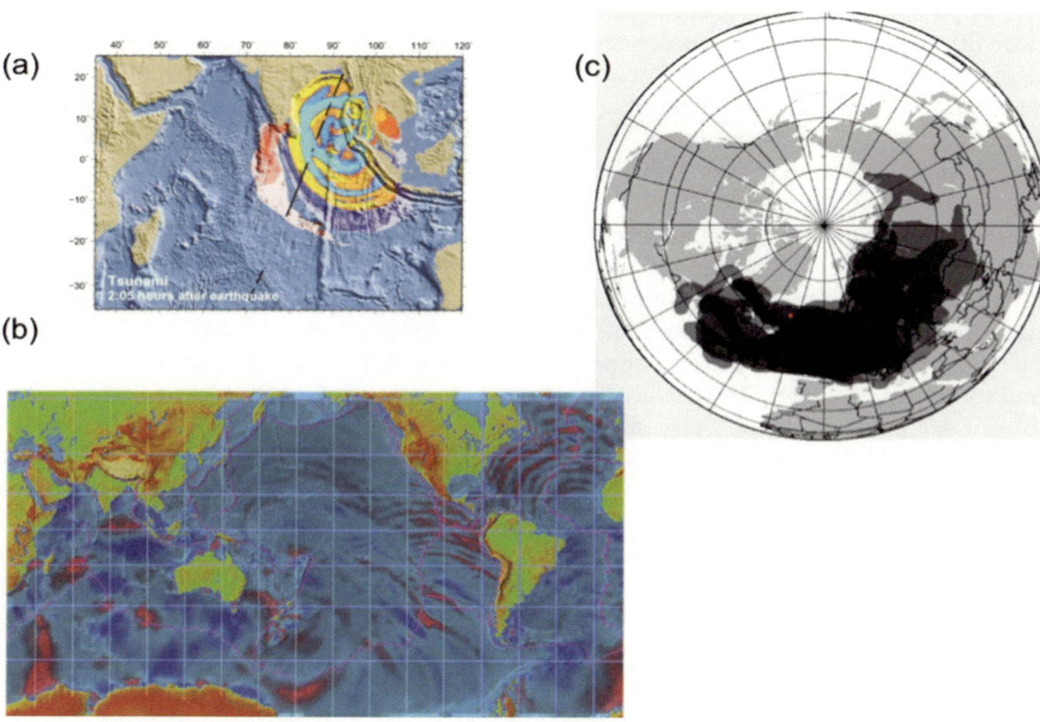

Fig. 6. (a) Tsunami in 2004 in the Indian Ocean began as 9.0 magnitude earthquake that (b) propagated globally within 44 hours (darker oceanic colors indicate greater intensity). As the intensity dissipated, the ecological and societal impacts decreased. Initial spread was governed by physical processes whereas impact through time became increasingly influenced by landscape structure and biotic processes. Images from National Oceanic and Atmospheric Administration (http://noaa.gov). (c) Icelandic volcano in 2010 exhibited high intensity dynamics followed by global transmission and dissipation of intensity and energy through time and space "(darker colors indicate greater intensity). Based on maps found at http://www.metoffice.gov.uk/ aviation/vaac/vaacu). Daily layers from 14-25 April 2010 combined into one image.

Examples of this behavior that can emerge across scales include wildfire that starts with a single ignition source, often from lightning or human causes, and cascades to influence large landscapes (e.g., Fig. 8a; Yellowstone National Park). Large fires often generate their own weather that leads to multiple ignition sources with inputs to the atmosphere that connects broad spatial extents (Fig. 8b). Nonlinear spread of invasive species across continents, water and sediment redistribution from small river channels to the ocean, and desertification dynamics from small, isolated patches to inter-continental transport of dust are additional dynamics that follow this model (Allen, 2007; Crowl et al., 2008; Marshall et al., 2008; Peters et al., 2006b; Williamson et al., 2008).

These cross-scale interactions can result in surprising behavior that cannot be predicted based on historical drivers or local inputs. For example, small thunderstorms in northwestern Africa can develop through time into hurricanes that influence North America after passing through a series of storm stages with increasing intensity and spatial extent (Fig. 9) (Dunn, 1940; Goldenberg et al., 2001; Landsea, 1993). Some African thunderstorms move off-shore to create tropical depressions in the Atlantic Ocean (Avila & Clark 1989). Of these, some develop into tropical storms and some storms build into sufficient intensity and extent to develop into hurricanes that strike the coast of North America. Each stage is controlled by a different set of physical-atmospheric-chemical processes, including teleconnections between storms in Africa and the El Niño Southern Oscillation in the tropical Pacific (Glantz et al., 1991). A shift to a new stage results in the crossing of a threshold and fundamental change in the behavior of the storm (Landsea et al., 1998), similar to wildfire and other cascading events (Fig. 9a). Furthermore, each storm is influenced by the atmospheric conditions at the time such that each follows its own storm track. Most hurricanes follow a landfall track similar to Hurricane Hugo (Fig. 9a), although the band of landfall can stretch to central Texas. However, in rare cases, a hurricane can hit land in extreme southern Texas and move to the northwest before heading eastward (Fig. 9b). For example, Hurricane Dolly in 2008 created extremely wet summer conditions as far inland as the Chihuahuan deserts of North America with 86% of the total annual rainfall falling in July (Fig. 9c). This surprising amount of rainfall initiated perennial grass recruitment events with legacy effects to the present (Peters et al., submitted). Although Hurricane Dolly did not start in western Africa, future hurricanes that connect deserts in North America with northwestern Africa under climate change are under-appreciated, yet may provide explanations for extreme system behavior and opportunities for future regime shifts or the development of novel ecosystems (Hobbs et al., 2006).

4. Approaches to understanding and prediction of connected systems

As evidence mounts that ecological systems are becoming increasingly connected through the transport of materials, resources, and information by a variety of transport vectors (animals, wind, water, disturbance), the challenges associated with understanding and predicting these complex dynamics are also increasing. Because errors of commission increase with the number of measurements, transport of materials from adjacent and non-adjacent locations should first be examined for importance relative to local inputs (Peters et al., 2004b). If redistribution across locations is important to ecological dynamics, then there are four main approaches to measuring or sampling both local inputs and fluxes or flows through time across a defined spatial extent: (1) Cross-location comparisons of existing data can provide important insights into patterns in driver and response data that may be

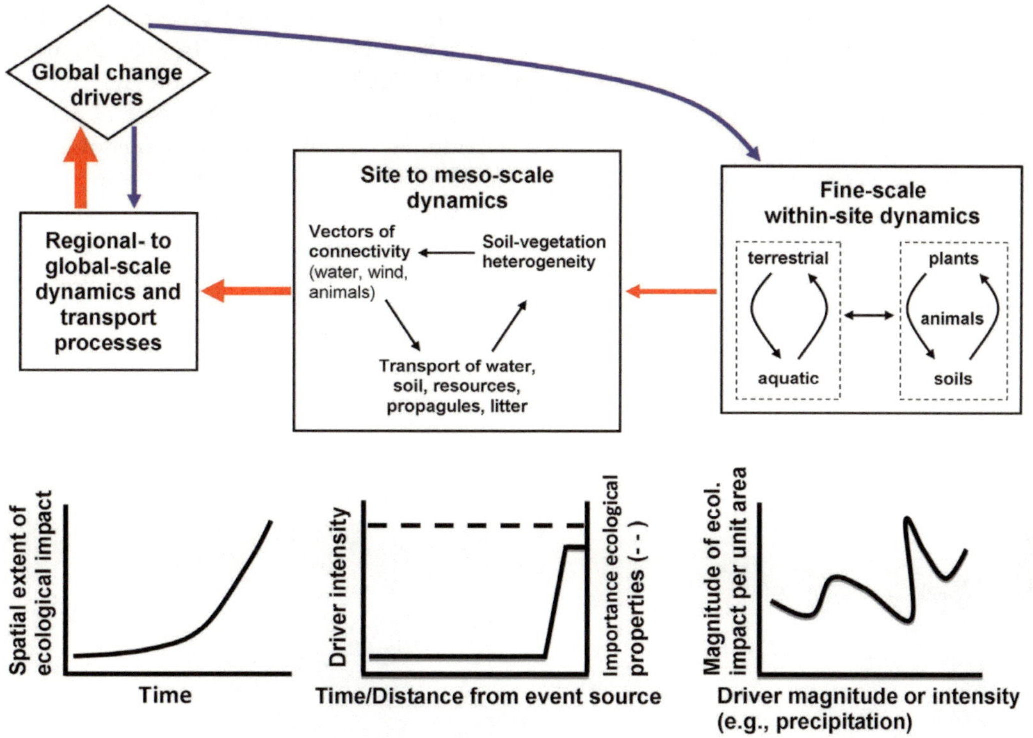

Fig. 7. Amplification occurs when low intensity drivers interact with properties of the ecological system, in particular transport processes at multiple, interacting scales, to modify pattern-process relationships through time and space (Peters et al., 2004a) The result is that ecological responses propagate non-linearly to affect a broad spatial extent (increasingly thicker red arrows). Driver intensity is low until land-atmosphere interactions become the dominant process that feed back to fine-scale patterns and processes. These feedbacks amplify the influence of the driver.

synchronized across locations (e.g., Figs. 3, 4). Analyses can also be used to determine if responses at one location are correlated with drivers or responses at another location as an indicator of synchronicity. Recently, hundreds of long-term data sets from 50 sites in the US were examined in this screening approach to determine both broad-scale patterns in drivers and responses, and potential connectivity among locations (Peters, 2010; Peters et al., 2011); (2) Experimental manipulations can be used to examine the role of similar events of a driver in different systems across a range of scales. Most experiments to-date are short-term (< 5 years) and have focused on local inputs rather than the horizontal transport of materials (e.g., Fay et al., 2008; Heisler-White et al., 2009). Notable exceptions are experiments that modify vegetation structure in order to alter resource redistribution (Jones & Post, 2004; Li et al., 2009a, 2009b) and tracer experiments used in streams (Mulholland et al., 2008; O'Brien et al., 2007); (3) Simulation models can be used to compare dynamics within and among ecosystem types to a variety of drivers, and to tease apart the relative importance of local inputs and transport of materials. Most ecosystems models simulate local climate inputs, although fire spread models, wind erosion, and hydrologic models examine the importance of transport to ecological dynamics (Daly et al., 2000l; Ivanov et al., 2008; Okin, 2008); (4)

One of the most promising approaches is provided by network-level observatories that collect similar types of measurements in similar ways (Peters, 2010). In the US, these national-level networks include sites operated by the USDA Forest Service and Agricultural Research Service, and the Long Term Ecological Research Program (Peters et al., 2011). Multi-site comparisons of historic data have proven to be very insightful (Lugo et al., 2006; Moran et al., 2008), and have led to the development of emerging networks with standardized data protocols across diverse ecosystems (e.g., the National Ecological Observatory Network). Comparable standardization in cyberinfrastructure is being developed to promote data and metadata protocols for archival and retrieval that are necessary for open data access and multi-site comparisons globally (Reichman et al., 2011).

Fig. 8. (a) Small ignition sources (e.g., a lightning strike) can initiate a wildfire that spreads nonlinearly to influence very large landscapes (Allen, 2007). The 2009 fire in Yellowstone National Park started by lightning on 13 September grew to 9300 ha by 1 October. Photo taken from the International Space Station looking southwest towards Teton Range showing Yellowstone Lake in center with reflection of smoke plume (http://earthobservatory.nasa.gov). (b) Multiple ignition sources are common as fires increase in size regionally with large smoke and particulate plumes released to the atmosphere to connect region, continents, and the globe. Fires in southern California in October 2003 were fueled by hot, dry winds: at least one fire grew 10,000 acres in just 6 hours (http://earthobservatory.nasa.gov).

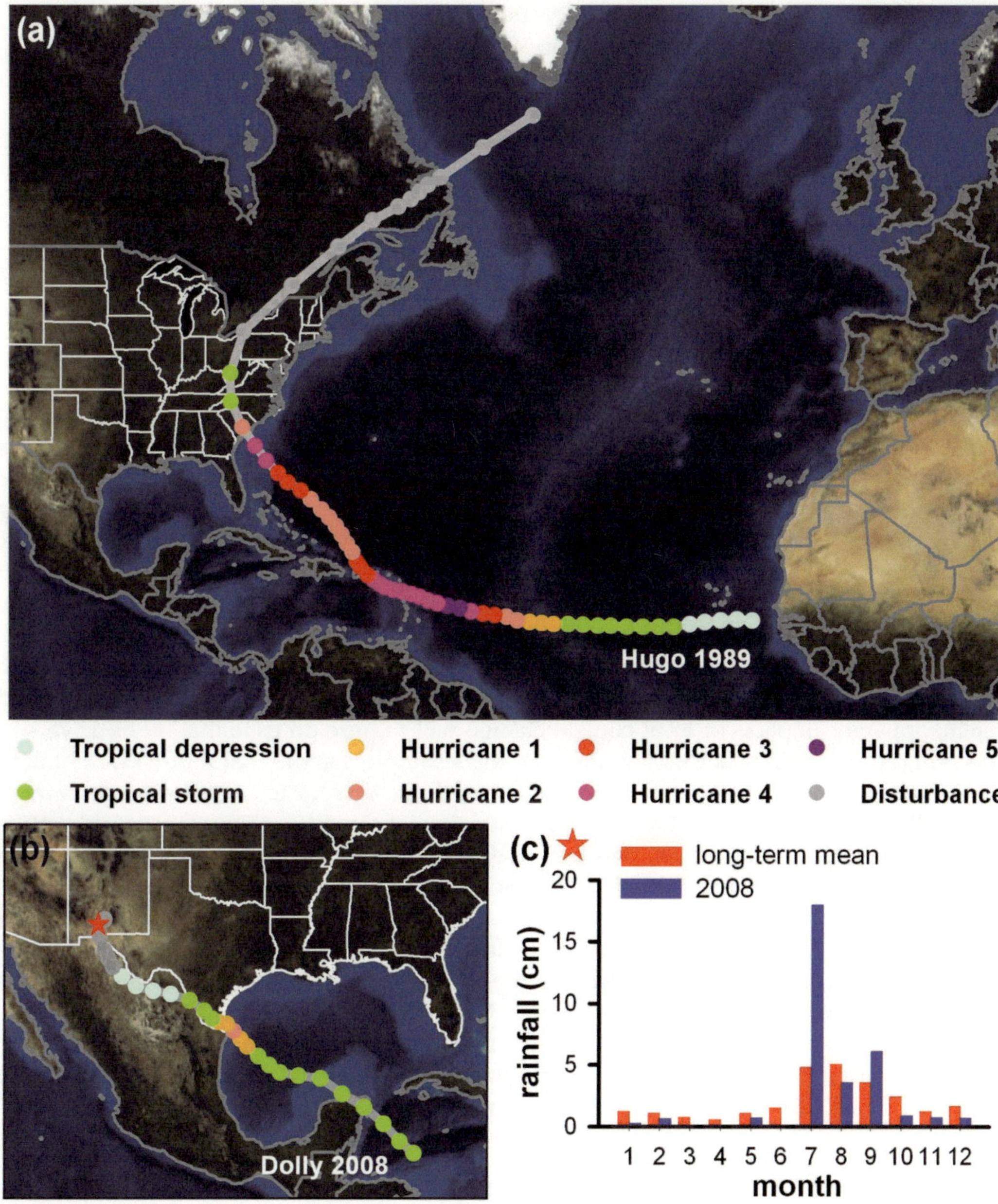

Fig. 9. Hurricanes are one example of an amplification event that starts small and propagates nonlinearly through time and space to influence very large areas that can connect continents on non-intuitive ways. (a) Hurricanes in North America start as thunderstorms in west Africa that move off-shore to create tropical depressions. As the depression builds in size and intensity, a tropical storm results that continues to build until a hurricane develops. Each stage is driven by a different set of linked atmospheric-oceanic processes with thresholds occurring between stages (http://maps.csc.noaa.gov; http://ww2010.atmos/uiuc.edu). (b) Although most hurricanes follow a similar track as

Hurricane Hugo, in some cases, hurricanes begin in the Gulf of Mexico and strike land in extremely south Texas and move to the northwest before heading east. These hurricanes (e.g., Hurricane Dolly: http://www.hpc.ncep.noaa.gov/) can result in very large amounts of rainfall over short periods of time in locations that are typically very dry. (c) For example, Hurricane Dolly produced 86% of the total annual rainfall in one month in locations in the Chihuahuan Desert (http://usda-ars.nmsu.edu). This large pulse of rainfall resulted in a broad-scale perennial grass recruitment event that has persisted to the present (Peters et al., submitted). Infrequent connectivity between locations on different continents may become more common in the future as the intensity of hurricanes increases with climate change, and may overwhelm dynamics driven historically by local rainfall inputs.

5. Conclusions

In an era of globalization, it is imperative that ecologists consider the possibility that local inputs are not governing observed dynamics, but rather that the redistribution of materials from adjacent or non-contiguous locations are overwhelming these local effects. This realization will require a "mind shift" away from the traditional approaches of relating ecological dynamics to local drivers, such as precipitation, with high unexplained variation. Conceptualizing ecological systems as inter-connected across many scales in the Earth System is one way to explain this high variation. Three classes of events were described here as ways to accomplish this shift in thinking and application. For example, extremely high precipitation amounts leading to unusual grass recruitment in the Chihuahuan Desert in 2008 resulted from a hurricane in the Gulf of Mexico. Under such a highly connected system, apparent impacts of local climate change will require an examination of drivers in non-contiguous locations across the globe. In this example, factors that influence rainfall in the Gulf of Mexico may be equally important as local drivers to future extreme rainfall events in the Chihuahuan Desert and the American Southwest regions. Future research is needed to identify where, when, and how the different elements of the Earth System are connected. Experimental manipulations across locations and biomes that include transport vectors at multiple scales are critically needed. Simulation models with an explicit consideration of thresholds and cross-scale interactions of the linked land-atmosphere-surface water system will be required for prediction. These challenges are large, but the development of cyberinfrastructure software, hardware, and accessibility tools are on the near horizon that will allow global information transfer and use that are needed for synthesis (Carpenter et al., 2009). Ecologists need to be ready (conceptually and quantitatively) to take full advantage of these tools.

6. Acknowledgements

Funding support was provided by the National Science Foundation to New Mexico State University as part of the Jornada Basin Long Term Ecological Research Program (DEB-0618210). Jin Yao assisted in figure preparation.

7. Reference

Albertson, F.W., & Weaver, J.E. (1942). History of the native vegetation of western Kansas during seven years of continuous drought. *Ecological Monographs,* 12, 23-51.

Allen, C.D. (2007). Interactions across spatial scales among forest dieback, fire, and erosion in northern New Mexico landscapes. *Ecosystems,* 10, 797-808.

Allen, T.F.H., & Starr, T.B. (1982). *Hierarchy theory: perspectives for ecological complexity.* University of Chicago Press, Chicago, IL, USA.

Avila, L.A., & Clark, G.B. Clark. (1989). Atlantic tropical systems of 1988. *Monthly Weather Review,* 117, 2260-2265.

Bender, E. A., Case, T. J., & Gilpin, M.E. (1984). Perturbation experiments in community ecology: theory and practice. *Ecology,* 65, 1–13.

Carpenter, S.R., Armbrust, E.V., Arzberger, P.W., Chapin, F.S. III, Elser, J.J., Hackett, E.J., Ives, A.R., Kareiva, P.M., Leibold, M.A., Lundberg, P., Mangel, M., Merchant, N., Murdoch, W.W., Palmer, M.A., Peters, D.P.C., Pickett, S.T.A., Smith, K.K., Wall, D.H., & Zimmerman, A.S. (2009). Accelerate synthesis in ecology and environmental sciences. *BioScience,* 59, 699-701.

Crowl, T.A., Crist, T.O., Parmenter, R.R., Belovsky, G., & Lugo, A.E. (2008). The spread of invasive species and infectious disease as drivers of ecosystem change. *Frontiers in Ecology and the Environment,* 6, 238-246.

Dale, V.H., Joyce, L.A., McNulty, S., Neilson, R.P., Ayres, M.P., Flannigan, M.D., Hanson, P.J., Irland, L.C., Lugo, A.E., Peterson, C.J., Simberloff, D., Swanson, F.J., Stocks, B.J., & Wotton, B.M. (2001). Climate change and forest disturbances. *BioScience,* 51, 723-734.

Daly, C., Bachelet, D., Lenihan, J.M., Neilson, R.P., Parton, W.J., & Ojima, D.S. (2000). Dynamic simulation of tree-grass interactions for global change studies. *Ecological Applications,* 10, 449-469.

Dennis, R., Haeuber, R., Blett, T., Cosby, J., Discoll, C.T., Sickles, J., & Johnston, J. (2007). Sulfur and nitrogen deposition on ecosystems in the United States. *Environmental Management,* 2007, 12-17.

Dietz, T., Rosa, E.A., York, R. (2007). Driving the human ecological footprint. *Frontiers in Ecology and the Environment,* 5, 13-18.

Driscoll, C.T., Whitall, D., Aber, J., Boyer, E., Castro, M., Cronan, C., Goodale, C.L., Groffman, P., Hopkinson, C., Lambert, K., Lawrence, G., & Ollinger, S. (2003). Nitrogen pollution in the northeastern United States: Sources, effects, and management options. *BioScience,* 53, 357-374.

Driscoll, C.T., Groffman, P.M., Blair, J.M., Lugo, A.E., Laney, C.M. & Peters, D.P.C. (2011). Cross-site comparisons of precipitation and surface water chemistry. In: *Long-term trends in ecological systems: a basis for understanding responses to global change.* Peters, D.P.C., Laney, C.M., Lugo, A.E., Collins, S.L., Driscoll, C.T., Groffman, P.M., Grove, J.M., Knapp, A.K., Kratz, T.K., Ohman, M.D., Waide, R.B., & Yao, J. (eds). pp. xxx-xxx. USDA Agricultural Research Service Publication No. XX. Washington, D.C.

Dunn, G.E. (1940). Cyclogenesis in the tropical Atlantic. *Bulletin of the American Meteorological Society,* 21, 215-229.

Emanuel, K.A. (2005). Increasing destructiveness of tropical cyclones over the past 30 years. *Nature,* 436, 686-688.

Fagre, D.B., Charles, C.W., lead authors. (2009). *Thresholds of climate change in ecosystems.* U.S. Geological Survey, Department of the Interior, Washington, DC.

Fay, P.A., Kaufman, D.M., Nippert, J.B., Carlisle, J.D., & Harper, C.W. (2008). Changes in grassland ecosystem function due to extreme rainfall events: implications for responses to climate change. *Global Change Biology*, 14, 1600-1608.

Fernando, H.J.S. & McCulley, R. (2005). Coral poaching worsens tsunami destruction in Sri Lanka. *Eoc*, 86, 301-304.

Field, J.P. Belnap, J., Breshears, D.D., Neff, J.C., Okin, G.S., Whicker, J.J., Painter, T.P., Ravi, S., Reheis, M.C., & Reynolds, R.L. (2010). The ecology of dust. *Frontiers in Ecology and the Environment*, 8, 423-430.

Glantz, M.H., Katz, R.W. , & Nicholls, N. (1991). Teleconnections linking worldwide climate anomalies: scientific basis and societal impact. Cambridge University Press, Cambridge. 534pp.

Goldenberg, S.B., Landsea, C.W., Mestas-Nuñez, A.M., & Gray, W.M. (2001). The recent increase in Atlantic hurricane activity: causes and implications. *Science*, 293, 474-479.

Heisler-White, J.L., Blair, J.M., Kelly, E.F., Harmoney, K., & Knapp, A.K. (2009). Contingent productivity responses to more extreme rainfall regimes across a grassland biome. *Global Change Biology*, 15, 2894-2904.

Hobbs, R.J., Arico, S., Aronson, J., Baron, J.S., Bridgewater, P., Cramer, V.A., Epstein, P.R., Ewel, J.J., Klink, C.A., Lugo, A.E., Norton, D., Ojima, D., Richardson, D.M., Sanderson, E.W., Valladares, F., Vila, M., Zamora, R., & Zovel, M. (2006). Novel ecosystems: theoretical and management aspects of the new ecological world order. *Global Ecology and Biogeography*, 15, 1-7.

Hopkinson, C.S., Lugo, A.E., Alber, M., Covich, A.P., & Van Bloem, S.J. (2008). Forecasting effects of sea-level rise and windstorms on coastal and inland ecosystems. *Frontiers in Ecology and the Environment*, 6, 255-263.

IPCC. (2007). *Climate Change 2007: The Physical Science Basis.* In: Contribution of Working Group I to the Fourth Assessment Report of the Intergovernmental Panel on Climate Change. Solomon, S., Qin, D., Manning, M., Chen, Z., Marquis, M., Avery, K.B., Tignor, M., & Miller, H.L. (eds.) Cambridge University Press, Cambridge, United Kingdom and New York, NY, USA.

Ivanov, V.Y., Bras, R.L., & Vivoni, E.R. (2008). Vegetation-hydrology dynamics in complex terrain of semiarid areas: 1. A mechanistic approach to modeling dynamic feedbacks. *Water Resources Research*, 44, W03429, doi:10.1029/2006/WR005588.

Jaffe, D., McKendry, I., Anderson, T., & Price, H. (2003). Six "new" episodes of trans-Pacific transport of air pollutants. *Atmospheric Environment*, 37, 391-404.

Jones, J.A., & Post, D.A. (2004). Seasonal and successional streamflow response to forest cutting and regrowth in the northwest and eastern United States. *Water Resources Research*, 40, W05203, doi:10.1029/2003WR002952.

Kitzberger, T., Brown, P.M., Heyerdahl, E.K., Swetnam, T.W., & Veblen, T.J. (2007). Contingent Pacific-Atlantic Ocean influence on multicentury wildfire synchrony over western North America. *Proceedings of the National Academy of Sciences*, 104, 543-548.

Landsea, C.W. (1993). A climatology of intense (or major) Atlantic hurricanes. *Monthly Weather Review*, 121, 1703-1713.

Landsea, C.W., Bell, G.D., Gray, W.M., & Goldenberg, S.B. (1998). The extremely active 1995 Atlantic hurricane season: environmental conditions and verification of seasonal forecasts. *Monthly Weather Review,* 126, 1174-1193.

Li, J.R., Okin, G.S., Alvarez, L.J., & Epstein, H.E. (2009a). Sediment deposition and soil nutrient heterogeneity in two desert grassland ecosystems, southern New Mexico, southern New Mexico. *Plant and Soil,* 319(1-2), 67-84.

Li, J.R., Okin, G.S., & Epstein, H.E. (2009b). Effects of enhanced wind erosion on surface soil texture and characteristics of windblown sediments. *Journal of Geophysical Research-Biogeosciences,* 114, DOI:10.1029/2008JG000903.

Luck, M.A, Jenerette, G.D., Wu, J., & Grimm, N.B. (2001). The urban funnel model and spatially heterogeneous ecological footprint. *Ecosystems,* 4, 782-796.

Lugo, A.E., Swanson, F.J., Gonzalez, O.R., Adams, M.B., Palik, B., Thill, R.E., Brockway, D.G., Kern, C., Woodsmith, R., & Musselman, R. (2006). Long- term research at the USDA Forest Service's experimental forests and ranges. *BioScience,* 56, 39–48.

Marshall, J.D., Blair, J.M., Peters, D.P.C., Okin, G.S., Rango, A., & Williams, M. (2008). Predicting and understanding ecosystem responses to climate change at continental scales. *Frontiers in Ecology and the Environment,* 6, 273-280.

Merrifield, M.A., Firing, Y.L., Aarup, T., Agricole, W., Brundit, G., Chang-Seng, D., Farre, R., Kilonsky, B., Knight, W., Kong, L., Magori, C., Manurung, P., McCreery, C., Mitchell, W., Pillary, S., Scindele, F., Shillington, F., Testut, L., Wijeratne, E.M.S., Caldwell, P., Jardin, J., Nakahara, S., Porter, F-Y., Turetsky, N. (2005). Tide gauge observations of the Indian Ocean tsunami, December 26, 2004. *Geophysical Research Letters,* 32, L09603, doi:10.1029/2005GL022610.

McConnell, J.R., Aristarain, A.J., Banta, J.R., Edwards, P.R., & Simones, J.C. (2007). 20th-Century doubling in dust archived in an Antarctic Peninsula ice core parallels climate change and desertification in South America. *Proceedings in the National Academy of Sciences USA,* 104, 5743–5748.

Millenium Ecosystem Assessment (MEA). (2005). *Ecosystems and human well-being: synthesis.* Island Press, Washington, D.C.

Moran M.S., Peters, D.P.C., McClaran, M., Nichols, M.H., & Adams, M. (2008). Long-term data collection at USDA experimental sites for studies of ecohydrology. *Ecohydrology,* 1, 377-393.

Mulholland, P. J., Helton, A.M., Poole, G.C., Hall, R.O. Jr., Hamilton, S.K., Peterson, B.J., Tank, J.L., Ashkenas, L.R., Cooper, L.W., Dahm, C.N., Dodds, W.K., Findlay, S., Gregory, S.V., Grimm, N.B., Johnson, S.L., McDowell, W.H., Meyer, J.L., Valett, J,M., Webster, J.R., Arango, C., Beaulieu, J.J., Bernot, M.J., Burgin, A.J., Crenshaw, C., Johnson, L., Merriam, J., Niederlehner, B.R., O'Brien, J.M., Potter, J.D., Sheibley, R.W., Sobota, D.J., & Thomas, S.M. (2008). Stream denitrification across biomes and its response to anthropogenic nitrate loading. *Nature,* 452, 202-205.

Neff, J.C., Ballantyne, A.P., Farmer, G.L., Mahowald, N.M., Conroy, J.L., Landry, C.C., Overpeck, J.T., Painter, T.H., Lawrence, C.R., & Reynolds, R.L. (2008). *Nature Geoscience,* 1, 189-195.

O'Brien, J.M., Dodds, W.K., Wilson, K.C., Murdock, J.N., & Eichmiller, J. (2007). The saturation of N cycling in Central Plains streams: 15N experiments across a broad gradient of nitrate concentrations. *Biogeochemistry,* 84, 31-49.

Okin, G.S. (2008). A new model of wind erosion in the presence of vegetation. *Journal of Geophysical Research-Earth Surface*, 113, F02S10, doi:10.1029/2007JF000758.

Okin, G.S., Parson, A.J., Wainwright J., Herrick, J.E., Bestelmeyer, B.T., Peters, D.P.C., & Fredrickson, E.L. (2009). Do changes in connectivity explain desertification? *BioScience*, 59, 237-244.

Palmer, W.C. (1965) *Meteorological Drought*. Research Paper No. 45, Dept. of Commerce, Washington, D.C.

Perrings, C., Mooney, H., & Williamson, M. (2010). *Bioinvasions and globalization: ecology, economics, management, and policy*. Oxford University Press, Oxford.

Peters, D.P.C. (2010). Accessible ecology: synthesis of the long, deep, and broad. *Trends in Ecology and Evolution*, 25, 592-601.

Peters, D.P.C., Bestelmeyer, B.T., Herrick, J.E., Monger, H.C., Fredrickson, E., & Havstad, K.M. (2006a). Disentangling complex landscapes: new insights to forecasting arid and semiarid system dynamics. *BioScience*, 56, 491-501.

Peters, D.P.C., Groffman, P.M., Nadelhoffer, K.J., Grimm, N.B., Collins, S.L., Michener, W.K., & Huston, M.A. (2008). Living in an increasingly connected world: a framework for continental-scale environmental science. *Frontiers in Ecology and the Environment*, 5, 229-237.

Peters, D.P.C., Laney, C.M., Lugo, A.E., Collins, S.L., Driscoll, C.T., Groffman, P.M., Grove, J.M., Knapp, A.K., Kratz, T.K., Ohman, M.D., Waide, R.B., & Yao, J. (2011). *Long-term trends in ecological systems: a basis for understanding responses to global change*. USDA Agricultural Research Service Publication No. XX. Washington, D.C.

Peters, D.P.C., Pielke, R.A. Sr, Bestelmeyer, B.T., Allen, C.D., Munson-McGee, S., & Havstad, K.M. (2004a). Cross-scale interactions, nonlinearities, and forecasting catastrophic events. *Proceedings of the National Academy of Sciences USA*, 101, 15130-15135.

Peters, D.P.C., Pielke, R.A. Sr, Bestelmeyer, B.T., Allen, C.D., Munson-McGee, S., & Havstad, K.M. 2006b. Spatial nonlinearities in the Earth System. In: *Terrestrial ecosystems in a changing world*, Canadell, J., Pataki, D., & Pitelka, L., eds, pp. 165-173, Springer, Berlin.

Peters, D.P.C., Urban, D.L., Gardner, R.H., Breshears, D.D., & Herrick, J.E (2004b0. Strategies for ecological extrapolation. *Oikos*, 106, 627-636.

Peters, D.P.C., Yao, J., Sala, O.E., Anderson, J. (submitted). Directional climate change and potential reversal of desertification in arid ecosystems. *Global Change Biology*.

Reichman, O.J., Jones, M.B., & Schildhauer, M.P. (2011). Challenges and opportunities of open data in ecology. *Science*, 331, 703-705.

Rial, J.A., Pielke, R.A. Sr, Beniston, M., Claussen, M., Canadell, J., Cox, P., Held, H., de Noblet-Ducoudé, N., Prinn, R., Reynolds, J.F., & Salas, J.D. (2004). Nonlinearities, feedbacks, and critical thresholds within the Earth's climate system. *Climatic Change*, 65, 11-38.

Tanaka, T.Y. & Chiba, M. (2006). A numerical study of the contributions of dust source regions to the global dust budget. *Global Planetary Change*, 52, 88–104.

Trenberth, K.E. (2005). Uncertainty In hurricanes and global warming. *Science*, 308, 1753-1754.

Weaver, J.E., & Albertson, F.W. (1940). Deterioration of Midwestern ranges. *Ecology*, 21, 216-236.

Williamson, C.E., Dodds, W., Kratz, T.K., & Palmer, M.A. (2008). Lakes and streams as sentinels of environmental change in terrestrial and atmospheric processes. *Frontiers in Ecology and the Environment,* 5, 247-254.

Yates,T.L., Mills, J.N., Parmenter, C.A., Ksiazek, T.G., Parmenter, R.R., Vande Castle, J.R., Calisher, C.H., Nichol, S.T., Abbott, K.D., Young, J.C., Morrison, M.L., Beaty, B.J., Dunnum, J.L., Baker, R.J., Salazar-Bravo, J., & Peters, C.J. (2002). The ecology and evolutionary history of an emergent disease: hantavirus pulmonary syndrome. *BioScience,* 52, 989-998.Dennis, R., Haeuber, R., Blett, T., Cosby, J., Discoll, C.T., Sickles, J., & Johnston, J. (2007). Sulfur and nitrogen deposition on ecosystems in the United States. *Environmental Management*, 2007, 12-17.

Dietz, T., Rosa, E.A., York, R. (2007). Driving the human ecological footprint. *Frontiers in Ecology and the Environment*, 5, 13-18.

Driscoll, C.T., Whitall, D., Aber, J., Boyer, E., Castro, M., Cronan, C., Goodale, C.L., Groffman, P., Hopkinson, C., Lambert, K., Lawrence, G., & Ollinger, S. (2003). Nitrogen pollution in the northeastern United States: Sources, effects, and management options. *BioScience,* 53, 357-374.

Driscoll, C.T., Groffman, P.M., Blair, J.M., Lugo, A.E., Laney, C.M. & Peters, D.P.C. (2011). Cross-site comparisons of precipitation and surface water chemistry. In: *Long-term trends in ecological systems: a basis for understanding responses to global change*. Peters, D.P.C., Laney, C.M., Lugo, A.E., Collins, S.L., Driscoll, C.T., Groffman, P.M., Grove, J.M., Knapp, A.K., Kratz, T.K., Ohman, M.D., Waide, R.B., & Yao, J. (eds). pp. xxx-xxx. USDA Agricultural Research Service Publication No. XX. Washington, D.C.

Dunn, G.E. (1940). Cyclogenesis in the tropical Atlantic. *Bulletin of the American Meteorological Society*, 21, 215-229.

Emanuel, K.A. (2005). Increasing destructiveness of tropical cyclones over the past 30 years. *Nature,* 436, 686-688.

Fagre, D.B., Charles, C.W., lead authors. (2009). *Thresholds of climate change in ecosystems.* U.S. Geological Survey, Department of the Interior, Washington, DC.

Fay, P.A., Kaufman, D.M., Nippert, J.B., Carlisle, J.D., & Harper, C.W. (2008). Changes in grassland ecosystem function due to extreme rainfall events: implications for responses to climate change. *Global Change Biology*, 14, 1600-1608.

Fernando, H.J.S. & McCulley, R. (2005). Coral poaching worsens tsunami destruction in Sri Lanka. *Eoc,* 86, 301-304.

Field, J.P. Belnap, J., Breshears, D.D., Neff, J.C., Okin, G.S., Whicker, J.J., Painter, T.P., Ravi, S., Reheis, M.C., & Reynolds, R.L. (2010). The ecology of dust. *Frontiers in Ecology and the Environment,* 8, 423-430.

Glantz, M.H., Katz, R.W. , & Nicholls, N. (1991). Teleconnections linking worldwide climate anomalies: scientific basis and societal impact. Cambridge University Press, Cambridge. 534pp.

Goldenberg, S.B., Landsea, C.W., Mestas-Nuñez, A.M., & Gray, W.M. (2001). The recent increase in Atlantic hurricane activity: causes and implications. *Science,* 293, 474-479.

Heisler-White, J.L., Blair, J.M., Kelly, E.F., Harmoney, K., & Knapp, A.K. (2009). Contingent productivity responses to more extreme rainfall regimes across a grassland biome. *Global Change Biology,* 15, 2894-2904.

Hobbs, R.J., Arico, S., Aronson, J., Baron, J.S., Bridgewater, P., Cramer, V.A., Epstein, P.R., Ewel, J.J., Klink, C.A., Lugo, A.E., Norton, D., Ojima, D., Richardson, D.M., Sanderson, E.W., Valladares, F., Vila, M., Zamora, R., & Zovel, M. (2006). Novel ecosystems: theoretical and management aspects of the new ecological world order. *Global Ecology and Biogeography,* 15, 1-7.

Hopkinson, C.S., Lugo, A.E., Alber, M., Covich, A.P., & Van Bloem, S.J. (2008). Forecasting effects of sea-level rise and windstorms on coastal and inland ecosystems. *Frontiers in Ecology and the Environment,* 6, 255-263.

IPCC. (2007). *Climate Change 2007: The Physical Science Basis.* In: Contribution of Working Group I to the Fourth Assessment Report of the Intergovernmental Panel on Climate Change. Solomon, S., Qin, D., Manning, M., Chen, Z., Marquis, M., Avery, K.B., Tignor, M., & Miller, H.L. (eds.) Cambridge University Press, Cambridge, United Kingdom and New York, NY, USA.

Ivanov, V.Y., Bras, R.L., & Vivoni, E.R. (2008). Vegetation-hydrology dynamics in complex terrain of semiarid areas: 1. A mechanistic approach to modeling dynamic feedbacks. *Water Resources Research,* 44, W03429, doi:10.1029/2006/WR005588.

Jaffe, D., McKendry, I., Anderson, T., & Price, H. (2003). Six "new" episodes of trans-Pacific transport of air pollutants. *Atmospheric Environment,* 37, 391-404.

Jones, J.A., & Post, D.A. (2004). Seasonal and successional streamflow response to forest cutting and regrowth in the northwest and eastern United States. *Water Resources Research,* 40, W05203, doi:10.1029/2003WR002952.

Kitzberger, T., Brown, P.M., Heyerdahl, E.K., Swetnam, T.W., & Veblen, T.J. (2007). Contingent Pacific-Atlantic Ocean influence on multicentury wildfire synchrony over western North America. *Proceedings of the National Academy of Sciences,* 104, 543-548.

Landsea, C.W. (1993). A climatology of intense (or major) Atlantic hurricanes. *Monthly Weather Review,* 121, 1703-1713.

Landsea, C.W., Bell, G.D., Gray, W.M., & Goldenberg, S.B. (1998). The extremely active 1995 Atlantic hurricane season: environmental conditions and verification of seasonal forecasts. *Monthly Weather Review,* 126, 1174-1193.

Li, J.R., Okin, G.S., Alvarez, L.J., & Epstein, H.E. (2009a). Sediment deposition and soil nutrient heterogeneity in two desert grassland ecosystems, southern New Mexico, southern New Mexico. *Plant and Soil,* 319(1-2), 67-84.

Li, J.R., Okin, G.S., & Epstein, H.E. (2009b). Effects of enhanced wind erosion on surface soil texture and characteristics of windblown sediments. *Journal of Geophysical Research-Biogeosciences,* 114, DOI:10.1029/2008JG000903.

Luck, M.A, Jenerette, G.D., Wu, J., & Grimm, N.B. (2001). The urban funnel model and spatially heterogeneous ecological footprint. *Ecosystems,* 4, 782-796.

Lugo, A.E., Swanson, F.J., Gonzalez, O.R., Adams, M.B., Palik, B., Thill, R.E., Brockway, D.G., Kern, C., Woodsmith, R., & Musselman, R. (2006). Long- term research at the USDA Forest Service's experimental forests and ranges. *BioScience,* 56, 39–48.

Marshall, J.D., Blair, J.M., Peters, D.P.C., Okin, G.S., Rango, A., & Williams, M. (2008). Predicting and understanding ecosystem responses to climate change at continental scales. *Frontiers in Ecology and the Environment,* 6, 273-280.

Merrifield, M.A., Firing, Y.L., Aarup, T., Agricole, W., Brundit, G., Chang-Seng, D., Farre, R., Kilonsky, B., Knight, W., Kong, L., Magori, C., Manurung, P., McCreery, C.,

Mitchell, W., Pillary, S., Scindele, F., Shillington, F., Testut, L., Wijeratne, E.M.S., Caldwell, P., Jardin, J., Nakahara, S., Porter, F-Y., Turetsky, N. (2005). Tide gauge observations of the Indian Ocean tsunami, December 26, 2004. *Geophysical Research Letters*, 32, L09603, doi:10.1029/2005GL022610.

McConnell, J.R., Aristarain, A.J., Banta, J.R., Edwards, P.R., & Simones, J.C. (2007). 20th-Century doubling in dust archived in an Antarctic Peninsula ice core parallels climate change and desertification in South America. *Proceedings in the National Academy of Sciences USA*, 104, 5743–5748.

Millenium Ecosystem Assessment (MEA). (2005). *Ecosystems and human well-being: synthesis.* Island Press, Washington, D.C.

Moran M.S., Peters, D.P.C., McClaran, M., Nichols, M.H., & Adams, M. (2008). Long-term data collection at USDA experimental sites for studies of ecohydrology. *Ecohydrology*, 1, 377-393.

Mulholland, P. J., Helton, A.M., Poole, G.C., Hall, R.O. Jr., Hamilton, S.K., Peterson, B.J., Tank, J.L., Ashkenas, L.R., Cooper, L.W., Dahm, C.N., Dodds, W.K., Findlay, S., Gregory, S.V., Grimm, N.B., Johnson, S.L., McDowell, W.H., Meyer, J.L., Valett, J,M., Webster, J.R., Arango, C., Beaulieu, J.J., Bernot, M.J., Burgin, A.J., Crenshaw, C., Johnson, L., Merriam, J., Niederlehner, B.R., O'Brien, J.M., Potter, J.D., Sheibley, R.W., Sobota, D.J., & Thomas, S.M. (2008). Stream denitrification across biomes and its response to anthropogenic nitrate loading. *Nature*, 452, 202-205.

Neff, J.C., Ballantyne, A.P., Farmer, G.L., Mahowald, N.M., Conroy, J.L., Landry, C.C., Overpeck, J.T., Painter, T.H., Lawrence, C.R., & Reynolds, R.L. (2008). *Nature Geoscience*, 1, 189-195.

O'Brien, J.M., Dodds, W.K., Wilson, K.C., Murdock, J.N., & Eichmiller, J. (2007). The saturation of N cycling in Central Plains streams: 15N experiments across a broad gradient of nitrate concentrations. *Biogeochemistry*, 84, 31-49.

Okin, G.S. (2008). A new model of wind erosion in the presence of vegetation. *Journal of Geophysical Research-Earth Surface*, 113, F02S10, doi:10.1029/2007JF000758.

Okin, G.S., Parson, A.J., Wainwright J., Herrick, J.E., Bestelmeyer, B.T., Peters, D.P.C., & Fredrickson, E.L. (2009). Do changes in connectivity explain desertification? *BioScience*, 59, 237-244.

Palmer, W.C. (1965) *Meteorological Drought*. Research Paper No. 45, Dept. of Commerce, Washington, D.C.

Perrings, C., Mooney, H., & Williamson, M. (2010). *Bioinvasions and globalization: ecology, economics, management, and policy*. Oxford University Press, Oxford.

Peters, D.P.C. (2010). Accessible ecology: synthesis of the long, deep, and broad. *Trends in Ecology and Evolution*, 25, 592-601.

Peters, D.P.C., Bestelmeyer, B.T., Herrick, J.E., Monger, H.C., Fredrickson, E., & Havstad, K.M. (2006a). Disentangling complex landscapes: new insights to forecasting arid and semiarid system dynamics. *BioScience*, 56, 491-501.

Peters, D.P.C., Groffman, P.M., Nadelhoffer, K.J., Grimm, N.B., Collins, S.L., Michener, W.K., & Huston, M.A. (2008). Living in an increasingly connected world: a framework for continental-scale environmental science. *Frontiers in Ecology and the Environment*, 5, 229-237.

Peters, D.P.C., Laney, C.M., Lugo, A.E., Collins, S.L., Driscoll, C.T., Groffman, P.M., Grove, J.M., Knapp, A.K., Kratz, T.K., Ohman, M.D., Waide, R.B., & Yao, J. (2011). *Long-*

term trends in ecological systems: a basis for understanding responses to global change. USDA Agricultural Research Service Publication No. XX. Washington, D.C.

Peters, D.P.C., Pielke, R.A. Sr, Bestelmeyer, B.T., Allen, C.D., Munson-McGee, S., & Havstad, K.M. (2004a). Cross-scale interactions, nonlinearities, and forecasting catastrophic events. *Proceedings of the National Academy of Sciences USA,* 101, 15130-15135.

Peters, D.P.C., Pielke, R.A. Sr, Bestelmeyer, B.T., Allen, C.D., Munson-McGee, S., & Havstad, K.M. 2006b. Spatial nonlinearities in the Earth System. In: *Terrestrial ecosystems in a changing world,* Canadell, J., Pataki, D., & Pitelka, L., eds, pp. 165-173, Springer, Berlin.

Peters, D.P.C., Urban, D.L., Gardner, R.H., Breshears, D.D., & Herrick, J.E (2004b0. Strategies for ecological extrapolation. *Oikos,* 106, 627-636.

Peters, D.P.C., Yao, J., Sala, O.E., Anderson, J. (submitted). Directional climate change and potential reversal of desertification in arid ecosystems. *Global Change Biology.*

Reichman, O.J., Jones, M.B., & Schildhauer, M.P. (2011). Challenges and opportunities of open data in ecology. *Science,* 331, 703-705.

Rial, J.A., Pielke, R.A. Sr, Beniston, M., Claussen, M., Canadell, J., Cox, P., Held, H., de Noblet-Ducoudé, N., Prinn, R., Reynolds, J.F., & Salas, J.D. (2004). Nonlinearities, feedbacks, and critical thresholds within the Earth's climate system. *Climatic Change,* 65, 11-38.

Tanaka, T.Y. & Chiba, M. (2006). A numerical study of the contributions of dust source regions to the global dust budget. *Global Planetary Change,* 52, 88–104.

Trenberth, K.E. (2005). Uncertainty In hurricanes and global warming. *Science,* 308, 1753-1754.

Weaver, J.E., & Albertson, F.W. (1940). Deterioration of Midwestern ranges. *Ecology,* 21, 216-236.

Williamson, C.E., Dodds, W., Kratz, T.K., & Palmer, M.A. (2008). Lakes and streams as sentinels of environmental change in terrestrial and atmospheric processes. *Frontiers in Ecology and the Environment,* 5, 247-254.

Yates,T.L., Mills, J.N., Parmenter, C.A., Ksiazek, T.G., Parmenter, R.R., Vande Castle, J.R., Calisher, C.H., Nichol, S.T., Abbott, K.D., Young, J.C., Morrison, M.L., Beaty, B.J., Dunnum, J.L., Baker, R.J., Salazar-Bravo, J., & Peters, C.J. (2002). The ecology and evolutionary history of an emergent disease: hantavirus pulmonary syndrome. *BioScience,* 52, 989-998.

12

Brightness and Austerity of the Globalization Theory: The Ideological Foundations of Cognitive Capitalism

Zlatan Delic
University of Tuzla
Bosnia and Herzegovina

1. Introduction

The term globalization began to be used only a few decades ago. There have been hundreds of the definitions of the term globalization and dozens of different classifications of these definitions. However, the very processes and activities we classify under the term globalization today have been present in action for centuries, along with a few interruptions. Still, the discussion on globalization focuses on a a relatively close time and the debate is linked to the nature and forms of modernity to certain extent. Thus, the globalization refers directly to recent events (Robertson, 1992). It is difficult to place all the discussions on globalization into one frame, even though it appears that it should be done that way. Mostly, we talk about the different dimensions or aspects of globalization that are more or less intertwined. When it comes to dimensions of globalization we can draw a line between economic, cultural, political, technological, environmental, ethical, bioethical, and other dimensions. It is less frequent to analyse deeper cognitive, autoreferential dimensions related to the language itself, which stands as a signifying system describing globalization in different scientific disciplines (Steger, 2005). This dimension can be called a discursive (symbolic) one. It refers to the transformation of the very idea of knowledge (it is symptomatic to often identify globalization with the "society of information" or "society of knowledge"). Such identification is most often present in a privileged economic discourses on globalization, especially in the discourse on the so-called new knowledge-based economy (Giddens, 2009). The discourse of the new knowledge-based economy has a large real, institutional and symbolic, in other words discursive power. Given the power at its disposal, it is trying to impose all the other discourses on globalization. As a consequence of excessive commercialization and economization of the very idea of knowledge, many normative globalization critiques occur. (Castells; 2003; Swedberg, 2006; Rifkin, 2006; Sen 2007; Zizek, 2008; Neumann, 2009). A critical analysis of the globalization discourse tends to be more interdisciplinar or shall we say transdisciplinar (Hart & Negri, 2003). Unfortunately, the division of social sciences to a variety of different ones, still poorly related disciplines, as a result of administrative and bureaucratic disciplinary knowledge, emerges as an obstacle to inter-disciplinary research on the negative consequences of globalization. Such research is still developing, especially through the events of the most discursive, environmental and bioethical consequences of globalization (Covic, 2004). The negative consequences of globalization are seriously staggering preferred methodology and reductionistic understanding of globalization. In addition, over the last ten years, different social movements have been acting under different names in reality, as a result of expressing dissatisfaction and resistance to globalization. (Wallerstein, 2004; Dow, 2005; Klein, 2008). The protests were mainly directed against the most global institutions. These institutions are sometimes mistakenly considered to deliberately control the process of globalization (Monbiot, 2006; Shiva, 2006; Chossudovsky, 2008; Stiglitz, 2009.). In general, globalization, therefore, has positive and negative aspects. In a positive development, it can be counted as the world's community in science, education and various areas of civil society, and the negative aspect is the "phenomenon of the world's risk-prone society" (Beck, 2007). In this paper we will not provide an overview of different approaches to globalization, or the presentation of different definitions of globalization, since there are already many classifications of these approaches as well as many interpretations of certain elements of these definitions. It is impossible to bypass the problem of globalization, but it is difficult to specify what it includes. It is clear, however, what is excluded. It excludes non-economic vocabulary (discourses), non-economic forms of knowledge and experiences of the world. That is considered to be one of the largest autoreferencial, conceptual problems of the very theory of globalization.

2. How to put the problem of globalization in context?

One of the most difficult issues related to this topic refers to the dilemma, therefore how can we learn to understand what is meant by this opaque context? Do we go to far or recent past, or rather, should we be focused only on the future? There is no single answer to this question. The problem of time and the problem of the area, are probably the most important elements to which numerous definitions of globalization are pointed at, there is no need to mention them here. Although, there is a fascinating number of different definitions of globalization, it should be noticed that not all definitions are equally influential. Main currents of science have the opportunity to act on certain definitions, created in the mainstream, to achieve a greater impact compared to others. Globalization is "the increasing interdependence of different nations, regions and countries, which arises because unique social and economic relations are beginning to include the whole world" (Giddens, 2007: 687). Globalization connects three concepts: globalization (Globalisierung) as a process, globality or globalism (Globalität) as an empirical state and globalism (Globalismus) as an ideology (Beck & Grande 2006). There are, of course, many different definitions and different analysis on the concept of globalization, which must be taken into account.

Globalization has not appeared out of nothing. Also, discussions on globalization, driven over the last twenty years, have got us nowhere. But only in the last ten years, have we seriously discussed explanatory theory on globalization of misery. Neoliberal concept of globalization has been particularly criticized. The new knowledge-based economy (in the form of new management, marketing, etc.), has suddenly been declared to be universal wisdom for humanity. The economy in the existing regimes of the so-called "global knowledge society", already in language, enjoys exalted, privileged status. The preferential flow of economic knowledge often identifies the globalization with the paradigm of "information society". As a result of a misidentified identification there is generally unacceptable reduction of knowledge to information society. (Castells, 2003). However, the problem with globalization is not (only) in it. It's not completely wrong to identify specific knowledge with information. But it is wrong to reduce the very idea of knowledge (knowledge as such) to the information. However, contextualizing the problems of globalization, integrating or differentiating the globalization from other problems - becomes a problem. Where should we begin during the contextualisation? Is there any global knowledge on globalization that would differentiate from the sum of different or the same information on globalization? Would our old holistic philosophy of consciousness, that we learn about from the Eastern and Western philosophies, be able to tell us about the globalization more than the modern, specialized, commercialized and instrumental knowledge, which have become quite popular over the past few decades? In this chapter we are not headed towards redescription of philosophy of consciousness in order to offer you an answer to such important issues. We started off gradually, in the direction of the economic literature, which many of you find to be far more attractive and desirable when compared to the tedious and abstract philosophical discussions.

Moreover, we headed towards one of its very popular parts that has been criticised, because today we have a new economic science and new knowledge-based economy which are quite popular. Although, we believe that this is not about popularity, but rather something else. In this chapter, therefore, we will try to talk about the new knowledge-based economy, the deeper meaning of its speech, about the prestige globally institutionalized speech, that is repeatedly and constantly without a break and an end, telling us about the new economy based on knowledge. This will be our base and general context. The inescapable context that pervades the entire text in some way (even when talking about something else), such as the new economy and economization of life that permeates the world as well as many other articles on globalization, particularly on economic globalization. Here we talk about that because the new economy of knowledge which we may consider to be the broadest and most comprehensive and consequently, we may as well refer to it as a global cognitive and valuable matrix – that has imposed itself to be the basis of our whole knowledge – to be such knowledge itself. However, the basic problem that we would like to discuss is not anywhere near that. The new knowledge-based economy is associated with the global economy of violence in many ways that don't seem to be visible at first. The violence is symbolic and real: and that is what we consider to be the biggest issue that the globalisation is most concerned of. It is necessary, not only in our case, to take into account the discursive and symbolic aspects of speech on globalization again and again. Consequently, we shall see the question of ideology re-emerging into the foreground.

Globalisation has a significant impact on a number of ideological traditions, especially nationalism, socialism and religious fundamentalism, but also it has broader implications on the ideology as a whole. Globalization is therefore impossible to present to be value-neutral. There are two basic, alternative versions of globalization that are essential for our theme. The first one is a neo-liberal globalization in which globalization is linked to the expansion of economic structures and values based on the market. It consists of so-called hyperglobalists. From this perspective, the essence of globalization is to build a global capitalist economy that serves the interests of transnational corporations, which significantly reduces the power of the state, particularly its power to transform the social structure. The globalization itself claims to be based on knowledge (hence the term cognitive capitalism). Globalization is thus a mechanism that enables us to achieve "the end of history" in terms of the final victory of neoliberal capitalism (Heywood, 2005). The second version is a critical alternative - opposed the first version. However, this alternative is neither conceptually nor practically homogeneous. Its basis lies in the power of many people (Hardt, Negri, 2003) who oppose market fundamentalism of a dominant model of globalization. They also oppose cognitive basis of a new knowledge-based economy or/and basis of the very global society of knowledge. Some authors believe that there is the third version, written by different authors, consisting of different concepts, attitudes, practices and interpretations. Many of these interpretations can be categorized in non-categorized, indefinite crowds, but the meaning of this work is not found in it. Neoliberal globalization has its own guards (soldiers). Keepers of the strategic work to defend a dominant model of globalization. These guardians tend to believe that between those who support, protect, defend and promote the first version of globalization (such as hyperglobalists), and between critics, who oppose it, there cannot be a true dialogue.

While *hyperglobalists* ignore the distinction between "theory" and "practice" (and the difference between "word" and "things"), arguing that globalization is no longer a theory but that "globalization has become the reality itself" (Ohmae, 2007), discourse analysts, critically oriented economists, anarchists, deep ecologists, theologians, feminists, and many activists are prone to various criticisms of globalization. It is impossible to consolidate their discourse in one place. Critics point at a number of serious arguments when associating globalization with the ideology of the rich and the powerful at the expense of the poor and the powerless. What they have in common is resistance to the dominant model of globalization. Discourse analysts who are looking for responsible theory and practice of globalization in particular, are sending us a warning of the ideological basis of globalization and the so-called global knowledge society. In this sense, it is justified to speak about the need for serious critical recontextualisation and redescription of global cognitive capitalism. In this paper we will focus on a critical stance on globalization, and we believe that the global economy, in the shape of the new knowledge-based economy, is a deeply ideological economy.

Te *critics* have proved that the "end of history" or the "end of ideology" still hasn't come. To claim the opposite means to represent an ideology, no matter how paradoxal it may seem to appear (Sim, 2001: 20). In its most general sense, ideology is a system of beliefs according to which society is organized. One of the most influential concepts of ideology in the 20-th century is one presented by Louis Althusser, and according to which the ideology is a system of believes that tries to hide (mask) its internal contradictions. So, let's say, liberal democracy, which is basically a cognitive capitalism and the new economy of knowledge, can claim that - since we live in a society of free market economy, in which all can compete under the same rules – thus, we live in the knowledge society. However, in reality, the market is not a natural mechanism, but can be understood as an exploitative system, designed to work in favor of those who have the greatest economic and symbolic power. For in case of eventual failure, the blame is always on the inability of an individual, and not on a contradiction within the economic system (Sim, 2001: 55-56). While the (hyper) globalists believe that we live in a "knowledge society", anti-globalists (alterglobalists) consider such a coincidence to be mere ideology. However, globalization defenders and their critics share a common view that globalization in itself is an incredible force for change in the world.

It is well known that the proponents of the neoliberal concept of globalization represent a firm view that the market is the main driver of human progress, freedom, democracy and peace. State regulation, or any invasion of (abstractly and imprecisely proclaimed) "freedom" of the market, are considered to be retrograded recurrence of a communist ideology. Hyperglobalists generally consider that the global markets must be left to operate without any restrictions, while the role of governments and multilateral institutions comes down to creating a favorable environment for business, or facilitating directed neo-liberal globalization. Ideologically compromised Communist legacy, whose deconstruction was unstoppable, has given way to unreserved neoliberal paradigm as a universal remedy that promises to establish a quick and unconditional enrichment of venture minorities who have abilities as well as the general prosperity of the majority or the whole nation (Kalanj, 2008: 167:168).

3. Different globalisation issues

In this paper, we try to contribute to an ongoing discussion on the consequences of globalization (and transition), thus we wish to point out the fact that the experience of globalization - as well as the experience of transition from socialism to capitalism - are not identical but are different. To do this, we believe that we first need to expand social and epistemological critique of the neoliberal concept of globalization further. This concept is closely associated with the dominant discourse of the new knowledge-based economy and consequently it is believed that it can produce the global knowledge society. A key methodological limitation of access through the knowledge-based economy - as shown below - is that it forgets that the novelty of the current historical conjuncture does not only consist of the simple application of knowledge-based economy, but it also includes the fact that the economy based on knowledge is disadvantaged and limited by institutional forms that define capital accumulation. In our opinion, it is entirely out of this "forgetting" that the difficulty arises and precisely defines the notion of *knowledge-based economy,* as well as an overall meaning and importance of this transition. The concept of *cognitive capitalism* which is - in the semantic sense closely related to institutional forms through which it imposes and promotes new economy of knowledge – is the concept that has been proposed, in the context of analysis of the negative consequences of globalization, to make an effort (in future research) to specify and understand the meaning and background of the current practice of knowledge (as a general resource of humanity) that is reduced to the economic idea of instrumentalized knowledge which is subordinated to the narrow interests of privatization and the inexorable logics of profit.

The economic globalization is one of the most important dimensions of globalization. It is closely related to the new global economy and the transformation of the very idea of knowledge. The economy is sometimes called information economy, and sometimes new cognitive economy or simply the economy of knowledge. It is also closely related to the revolution in information technology. The information economy is the global economy. The global economy is a historically new reality, which differentiates from the world economy. The world economy is an economy in which capital accumulation progresses throughout the world. It was present in the West in the sixteenth century, as we can learn from Fernand Braudel and the known theorist of world systems, Immanuel Wallerstein. The global economy is something different: it is the economy that has the ability to work as a unit of real time on a planetary level. While the capitalist mode of production marks its relentless expansion, which is always trying to cross the boundaries of time and space, so in the late 20th century, the world economy has been able to become truly global on the basis of a new infrastructure that has made information and communication technology. This globality concerns the core elements of the process of the economic system. Capital is controlled regularly on globally integrated, financial markets that are working in real time for the first time in history: transactions worth billions of dollars are taking place in a second through the electronic transport through the whole world.

Disputes on globalization have been discussed on the conceptual-pragmatic level, in the field of the meaning of the term. They have been also discussed when it comes to considering the actual effects of the activity of key concepts that are built using the building of globalization theory. Such situation is explained by the experience of globalization for different theorists, belonging to different habitats. They are different but also sometimes incommensurable. While for instance, Anthony Giddens, one of the main initiators of the project, sees globalization as a direct consequence of *modernity*, some authors, like Michael Hardt and Antonio Negria, will talk about *postmodernization* of the global economy in general. They argue that: "In postmodernization of global economy creating wealth tends to be more prone to what we will call biopolitical production, that is the production of social life, in which economic, political and cultural increasingly overlap and embraces one another» (Hardt, Negri, 2003: 9) In order to illustrate this, they will use a broad, interdisciplinary approach, and claim: "Our arguments tend to be equally philosophical and historical, cultural and economic, political and anthropological (...) In the imperial world, an economist, for instance, needs a basic knowledge of cultural production to understand the economy and the same applies to the cultural critic. He also needs a basic knowledge of economic processes in order to understand the culture" (Hardt, Negri, 2003: 11).

Some other influential theorists also rely on broad interdisciplinary approach of globalization: in order to accentuate the different experiences of globalization, that is the experiences they care about. By using these approaches, they are trying to look into many different perspectives of the phenomenon of globalization at the same time, and thus explain it as objectively as possible. It is possible to show through a series of examples that an attempt of the objective, value-neutral analysis of globalization, produces enormous difficulties. Some of these difficulties arise from the ideological reasons, and some out of the unevenness of the methodological instruments. Sometimes it is very difficult to distinguish whether these "thickets" that "confusing places» (Rosenberg, 2000), belong to the battlefield of ideology, or else they can be attributed to a purely scientific reasons.

Without intending to definitively draw a conclusion on these dilemmas, regarding the different experiences of globalization, we can say that each interdisciplinary research is burdened with some kind of methodological inconsistencies at the level of meanings of basic terms, without any exception. Methodological inconsistency is particularly evident in recent disputes over the *global society of knowledge* and *knowledge-based economy*. These disputes are certainly not in favor of methodological monism. Neither are they in favor of an attempt to achieve unity. However, there is a question arising: Is the meaning, for instance, knowledge-based economy dependant on whether the phrase is used by an economist, or whether the meaning of the phrase is attributed to someone who deals with the new economic sociology or materialistic theory of discourse. The preliminary answer to this question is that the meaning of the term should be designed not only within one discipline, but a critical focus on issues of meaning grows in proportion to the sensitivity that we have towards the critical aspects of science as well as towards the epistemological issues. Considering that we are starting from the principal thesis that the experience of globalization are different in general makes the difference become even more complex, depending on what we mean by knowledge that might help us to learn about globalization itself.

4. Several methodological suggestions – back to the epistemology

Here we try to apply an interdisciplinary, or more precisely, transdisciplinary approach to the above issues. Generally, we advocate for equal combination of quantitative and *qualitative methodologies*. We combine multiple qualitative research methods. At the same time, we consider *epistemological* issues related to the analysis of the social conditions of knowledge, prior to the methodological and methodological issues. One of the key aspects of the cognitive system is the basic notion of the knowledge, or what philosophers call a formal epistemology. Epistemology (that people are often aware of only to the minimum extent) determines what is considered to be a "fact", "explanation" and "understanding" (Scholte, 2009: 258). In this context, it becomes a question of principle: has the globalization altered the conception of the nature of knowledge? Our response, which can not be linear, is the following: globalization is dramatically changing the stable performance of knowledge and experience of the world. However, this conclusion is part of the problem, and not an answer to the riddle of globalization. It is therefore necessary to encourage emancipatory possibilities for methodological doubt towards all of the dogmatic and preferred conceptions of knowledge. It is on this crucial point, that the elements of cognitive philosophy and ideology of sociology overlap along with some not fully integrated, elements of sociosemiology, critical analysis of discourse and new economic sociology. In this sense, we advocate for an open and pluralistic epistemology. We suspect that there is (only) a model of knowledge-based economy on which it would be possible to simply implement a global society of knowledge. Steger also believes that it is best to think of globalization as a multidimensional series of social processes which can not be restricted to a single thematic framework (Steger, 2005).

The transforming effects of globalization strongly affect the economic, political, cultural, technological and ecological dimensions of contemporary social life. Considering that globalization - or hyperinflation of the globalization discourse - breaks the established framework and stable meanings, there is a danger that the word "globalization" becomes a mere buzzword, a device for something else. Regarding this, here we primarily want to demonstrate that globalization contains important aspects of *discourse* in the form of *ideologically-coloured view that presents* a certain scheme of topics for discussion to the public. The existence of these views shows that globalization is not only a fair process but also a lot of statements that define, describe and analyze the actual process. Social forces from these opposing views of globalization tend to enrich this new buzzword with norms, values and meanings that not only legitimize and promote the specific interests of power, but also shape the personal and collective identity of billions of people.

In order to illuminate these rhetorical maneuvers, Steger believes that any introduction to globalization should investigate its ideological dimension. Steger's attitude is partly identical to our query. Over the recent years, it has been increasingly indicated that the study of globalization is born as a new field that cuts across traditional disciplinary boundaries (Steger, 2005). The biggest challenge that today's researchers of globalization are facing lies in connecting and synthesising of the different categories of knowledge in a way that provides a fair access to fluid and interdependent nature of our world, whether it we refer to modernism or postmodernism. Each categorical terminology defining the time in which we live ("modern", "postmodern," "political", "postideological", "postdemocratic", "Age of doctrines", "Age of control" and so on), implies certain value assumptions, which greatly affects the management of globalization. Therefore, globalization is, first of all and after all, still an unfinished and open process, a subject to various forms of reform. According to David Held and Anthony McGrew, globalization is a set of processes that alter the spatial organization of socio-economic relations and transactions, and from the reformist perspective, it is neither new nor inherently unfair or nondemocratic (Held, McGrew, 2002: 107).

Nevertheless, we believe that over the recent years, at least when it comes to methodological terms, there is some kind of balance between the privileged and critical discourse on globalization. The discourse on globalization - especially economic globalization, neo-liberal type – has been developed by a positivist, overly reductionist epistemology. This epistemology is in the service of unbridled, neo-liberal capitalism that has spread through violence to nature and the living world. To sum up, it's about ideologised epistemology. The trademark of this epistemology is the so-called "society of knowledge and skills" (Giddens, 2009: 36), and therefore as a result of constant, recursive, refering to knowledge, we can as well call it an ideology of cognitive capitalism. Due to the fact that privileged discourses of the new economy of knowledge avoid a critical analysis of the concept of knowledge, and review their own methodological assumptions, the whole building of globalization theory is in the "quicksand". By the term discourse, we mean a system for the production of statements and practices. Once they get established institutionally, they can be performed as more or less normal. As a response to the explanatory shortcomings of positivist, privileged discourses on globalization we have been warned by Justin Rosenberg (2000), especially in *The Follies of Globalisation Theory*.

The critical approaches, which have been present ever since, are combining different methods. In this paper, therefore, let us repeat once again that our focus is on postpositivist, pluralistic approach that combines (1) an in-depth analysis of the transformation of social relations, (2) critical theory of knowledge (3) transdisciplinar analysis on discourse of the new 'knowledge-based economy'. This combination arises from the need to overcome some limitations in the discussion of the knowledge economy that prevents clear understanding of the logics and consequences of globalization. The focus of the biggest controversies about globalization and the transition seems to be a misunderstanding, or deliberate misunderstanding of economic globalization, or in other words misunderstanding of the defense of knowledge on which economic globalization is based.

5. The defense of the global knowledge economy and the critics

It is well known that the simplest but also the most dangerous way to address the specific phenomenon is to act as a fan - when something is classified through the model of bipolar opposition: "for" or "against". In such circumstances, we reduce the complexity of the phenomenon to a "Prokrust's bed," and as a result there can be violence directed towards that what we are talking about. Jagdish Bhagwati (2008), for instance, recognizes that globalization can mean several things, and at first glance is focused solely on the economic globalization. Economic globalization represents the integration of national economies into the international economy through trade, direct foreign investment (which consists of corporations and multinational companies), short-term capital movements, international movement of workers and people in general as well as technology trends. This raises the question: Why are the critics of globalization so frustrated? What is it that really upsets them? Bhagwati believes that there are two groups. Firstly, there are a lot of hard-line opponents who have deeply grown antipathy towards globalization. They come from different intellectual and ideological backgrounds and they do not all share same ideas and feelings. However, many will give in to the obligatory triad of discontent, which represents an ethos, composed of anticapitalist, antiglobalist and anticorporated orientations. Bhagwati argues that, in addition to understanding the origin of their discontent, in a dialogue with the critics of globalization not a lot can be achieved (Bhagwati, 2008: 16).

Ideological nature, which is attributed to the critics of globalization in the defense of globalization, is not defined. However, it can be proved that any uncritical defense of globalization, which is reportedly opposed to ideology, is also the only one, and it is a very dangerous form of ideology. Stuart Sim (2006, 9-38) considers to live in an age of free market ideology (market fundamentalism), and that ideology is a form of global and corporate fundamentalism. Sim argues that we have entered a "new dark age of dogma." Moreover, the problem "lies not so much in dogmatism, but in the force it uses to push people" (Sim, 2006: 37).

This dogmatic era (which we could also consider not to be the age of knowledge, but rather the age of ignorance), is characterized by mutually complementary forms of fundamentalism: the market fundamentalism, nationalist fundamentalism and religious fundamentalism. Although, it doesn't claim that there is a global conspiracy of fundamentalism, Sim noticed that each of these parties claimed that only they "have the truth" (Sim, 2006: 17). According to Sim, fundamentalism has replaced communism in a form of a ghosts that haunts the conscience of the West (Sim, 2006: 13). The defense of globalization by Bhagwati, has minimized, or completely negated the negative consequences of globalization. On the contrary, he is trying to prove that there is no explicit link between globalization and economic prosperity. The defense did not show a perverse relationship between globalization, on one hand and poverty, unemployment, social psychology, social exclusion, violence, child labor, organized crime, corporated espionage or technologically produced ecological disaster on another hand. Bhagwati generally considered that globalization has nothing to do with it. His central thesis is that globalization promotes democracy (Bhagwati, 2008:47) and that it already has a human face (Bhagwati, 2008: 48). Therefore, he attacks alterglobalist, and especially feminist movements, considering their complaints on globalization to be unfounded. Problems such as child labor, poverty, unemployment, global pollution, destruction of the ozone layer and acid rain are global problems, but they are not necessarily a consequence of globalization (Bhagwati, 2008:195.). If we proceeded from there, it would be possible to reverse the question and ask what is the connection between global issues and globalization, and what are the discursive consequences of denying the fact that this relationship really exists.

The defense of globalization is opposed to the concept of "sustainable development" as well: "No one who is alive knows what sustainable development actually means. It has become a meaningless term which can be understood in any way today, like the notion of the former concept of socialism to which the adjective Arab or African was added. It is this notion that was heavily used by leaders of the Third World during the sixties and seventies, by adding a rule, the adjective Arab or African" (Bhagwati, 2008: 192). Bhgwati also believes that America stands out when it comes to a society that is most prone to experimentation in the field of technology. To Americans technique represents a device for solving problems, whereas to others it is a device for creating problems. Bhagwati considered this difference in attitudes to be a primarily cultural difference, and it is found on the grounds of conflicting positions of both Americans and Europeans in terms of hormone-fed cattle meat and genetically modified (GM) products. Unlike authors such as Rifkin (2006), who approaches analysis of differences between America and Europe on a higher level, Bhagwati, for instance, argues that "the widely spread use of silicone implants for women and Viagra for men has turned America into a society where artificially excited men are chasing women who are artificially enlarged" (Bhagwati, 2008: 153.).

The former critical analysis, particularly the economic aspects of globalization, which have been carried out separately by Amartya Sen, Joseph Stiglitz, Jeremy Rifkin, Naomi Klein, Sandra Harding, and many others - were particularly critical about the methodological reductionism of the new economy of knowledge. According to our insights, reductionism is based upon the concept of knowledge-based economy that wants to be defined as a "category of the history of economic growth," but it is still considered to be just normal expansion of economic variables of "knowledge". The largest part of the approach to the knowledge-based economy, is characterized by a positivist and non-conflict vision of knowledge and technology, which leads us to bypass the social, cultural and ethical contradictions that are inherent in a knowledge-based economy. From this point of view, there is a strong tendency to treat the production of knowledge and technological achievements independently of the analysis of social relations and the conflicts that have merged throughout the entire history of capitalism that are connected with the substantive issue of control, "the intellectual forces of production" (Lebert , Vercellone, 2007: 17).

The term of knowledge-based economy is still not properly defined (Guellec, 2002: 131). The first difficulty arises from the errors to approach the subject of knowledge on the basis of general theoretical models that are valid at any time and space, based on the separation of economic analysis from the analysis of social relations. According to Howitt (1996), the novelty in this approach is not a historic affirmation of knowledge-based economy, but only the formation of the economy of knowledge as a subset of economics focused on the study of knowledge production, which is considered to be a new factor of production. It is one of the greatest paradoxes we got accustomed to through the economic science in its attempt to formulate a single model for the functioning of economic systems: the theory ignores or denies the importance of structural changes that are in the very base of the birth of new areas of research, that is the theme of knowledge, in this case.

Another difficulty lies in the reductive vision of the role of knowledge in most of the interpretations relating to the occurrence of knowledge-based economy. These approaches are interesting because they highlight the existence of historical discontinuity. However, the origin of knowledge-based economy is mainly explained by changing the width of the phenomenon, a kind of a transition where we move from quantity to quality. This acceleration of history is the result of a shocking encounter of two factors: on the one hand, long-term trend of relative increase in the share of so-called "intangible capital" (education, training, research, development and health), and changes in the conditions of reproduction and transmission of knowledge and information through "spectacular spreading of new communication and information technology", on the other hand. There is certainly some truth in the second one, but there are two risks.

The first is the technological determinism. Communication and information technologies, given the leading role in tranzit to "mass production of knowledge and intangible assets" on the basis of a mechanistic scheme similar to the approach where vector is made out of a steam engine, which after the first industrial revolution leads to the formation of the working class and mass production of material goods. These distortions - as indicated by

Paulré (2000) and Castells (2002) is typical of many approaches in the New Economy, which tends to identify knowledge-based economy with the computer revolution. This vision is fully in line with the inability to derive a clear distinction between the concept of information and the concept of knowledge, given that the concept of knowledge is based on cognitive ability to interpret information and mobilization, which would otherwise represent unused resource. Theoretical and epistemological debates about the meaning of the new knowledge-based economy are not always abstract. They are not far from the real problems of moral and ethical challenges that we, human beings are confronted when thinking about the consequences of the progress of biotechnology and technoscience.

6. Should we try to avoid ethical dilemmas?

When speaking about the gene trade at the dawn of the brave new world, Rifkin (1999: 15) has set before us several far-reaching questions related to our theme: what will be the consequences for the global economy and society, if the world's gene bank turns into a patented intellectual property that will be controlled by only a handful of multinational corporations? How will the patenting of life affect our deepest beliefs about the pure nature and true values of life? What is the emotional and intellectual impact of growing up in a world where everything that is connected with life is considered to be an "invention" and "commercial property"? What does it mean to be a human being in a world where an infant is genetically created within the mother's womb to meet the customer's wishes? And what does it mean to be a human being in a world where people recognize and differentiate according to their genotype? These issues can be analyzed with regards to changing epistemological and ethical status of knowledge in the global knowledge society, which we call cognitive capitalism. Different authors take different experiments. Some will looks backwards while others will look forwards. The consequences of the progress of technoscience support unlimited confidence in scientific rationality. They cause a number of ethical dilemmas related to human self-understanding and nuanced approaches are needed for their contextualization. The progress in the field of biotechnology has created a gap in already existing regimes of regulation of the progress of biomedicine (Fukuyama, 2003: 234). George Myerson (2001: 38), has examined the consequences of gene manipulation. The dilemma is this: Aren't the gene manipulators associated with racists in a way? race? Aren't they the ones who keep old dreams of extermination of degenerics through the reprogramme of genes? Many theologians, bioethicists and other experts expressed their doubts concerning the moral and ethical aspects of progress of technoscience and biomedical research. In 1987, the Supreme Court of the United States approved "patent on life" - right to the patenting of species, genes, or herbal ingredient, which has not been created in the mind of man but is rather a creation of Nature. The U.S. PTO (Patent and Trade Office) issued a statement that the parts of living things (genes, chromosomes, cells and tissues) can be considered patent and intellectual property of those who first isolated them and found usable application. The multinational corporations collect knowledge on plant species and their use from indigenous people through biopiracy, for industrial production and sales.

Therefore, the question of strengthening intellectual property rights and its spreading into the area of the living world as well as on the results of fundamental research seems to be a crucial aspect of the current regulation of cognitive capitalism. This restructuring of the intellectual property suits the policy of creating positional rents which are supposed to encourage innovation and synergy between the private and public research sectors. This policy is often justified by an argument according to which the main costs in the sector with intensive amount of knowledge are fixed ones relating to investment companies in research and development. However, - as Lebert and Vercellone demonstrated – the foundation of this argument is rather questionable. Moreover, they believe that strengthening the system of intellectual property rights, even when racing for a patent between some companies is presented before us as a matter of life and death, is actually a mechanism that blocks the flow of circulation and production of knowledge. François Chesnais believes that we are far from the optimistic visions of the transformation of "cognitive" potentials, which offers us the use of new technology: "In the scientific and technical disciplines that industry and financial speculation put the highest price on and that is biology, medicine and computer science, we noticed that the system of "compensation" from the Finance (wages and social recognitions) is expanding and it now includes highly advanced research. This resulted in a strong strengthening of opportunistic behavior in relationships between researchers and the academic community. We concluded that there is some fierce rivalry in which the bait is a gain. It damages the scientific cooperation, and sometimes even leads to separation of research teams " (Chesnais, 2007: 126).

In addition, temporary and individual wage relations, the destabilization of the collective services of the welfare state and excessive privatization of knowledge associated with the strengthening of intellectual property rights, affects the current regulation of cognitive capitalism to be some kind of potential obstacles to the development of knowledge-based economy. Consequently, according to the recent research the current changes of capitalism, characterized by changes in the cognitive capitalism, appears to be a conflicting phenomenon that in many of its aspects moves and intensifies the contradictions at both the relationship capital / labor, as well as in the effects of dominance that structures the new international division of labor. The crisis, which currently affects the world economy, is believed by these authors to be interpreted as the first "big crisis" of the regulation of cognitive capitalism. Finally, everything that happens confirms in some way the crisis and the new form of regulation and therefore some will legitimately question not just a crisis of cognitive capitalism, but will also wonder if the there is crisis of capitalism that deeply affects the Society. The history of other major crises that capitalism has experienced is a lesson for us today. The end of this great crisis is quite indefinite and depends on the game of complex dynamics of conflict / innovation. The investments are clear and therefore, Lebert and Vercellone want to draw attention to the dynamics of social transformation and power which is its integral part. This way the society of knowledge would be truly emancipated from the capitalist logics that it summs up, thus would set free the potential for emancipation - the potential added to the economy based on the free circulation of knowledge and democracy represented by the general mind (Lebert, Vercellone, 2007: 28).

Other researchers came to similar research results. Antonella Corsán believes that capital no longer subjects the science to make it suitable to its logic accumulation. It is immediately aiming at the field of knowledge production through knowledge, on the inside. It is not only that attitude towards science, technology and industry that is not linear, but it is rather about a deeper turn of a relationship between knowledge and accumulation of capital. This reversal reveals the fact that it is not only scientific knowledge that is suitable to be finalized for the industry and evaluation of industrial capital. Doesn't the change in the structure and status of knowledge, which is in political economy and has not found the conceptual tools for its analysis, force us to change the way of understanding the consequences of globalization? Philosophical reflection on the internal logics, upon which the transformation runs from industrial to a postindustrial society of knowledge, does not offer us a simple answer to the most important epistemological question: who decides what knowledge is and who knows what to choose? If it is true that we have stepped into the uncertain field of postpositivist epistemology, it is still not clear what that really means.

Finally, it seems that the most important thing is clear: cognitive capitalism works to turn all knowledge, regardless of whether it is artistic, philosophical, cultural, linguistic or scientific, into a commodity (Corsani, 2007.). However, the problem is that knowledge is not as good as other goods, and not reducible to a commodity. Knowledge is, therefore, not good or can not be good in the strict sense of the word. Therefore - as was noticed by other critics of the concept of knowledge-based economy - many problems arise when trying to apply the knowledge of the laws of valorization of capital that are inherent in industrial capitalism.

Entry into the knowledge-based economy, is not a homogeneous process in space and time (Mouhoud, 2007: 89), although the preferred concept of the new knowledge-based economy is imposed as if it is valid for all places and all times. Considering that historically, geographically and technologically different national economies, didn't have the same initial conditions for the creation of knowledge-based economy, and neither can the cognitive capitalism contribute to the true planetar integration of goods, capital and technology. Categories and terms used by the critics of cognitive capitalism have not been proposed to appoint or give authority to globalization *as such*. As a result, new critical sciences emerge out of a need to uncover the myths of valuable neutrality of privileged forms of knowledge. The new knowledge-based economy and global society of knowledge and skills that the economy is constantly talking about, already represent cognitive capitalism as a universal and immutable framework of any possible concept of knowledge.

Authors such as Rifkin (2006: 404) advocate a new vision of science that appears in this era of globalization. As science and technology are becoming more powerful, it is more complex and harder to predict its consequences. Many members of the scientific community are concerned that science, due to its greater innovative power, is lost. It seems, the ability to predict the effects of implementation of these innovations, and that because of increasing man's power to change the nature, the chances that it will eventually be a serious and global nuisance are on the increase. It seems that in the old educational science the answers to questions on how to deal with these new circumstances are simply not there (Rifkin, 2006: 405). Unfortunately, the way we think about the economy, politics and society and our attitude towards the environment are still bound by the old scientific paradigm. The new science should impose to public and public policy stronger in order to achieve real change (Rifkin, 2006: 412) .

New science needs a new philosophy of sustainability of global and local community, that will not be dictated by the rich and powerful who impose a *global definition as a global definition of knowledge*. Globalization is, in general, expressed through the circulation of capital (the capital of base knowledge) between and within rich countries. This is in accordance with the logics, although it includes several countries that are emerging, though most countries rich in natural resources are violently excluded, since their only advantage lies in the natural resources and cheap labor (Mouhoud, 2007: 95). To that extent the cognitive capitalism, regardless of polysemic meaning of this phrase, in general refers to the establishment of new rules of ownership of the living world. Consequently, the ethical and moral issues become as important, if not even more important than epistemological. However, the problem is that the innovative theory of success of cognitive capitalism has turned the neglect of ethical and epistemological issues into a strategic methodological virtue.

The theory of innovation systems, upon which the building of the new knowledge-based economy is rising, does not have its own foundation in any scientifically proven knowledge. As Chesnais points out, the innovation system theory is placed not in a complete hell of theory but rather on a lower status. Nobel prize for economics has never been awarded for contribution inside this theory. The theory of systems of innovation is nothing but a clumsy attempt of recognition of positive and free production effects - defined as a positive "externality" of a multitude of interactions, out of which only the most visible are noticed, more socialized labor research, development and production. The emergence of new information and communication technology and technological management of living beings marks the end point of a long-term social accumulation of scientific and technical knowledge.

According to Chesnais, the main investment for capitalism has always been to do whatever is possible so that the social character of labor largo sensu is not recognized as such in order to keep a private property to be the inevitable form of creation, appropriation and use of knowledge. That is, during the age of so-called cognitive capitalism, has become even more obvious than before. Every time an international group puts a medicine under its license, they turn it into an element of strengthening their monopolistic position and the basis for an adequate flow of profits and fees, licensing rights, socially produced scientific knowledge that are publicly funded (Chesnais, 1994). Lawyer' fees for the identification of global right of intellectual property cost a fortune, which in practice means that they are only available to corporations with greater ability to pay. In all the sectors where intellectual property is a major determinant of value - in the media, information technology, pharmaceutical companies, biotechnology and seed breeding – the main role belongs to a few large companies, whose headquarters are mainly in industrialized countries. Ninety-seven percent of patents are owned by corporations from the rich part of the world. Due to recent legislation on intellectual property, poor countries will have to pay 40 billion dollars a year in the form of fees for licenses, and half of that amount will be payable to companies based in the United States (Monbiot, 2006: 134.) .

Ha-Joon Chang (2002), the economist who specializes in the development, has dedicated the past ten years to uncovering the myth of the origin of the industrialized countries. Like all the stories that invading forces are saying about themselves - the compassionate heroism, the power in the service of the conquered - not even a single story about the development based on free trade and equal opportunity that the rich countries introduced and which is, quite obviously, not true. It can suppress an unpleasant historical fact, and that is that free trade policies have been introduced only after industrialized countries have achieved economic dominance. They have been fiercely defending their economies in the most important stages from the competition of other countries. (Monbiot, 2006: 135-136). One very interesting but little known fact is that no country that has been successfully industrialized and therefore can be considered to be developed today, has not achieved it through free trade, but through protectionism.

7. How is globalization related to violence?

Many believe that the trade policies imposed by the rich to the poor today are in accordance with the unfair rules that were adopted by the imperialist forces in the past. From the time of protests against the World Trade Organization, held in the late 1999, the international debate on the most unavoidable issue of our time has become really serious and the issue itself is: what kind of values will rule the global age? There are many reasons to suggest that it is impossible to ignore the failures of a dominant economic model based on the concept of unlimited neoliberal globalization. Governments around the world have failed to meet the needs of the people who elected them. At the turn of the 20th to the 21st century there was a need for non-profit cultural room where you can communicate non-violently. The beginning of a new century has been marked by features of horrific violence and, of course, by a new economy based on knowledge. There have been movements against the global corporated organization of society. It seemed that the fences that protect the general interests are increasingly disappearing, while those that restrict fundamental human freedoms repeatedly multiplied. Another limit of general interest that faces a serious danger is the one that separates the genetically modified crops from the crops that have not yet been reconstructed. Climate change is probably the most serious problem the world faces, and it is largely affected by the sector of transportation. The movement of goods around the world is extremely wasteful and inefficient: cargo ships carrying grain from one side of the globe to another bypass with the same ships that transport it in the opposite direction (Monbiot, 2006: 145).

The political philosophy of global institutions became affected by "metaphysical mutation" of its own "subjects" of research that pervades critical reflection. Slavoj Zizek, the philosopher who lists a number of arguments from the globalization as we know it, and associates it with cognitive (discursive, symbolic) and actual violence. He believed that the fundamental systemic violence of capitalism, is far more seducive than the pre-capital direct socio-ideological violence: It is the violence that cannot be attributed to certain individulas or their evil intentions. It is rather objective, sistematic and anonymous. It spontaneously creates excluded and unnecessary individuals, starting from the idle to the homeless. This violence is favored for the birth of new ethnic and / or religious (in short: racist) fundamentalisms. It is very easy to find a scapegoat in it all, put the blame on the Party, Stalin, Lenin and eventually Marx himself for the millions of dead, the gulags and terror whereas in capitalism, there is no one on whom we can lay the guilt and responsibility. Although capitalism was not less destructive when they it came to the loss of millions of human lives, destruction of the environment, destruction of the original tribal culture –the system appeared to work spontaneously, without naming the culprits.

Naomi Klein, the famous activist believes that during the protest in Seattle it was not the trade or globalization that was on trial, but there was a global attack on citizens' right to set rules that protect people and the planet (Klein, 2003: 20). However, protests against market fundamentalism, or against the so-called "free trade" are not always antiglobalist: "When the protesters shout about the sins of globalization, most of them do not call back for narrow-minded nationalism, but rather they call for the expansion of the globalization borders, linking trade with the labour rights, and protection of the Environment and Democracy (Klein, 2003: 20). In this respect, we should understand the views of Jeremy Riffkin, who committed to making biopatents to be in the ownership of the whole world, that is the humanity. The World Trade Organization, International Monetary Fund and World Bank, are subject to continuous attacks by many activists and protesters.The critics argue that these institutions became so domesticated in poor countries that they even give themseves the right to determine which computer brand are schools to buy.

Whether we will live in peace, or under the constant threat of terrorism and war is dependent on the decisions of the Security Council. However, we we cannot escape climate change, financial speculation, debt bondage and deregulation, wherever you live. Since everything is globalized except democracy, the rulers of the world can deal with their affairs without paying attention at us. It is therefore not surprising that most of their decisions are against the interests of the majority and only reflect the interests of the overwhelming minority (Monbiot, 2006: 63). According to one of the senior World Bank officials, the new project is a "mandatory programme, which enables those who have money to give orders to those who do not have on what they must do to get it" (Monbiot, 2006: 105).

Zizek believes that the big news of today's post-political age, the "end of ideology" is a radical de-politicization of the economic sphere: the way the economy works (the necessity of cutting welfare, etc.) It has been accepted as a true insight into the objective of things, in neoliberal globalization. However, so long as we accept the fundamental depoliticization of the economic sphere, each discussion on active citizenship, public discussion that leads to common decisions, etc. will remain limited to "cultural" issues of religious, sexual, ethnic and other differences of lifestyle, without any real interfering on the level where long-term decisions are made that affect us all. The return of former communists to power (in some post-socialist countries in transition), for Zizek is a sign that socialism is really canceled, or what political analysts (wrongly) perceived as a "disappointment capitalism" is in fact a disappointment of ethnic and political enthusiasm which has no place in "normal" capitalism.

Thus, the depoliticization of the economy is in a way some kind of depoliticization of the political sphere: a political struggle turned into a cultural struggle for recognition of marginal identities and tolarance of diversity. The ideological dream of a united Europe aims to achieve (an impossible) harmony between the two components: the full integration into the global market and maintenance of specific national and ethnic identities. What we get in the post-communist Eastern Europe is a kind of negative, dystopian realization of that dream - in short, the worst of both worlds, unfettered market coupled with an ideological fundamentalism. Even George Soros (2002) one of the richest people on the planet, considers that the market fundamentalism is more dangerous than the totalitarian ideologies, and that the market itself is not a moral force, while Misha Glenny believes that "the widely unregulated economic field, reminds of a swamp full of nutrients for growing security problems" (Glenny, 2008: 14).

If the economy based on knowledge could make a thought experiment in which they could trace the discovery of the origin of their own knowledge they would discover that knowledge cannot be possessed. The only exception to the tendency of disciplinary and methodological vulgarization of the ideas of knowledge, is the emergence of economic sociology. Apparently, economic sociology has made a "revolutionary" (in Kuhn's sense of the word) epistemological and methodological shift. What makes it a novelty is that it is the economy and economic activity, analyzed in a critical and multi-disciplinary context, as an integral part of an overall social activity, and not isolated as it is represented by the conventional economic science, or more precisely by preferential aspects of the conventional economic science. Economic sociology is a kind of analysis that is very promising, considering the speed with which it has developed over the past ten years. It could easily become one of the key competitive methods in the analysis of economic phenomena - on the same level with neoclassical economics, the game theory and behavioral economics, in the 21 century.

8. Do we live in a knowledge-based society or we commercialise life?

It is necessary to briefly examine the negative social and (anti) educational effects of *commercialization of knowledge*, which we consider to be a consequence of the institutional and cognitive manipulation of the idea of knowledge, and even the "science". Globalization, especially economic globalization and the new economy of knowledge, are deeply associated with commercialization, or more precisely, with the *commercialization of knowledge*. Basically, the core of commercialization, or whatever you may consider by that term, is a *commercial logic*, a commercial mindset or attitude towards the people and the world. French sociologist Pierre Bourdieu, and several other authors are the ones who gave us inspiration for criticism of the commercialization of knowledge. As a result of criticism of commercial television broadcasts and commercialization in the broadest sense, he says: "It is important to look back on the fact that in history, all the cultural products that I consider to be - I hope I'm not alone in this - and that a number of others consider to be, are the highest achievements of mankind in areas of mathematics, poetry, literature, philosophy - were created to resist or neglect the level of viewership and commercial logic. Bourdieu, indeed, was not the only one to see "a very worrying fact" in the global process of commercialization of knowledge (Bourdieu, 2000: 44).

Whether the care and concern are good allies to fight against the commercialization of knowledge, is the question here. In addition, for the main ideological promoters of economic globalization and knowledge-based economy, commercialization of knowledge is not a problem, but a desirable thing, that the global society of knowledge entails. However, let us look back for a moment, at the very core of a problem. It is well known, for instance, that Martin Heidegger, the philosopher who was in the fundamental ontology, thought that it is pure care that is the main modus of us human beings. It is also well known, why it is his philosophy that was heavily criticized, by other great philosophers such as Richard Rorty (1995), Jacques Derrida (2007) and Peter Sloterdijk (1992).

Let us ask ourselves: "what is the prevailing conception of philosophy today, at least in the West?" Surely it is no longer thinking of a concept of being and time, as the philosopher Martin Heidegger claimed in his (for some thinkers even today a significant) book 'Sein und Zeit' (Heidegger, 1927). We shall probably agree that in this day and age, for today's understanding of the concept of time, the prevailing conception of philosophy, is the one that treats philosophy as a *business philosophy* (philosophy of success), or, simply, "management" (Drucker). In that kind of philosophy, there is no trace of Heidegger's *interpretation of being* (human being) *with respect to temporality*, nor is there, *explication of time as the transcendental horizon when it comes to a questions* about the being. Also, in today's business philosophy, management, as a modern story on success, does not contain any trace of *the main line of metaphysical destruction in the history of ontology on the guideline of a temporality related issue*, as is named a title of one chapter that the philosopher Heidegger wrote. In today's business philosophy - which definitely should pave its way towards the "global society of knowledge" - with a "knowledge-based economy" (which, therefore, serves as a device of arriving at the magnificent goal) - things related to philosophy, metaphysics, ontology and knowledge as a whole, appear to be quite different. To be more precise, the difference between those two philosophies is incomensurable. This difference speaks of "absolute anarhy of our time,"division of each modernity" (Derrida, 2001: 28). If we asked ourselves today, like Martin Heidegger, whether we are in trouble because we forgot to ask about being and time, perhaps our response should be: no way.

The business philosophy is, finally, after the hard travel times, after 2500 years of such a thinking in the West and at least a thousand years long period of philosophical (and Theosophical) thinking in the East, finally revealed the truth. To simplify it: *time* is *money, the space* is transformed into a *market* and a *thought* turns into *calculations*. (Of course, the story here is not over yet. The question of all questions that still remains after the end of times is what to do with humans, or more specifically, with what is left of him?). Since that day it was not popular to speak of a man as simply as it used to be before (or long ago), because it no longer was cool to talk about man as a man - the man alone has finally turned into a resource (goods). However, it became a human resources (human goods), but in the end, it is just a commodity. According to Wallerstein "it is necessary to be aware of the historical system in which we live and which is sustainable only thanks to an attempt to to turn everything in the goods (Wallerstein, 2004:102).

We cannot go into the semantic nuances and identify the range of variation within the new economy of knowledge in which there are rumours about a man, or people in general (in order to make the speech adapted to "natural" laws of the market and, of course, standards of "excellence" and "quality"), to be systematically, strategically and programmatically (which is, of course, very innovative), the capital: *human capital, intellectual capital, social capital, cultural capital* and of course *transcultural (global) capital*. It is sufficient to notice that the hyperinflation of the expansive, commercialized (posthumous) speech, for instance about a human, and generally "social capital", was strategicaly launched in the 90-ies of the 20-th century (Putnam and others, 1993). It happened just in time when other changes were on the lookout (not only in discourses and ways of naming our changing social reality), which can be considered global, far-reaching changes.

We have selected these examples so that we could indirectly, partly interdisciplinary, partly sociosemiologically, particularly with regards to the "anachronistic simultaneousness", in which we find ourselves, trying to draw attention to the indicative, disturbing fact (which in today's "knowledge society" is usually caused by indifference) that the meaning of what is meant by philosophy - wisdom or knowledge - changes over time. Our triumphantly cry "we live in a society of knowledge" has become a common place. "Common Places" that Flaubert spoke about, are those ideas that all people accepted, they are banal and common and chosen. These are the ideas that, once you have accepted them, already have been accepted in advance so that the problem of their reception does not exist. When you expose an already accepted idea, you seem to have done it already and the problem is resolved in advance. Communication is immediate, because, as Bourdieu observes, it is in a certain sense, not there. Or it seems to be only apparent.

A general exchange of communication whose only content is the mere fact that something, which is already understandable to be that way, relentlessly repeats. This is precisely the case with self-satisfied repetition of the airy, soothing slogans: we live in a society of knowledge. It is a catchword on whose wings flies a long prepared absence of thinking of new management, new economy of knowledge, commercialization, consumerism and much more. "The global society of knowledge" can be analyzed as the latter form of knowledge (and enjoyment), which enjoys an exalted - almost metaphysically exalted status. On the contrary, if we return to reason, we shall agree with those authors who argue that by definition a thought is subversive: it, therefore, must begin with the dismantling of "common places" and then it has to be demonstrated (Bourdieu, 2000: 46).

If there was enough time, it would be necessary to disassemble, ' deconstruct', or at least critically explain the background assumptions that enable one form of science, which functions in the form of a new economy (of knowledge), to get identified and self-identified through (again and again, regardless of the circumstances in which we live, no matter what "happens" in the world) production and reproductionand that way gets recycled, is recursively renewing. It's always the same one, the identical one which has not been proved yet but claims that we live in a society which (again and again, regardless of the circumstances in which we live, no matter what "happens" and "happening" in the world), produces and plays and so recilklira, recursively restores, spins, this one and the same, always identical, nothing proven, tautologični attitude, which is that we live in a knowledge society.

Liessman warned that "scientific" is often not more than labels that you put the prestige associated with it, wanting to improve the credibility and the likelihood of success. Among theorists of science, but is controversial whether such venerable disciplines such as economics or psychoanalysis in general science (Liessman, 2008: 39). The same argument but in cynical interpretations: "We live in a society of knowledge. This sentence haunts educators and politicians, educators, university reformers and trustees of the European Union: it movess researchers, markets and enterprise. Knowledge and education are the most important raw resource material of the poor Europe, and whoever invests in education, is investing in the future. With less emotions, we evoke the end of the industrial work, and the overall energy focuses on the activities of "knowledge-based"... At first glance it may seem that the supposed Enlightenment dream of a completely educated man in a truly informed society, finally, becomes a reality, although a second look at the actual formation is far more realistic. We will notice that much of what is being propagated and proclaimed under the title of a 'society of knowledge' is seen as a rhetorical gesture that owes less to the idea of education and more to a strong political and economic interests, if we observe carefully" (Liessman, 2008: 7). The idea that we live in a society of knowledge has become a commercially viable idea and it is worth repeating it but if you decide to deny it you can do it. However, considering the widely accepted and based view that we live in a society of knowledge, says Liessmann, it will only do us harm. Commercialization of knowledge is, therefore, not only a rhetorical gesture. It leads to commercialization of private and public institutions - such as, for instance, the university - and goes far to bring us to the commercialization of life itself.

The commercialization of universities, as the highest institutions of knowledge, represent a symptom of disorders of self-regulated idea of knowledge. Stanley Aronowitz, the sociologist, point out that "the learning has come under the service of a stronger administration, which does not suit many teachers and students, except in borderline cases, but tends to suit more policies and market forces that require the power over the higher education" (Aronowitz, 2000: 164).

For the cultural anthropologist Wesley Shumar, learning and research "began to be valued according to its ability to be converted into cash or goods, and not some other ways, such as aesthetics or satisfaction you gain from doing them. In the end, you lose the idea that there are other types of values as well" (Shumar, 1997: 5). Many fear that commercially oriented activities overshadow other intellectual values and that university programmes will be assessed through the money that students bring and not by their intrinsic intellectual quality (Bok, 2005: 22). Members of the university, who oppose the excessive expansion of the commercial impact of torture, are concerned. They fear that money and efficiency can gradually get too much prominence in the academic decision-making and that the verdict of the market will get rid of the judgement of scientific workers when it comes to deciding on the teaching school methods and the setup of education board staff (Bok, 2005: 25).

The modern science does not allow clear separation of scientific, industrial, technological or commercial aspects of research. If under the influence of the new economy of knowledge, marketing and management, the administrators are tirelessly repeating that "we live in a society of knowledge", but in reality (in addition to so present will of ignorance, trance or ecstasy), we see domination of dogmas and imitations, it is a symptom of the dramatic transformation of the very idea of knowledge which reaches its climax with the crisis of the neoliberal concept of globalization. The increasing closeness of university science and profit-oriented industry produces a variety of risks to compromise, openness and objectivity of academic research (Bok, 2005: 145).

As one of the authors put it down: we do not know what we need to know until we ask the right question, and we can identify the real question only if we put our own ideas about the world on the test of public controversy (Lasch, 1996). The essential question is what should be and what may become the subject of scientific research. How and by which qualitative (interpretative) methods will be interpreted the results of a socially sensitive research? What will be highlighted as a potential risk, what is left out, what will remain open, and what problem will be (and whether it will ever be, and how) anticipatory named as a possible or desirable direction of future research? - All of these are very complex, epistemological, ethical and commercially open and challenging questions. For instance, if the pharmaceutical companies become major sponsors of medical research, it raises an obvious question - and that is exactly what happens in the moment. The government encourages universities to get the sponsorships rather than to rely on the public funding (Crouch, 2007:54).

Some scientific problems deserve to be explored, although they do not have a predictable commercial value, while other areas, such as Egyptology or epistemology, deserve the greatest and highest scholarships, although only a few people read about them. Also, universities must be careful when it comes to looking up to venture models for achieving greater efficiency in their activities. We can find the useful suggestions among the business methods on how to reduce costs in maintaining buildings and providing support services. However, efficiency is not a very useful guide on teaching and research. The ways according which the markets function are not always useful in attempts to improve the work of research universities. The high risk lies in a fact that companies can influence the results of research (Bok, 2005:73). More troubling is the multitude of cases where pharmaceutical companies are trying to suppress unwanted results that were identified by university researchers (Bok, 2005: 74). Testing drugs for pharmaceutical companies is not the only example of high-risk research. Nutritionists who are investigating the effects of certain foods on human health can reduce the chances of entire companies, the way epidemiologists changed the lives of tobacco producers and demonstrated a link between cigarettes and cancer. Scientists that are working on environment and assess the impact of exhaust gases can bring to release the results which lead to extremely costly regulations for manufacturers. Researchers who study the existence of global warming could drastically alter the future of the energy industry (Bok, 2005:76).

The most obvious danger is that researchers who receive money from the companies for their research can be under the influence of that company. They do not need to deliberately change their results of research in order to keep the favor of the company's sponsors. However, when you have received such support, it can be a subtle way to influence you, when deciding on how to draft conclusions, how much to highlight the qualifications and contrary interpretations (or whether to mention the potential (but unproven) new risks (Bok, 2005: 77). It has been the case that more and more scientists are becoming businessmen rather than remaining scientists. Due to the process of commercialization of knowledge, triggered by global trends, scientific truth that we have spoken about becomes less important than economic success. The ethics loses appeal in relation to politics and business. This is confirmed by the evidence of that fact, that the ethics, where it exists, is taught and referred to a business ethics. The traditional ethics was such forms of unity. Nevertheless, there is still faith in the ability of humanity. There is a measure of that that is human that we cannot change, but only lose (Valjan, 2004: 360).

9. Are we living in a postdemocratic or predemocratic period?

Colin Crouch's attitude from Postdemocracy (2007) is congruent with our experience that democracy is going through a period of significant paradox. In the post-socialist transition countries it is widely believed that globalization imposes itself on the consumerist culture of egocentric consumer who gets promoted on a wave of theft (predatory) privatization and environmental degradation. When the masses have the opportunity to actively participate in defining priorities of public life, the democracy is making a progress. But the question, which refers to the paradox of democracyas well, is that the masses have the necessary knowledge to understand the priorities to establish a healthy democratic society. The experience of former Yugoslavian countries that are now in transit is negative. It claims that the newly-ethnic democracy, is in fact, only a formal democracy. They encourage discrimination, alienation between people, and various forms of deviant and criminal behavior. Lack of transparency has become a synonym for the transition and privatization. Such democracy is not a true democracy, but pre-democracy. They reduce and cripple the human creative potential. They reduce the plurality of human identity to a single - "killer identity" (Maalouf, 2002: 12). Questions of identity, essentially conceived identity, which in post-socialist societies, over the last 20 years imposed as the most important existential questions - questions were false. These issues are suitable for manipulating the masses.

It is a well known fact that the masses are generally more prone to cheering than reading the critical literature on the manipulation of the mind, will and emotions, manipulation of needs and desires and the manipulation of collective and personal identities. Guy Debord talks about the type of "integrated spectacle" as a stage in which the West is a postindustrial, and postmodern society. Model of integrated spectacle, as the logic that leads to cultural practices of consumption, unites the two types of spectacles that have preceded him. The first is the concentrated spectacle, marked by dictatorial totalitarian ideology of a dictatorial type, whether it is a Nazi or Stalinist style, and the other is diffuse spectacle, the so-called Americanization of the world on principles of an intrusive market offer of competitive goods and services (Debord, 1999: 152). When a society which proclaims democracy comes to the level of the integrated spectacle, it seems as if fragile achieving perfection is considered everywhere. Therefore, no longer is it exposed to attacks, because it is fragile and cannot be attacked any more and also it seems to be perfect, as no society has ever been. This society is fragile because it is very difficult to manage their hazardous technological expansion.

However, such a society is also quite appropriate to rule the world. The evidence of this is that those who aspire to power want to rule it exactly as it is, by the same procedures and keep it just as it was. For the first time in modern Europe, no party or faction is no longer trying to pretend to make any changes. No one can criticize the goods (Debord, 1999: 190). Giorgio Agamben adds to this diagnosis, when talking about the "decadence of modern democracy and its gradual convergence towards the totalitarian states in postdemocratic society of the spectacle" (Agamben, 2004: 18). Colin Crouch also believes that the more we move towards the postdemocratic sex, the more this explains the widespread feeling of disillusionment and dissatisfaction with the level of participation among the political class and the masses of citizens. While the framework of democracy remain fully in force, politics and government are increasingly rolling back into the hands of the privileged elite in a way that is typical for pedemocratic period. An important result of this process is the growing weakness of the ideals of equality (Crouch, 2007: 12).

A large number of people in democratic regimes, and an even larger number in non-democratic regimes, suffers an enormous amount of pain while living in misery, poverty and hopelessness. It is the living, everyday paradox of so-called developed democracy and ethnic democracy, which mark most of the countries in transit. Finally, "if we go back to the beginning, we still do not know what democracy means, or what democracy is. For democracy is not yet presented, it has not yet been proved, it is to come" (Derrida, 2007: 25). The question is how to set free the opportunities for true, global democracy. The need for an answer to what is so urgent that it cannot wait any longer for an answer may cause blockage of opinion. If you do not know what globalization is, then you cannot be sure what the global democracy is either. Who is the true subject of the global democracy? Is it a working man who works, one that earns his bread by labouring with his own hands? Or is it a man who does not work, because the work, the very concept of work, seems to have become obsolete - insufficient? What if the global democracy is not an appropriate subject? What if the fascinating progress of micro-computer technology, biotechnology and robotics, and man has made democracy insufficient in an irreversible way? What if Rifkin and Derrida were right to speak about our posthuman future, for instance, to talk about the different micro-information revolution and the revolution in robotics, that is actually happening. Rifkin's book 'The End of Work', creates a separate place for what he calls the "division of knowledge" and that way referring to the change that is underway. Derrida goes even further than that. He is interested in the problem of consumer culture, the loss of meaningful work, and culture of idleness. Derrida connects the problem of "the end of work" to "globalization", "mondialisation". He does so in the context of the transformation of the university and the transformation of the very idea of knowledge, which disrupts any stable notion of knowledge, as well as in the context of future social sciences, which could happen tomorrow. Thus, in the case of the "end of work" and in the case of the "globalization", which are closely linked, Derrida emphasizes the need to distinguish between extensive and firmly set phenomenon which we under under these words on one hand, and between the non-conceptual use of the word, on the other hand. Derrida argues that "renewed and revised idea of the "human rights" (1948) and the institutions of the legal term crimes against humanity" 1945) shape the vision and mondialisation of the international law for which it is assumed to watch over this idea.

Derrida kept the French word "mondialisation", in terms of "globalization", a reference to preserve the "world" ("monde") [World, Welt, Mundus, which is neither globe nor cosmos.] The concept of man, human distinctiveness, human rights, crimes against humanity, as we know, is organizing the mondialisation. The notion of man is, at the same time, necessary but is, still, always problematic... We can discuss about it or consider it the way it is but only within the frame of new Social Sciences" (Derrida, 2002: 83). However, in order to make these debates critical or deconstructive, in what regards the question of history and truth in relation to the question about man, human distinctiveness, human rights, crimes against humanity, etc. - all of this should be, in principle, to find its place in unconditional discussion without preconceptions or assumptions, to find its legitimate place of work and reconsideration at the university, and in it, primarily within the social sciences (Derrida, 2002: 83).

Wallerstein also considered that the first thing you should do is completely delete the category of social sciences from the head, which the legacy of the existing world system has left to us and which has been an obstacle not only on the way to analyse current realities but also when it comes to creating possible alternatives to it. The first step is to understand that there are multiple temporalities, a multiple spectrum of universalism and particularism. However, it is necessary to do much more than simply accept that they exist. We must begin to discover how they fit together and what is the optimum combination and in what circumstances. This is a serious plan of reconstruction for our system of knowledge. In this opening, future-oriented context (asking an autoreferential question who we are, when talking about globalization, when speaking to each other), Wallersten believes that "we need to focus our students to think about the fundamental epistemological issues" (Wallerstein, 2004: 137). Unfortunately, as Wallersten claims, "we are all just talking about globalization - regardless of political affiliation, as if this concept is a far more then just a passing rhetorical device for continuing conflict within the capitalist world economy, which is unauthorized and excessively used.

This is the dust that we had thrown in our eyes. The endless litany on ethnic violence, for which not only sociologists are responsible but also activists fighting for human rights, and that also is the dust that we had thrown in our eyes. I will not deny that the ethnic violence is a horrific and frightening reality, but I want to point out that it is obviously not the domain of some other people who are less happy, less intelligent, less civilized. It is an absolutely normal result of deep and growing inequality in our world system... Social science has not offered us a useful tool for analyzing what is happening in the world system since the 198th year" (Wallerstein, 2004: 74). This internationally recognized, a longtime researcher of the world system, proves that the world economy is in structural crisis and that we are in the midst of chaotic period. He believes that we are in the period of bifurcation, and that by mid-21st century, not only will our present world system cease to exist this, but he predicts that a new one will generate (Wallerstein, 2004: 133).

Attali (Attali, 2010: 7) offered a simple diagnosis of the present: *market forces take over the planet*. If this development continues until the end, it is anticipated that the money will remove anything that might hurt, and will even gradually destroy the country, including the United States. We shall experience the decline in U.S. omnipotence, and the distribution of the world order among several regional powers. Lastly, when it gets to rule over the world, the market will educate an entity called *hyperimperialism*, which will be intangible and planetary, which will create market value and the new alienation, extreme wealth and poverty; the nature will be strictly divided, it will all be privatized, including the army, police and legal system. The man himself will perform the intervention of plastic surgery, after which he himself will become an artifact of the standard sales, intended for consumers who have also become artifacts. After becoming unnecessary to his creations, the man will disappear. Although mankind has withdrawn before such a future and violently opposed to globalization, before it releases of all of its earlier alienation, it will fall into a series of regressive and destructive wars, it will used the weapons unthinkable for us today, confronting the states, religious groups, terrorist units and private pirates.

Attali called this war a hyperconflict, and believes that such a war could lead to the extinction of mankind. There is, however, more optimistic scenario. If the globalization can be controlled and accepted, if the market could be limited without being lifted, if democracy could have planetary dimensions and still remain concrete, if the domination of one empire could be prevented, only then will open up a new infinity of freedom, responsibility, dignity, overcoming and respect for another. This period is called *hyperdemocracy* (Attali, 2010: 8). The first global financial crisis of the 21st century confirmed that we are in the midst of chaotic period. The crisis was initially detected in the U.S. mortgage market. This crisis, in 2007. and 2008. spread outside the U.S. and outside the mortgage market crisis in the international banking system (Snower, 2008. 140). It is a widespread belief that the global financial crisis is not just financial, but also moral and political and environmental, etc.

This global crisis has additionally burdened the processes of globalization, transition and democracy. After the terrible experience of the global crisis, many believe that the current crisis will not prevail: if economic and financial information are not distributed equally and simultaneously available to everyone, if financial markets that are ipso facto - world markets are not balanced by global rule of law and thus cease to be financial casino, if bank interest does not become "modest and boring again (which was supposed to be the case), if there is not an established global and real surveillance of the risk, if the system of personal income is not revised,"if we do not separate the market and banking activities," "if we do not introduce an obligation of risk-taking for the one that imposes on others," "unless we turn to larger, environmentally sustainable work on a global level, as it is already does in some countries" (Attali, 2009: 21).

It has been suggested that we should consider replacing the banking supervision at the state level by banking supervision at EU level, because the supervisory failure was caused by mutual competition of national authority and supervision requires a united EU authority (Tabellini, 2008: 61-64). Analysis of the current global economic crisis shows that this crisis began with the increased losses that turned into a crisis in U.S. subprime mortgage market. There are many macro and micro economic causes of the crisis. We should let experts explain to the general public – based on the background of a society of knowledge or the new knowledge-based economy in other words - the meanings of key terms which explain the causes of the crisis, such as for instance: ignorance, bad judgments, speculation, creating bubbles, credito mania (strategy at which the old loans are repayable by new loans), bad practice on the border of negligence, trusting to (wrong) people from credit rating agencies, excessive extravagance, incompetence, greed for quick wealth. It seems that there is a multitude of evidence that there is no organic link between capitalism (cognitive capitalism) and democracy, though, in the dominant political rhetoric, these two concepts are treated almost like Siamese twins (Hobsbawm, 2007: 97).

10. Apocalyptic tone in philosophy, theology and critique

The global economic crisis, population growth, resource consumption, environmental pollution, mass extinction of species, and ontological uncertainty, and new security risks -

these are all the phenomena related to globalization. That does not mean that we have listed it all. What determines initial definition as globalization, is a subject to subsequent changes based on different experiences. Many definitions have been suggested for the start of globalization. There are only a few that have declared its end. One definition says: "Globalization is the beginning of broadening, deepening and speeding up of the global interconnectedness in all the aspects of contemporary social life, from cultural to criminal, from the financial to the spiritual" (Held, McGrew, 1999: 2). Unlike the privileged discourse, where the leading discourse is the discourse of the new economy, spreading the mantra that we live in a „society of knowledge and skills" (Giddens, 2009: 38), many critics believe that we have entered a new era of dogmatism (Sim, 2006: 22), darkness and ignorance (Zizek, Gunjevic, 2008: 25).

Faced with that kind of threat, our collective ideology has launched a cover-up mechanisms and self-deception, including the direct will to ignorance, 'it is the general pattern of vulnerable human societies: instead focusing on the crisis, while declining, they are becoming more and more blinded. "Also, there are re-appearing variants of apocalyptic discourse. This time, the apocalyptic tone in philosophy and theology of liberation, became very close. Zizek believes that the apocalypse is characterised by the special weather mode, which is clearly opposed to the other two main modes - traditional circular time (which is established and governed by the principles of the universe, and reflects the natural and celestial order, as the time format in which microcosm and macrocosm resonate harmoniously in the second one) and the straight line modern time (as a time of gradual progress and development) is an apocalyptic time 'time of the end of time', 'time of an emergency', when we should get prepared for the end that is closer.

There are three variants of apocalyptism: Christian-fundamentalist, new age and techno-digital-posthumous apocalyptism. Although sharing the basic idea that humanity is approaching the zero point of radical transformation, their ontologies differ radically: the techno-digital apocalyptism (whose main representative is Ray Kurzweil) moves within the boundaries of scientific naturalism and, at the level of evolution of human kind, recognizes the contours of the conversion of people in 'post-human beings'; new age apocalyptism gives spiritualist reversal to the conversion, interpreting it as a shift from one mode of 'cosmic consciousness' to another (usually from the modern dualistic-mechanistic attitude to an attitude of a holistic immersion); Ultimately, the Christian fundamentalists read the apocalypse in the strictly biblical terms, ie, seek (and find) in the modern world of wonders to be closer to the final battle between Christ and Antichrist, and a critical turning point inevitably awaits us. Although the latter option, despite its dangerous contents, often considered laughable, is the closest 'millenium's' radically emancipatory logics (Zizek, 2008).

Apocalyptic discourse becomes a newly discovered area of productive encounter of philosophy and theology - the meeting that simultaneously transcends both of these areas. Gunjević believes that apocalyptic discourse transcends all other forms of theology, because the only revolutionary apocalypse has enough potential to radically revise and change reality. The apocalyptic discourse constructs doxolic practice not only to see the reality differently, but it evokes it into existence. Hence the importance, power and beauty of the apocalyptic vision of reality (Gunjevic, 2008). Hence the talk about diabolic relationship between capital and terror, to which Hardt and Negri are coming based on the deconstruction of the works of Aurelius Augustine, *Civitate Dei*, "as Saint Augustine, the great kingdoms are only projections of small thieves. However, Augustine of Hippoa is so realistic in his pesimistic concept of power that he would be stunned in front of today's small thieves of the monetary and financial power. Indeed, when capitalism loses its relationship with the value (as measured by a single operation as well as the norms of collective progress) it appears as a corruption" (Hardt, Negri, 2003: 14).

The problem with capitalism in the above mentioned perspective is that it successfully captures the desire and discipline. Micro-politics of desire has developed a technique of desire so we want what others want and the way others want it, noticed Gunjević. Augustine in 'City of God', from the second until the nineteenth chapter, calls for a certain shape, desertion, exodus, nomadism. He call for specific disciplined asceticism. That is what is missing not only to Negri's anti-imperial activist, but also to the multitude that is constituted as a political subject (Gunjevic, 2009: 71). Also, the final page of the Empire are more mysterious than incomplete. A person who embodies joy of non-communist struggle against the Empire, is none other than Francis of Assisi. Other authors have taken a serious anti-capitalist critique. They diagnosed negative consequences of globalization, especially the increase of social inequalities, both within countries and globally, and they gave an open contribution to the anti-capitalist movement, which is thought to be activated during the protests in Seattle in 1999.

Callinicos admits that the main intellectual danger is the fact that critical thinking may be driven into a torrent of aggressive propaganda of the "new economy" (Callinicos, 2009: 31). We recognize the apocalyptic tone in his book '*Against The Third Way: Anti-Capitalist Critique*', where he says: "The deception of the Wall Street is a key component of a long boom of the early 1990s: thanks to the so-called "welfare effect", the middle-class Americans reacted to the increase in the value of their stock investments by more borrowing and spending. This has allowed the U.S. to act as a "consumer" and thus contribute to re-stabilize the world and Asian economies after the Asian and Russian the collapse of 1997-98 (Callinicos, 2009: 559).

Samuel Brittan and Martin Wolf, the two economists and commentators of the Financial Times, are both loyal to the neo-liberal orthodoxy, rejecting claims of "Wall Street's ability to reach stratosphere. Brittani adds that "no one can tell whether the failure will happen in a week, year or five years' time" (Callinicos, 2009: 56). An interesting phenomenon, which could be a good landmark for future research associated with globalization (glocalization) is the collision of fake and real sense of urgency. Since the crisis is global, it often imposes a sense of urgency, that is a need that something urgent must be done in order for humanity and the planet to be saved. A preliminary analysis of individual proclamations, bordering with the badly pretended panic-spreading, shows that it is often to do with a false sense of urgency. Therefore, how shall we responsibly rationalize this false sense of urgency? An interesting phenomenon, which could be a good landmark for future globalization (glocalization) associated research is the collision of fake and real sense of urgency. As Bill Gates recently said: "What is the use of millions of computers when there are people still needlessly dying of dysentery?" (Soros, 2002). Contrary to this request for urgency, Zizek reminds us of Marx's letter to Engles from 1870 in which, at least for a moment, it seemed as if the revolution in Europe once again was knocking on the door. Marx's letter reveals his panic-stricken fear: why couldn't revolutionaries wait several years, given that he had not yet completed his Capital? Mass protests of Croatian citizens against the Croatian

Government, which began in March of 2011 under the motto THIS IS NOT THE REVOLUTION THIS IS THE EVOLUTION.

According to some analysts, such protests represent a symbolically significant expression of socially discontent people. They are discontent with the way the post-war transition is made as well as the privatization of public goods. The social consequences of transition and ethnic privatization are even worse in Bosnia and Herzegovina. Because the multi-ethnic and multi-religious Republic, with significant social capital and major European, civil, cosmopolitan potential - exposed crime against humanity, genocide against Bosnian Bosniaks in Srebrenica in 1995. – and was parallel to the impact of "economic genocide." After the terrible experiences - such as the Holocaust and genocide - Zizek thinks that Adorno should be corrected: it is not poetry but the prose, that became impossible after Aushwitz. Zizek, for instance, believes that the constantly present violence and terror as well as sympathy for the victims are relentlessly acting as a decoy that prevents us from thinking (Zizek, 2008: 9). In this respect, one of the author who did not participate in the conflicts and who acknowledges that he cannot enter into any of the official policies of collective identities, expressed his doubt regarding the official bureaucratic language used to describe post-conflict societies, when he said: "it can happen to us to talk about the reconciliation without really knowing what we are talking about". Politics of ethnic representation, which I have elsewhere called democracies of ethnomathematics - which are based on the endless counting and counting, sorting and classification and exclusively on the so-called ethnicity, ignoring the plurality and multiple interweaving of the human identity – produce the dissatisfaction of the same people who have voted for them and elected them, 20 years ago... The experience of transition in Bosnia and Herzegovina is very specific and reveals a number of paradoxes, related to global, regional and local identity politics, but also paradoxes that are the result of international continuity in a symbolic and actual space that not even the so-called international community understands herself.

To make things that relate to the installation of globalization on Bosnian soil worse, here comes the following fact: The Dayton Constitution recognizes only the ethnic identities: Bosniaks, Serbs, Croats and others, while the Bosnians or Herzegovians as civils and citizens, are eliminated upon mentioning their name, and thus, symbolically, and actually switched off - declared non-existent. This is a textbook example that speaks about how the symbolic and actual violence are, in fact, inextricably linked. This can also be an example of how the economy of violence is reproduced in our everyday speech forms, as an integral part of symbolic violence that is embodied in language and institutional forms. The symbolic and actual elimination of multiple, plural, open, multicultural identity - which are exposed to the residents of Bosnia and Herzegovina - can be analyzed as a symbolic blow to the most terrible idea and the reality of European and global multiculturalism. The elimination would bring to a fatal administrative protocol error made during an attempt to stop the aggression on the Republic of Bosnia & Herzegovina. There will be a mistake, at the international level, that needs to be corrected. And not only because of citizens of Bosnia and Herzegovina, but for the ideas of cosmopolitanism, in order to preserve the universal values of civil society, universal rights and freedoms upon which the idea of living together, or the very idea of humanity is based. The logic is very simple: if the common life in Bosnia and Herzegovina is impossible, why should life together be possible anywhere else on the globe? Because of the hope that the idea is Justice, even in this world where it is the possible landmark of work of international institutions, it is worth to fight for the idea of living together in Bosnia and Herzegovina and for the idea of freedom and common life anywhere in the globalized world.

Since Bosnia and Herzegovina has a cosmopolitan potential to be globalized, it can also serve as a paradigm of the global crisis, but it van also serve as a paradigm of a hope to restore the ideas of cosmopolitanism and universal respect for human rights. As Michel Chossudovsky writes: "Relying on the Dayton agreement, which created the Bosnian "Constitution," U.S. and the European allies have introduced a complete colonial rule over Bosnia ... The new "constitution", which is a separate annex attached to the Dayton Agreement, gave the reins of economic policy into the hands of institutions that emerged from Bretton Woods and the European Bank for Reconstruction and Development (EBRD), based in London. The International Monetary Fund had the authority to appoint the first governor of the Bosnian Central Bank, as well as the High Representative, "who will not be the citizen of Bosnia and Herzegovina or any neighboring country"... From the very beginning, Bosnia didn't get the possibility to self-finance its own reconstruction, starting from an independent monetary policy... While the West has pleaded in support of building democracy, real political power has crossed the parallel to the Bosnian "state" where executive power was in the hands of foreigners and not Bosnian nationals.

The Bosnian Constitution, which was quickly written by the Western creditors on their behalf, contained their interests as well. They managed to do this without convening a constituent assembly and without a participation of an organization of Bosnian citizens." (Chossudovsky, 2008.) The inability of multilateral institutions to renew the possibility on the globally deterritorialized points of the symbolic encounter of civilizations and cultures of the world (for us it is Bosnia and Herzegovina, for Iraqi it is Iraq, for Tibetan Buddhists it might be Tibet, for Africans probably a whole, not just sub-Saharan Africa, and so on) and therefore to build a global solidarity and so bring hope to the excluded, subordinated, poor, excommunicated, eliminated and disenfranchised – brings back to lie those who persistently claim that we live in a global society of knowledge - the best of all the possible worlds. Resemantization discourse on globalization, in a variety of interdisciplinary, transdisciplinary and subdisciplinary contexts, can be a good way to open up critical opportunities to build new value related orientations that could facilitate the construction of a better world with more justice for all the people.

11. Conclusion

The transforming effects of globalization strongly affect the economic, political, cultural, technological, environmental, ethical and other aspects of the modern world of life. In this section we will try to show that what we call globalization is so loaded with different meanings that the incomensurability of these meanings is hard to place in one discursive framework. We we shall therefore focus on the analysis of the underlying assumptions of economic globalization. We analyse the nature of knowledge on which the new knowledge-based economy in detail. It is the most dominant form of knowledge that has tremendous power and impact on all other dimensions of globalization. We partly compare "central" and "peripheral" or marginal flow of science. We show that the new knowledge-based economy (and knowledge paradigms close to her) enjoy very high status within the mainstream of science. Based on the symbolic power that they possess, the main flows of science have the opportunity to make the certain definitions and practices of globalization, which occurred just within these flows, on the outskirts, achieve greater impact in comparison to some others. While the positivist, commercial discourses, very superficially speak about the discursive preconditions and effects, we headed in the different direction. We investigated deeper: epistemological, cognitive, discursive and symbolic aspects of globalization, starting from the sociosemiotic and discursive critique of economic globalization. We were interested to know, above all, how it is possible that the economic aspects of globalization, in most discussions (except perhaps in economic sociology), act as dominant in relation to some essential problems, such as the destruction of biological diversity or multiculturality. We searched for an answer to the question of whether and how globalization, namely economic globalization, affect the structure of knowledge, for instance, the transformation of the very idea of knowledge. The answer to that question is yes. Globalization, in general, leads to the commercialization of knowledge (philosophy turns into a "business philosophy"). At the same time, it promotes consumerism (extravagance and consumption became a virtue). However, we have focused on the internal, intrinsic aspects of the economic effects of discourse, which allow institutional consumerism of knowledge. These aspects are, in positivist analysis of economics and economic activities as well as in a pragmatic system of "knowledge and skills", considered to be as self-evident, and are rarely subjected to any criticism. On the contrary, we started from the criticism of the positivist and econometric methodology on which the new knowledge-based economy is founded. We applied postpositivist, qualitative methodology, in order to comprehend how a more comprehensive discourse actually functions based on the new knowledge-based economy and the scientific, ideological and real consequences of uncontrolled spreading in all the spheres of knowledge and education. We have shown that the new knowledge-based economy (as a concept, approach, paradigm), is a dangerous form of methodological reductionism. We believe that this kind of reductionism is linked to the specific institutional, political, cultural, and psychological factors that suit the corporate fundamentalism and neoliberal concept of globalization. The economic dimension of globalization we consider to be the most important dimension of globalization because it is based on these dimensions, starting from the economic language and the economic criteria of rationality, and it is on the level of these dimensions that all the other phenomena that are associated with globalization are analysed and evaluated. According to our insights, globalization provokes both positive and negative effects, although we shall focuse more on the negative effects of globalization. We tried to contribute to ongoing discussions about the consequences of globalization (and transition), so we are focused primarily on transdisciplinary critical connection of a knowledge-based economy and ideology. The largest part of the approach to knowledge-based economy, is characterized by positivist, non-conflict vision of knowledge and technology, which leads us to avoid the social, cultural and ethical contradictions inherent in a knowledge-based economy. We came to the insight that the new knowledge-based economy is a deeply ideological economy, which serves as a strategic tool for the production of so-called "global society of knowledge", and that makes an ideological foundation for cognitive capitalism. We talked about the background speech assumptions, about the new knowledge-based economy and the global knowledge-based society and the deeper meaning of this very powerful discourse. We searched for an answer to the question of why - and how - a new knowledge-based economy - a broad, comprehensive matrix, as a global matrix - imposed to all the other forms of knowledge, and works as the inevitable basis of a global knowledge-based society - as the knowledge itself. The concept of cognitive capitalism, which is - in the semantic sense, inextricably linked to the institutional forms through which it imposes and self-promotes the new knowledge-based economy – has been proposed to make an effort for the future research, so that in the context of analysis of the negative consequences of globalization which we have more, it can be rationally understood. It is necessary to have clearly precise meaning and background of the current practice of knowledge, as a general resource of humanity reduced to the economic idea of instrumental knowledge which is subjected to the narrow interests and the logics of privatization of profits. The issue of strengthening intellectual property rights and its expansion in the area of wildlife and owards the results of fundamental research is a crucial aspect of the current regulation of cognitive capitalism. We have shown that there is not (just) a model of knowledge-based economy on which it would be possible to simply implement a global knowledge-based society. Globalisation has a significant impact on a number of ideological traditions, especially nationalism, socialism and religious fundamentalism (though we speak more about the social consequences of "market fundamentalism"), but also has broader implications for the ideology as a whole. The experiences of globalization, as well as experiences of transition from socialism to capitalism are not identical, but different. Theoretical and epistemological debates about the meaning of the new knowledge-based economy are not always abstract. They are not far from the real problems of moral and ethical challenges that we, human beings are confronted when thinking about the consequences of the progress of biotechnology and technoscience. As the world of science grew in size and power, its deepest problems ranged from the epistemological to the social and ethical issues. Because historically, geographically and technologically different national economies, did not have the same initial conditions to create the economy and knowledge-based society. Therefore, cognitive capitalism does not contribute to a true planetary integration of goods, capital and technology. Ethics of responsibility for the consequences of the application of science we consider to be the royal path of knowledge. We are committed to new critical science, an open, multicultural epistemology that recognizes the various intellectual and spiritual traditions of knowledge that can not exclude the so-called ordinary people (laities). Knowledge should be understood as a public good in the service of peaceful ideas of humanity. Commercialization of universities, as the highest institutions of knowledge, is a consequence of disorders of self-regulation of the idea of knowledge. Science and scientific results do not pertain just science, but concern all people. When dealing with a variety of ethical and moral dilemmas, in which Western science itself is necessary in order to establish a balance between the authority of science and the public. It is necessary to develop intelligent and responsible dialogue between those who have the power and the movement for global justice and solidarity with those who are subordinated, excluded, excommunicated, removed. Finally, we give a brief overview of Bosnia and Herzegovina, a country that does not lose hope when it comes to the idea of love and coexistence between people in a global context. Since Bosnia and Herzegovina was globalized with the help of the international community, it now has a multicultural cosmopolitan potential. Some authors consider Bosnia and Herzegovina to be the first (post) modern state in Europe, though it can also serve as a paradigm of the global crisis of a (post) modern idea of humanity, but it can also deliver hope for the recovery of the ideas of cosmopolitanism and universal human rights and responsibilities.

12. References

Agamben, G. (2004). *Homo Sacer: Sovereign Power and Bare Life*, ISBN 961-6446-63-0, Kodo, Ljubljana

Aronowitz, S. (2000). *The Knowledge Factory, Dismantling the Corporate University and Creating True Higher Learning*, ISBN-10: 0807031224; ISBN-13: 978-0807031223, Beacon Press

Attali, J. (2010). *Une brève histoire de l'avenir*, ISBN, 978-86-86933-97-3, Arhipelag, Beograd

Beck, U. & Grande, E. (2006). *Das kosmopolitische Europa: Gesellschaft und Politik in der Zweiten Moderne*, ISBN, 953-0-61451-9, Školska knjiga, Zagreb

Beck, U. (2007). *Weltrisikogesellschaft*t: *Auf der Suche nach der verlorenen Sicherheit*, ISBN-103518414259 ISBN-139783518414255, Suhrkamp, Verlag, Frankfurt am Main

Bhagwaty, J. (2008). *In Defense of globalization*, ISBN, 978-86-7549-544-4, Glasnik, Beograd

Bourdieu, P. (2000). *Sur La télévision, suivi de l' emprise du journalisme*, ISBN-13: 978ID86288396, Clio, Beograd

Callinicos, A. T. (2009). *Against The Third Way: An Anty-Capitalist Critique*, ISBN, 953-316-064-7, Jesenski i Turk, Zagreb

Castells, M. (2003). *The Information Age: Economy, Society and Culture*, Volume 3, *The End of Millennium*, ISBN, 953-212-000-9, Golden marketing, Zagreb

Chesnais, F. (2007). In: *Soomes-nous sortis du capitalisme industriel?*, (Ed.) Carlo Vercellone, ISBN 953-258-014-x, Politička kultura, Zagreb

Chossudovsky, M. (2008). *The Globalization of Poverty and the New World Order*, ISBN, 978-953-6460-83-0, Prometej, Zagreb

Corsani, A. (2007.) In: *Soomes-nous sortis du capitalisme industriel?*, (Ed.) Carlo Vercellone, ISBN 953-258-014-x, Politička kultura, Zagreb

Crouch, C. (2007). *Postdemocrazia*, ISBN - 10 953-203-274-6; ISBN 13 978-953-203-274-1, Izvori, Zagreb

Čović, A. (2004). *Ethics and Bioethics*, ISBN 953-6576-17-1, Pergamena, Zagreb

Debord, G. (1999). *La Société du spectacle*, ISBN 953-6542-11-0, Arkzin, Zagreb

Derrida, J. (2001). *Foi et Savoir, suivi de* Le siècle et le Pardon, *entretiens avec Michel Wievorka „Point Essais"*, n. 447, Svetovi, Novi Sad

Derrida, J. (2007). *L' écriture et la difference*, ISBN 978-9958-41-189-2, „Šahinpašić", Sarajevo, Bosna i Hercegovina

Derrida, J. (2002). *L' avenir de la profesion ou l' université sans condition* (*grâce aux „Humanités" ce qui pourrait avoir lieu demain*), ISBN 86-7979-016-8, Stubovi kulture, Beograd

Derrida, J. (2007). *Voyous* (*Deux essais sur la raison*), Beogradski krug, Beograd, 2007. ISBN 978-86-82299-78-3.

Dow, S, C. (2005). *Economic Methodology: An Inquiry*, ISBN 953-6213-87—7, Politička kultura, Zagreb

Dracker, P. (1993). *Post- capitalist Society*, ISBN 0887306209 ISBN 9780887306204, HarperBusiness, New York

Fukuyama, F. (2003). *Our Poshuman future: Concequences of the Biotechnology Revolution*, ISBN 86-495-0190-7, CID, Podgorica

Giddens, A. (2009). *Europe in the Global Age*, ISBN 978—86-7102-352-8 , Clio, Beograd

Giddens, A. (2007). *Sociologija*, ISBN, 978-953-167-200, Globus, Zagreb

Glenny, M. (2008). *McMafia: Crime Without Frontiers*, ISBN, 978-86-7963-318-7, „Samizdat B92", Novi Beograd

Guellec, D. (2002). L' émergence d' une économie fondée sur le savoir, in J. -P. Touffut (ed), *Institutions et innovation: de la recherche aux sysstèmes sociaux d'innovation*, Albin Michel, Paris

Gunjevic, B. (2009). The virtue of Empire between the capital and terror, in *Philosophical research*, Vol 29. pp. 63-74. Zagreb,

Ha-Joon Chang (2002). *Kicking Away the Ladder: Development Strategy in Historical Perspective*, ISBN 978 1 84331 027 3, Anthem Press, London,

Hardt, M. & Negri, A. (2003). *Empire*, ISBN, 953-98699-2-7, Multimedijalni institut, Arkzin, Zagreb

Held, D. and McGrew, A. (2002). *Globalization/Anti-Globalization*, ISBN, 074562989x, Polity Press, Cambridge

Heywood, A, (2005). *Political Ideologies: An Introduction*, ISBN, 86-17-12841-0, Zavod za udžbenike i nastavna sredstva, Beograd,

Hobsbawm, E. (2007). *Globalisation, Democracy and Terrorism*, ISBN 978-86-86933-22-5, Artprint, Novi Sad

Howitt, P. (1996). *The implications of knowledge-based growth for micro-economic policies*, University of Calgary Press, Calgary

Kalanj, R. (2008). *Modernisation and Identity*, ISBN, 978-953-258-022-8, Politička kultura, Zagreb

Klein, N (2008). *The Shock Doctrine: The Rise of Disaster Capitalism*, ISBN, 978-953-201-987-2, V.B.Z. Zagreb

Klein, N. (2003). *Fences and Windows: Dispatches from the Front Lines of the Globalization Debate*, ISBN 0312307993; ISBN 953-201-261-3

Lebert & Vercellone (2007). *Soomes-nous sortis du capitalisme industriel?*, (ed) Carlo Vercellone, ISBN 953-258-014-x, Politička kultura, Zagreb

Liessmann, K. P. (2008) *Theorie der Unbildung: Die Irrtümer der Wissensgesellschaft*, ISBN 3552053824, Jesenski i Turk, Zagreb

Monbiot, G. (2006). *The Age of Consent: A manifesto for a new world order*, ISBN, 953-220-465-2, Algoritam, Zagreb

Mouhoud, M. (2007). In: *Soomes-nous sortis du capitalisme industriel?*, (Ed.) Carlo Vercellone, ISBN 953-258-014-x, Politička kultura, Zagreb

Myerson, G. (2001). *Donna Harraway and GM Foods*, ISBN 953-6483-82-3, Jesenski i Turk, Zagreb

Neumann, I. B. (2009). *Mening, materialitet, makt: en innføring i diskursanalize,* ISBN 978-86-83275-48-9, Alexandria Press, Beograd

Ohmae, K. (2007). *The Next Global stage: Challenges and Opportunities in Our Borderless World,* ISBN, 978-953-246-032-2, Mate, Zagreb

Patnam, R. (1993). *Making Democracy Work: Civic Traditions in Modern Italy,* ISBN–10: 978069 1037387; ISBN 13: 978-0691037387, Princeton University Press

Paulré, B. (2000). De la New Ekonomy au capitalisme cognitif, *Multitudes* 2, pp. 25-42, Exils Editeur, Paris,

Rifkin, J. (1999). *The Biotech Century: Harnessing the Gene and Remaking the World,* ISBN 953-6483-44-0; ISBN 953-6552-21-3, Hrvatsko sociološko društvo, Zagreb

Rifkin, J. (2006). *The European Dream: How Europe's Vision of the Future is Quietly Eclipsing the American Dream,* ISBN, 953-0-61437-3, Školska knjiga, Zagreb

Robertson, R. (1992). *Globalisation: Social theory and Global Culture,* ISBN 9780803981874, Sage, London

Rorty, R. (1995). *Contingency, Irony and Solidarity,* ISBN 1780366000, Naprijed, Zagreb

Rosenberg, J. (2000). *The Follies of Globalisation Theory,* ISBN, 1-85984-611-4, UK: 6 Meard Street, London, USA: 180 Varick Street, New York

Scholte, J. A. (2009). *Globalization: A Critical Introduction,* ISBN, 978-86-495-0400-4, CID, Podgorica, Crna Gora

Sen, A. (2006). *Identity and Violence: The Illusion of Destiny,* ISBN, 9780393060072, Masmedia, Zagreb,

Shiva, V. (2006). *Water Wars: Privatisation, Pollution and Profit* ISBN, 953-6956-07-1, DAF, Zagreb

Shumar, W. (1997). *College for Sale: A Critique of the Commodification of Higher* Education, Falmer Press, London

Sim, S. (2001). *Derrida and the End of History,* ISBN 953-6483-75-0, Jesenski i Turk, Zagreb

Sim, S. (2006). *Fundamentalist World: The New Dark Age of Dogma,* ISBN, 953-257-002-0, Planetopija, Zagreb

Sloterdijk, P. (1992). *Kritik der zynischen vernunft,* ISBN, 86-343-0654-2, Globus, Zagreb

Snower, J. D. (2009). Four mega-dangers international financial markets face, In: *The First Global Financial Crisis of the 21th Century,* pp. 107-109, ISBN 978-953-6808-17-5, Novum, Zagreb,

Steger, M. B. (2005). *Globalisation: A Very Short Introduction,* ISBN 9958-41-119-9, „Šahinpašić", Sarajevo, Bosna i Hercegovina

Stiglitz, J. (2009). *Making GlobalizationWork: The Next Steps to Global Justice,* ISBN, 978-953-220-588-6, Algoritam, Zagreb

Soros, G. (2002). *On Globalization,* ISBN 86-7963-181-7, Samizdat, Beograd

Swedberg, R. (2006). *Principles of economic sociology,* ISBN, 953-246-011-x, Mate, Zagreb

Tabelini, G. (2009). Why did bank supervision fail?, In: Felton, A. & Reinhart, *The First Global Financial Crisis of the 21th Century,* pp. 45-48, ISBN 978-953-6808-17-5, Novum, Zagreb,

Valjan, V. (2004). *Bioethics,* ISBN, 9958-741-29-6 ISBN, 953-7081-11-2, Sarajevo-Zagreb

Wallersten, I. (2004). *The Decline of American Power,* ISBN, 86-495-0232-6, CID, Podgorica

Zizek, S. & Gunjević, B. (2008). *God in pain / The return of the apocalypse*, ISBN 978-953-6932-35-I ISBN 978-9958-587-21-4, Biblioteka Ars haeretica, Ex Libris Rijeka i Synopsis, Sarajevo

Zizek, S. (2008). *Violence: Six Sideways Reflections*, ISBN, 878-953-178-940-0, Ljevak, Zagreb

Tourism: Analysis of a Global Phenomenon from a Perspective of Sustainability

Juan Ignacio Pulido-Fernández and Yaiza López-Sánchez
University of Jaén
Spain

1. Introduction

Many international institutions have highlighted the importance of tourism as a motor of social transformation and a instrument for promoting economic development (OECD, 2009; UNWTO, 2005; WTTC, 2005). Its potential for growth is considered to be such that, at a horizon of no more than ten years, tourism is expected to generate 11.3 per 100 of world GDP and 8.3 per 100 of employment (WTTC, 2005). The economics literature concurs with this view. From analyses of the role of international tourism in the provision of foreign exchange and its contribution to compensating trade deficits in the balance of payments, to its capacity to generate employment or to increase tax revenues and with them the possibilities of public intervention to improve the welfare of the country's citizens, there have been many contributions that recognize the potential of tourism as an instrument of economic development (among others, see Cooper, Fletcher, Fyall, Gilbert & Wanhill, 2008; Cortés-Jiménez & Artis, 2005; Goded, 2002; Lanza & Pigliaru, 1994; Lanza et al., 2003; Lickorish & Jenkins, 2000; Pearce, 1989; Pulido & Sánchez, 2010; Sinclair 1998; Sinclair & Stabler, 1997; Tribe, 2005; Vanhove, 2005).

The concept of "globalization" has been the subject of considerable debate, which has still not come up with a clear and widely accepted definition. Some argue that the driving force behind the process is economic, while others stress political and even cultural aspects. Whatever the case however, there is a certain consensus on understanding globalization as a dynamic phenomenon which has accelerated noticeably in the last decade (Randolph, 2007), which is multidimensional (Martin, 2001; Shademan, 2009), and which affects the world as a whole thus distinguishing it from the other ways in which countries open up to the international arena. As Vujakovic (2009: 5) notes: "*Globalization is a process of growing interaction and interdependence between economies, societies and nations across large distances.*"

In synthesis, there are seen to be three fundamental benefits of globalization: (i) it promotes global economic connectivity, revolutionizing trade flows and conditioning business strategies (Morrison, 2002); (ii) it contributes to the interchange of information, improving comprehension between different cultures and fostering democracy (Bagchi, 2007); and (iii) in the more globalized countries, it generates growth in revenues and in the quality of life of its inhabitants (Randolph, 2007). Some of the major arguments against globalization are: (i) the "improvement" in living standards in fact occurs in developed countries at the expense of developing countries; (ii) business relocation is directed towards those developing countries that have the lowest labour costs and least social protection; (iii) the primacy of the pursuit of increased profits generates abuses of the local population's social and environmental rights; (iv) local people's cultural identity is at continual risk due to the abuse of the Internet and the generalization of consumerism; etc.

With respect to tourism in particular, the last decade has seen an interesting debate about whether the sector has already reached a high level of globalization. As noted above, most of the literature assumes that tourism is an activity which connects the richest parts of the world to peripheral areas, and can thus contribute to improving the wealth and living standards of the less developed countries. Nevertheless, there are those who have questioned this role, identifying a number of aspects that they see as evidence that tourism is not an example of globalization. Above all, they believe that tourism generates a set of negative impacts on the destination territories which merit an overall evaluation of the effect of promoting tourism in them. As Aramberri (2009: 367) notes: "*While it is an activity practised all over the world, it is scarcely global.*"

A twofold hypothesis is defended in the present chapter. On the one hand, while tourism will undoubtedly be one of the activities contributing to intensifying the phenomenon of globalization in the coming decades, this contribution will be asymmetrical since it will not affect all geographical areas equally. And on the other, as a global phenomenon, tourism is facing a major, also global, challenge which is to ensure sustainability, especially if one considers that, as acknowledged by the World Tourism Organization (UNWTO), in 2020 the number of international arrivals will reach 1.6 billion.

With this as the goal, the following sections will address three main topics. First, using official figures from the UNWTO, we shall examine the process of growth and simultaneous globalization of tourism which is involving ever more countries. Second, we shall analyze the principal motors of global change faced by tourism which will shape its evolution as a global phenomenon. And third, we shall identify the characteristics that a new flexible, adaptive, and experimental tourism management model should have, based on the principles of sustainability so as to respond to this new scenario of global change.

2. The globalization of tourism: facts and figures

Tourism has undergone significant growth worldwide (over 6 per 100 per annum in terms of international tourist arrivals) since its emergence as a mass phenomenon in the 1950s. As well as this overall growth, the other striking aspect is its steady expansion as a global phenomenon, progressively spreading into all regions of the world and most countries.

Indeed, there have been some interesting changes since the 1950s in the direction of tourist flows worldwide, with an especially noticeable steady increase of arrivals of international tourists in Asia and the Pacific (which in 2010 received 21.8 per 100 of the total, compared with 0.8 per 100 in 1950), and to somewhat lesser extents in the Middle East (6.4 per 100 in 2010 compared to 0.8 per 100 in 1950) and Africa (5.2 per 100 compared to 2 per 100 in 1950). At the same time, Europe continues to maintain a far from negligible market share of 50.4 per 100 in the volume of tourist flows worldwide, although in relative terms it has declined from 66.4 per 100 in the 1950s. The same relative downward trend has occurred in the Americas, which have gone from a market share of 29.64 per 100 in 1950 to 16.2 per 100 in 2010.

The year 2010 has been a turning point in the downward trend of the main global data on tourism in recent years (Table 1). Powered by improving economic conditions worldwide, international tourism has recovered faster than expected from the effects of the world financial crisis and economic downturn of late 2008 and 2009. International tourist arrivals increased by 6.7 per 100 compared with 2009, with positive growth in all regions of the world. In absolute terms, the number of arrivals reached 935 million, surpassing by 58 million the 2009 figure and by 22 million the pre-crisis peak of 2008 (913 million). In addition, although all regions recorded growth in international arrivals, the main drivers of the growth continued to be the emerging economies. This two-speed recovery, slower in the advanced (5 per 100) and faster in the emerging (8 per 100) economies, is a reflection of the global economic situation, and will dominate 2011 and the foreseeable future.

The sub-regional results also clearly reflect the different speeds of recovery. Some subregions, such as North and Sub-Saharan Africa and Southeast Asia, were unaffected by the global crisis, and showed continued growth throughout 2009 and 2010. Among the subregions that had been affected by the crisis in 2009, the 2010 arrivals in Northeast and South Asia, North and South America, and Western Europe fully offset the earlier losses, reaching levels equal to or even higher than the pre-crisis situation. The Caribbean and Central America, however, have barely recovered their 2008 levels, and the growth in Central and Eastern Europe, and Southern Europe and the Mediterranean has been insufficient to offset the tourist flow loss in 2009, and Northern Europe presented no positive figures in 2010.

Asia was the first region to recover, and was that with strongest growth (13 per 100) in 2010. International tourist arrivals in Asia reached a new record of 204 million, compared to 181 million in 2009. Africa (6 per 100, 49 million arrivals), the only region with positive figures in 2009, continued to grow in 2010, benefiting from the increased economic dynamism and events such as the World Cup in South Africa. The Middle East returned to growth with double-digit results (14 per 100, 60 million arrivals), with an increase of 10 per 100 or more in almost all of its destinations.

Recovery in Europe (3 per 100, 471 million arrivals) was slower than in other regions. This partially reflected the interruption of air traffic following the eruption of Eyjafjallajökull and the economic uncertainty affecting the euro zone. Although the sector has gained momentum in the second half of the year, with performances above the regional average in some countries, it has not been enough to revert the overall losses of 2009.

The Americas (with a growth of 8 per 100, 151 million arrivals) recovered from the fall of 2009 that had been caused by the economic difficulties of North America and the impact of the outbreak of influenza-A(H1N1). The return of the U.S. economy to growth has helped improve the performance of the region as a whole, as has the progress of regional integration in Central and South America, and the vitality of Latin American economies. The greatest growth corresponded to South America (10 per 100).

Together with international tourist arrivals, the other variable that is commonly used as a measure of the evolution of world tourism is the volume of receipts (Table 2). During 2010, the growth of international tourism receipts lagged somewhat behind that of arrivals, as is usual during periods of recovery. Among the main markets in terms of external tourism expenditures, it has been the emerging economies which have been driving growth: China (17 per 100), the Russian Federation (26 per 100), Saudi Arabia (28 per 100), and Brazil (52 per 100). Among the traditional source markets, there has been recovery in the cases of Australia (9 per 100), Canada (8 per 100), Japan (7 per 100), and France (4 per 100), with modest growth (2 per 100) in the U.S., Germany, and Italy. In contrast, external tourism expenditures of the U.K. during 2010 fell by 4 per 100.

	International tourist arrivals (millions)								Market share (%)	Change (%)		Mean annual growth (%)
	1990	1995	2000	2005	2007	2008	2009	2010	2010	09/08	10/09	2000-2010
World	**438**	**533**	**683**	**802**	**901**	**913**	**877**	**935**	**100**	**-4.0**	**6.7**	**3.35**
Advanced economies	300	339	423	451	496	489	468	493	52.7	-4.3	5.3	1.50
Emerging economies	138	194	260	351	405	424	409	442	47.3	-3.5	8.2	6.36
By WTO region												
Europe	**265.0**	**309.1**	**392.2**	**441.0**	**485.4**	**480.8**	**456.9**	**471.5**	**50.4**	**-5.0**	**3.2**	**1.84**
Northern Europe	28.6	35.8	43.7	52.8	58.1	56.4	53.4	53.3	5.7	-5.5	-0.1	2
Western Europe	108.6	112.2	139.7	141.7	153.9	153.2	148.6	156.1	16.7	-3.0	5.1	1.07
Central/Eastern Europe	33.9	58.1	69.3	87.5	96.6	100.0	89.9	93.7	10.0	-10.1	4.2	3.20
Southern/Medit. Europe	93.9	103.0	139.5	159.1	176.8	171.2	165.1	168.4	18.0	-3.5	2.0	1.88
Asia & the Pacific	**55.8**	**82.0**	**110.1**	**153.6**	**182.0**	**184.1**	**181.0**	**203.8**	**21.8**	**-1.7**	**12.6**	**7.74**
North-east Asia	26.4	41.3	58.3	86.0	101.0	101.0	98.1	111.7	11.9	-2.9	13.9	8.33
South-east Asia	21.2	28.4	36.1	48.5	59.7	61.8	62.1	69.6	7.4	0.5	12.1	8.44
Oceania	5.2	8.1	9.6	11.0	11.2	11.1	10.9	11.6	1.2	-1.6	6.0	1.89
South Asia	3.2	4.2	6.1	8.1	10.1	10.3	9.9	10.9	1.2	-3.4	10.1	7.15
Americas	**92.8**	**109.0**	**128.9**	**134.0**	**143.9**	**147.8**	**140.5**	**151.2**	**16.2**	**-4.9**	**7.7**	**1.57**
North America	71.7	80.7	91.5	89.9	95.3	97.7	92.1	99.2	10.6	-5.8	7.8	0.77
Caribbean	11.4	14.0	17.1	18.8	19.8	20.1	19.5	20.3	2.2	-2.8	3.9	1.70
Central America	1.9	2.6	4.3	6.3	7.8	8.2	7.6	8.3	0.9	-7.4	8.3	8.46
South America	7.7	11.7	15.9	19.0	21.0	21.8	21.3	23.5	2.5	-2.3	10.4	4.35
Africa	**14.8**	**18.9**	**26.5**	**35.4**	**43.2**	**44.4**	**45.8**	**48.7**	**5.2**	**3.2**	**6.4**	**7.62**
North Africa	8.4	7.3	10.2	13.9	16.3	17.1	17.6	18.6	2.0	2.5	5.8	7.49
Subsaharan Africa	6.4	11.6	16.3	21.5	26.9	27.2	28.2	30.1	3.2	3.6	6.9	7.70
Middle East	**9.6**	**13.7**	**24.9**	**37.8**	**46.7**	**55.9**	**52.7**	**60.0**	**6.4**	**-5.7**	**13.9**	**12.81**

Table 1. International tourist arrivals.
Note: 2010 data provisional. Source: UNWTO (2010) and UNWTO World Tourism Barometer.

Regarding the outlook for the future, the UNWTO (1995) published a study forecasting and evaluating the evolution of tourism in the first twenty years of the new millennium. It foresaw, besides the natural expansion of tourism flows and receipts, a consolidation of the process of globalization, with a significant percentage of the growth being directed towards regions that currently have lower market shares, and thus leading to a better distribution of tourism flows worldwide.

Notwithstanding the irregularity of tourism flows in recent years, the UNWTO for the moment maintains its long term forecast, considering that the structural trends underlying the forecast have not changed significantly. Indeed, experience has shown that, in the short term, there alternate periods of strong growth (1995, 1996, 2000, and 2004–2007) with periods of low growth (2001–2003, 2008, 2009), and indeed, for the period as a whole, the UNWTO expectation is being borne out.

The UNWTO foresees international arrivals reaching almost 1.6 billion in 2020, of which 1.2 billion will be intra-regional and 0.4 billion long-distance travelers. For the total of tourist arrivals by region, in 2020 the top three receptor regions will be Europe (717 million tourists), East Asia (397 million), and the Americas (282 million), followed by Africa, the Middle East, and South Asia.

	International tourism receipts				$ US			€ Euro		
	Local currency, constant prices (%)			Share (%)	Billions		Per arrival	Billions		Per arrival
	07/06	08/07	09/08	2009	2008	2009	2009	2008	2009	2009
World	**5.5**	**1.3**	**-5.6**	**100**	**941**	**852**	**970**	**640**	**611**	**690**
Advanced economies	4.9	1.9	-6.7	64.2	613	547	1160	417	392	830
Emerging economies	6.8	0.1	-3.7	35.8	328	305	740	223	219	530
By WTO region										
Europe	**2.7**	**-1.2**	**-6.6**	**48.5**	**473.7**	**413.0**	**900**	**322.0**	**296.1**	**640**
Northern Europe	4.0	-2.0	-2.9	7.1	70.2	60.9	1140	47.8	43.6	820
Western Europe	2.2	-2.3	-7.2	16.9	162.2	143.7	980	110.3	103.0	710
Central/Eastern Europe	8.9	2.1	-8.2	5.6	57.8	47.4	530	39.3	34.0	380
Southern/Medit. Europe	0.9	-0.8	-7.0	18.9	183.5	161.1	940	124.7	115.5	680
Asia & the Pacific	**10.0**	**4.6**	**-0.7**	**23.9**	**208.9**	**203.7**	**1120**	**142.1**	**146.1**	**810**
North-east Asia	8.3	8.4	0.7	11.8	99.9	100.3	1020	67.9	71.9	730
South-east Asia	16.0	-1.0	-6.3	6.4	59.8	54.3	870	40.6	38.9	630
Oceania	6.4	2.9	5.2	3.9	33.7	33.5	3080	22.9	24.0	2210
South Asia	6.8	7.4	-0.2	1.8	15.5	15.6	1150	10.6	11.2	1110
Americas	**6.6**	**4.9**	**-10.1**	**19.4**	**188.1**	**165.2**	**1180**	**127.9**	**118.5**	**840**
North America	7.6	6.9	-12.3	14.0	138.9	118.9	1290	94.5	85.2	930
Caribbean	0.9	-3.1	-4.9	2.6	23.6	22.2	1140	16.1	16.0	820
Central America	10.6	-1.1	-7.1	0.7	6.4	5.9	770	4.3	4.2	550
South America	6.8	2.4	-1.3	2.1	19.2	18.2	850	13.1	13.0	610
Africa	**9.7**	**-3.5**	**-4.3**	**3.4**	**30.2**	**28.9**	**630**	**20.5**	**20.7**	**450**
North Africa	7.4	-3.9	-4.3	1.2	10.8	9.9	570	7.3	7.1	410
Subsaharan Africa	10.9	-3.3	-4.2	2.2	19.4	19.0	670	13.2	13.6	480
Middle East	**9.4**	**0.8**	**-0.8**	**4.8**	**39.7**	**41.2**	**780**	**27.0**	**29.6**	**560**

Table 2. International tourism receipts.
Source: UNWTO (2010).

East Asia and the Pacific, South Asia, the Middle East, and Africa are expected to grow by more than 5 per 100 per annum compared to a world average of 4.1 per 100. The more mature regions of Europe and the Americas are expected to have growth rates below the average. Europe will maintain its position as having the greatest share of arrivals, although it will decrease from 60 per 100 in 1995 to 46 per 100 in 2020.

Globalization in tourism affects all aspects of demand, supply, and intermediation. Go & Van't Klooster (2006) argue that globalization helps to blur geographic and economic boundaries, the limits on firms accessing different markets, and the barriers to the free movement of persons. This is a radical change for which tourism managers need to be prepared, opening their minds to the move from local management of tourism to global management.

3. The motors driving the global changes facing tourism

There have been many reports on the recent trends that have affected the field of tourism. Most have focused on three main areas of analysis: changes in consumer behaviour in tourism, the influence of the technological revolution on the processes of production and consumption in the sector, and concern for the longer term effects of over-sizing tourism, especially for the pressure on the destination's natural capital. In recent years there has also been a growing concern about the compatibility between tourism development and the resident population's quality of life (Aguilar, 2007; Riera, 2009; Sharpley, 2003).

Apart from the many, and often very interesting, company and consultancy reports devoted to the analysis of trends in recent years, the analysis of the drivers of the global change which tourism is facing has predominantly used the literature of tried and tested authors in the field of tourism research (Cooper, Fletcher, Fyall, Gilbert & Wanhill, 2008; Dwyer, Edwards, Mistilis, Roman & Scott, 2009; Edgell et al., 2008; Goldin, 2010; Page, 2009; Riera, 2009). A brief review of this literature follows.

3.1 Economic motors of change

The current global economic crisis has shattered all earlier expectations about economic trends, and has made any analysis in the medium to long term particularly difficult. There does however seem to be a consensus among the most prestigious analysts and financial institutions that the crisis is shaping a different world, characterized by scarcity and by uncertainty about the future. To the enormous difficulties of the global financial system, there have to be added for the main source markets of tourist flows (the developed countries) four other negative factors: unemployment, the relative impoverishment of the middle classes (the real protagonists of what came to be called the "democratization of travel"), debt (in the private sector, but also sovereign debt and budget deficits), and the squeeze applied to business and family credit. This last has had the consequence of a growing fear that the difficulties may be here for the long stay, resulting in an overall reduction in consumption as an austerity measure in response to the uncertainty - a situation that the Slovenian philosopher Slavoj Zizek summed up as "purely and simply a way of life".

The reality is that, while the U.S., Japan, and even the European Union (in this case, with tremendous inequality between countries) have regained the path to growth in 2010, no one dares to predict flatly that this is the end of the problem, let alone in certain countries which are continuously threatened by an "attack" from the financial markets. And in any case, even if the crisis were definitively past, the last four years have revealed major weaknesses in the current model of growth (the scarcity of raw materials including oil, the demographic challenge, climate change, migration, the abuse of power on the part of financial markets, the globalization of threats to security and world peace, the radical change in many of the values that have underpinned global coexistence since the end of World War II, etc.) which require countries to react through deep structural reforms to modify the current patterns of the model of growth and to regulate certain aspects at a global scale. It is still of course too early to see how good the results of these policies are going to be. Indeed, in the view of some experts they are too little to tackle the change that is really needed. Consequently, it is presently very difficult to guess what the economic motors of global change will be.

Whatever the case, the phenomenon of globalization, driven by the technological revolution, leads to increased freedom of movement of capital, goods, services, and, of course, people.

For the travel industry, this means both greater mobility of global tourist flows and increased competition among international destinations (Dwyer et al., 2009).

Moreover, the stress that public finances have been subjected to during the crisis has led to stabilization policies that are already affecting, and will affect even more in the future, governments' capacity for intervention, since they find themselves forced to curtail public spending. One must not forget that, until now, a significant portion of the investment in the development and management of tourism has come from the public sector, whether in terms of stimulating the development of the activity, the provision of public services, or the promotion of the destination. Instead, governments are now beginning to see tourism as a sector to obtain financing from, rather than as an activity to invest in. Indeed, the justification given for the implementation of "green taxes" during 2010 in Germany, the U.K., and Austria (the Netherlands introduced it in 2008, but withdrew it a year later) in the form of an environmental air tax was the impact generated by tourism. It seems, however, merely to have been an effort to generate revenues, especially given that the receipts have no fixed destination, so that there is no guarantee that they will be spent on improvements in terms of sustainability[1]. The case is similar with the "tourism tax" recently implemented in Rome (and already being considered by other cities including Venice and Barcelona, although in the case of Spain the possibility has been rejected by the nation's Congress of Deputies). The justification given for this is the need to sustain the city's efforts in the organization of urban services and hence guarantee that tourists will benefit from better reception and services.

The credit crunch is another of the current situation's dangers both for companies, since it slows down their investment projects, and for consumers, because it affects their capacity to consume. In the latter case, price has become a key factor in tourists' purchasing decisions. The purchasing process has become lengthier, since customers shop around more carefully, compare, ask other people's opinion, and wait until the last minute to book and pay in instalments or by credit card. Experts agree that this trend is likely to be consolidated in the medium to long term, towards a more thoughtful consumer who seeks to maximize experiences, get the best service, and at the lowest price. And of course the Internet is playing a determining role throughout this process.

In contrast, developing countries are increasingly relevant as sources of tourists and business travelers. According to a recent Goldman Sachs report, two thirds of global economic growth over the next five years will take place in Brazil, Russia, India, and China (whose initials form the acronym BRIC). This growth will result in an increase in the middle classes of those countries, and consequently in a rise in their tourism. I.e., the North Americans and inhabitants of northern Europe who have traditionally dominated the travel industry will gradually give way to Brazilian, Russian, Indian, and Chinese tourists and business travelers. Indeed, according to the latest figures published by the WTO, two of the BRIC countries already figure in the world's top 10 source markets for tourism spending.

But the BRIC countries will not only have growing importance as sources of tourists, but also as receptor countries[2]. In this context, one must also consider the emergence of a

[1] It has even been suggested that the application of these taxes distorts competition in leading passengers to migrate to airports, airlines, and destinations unaffected by their implementation – hence the proposal that such decisions need to be taken within the framework of the European Union as a whole.

[2] In China, according to data released by the Chinese Government itself, 10 243 new hotels have opened between 1999 and 2008. In Brazil, according to Embratur data, in 2010 Spanish firms invested $157

growing number of new destinations around the world. This is a consequence of the expectations for development that this activity generates, changes in the habits of tourists, the need for travel multinationals to diversify their business, the efforts of developing countries to remove barriers to the entry of travelers, improved transport, and easier access to the source markets, with the last two reasons being the result of the revolution in technology.

This increasing international competition will end in generating an ever more dynamic private sector. The pressure of this growing competition, together with firms' reduced access to financing, stricter environmental constraints, and changes in the traveler's purchasing behaviour and expectations will result in increased demand for the more efficient use of resources (Dwyer et al., 2009).

3.2 Environmental motors of change

Tourism is closely related to the environment, a limited asset which has to simultaneously provide ecological functions that are vital for the survival of ecosystems, and services that are essential to human activities. The natural environment provides the physical territorial context in which tourism is developed and a significant portion of the resources required to support the tourism production process of any destination (basic resources such as water and power, and others that are available for tourism and recreational use), and receives much of the waste resulting from production and consumption (Riera, 2009). Indeed, the natural environment and climate have always been considered two of the principal competitive advantages of any tourism destination or business.

Traditionally, the main concerns regarding the relationship between tourism and the environment have focused on the role that the development of tourism might be able to play to help improve the effectiveness of the management of ecologically sensitive areas and the preservation of unique environments (both basically cases of protected areas). In recent years, however, interest has shifted to the analysis of the impact that tourism can have on the environment as a result of exorbitant increases in the use of resources. These concerns include climate change, depletion of natural resources, and loss of biodiversity.

Concern in the field of tourism about the effects of climate change and global warming has been very late in making itself felt (Pulido, 2008). Perhaps the fact that it is a global phenomenon and that its impacts respect no frontiers led to people forgetting that its main effects will be local and regional – rise in sea level, changes in ocean currents, melting glacier and polar ice, loss of snowpack, increased heat indices and high daytime temperatures, and changes in rainfall patterns (Viner & Nicholls, 2006). The foreseeable repercussions of climate change on tourism can be summarized in four main areas (Pulido, 2008: 110-111):

- **Repercussions on the geographic travel space:** It is estimated that in all coastal zones, beach-front infrastructure will be at jeopardy, and freshwater reserves will be affected, further aggravating the already difficult water supply situation in these tourist areas.
- **Repercussions on demand:** The climate is a central motivating factor in choosing a holiday destination. Tourists will try to avoid the places most affected by this phenomenon, replacing them with others or choosing other times of year for their visit.

---

million, behind only U.S. ($364 million), Dutch ($233 million), and French ($164 million) companies, and the Brazilian government plans to invest more than $9 billion dollars to modernize airports, roads, and ports, taking as targets the Football World Cup in 2014 and the 2016 Olympics.

- **Repercussions on supply:** Climate variability and changing weather patterns will generate higher levels of uncertainty than are considered normal for business activities. In principle, the source market tour operators and travel agencies will simply respond by offering travel to other places. The most negative and direct impact will affect firms located in the most vulnerable destinations, with the resulting reduction in revenue for these locations, and consequent increase in unemployment.
- **Repercussions on transport:** Transport has a considerable effect on the environment and the climate. The measures so far proposed to mitigate this impact[3] can be translated into different forms of increasing the cost of travel. This will result in a retraction of tourism demand for certain zones. Indeed, there is already a clear awareness of the need for destinations to develop sustainable mobility plans, to boost tourism from neighbouring areas, and to introduce less polluting modes of transport.

But tourism is of course not just a victim of climate change - it is also a vector. A study published by the UNWTO (2008) shows that in 2005 tourism generated 4.9 per 100 of total CO_2 emissions, with transport being responsible for the greater part (75 per 100), and air transport in particular accounting for approximately 40 per 100. The Fourth Evaluation Report of the IPCC (2007) estimated that total aviation (domestic and international) currently produces about 2 per 100 of global CO_2 emissions. If there are no radical changes, with an expected air traffic growth of 4.6 per 100 per annum, it is estimated that in 2050 emissions from air transport will have risen to 4.5 per 100 of the global total (Goldin, 2010).

The second major concern is the depletion of natural resources and the loss of biodiversity (Dwyer et al., 2009; Goldin, 2010). The increasing population and growth rates worldwide are conditioning the availability of natural resources. Declining oil production with a dramatic increase in demand will translate into higher fuel costs, generating a growing concern for energy efficiency and greater investment in renewable energies. At the same time, water scarcity will mean increased conflict for the control of water resources. Increased demand will lead to higher food prices, and hence large-scale land clearance in order to increase agricultural production. The result may well be over-cropping of current farmland and loss of original forests.

Moreover, most studies recognize that habitat loss will be the main threat to species conservation and biodiversity. The destinations that will most suffer from these effects will be those that specialize in nature-based tourism.

3.3 Technological motors of change

Technological advances create opportunities for the travel industry, but they also pose a threat. Today's tourism is of course highly dependent on ICT and transportation. The coming years will see the accession of the world of tourism to many technological innovations that will enhance the experience of travelers (David Burton Associates, 2010). The main changes will be through the combination of mobile Internet and the Web's social networks, which should provide travel companies with new opportunities to improve their

---

[3] From 2012, airlines based in EU territories will receive annually a number of emission permits based on the average of those produced between 2004 and 2006. If they exceed these permits, they will have to purchase new permits that have remained unused by the industry or from other firms (always ensuring that there is a part for new entrants). In particular, in 2012 airlines will have to reduce their emissions to 97 per 100 of those made in the aforementioned period, and in 2013 to 95 per 100.

customers' experience. "Telepresence" technologies will complement business travel without replacing it. The futurologist Ray Kurzweil has predicted that, within ten years, computers will for the most part be invisible, embedded in walls, furniture, clothing, and even our bodies. This new scenario will of course not only affect how travel is produced and consumed, but also how it is branded and marketed. Indeed, just this last decade has been prolific in the incorporation of technology into the processes of intermediation.

ICTs also facilitate the incorporation of sophisticated database management systems, providing travel firms with the tools they need to respond to individual preferences and stimulate the tourist's purchases. A result is a reduction in operating costs and an increased capacity to add value for their customers.

Technological advances in transportation have made journeys faster and more comfortable. These changes are taking place in the four basic elements of any transportation system – route, terminal, vehicle, and propulsion. They are leading to improvements in the speed and quality of the journey, minimize waiting times at the terminal, and, in sum, reducing the real cost of travel. The result is greater accessibility of destinations around the world (Cooper et al., 2008). However, the environmental constraints that the sector will have to adapt to in the coming years represent its main challenge in the sense that they will mandate a permanent reduction in the social and environmental costs associated with travel (pollution, congestion, safety, etc.). Likewise, transport will also be affected by future fuel price rises.

The incorporation of technology allows the travel industry to renovate and innovate in its products and services, adding value to them through the use of production technologies that generate competitive advantages (Dwyer et al., 2009). This, together with the ongoing process of disintermediation that the travel industry is living through, implies, as noted by Riera (2009: 129): "*An especially important organizational shockwave which, in consonance with its cross-sectional character, is spreading throughout the fabric of the travel business.*" Hence travel firms' are interested in achieving a greater degree of integration of their activities with the rest of the value chain of tourism, offering a "total travel experience" (Oxford Economics, 2010).

3.4 Political motors of change

Now that the block politics established after World War II has passed into history, a new geopolitical reality has been taking shape. The U.S. still has an important influence, but with an increasingly relative power due partly to the enlargement of Europe which will continue to increase in international influence, but above all to the emergence of China and India as new major global players who are transforming the geopolitical (and, as was seen above, the tourism) landscape worldwide.

In this new geopolitical scenario, peace, security, and political stability are prerequisites for sustainable tourism development. Countries in which there are conflicts, or areas in which there are conflicts between countries, have a severely limited potential to attract tourist flows (Dwyer et al., 2009). This situation may also of course benefit destinations that tourists perceive as "safe". Such was the case in Spain compared with other Mediterranean destinations, which has for years had a privileged position in this regard, broken only at specific times following attacks by the terrorist group ETA.

After the attacks of 11-S, and later in London, Madrid, Bombay, etc., international terrorism has become a major global threat, and has led to increased security measures, especially in airports and railway stations around the world. But, at least for the moment, it seems not to have affected international tourist flows which have continued to rise year after year despite the discomfort of these measures.

The other major safety threat has to do with the increased risk of the spread of infectious diseases and other health-related crises as a result of the massive displacement of people for reasons of leisure. The response to these increased risks will be stricter border controls, creating barriers or, at least, impediments to tourism[4].

Destinations will therefore find themselves forced to develop appropriate strategies to deal with such contingencies. Until now, the only approach has been to obviate these difficulties through strategies of "enclave tourism", i.e., isolating the tourists in everything-included resorts (Dwyer et al., 2009). This poses a serious threat to the economy and local society, apart from being a form of neo-colonialism, contrary to the basic principles of sustainability.

In the clearly political arena, as problems of access to basic resources (water, fuel, etc.) become increasingly acute in the years ahead, there will be a need for strategies to deal with regional and/or ethnic conflicts for the control of territories that contain valuable resources, preferably before they occur, by reducing the gap between countries with resources and those without, guaranteeing application of the principle of intra-generational and inter-regional equity.

Visa policies will also be the object of attention in the coming years, since they can cause significant distortion of competition between destinations. Thus, while developing countries, including those with non-democratic regimes, are maintaining an openness policy that facilitates the entry of tourists, in developed countries, and especially in the European Union, in just the last few years procuring a visa has been a brake on the growth of tourist flows from emerging outbound markets, and has been the cause of increased tension between travel multinationals and governments. In the case of the European Union, added to this polemic is another of no less importance. This has to do with the economic and environmental impact on airlines represented by having to pass through a fragmented airspace, hence their demand for a single European airspace (a "*single sky*"). According to SESAR (Single European Sky ATM Research), this would allow direct routes to be designed which, being more efficient, would save 12 million tonnes of CO_2 per annum, not to mention the reduction in departure delays and cheaper travel. The big problem will of course be if the Member States are obliged to cede sovereignty over their airspace, to which one must add the need to redesign the regulatory and institutional framework, and to organize cooperation among states to ensure a single management structure.

In sum, all of the this highlights the need to implement models of governance that ensure the involvement of all stakeholders in the decision making process for the development of tourism. This is the other major challenge facing policy makers in the coming years – to establish a new model of governance that will allow equitable sharing of responsibility for solutions to the problems facing the goal of sustainable management of tourist destinations. The challenge really is no trivial matter. If one really wants to advance in this agenda, it will require institutional reform, the establishment of new instruments of financing (and therefore a revision of existing tax systems), and the design of new juridical frameworks.

---

[4] At the last annual summit of the World Travel and Tourism Council held in Beijing in May 2010, tourism multinationals harshly criticized "*the mismanagement of these last pandemics*" by national governments. This shows how sensitive the tourism industry is to such decisions, and the need for public/private coordination in these matters.

3.5 Demographic motors of change

As recognized by Yeoman, Hsu, Smith & Watson (2010: 19): "*Demography affects everything and everyone in as much as it is the future of terrorism, health care, taxation, of niches in the tourism market, or of the food supply.*" Among the main drivers of global change related to demographic trends, two stand out - world population growth and ageing of the population. Indeed, the concept of age is becoming ever more complex: as noted by Dwyer et al. (2009), children become adults more quickly, while adults want to be teenagers.

The sociologist Michael Young coined the term "multi-generational family", also called the "vertical family" to refer to changes taking place in family structure. The increase in longevity and the existence of smaller households (a result of families having fewer children) are giving rise to a family structure that grows vertically rather than horizontally, in which three, four, and even five generations may be living together (Yeoman et al., 2010). This substantially modifies the possibilities and forms of travel - the whole family may travel together; parents do not necessarily have to travel with their children, since they can leave them in the care of grandparents; the grandparents can travel with the grandchildren; etc.

But, in addition to changes in family structure, social structures are also changing. Society is becoming increasingly feminized, with the traditional distinction between the roles of men and women being more diffuse. Women have a growing influence on all key consumption decisions, including tourism. And one also observes a process of feminization of holiday travel. Yeoman et al. (2010: 8-9) call it the "Bridget Jones effect": "*Thirtysomething single women trying to make sense of life and love*", independent, and with a medium-high income level.

Working patterns are also evolving. People want to work flexibly, and they will be less and less willing to sacrifice their personal life and family-related goals for the sake of their career. The distinction between work and leisure will blur, enabling greater flexibility in travel plans.

In short, the family vacation will still be one of the main drivers of change in global tourism, but the greatest growth will occur in holidays for pensioners and singles. As noted by Dwyer et al. (2009), success in attracting these segments will come from determining how they think, not just how they behave.

Another of the demographic motors of global change is a worldwide tendency towards urbanization. Already 50.5 per 100 of the Earth's inhabitants live in urban contexts, and the urban population is growing. Currently, there are 21 megacities (with more than 10 million inhabitants), representing 9 per 100 (324 million) of the world's urban population. It is expected that by 2025 the number of megacities will have reached 29, concentrating 10 percent of the world's urban population, and, by 2030, 60 per 100 of the population will be urban (United Nations, 2010). In this context, the management of large cities will be another significant problem.

From the perspective of tourism, this trend has two obvious consequences (Dwyer et al., 2009). On the one hand, one will have to satisfy the needs of the, mostly urban, tourists to vacation far from the crowds, looking during their trip to escape the congestion, noise, and stress of their daily lives. And on the other hand, as destinations large cities must generate an offer that is attractive enough to demonstrate to the tourist that they are really worth visiting over and above the problems that the urban agglomeration may cause.

Related also to the economic and political drivers of change, two major demographic trends have to be borne in mind. The first has to do with the evolution of pension systems in the principal developed countries. The baby boomer generation (born between 1943 and 1960) will be retiring with a relative wealth guaranteed by a pension system with adequate funding. As a result, this generation will give rise to a significant volume of tourism flows. However, the changes on the horizon regarding the pension systems of countries such as Germany, Italy, Spain, and the U.K. will reshape the patterns of foreign travel, with a particularly rapid and significant drop in tourists from Japan and Germany. As noted by Yeoman et al. (2010), from 2050 onwards, pensioners will have less spending power than previous generations, and consequently also less propensity to travel.

The second question is related to migratory movements. In the last decade of the twentieth century, the more developed regions of the world received 2.7 million immigrants per annum (1.6 million with North America had as their final destination). The greatest volume of employment in the tourism industry has traditionally been generated in low-skilled, low-paying jobs, which have been taken up by young immigrant workers. To the extent that the average qualification level of young people in developed countries is becoming ever higher, the tourism industry will be unable to compete with other industries to attract this skilled workforce, and this will be further exacerbated if, as seems likely, there is increased control of immigration (Yeoman et al., 2010). The result will be a strong pressure on the costs of tourism firms in these countries, which will find themselves forced to reduce their capacity so as to adapt it to their real possibilities of competing in the markets.

3.6 New citizen and business values

The changes and trends discussed so far will condition in the future (indeed, in some cases they already are doing so) the forms of production and consumption, and hence the behaviour of businesses and individuals. Citizens have new values and needs, aspirations and expectations, that will shape the way they travel, and this in turn will influence the production process, market access, and even the behaviour of tourism firms and managers.

Particularly noteworthy is that more and more tourists are tailoring the planning of their vacations to meet their specific needs, beyond the mere fact of taking a few days of holiday break. A growing number of experienced travelers will seek experiences that are authentic and out of the usual, but not shared, and therefore will fall outside the mass organization formulas of combined tours. Moreover, customers are showing increasing interest in discovering, experiencing, participating, and learning in a more intimate way aspects of the daily life of the destinations they visit. Consequently, they are demanding more options, more interactivity, and products that are more personalized.

Indeed, this is one of the most interesting aspects of the so-called "Experience Economy". It enables the travel market to be fragmented into subsets of unique experiences, based on tailored holidays and a personalized service that allows the traveler to participate more actively in the experience. In developed countries in particular, clients are strongly attracted by the call of new experiences, and are willing to try new products, food, and places of interest, but also are too impatient to give a product or service that does not initially meet their expectations a second chance (Dwyer et al., 2009).

There are two aspects that stand out in consumers' new values which will be crucial when it comes to positioning a successful tourism product in the market. The first is that consumers are increasingly interested in their travel experience contributing to their personal growth, to improving themselves, with the emphasis being on health, welfare, education, the development of skills, and developing themselves culturally. This implies a trend worldwide towards choosing vacations in which they learn something. In sum, they see their holiday, not as a form of consumption, but as an investment in themselves.

The second is that customers, particularly those from developed countries, are increasingly socially and environmentally aware. This leads them to seek tourism experiences that they see as "authentic", including the demand that the services and/or products that they consume respond to codes of ethical production and marketing ("ethical consumerism"). This implies a willingness to purchase beyond the stimulus of price comparison, looking for the quality and opportunities that are coherent with their environmental and social concerns. And it also implies that consumers have a growing need to actively participate in a variety of tourism experiences which are in line with this militant attitude towards certain causes and beliefs.

In both cases, what one sees approaching on the horizon is a new tendency to mix holiday leisure with personal education and a proactive stance towards health or environmental and social causes. In the same vein, it also appears that the boundaries between work and retirement will also become increasingly blurred.

Together with this militant attitude goes a certain belligerency. Increasingly, prior to purchase, tourists are demanding guarantees that they will be paying for products, services, and practices that are safe. Therefore, given that the purchase will be conditioned by any perception of risk, tourism firms and destination managers need to take a twofold approach. On the one hand, they will have to promptly address any perception that markets have of risk, trying to counter any negative image that may have arisen. And on the other, they will have to implement actions necessary to minimize, and better to eliminate, any risks that indeed exist (Dwyer et al., 2009).

In our examination of the economic motors of change, we foresaw a significant shift in tourists' purchasing habits. In the coming years, this new culture of austerity in consumption will be maintained, with spending being less impulsive, more thoughtful, and better informed. There will clearly be an increase in Internet searches and comparative shopping, especially in regard to prices. But in no sense does this mean that consumers will simply be looking for the cheapest offer. Rather, they will continue to demand a quality experience, looking for the best price-to-quality ratio. They will elect not just any destination, but one that can guarantee the experience they are looking for. At the same time, they will keep their high expectations, so that their focus will be on "value for money" rather than on to the lowest priced offer.

It is also interesting to observe the response of travel firms and tourism managers to these changes in tastes, motivation, and attitudes of the demand, and to what degree they will also change their production and management processes to adapt to this new scenario. One might distinguish here between the large tour companies and the rest, bearing in mind that the vast majority of tourism-related businesses are SMEs, and that a characteristic of the tourism industry is its lack of sectoral articulation. This conditions the potential to generate the sufficient economies of scale to address many of these challenges, and affects the likelihood of the emergence of local firms capable of setting the standards for others in the destination to follow (Exceltur, 2010). One also notes the confusion of policy-makers (including destination managers) who are finding it very difficult to understand the changes in their environment and to act accordingly. Their attitude for now has mainly been one of a reactive response to events as they happen, without any real criterion underlying their decisions. This is clearly an untenable situation in that the effects of these events are far exceeding the capacity of too many destinations to ensure the continuation of their current planning and management frameworks.

Travel firms are, however, beginning to accept that they must take on a growing social and environmental co-responsibility, with greater real and practical interest in the destination. They realize that their business will be increasingly conditioned by the ability of all stakeholders to ensure the sustainable management of tourism destinations and the conservation of their unique characteristics (Cooper et al., 2008). Hence there is a growing concern of large firms to create departments that can effectively manage their Corporate Social Responsibility strategies, although, as pointed out by various United Nations reports (Jiménez, 2007), the concern has of now been for these strategies to improve the image of the company, and hence its immediate financial results, rather than contributing to reducing the real negative impact of the company's activities on the territory of the tourism destinations it operates in.

In the immediate future, tourism firms, including tour operators, will begin to understand the importance of working together with other members of the destination's value chain, creating business networks or alliances that will improve business efficiency and the effectiveness of their communication strategies (Cooper et al., 2008). This trend implies a shift away from the traditional management practices of individual sectors of the tourism industry - airlines, accommodation, intermediation, etc. - to a new concept of integrated management, in which the value chain of the entire trip will become increasingly more important (Oxford Economics, 2010).

The growing importance of non-Western cultures in the composition of outbound tourism worldwide has major consequences for the travel industry. A report by The Economist Intelligence Unit (2009) suggests that this new context will require changes in how customers are segmented. An 18-year-old from China may have more in common with an 18-year-old from the U.S. than either of them with a 40-year-old adult of their own country. More than 80 per 100 of that study's panel of experts agreed with this assessment, and most of them were totally in agreement.

For the supply side of the travel market to address all these changes will inevitably require a more highly skilled workforce. Increasingly, education will be a determinant of success for destinations and travel firms (Dwyer et al., 2009): the most successful will be the innovators, those who can count on highly trained personnel capable of keeping the offer in tune with changing customer needs. Likewise, the employees themselves will value their firm's organizational culture, especially if the firm devotes part of its personnel's working time to further training and learning. One aspect that will be particularly valued is the involvement of enterprises in the creation in the destination of social infrastructures that maximize the opportunities for individuals and businesses to innovate, learn, and in general develop the skills they need to access knowledge services.

While each of the motors of global change that we examined above is important in itself, they all influence each other to a greater or lesser extent, depending on the characteristics of the destination and the sector of the travel industry being analyzed. While most of them will be mutually reinforcing, in some cases they will work at cross purposes.

In sum, the present analysis has been aimed at providing the context for discussion on the future of the tourist industry. The various agents involved need to be proactive instead of reactive in their strategic responses, and to continually monitor and develop understanding of the factors driving change in their sector.

4. The paradigm of sustainability in the global tourism phenomenon

As is the case with "globalization", few concepts have been taken up into the global collective consciousness so quickly and so little questioned as "sustainable development", even though debate continues on its content and scope. Indeed, it is still used with different meanings, even sometimes with conflicting connotations (Pulido, 2006a). Since it was coined by the Brundtland Commission just over twenty years ago, it has become a recurring term in the political agenda of most governments and international organizations, as well as of a growing number of large and small firms and other social groups (Redclift, 2005). It has also given rise to countless international declarations (Rodríguez, 2007; Quental, Lourenço & Da Silva, 2011), scientific papers, projects, tools, and management models.

Experts agree that we are still far from the time when it will be possible to implement the changes that sustainability will require, especially if the current model of development is maintained. Consequently, the main causes of unsustainability remain, even if some of its symptoms have been dealt with (Bass, 2007). Neither does there seem to be acceptance of the real need for urgent, firm action in this issue, whether by government institutions, the business world, civilian society, or even at the individual level. All this is despite the ever more worrying warnings in successive reports of the International Panel on Climate Change, the Stern Report (2006), and the recognition of the significance of this challenge represented by the award of the Nobel Peace Prize 2007 (Prats, 2007).

The situation is no different in the field of tourism. As pointed out by Jiménez (2007: 78), tourism "*has clearly been slow relative to other productive industries when it comes to environmental considerations and accepting the principles of sustainability from a strategic standpoint.*" Moreover, the concept of "sustainable tourism" itself has been subject to simplistic misinterpretations. Examples are its confusion with specific types of tourism such as eco-tourism or nature tourism, its denomination as "green tourism" or "ecological tourism", or, even worse, its coming to be regarded as a new alternative type of tourism[5]. In this sense, Lim & Cooper (2009: 90) recognize that: "*The concept of sustainable tourism has been the object of numerous definitions which have repeatedly been criticized as ambiguous, vague, sectoral, too conceptual, and prone to create confusion by linking it exclusively to environmental issues.*"

Despite the controversy, at least in recent years, it seems that in the scientific literature (Cerina, Markandya & McAleer, 2011; Edgell, Allen, Smith & Swanson, 2008; Gössling, Hall & Weaver, 2009; Leslie, 2009; Lim & Cooper, 2009; Lu & Nepal, 2009; Sharpley, 2009; Miller & Twining-Ward, 2005), and in publications of international organizations, institutions, etc. in general, it is broadly accepted that the paradigm of sustainability in tourism is multidimensional. It is not simply a goal that has to be reached or a strategy *per se*, but, in the words of Novo (2006: 152): "*Sustainable development means seeing things in a completely different light (...) it of course means a radical transformation in the relationships between economics,*

---

[5] Indeed, despite the progress of recent years made in the conceptualization of sustainable tourism, and UNWTO's own efforts in this direction, even today official publications as important as the strategic document prepared for the G-20 Summit held in the Republic of Korea in October 2010 inexplicably again fall into the same conceptual errors (Goldin, 2010: 46-47). One can thus understand why there is so much difficulty in specifying, within a spectrum of operational policies and actions, the content of the paradigm of sustainable tourism.

ecology, and ethics; it means starting to think and act with a different logic, taking into account the limits of the biosphere, social redistribution, and cultural diversity."

Consequently, progress towards sustainability requires profound changes in the current model of tourism development. One must expect a completely new setting for the relationships between the agents of tourism, the host society, the tourists themselves, and the resources that may be used, with these last being understood in a much broader sense than the traditional conception of their being exclusively associated with the idea of natural resources (Pulido, 2006a).

Indeed, one of the great mistakes that has been made since the concept was coined (although the Brundtland Report itself warned against it) has been to link it exclusively - at times even explicitly rejecting any other connection - with the environmental dimension. There has been discussion of "environmental sustainability", not understanding that achieving progress in sustainability requires an effort to be made to balance its three basic dimensions: efficient use of resources (economic dimension), intra- and inter-generational equity (social dimension), and maintenance and enhancement of the cultural and natural heritage (environmental dimension). And, as is already beginning to be recognized (Peris, Acebillo & Calabuig, 2010; Puhakka, Sarkki, Cottrell & Siikamäki, 2009; Pulido, 2006b), none of this is very likely to occur except in the context of a fourth dimension - the institutional.

One of the main challenges facing the current process of growth and globalization of tourism is its sustainability, which in recent years has generated an interesting debate about the approach that needs to be taken to the active sustainable management of tourism attractions and destinations. It is now accepted that the destination can not be a mere container for leisure practices and businesses - a simple backdrop against which tourism activities can be developed. Rather it has to be treated as a key substantial element of the entire process of production and consumption of tourism, and in particular as requiring proactive management (Cooper et al., 2008).

Tourism has traditionally been analyzed systemically, based on principles of stability, equilibrium, and predictability so as to be able to construct models in which any changes can be foreseen and therefore controlled. Under the assumptions of this approach, a tourism system functions like a machine in which stability, order, uniformity, and equilibrium are the norm - in a state which is seen as harmonious. Any change is seen as an unexpected perturbation to the system, something out of the ordinary to which a solution has to be found so as to restore everything to its natural state of equilibrium. Such systems have a linear behaviour, in which any change is predictable and can be foreseen and controlled with precision.

A quite different vision emerges from the scientific advances of this past decade concerning the concept of sustainability which have appeared in the fields of ecology, thermodynamics, ecological economics, and the so-called sciences of sustainability and of global change, among others. This sees tourism systems as being "*complex, adaptive, interdependent, and nonlinear*" (Farrell & Twining-Ward, 2004: 69). They are systems in which there is no one simple state of equilibrium, but different states of stability, instability, and even chaos. Moreover, various of these states may occur simultaneously. Consequently, management of these systems has to be flexible, adaptable, and experimental, in an ongoing process involving constant revisions and corrections (Page, 2009). There is thus a need for adaptive models of management that are based on accepting uncertainty as a working environment.

Through a process of social participation and learning, they will involve a progressive accumulation of the knowledge required to understand the changes that are occurring, and to react to them systematically, adapting, and indeed benefiting, from the new situation (Pulido, 2006a).

The challenge therefore lies in the implementation of new models of management of tourism destinations to ensure compliance with the, now widely accepted, principles of sustainability (GSTC, 2008; Sharpley, 2009).

5. Conclusions

This chapter has analyzed the growing importance of tourism as a global phenomenon. Despite the intense debate that has arisen in the last decade on tourism's role in a globalized world, the information that has been examined in this paper shows that, since the 1950s, both the production and the consumption of tourism have been characterized not only by a growth of flows and receipts, but also by their own steady process of globalization which now affects all the world's regions and most of its countries.

The data provided by UNWTO on future prospects confirm that the globalization of tourism will be even more marked in the coming years, since the greatest future growth rates are expected in regions of the world that currently have only minor shares of the market.

In this burgeoning process of globalization, tourism is facing a new scenario of global change that will condition all of its patterns of production and consumption. The impact will be very different depending on the type of destination and the sector of the industry concerned. It seems clear therefore that a key factor for success in the management of tourism destinations will be to identify and analyze these impacts, and to have the capacity to foresee the behaviour of many of the phenomena that affect the sector.

In this context, sustainability emerges as one of the great challenges for the development of tourism worldwide. With the expected horizon of continued growth and expansion into all regions and countries, tourism could well become in itself a serious global threat if it is not managed holistically and proactively. Principally, there is a need for new management models to cope with the conditions of stability, instability, and even chaos that every tourism destination may find itself subjected to.

It is urgent, therefore, that international agencies and institutions, governments, and the major multinational tourism companies commit themselves to leading this process of transition towards sustainability by adjusting their policies and actions to the now generally accepted principles of sustainable development. It will be important to avoid the mistake of the purely environmentalist orientation that has mostly been followed up till now. Its results have been at best sparse and incomplete, and the policies have generally been characterized by a proliferation of measures with considerable duplication, overlap, and unnecessary complexity.

6. References

Aguiló, E. (2007). *Actitud de los residentes frente al turismo: análisis para las Islas Baleares*, Fundación Antoni Maura, Mallorca.

Aramberri, J. (2009). "The future of tourism and globalization: Some critical remarks", *Futures*, 41: 367-376.

Bagchi, A.K. (2007). Migration and Morality: Sovereign Finance and Dehumanized Immigrants, *in* Calosz-Tschopp, M.C. & Dasen, P. (eds.): *Globalization, Migration and Human Rights: A New Paradigm for Research and Citizenship*, vol.1, Bruylant, Brussels, pp. 647–79.

Bass, S. (2007). *A New Era in Sustainable Development. An IIED Briefing*, International Institute for Environment and Development (IIED), London.

Cerina, F., Markandya, A. & Mcaleer, M. (2011) (ed.). *Economics of Sustainable Tourism*, Routledge, Oxon.

Cooper, C., Fletcher, J., Fyall, A., Gilbert, D. & Wanhill, S. (2008). *Tourism. Principles and Practice*, Fourth Edition, Pearson Education Limited, Essex.

Cortés-Jimenéz, I. & Artís, M. (2005). The role of the tourism sector in economic development: lessons from the Spanish experience, *Proceedings of 45th Congress of the European Regional Science Association*, Vrije Universiteit Amsterdam, 19 pp.

David Burton Associates (2010). *The Amateur-Expert Traveller*, Amadeus IT Group, S.A., Madrid.

Dwyer, L., Edwards, D., Mistilis, N., Roman, C. & Scott, N. (2009). "Destination and enterprise management for a tourism future", *Tourism Management*, 30(1): 63-74.

Edgell, D.L., Allen, M.D., Smith, G. & Swanson, J. (2008). *Tourism Policy and Planing. Yesterday, Today and Tomorrow*, Butterworth-Heinemann, Burlington.

Exceltur (2010). *Monitur 2009. Monitor de competitividad turística relativa de las Comunidades Autónomas españolas*, Exceltur, Madrid.

Farrel B.H. & Twining-Ward, L. (2004). "Reconceptualizing tourism", *Annals of Tourism Research*, 31(2): 274-295.

Go, F. & Van't Klooster, E. (2006). Managing globalization, *in* Buhalis, D. & Costa, C. (eds.): *Tourism Management Dynamics: Trends, Management and Tools*, Butterworth Heinemann, Oxford, pp. 137-144.

Goded, M. (2002). "La promoción de la actividad turística: ¿Una política de desarrollo acertada?", *Revista de Economía Mundial*, 7: 111-133.

Goldin, I. (2010). *Tourism and the G-20: T.20 Strategic Paper*, Document prepared for the 2nd T.20 Ministers Meeting, mimeo.

Gössling, S., Hall, C.M. & Weaver, D. (ed.) (2009). *Sustainable Tourism Futures: Perspectives on Systems, Restructuring and Innovations*, Routledge, New York.

GSTC (2008). *Global Sustainable Tourism Criteria*. The Partnership for Global Sustainable Tourism Criteria. URL: *http://www.sustainabletourismcriteria.org/images/Documents/Versions/global%20sustainable%20tourism%20criteria%20version%205.pdf* Acceded 10 January 2011.

Jiménez, L.M. (2007). "Hacia la sostenibilidad turística en España", *Estudios Turísticos*, 172-173: 73-79.

Lanza, A. & Pigliaru, F. (1994). The Tourism Sector in the Open Economy, *in* Nijkamp, P. & Coccossis, W. (eds.): *Tourism and the Environment*, Avebury, Aldershot.

Lanza A., Temple, P. & Urga, G. (2003). "The Implications of Tourism Specialisation in the Long Run: an Econometric Analysis for 13 OECD Economies", *Tourism Management*, 24: 315-321.

Leslie, D. (2009) (ed.). *Tourism Enterprises and Sustainable Development*, Routledge, New York.

Lickorish, L.J. & Jenkins, C.L. (2000). *Una introducción al turismo*, Editorial Síntesis, Madrid.

Lim, C. & Cooper, C. (2009). "Beyond Sustainability: Optimising Island Tourism Development", *International Journal of Tourism Research*, 11(1): 89-103.

Lu, J. & Nepal, K. (2009). "Sustainable tourism research: an analysis of papers published in the Journal of Sustainable Tourism", *Journal of Sustainable Tourism*, 17(1): 5-16.

Martin, M. (2001). "Globalisation, Corporate Governance and Competition", *Journal of the Malaysian Institute of Accountants*, 14 (11).

Miller, G. & Twining-Ward, L. (2005). *Monitoring for a sustainable tourism transition: the challenge of developing and using indicators*, CABI Publishing, Wallingford.

Morrison, J. (2002). *The International Business Environment*, Palgrave, New York.

Novo, M. (2006). *El desarrollo sostenible. Su dimensión ambiental y educativa*, Pearson Educación, S.A., Madrid.

OECD (2009). *The Impact of Culture on Tourism*. OECD, Paris.

Oxford Economics (2010): *The Travel* Gold *Rush 2020*, Amadeus IT Group, S.A., Madrid.

Page, S. (2009). *Tourism Management. Managing for change*, Third edition, Butterworth-Heinemann, Oxford.

Shademan, M. (2009). The impact of globalisation on Iran's tourism sector: a test of the demonstration effect, *Proceedings of the PhD Networking Conference*. "Exploring Tourism III: Issues in PhD Research", University of Nottingham: 117-131. URL: *http://www.nottingham.ac.uk/ttri/discussion/PhDConferenceProceedings.pdf* Accesed 4 April 2011.

Pearce, D. (1989). *Tourism Development*, Longman, Harlow, Essex.

Peris, J., Acebillo, M. & Calabuig, C. (2010). *La Agenda 21 local como instrumento para la gobernanza democrática local*. Colección Avances de Investigación, núm. 21, Fundación Carolina. Cealci, Madrid.

Prats, F. (2007). "Sostenibilidad y turismo, una simbiosis imprescindible", *Estudios Turísticos*, 172-173: 13-62.

Puhakka, R., Sarkki, S., Cottrell, S.P. & Siikamäki, P. (2009). "Local discourses and international initiatives: sociocultural sustainability of tourism in Oulanka National Park, Finland", *Journal of Sustainable Tourism*, 15(9): 529-549.

Pulido, J.I. (2006a). Turismo y sostenibilidad, *in* Sáez, A., Martín, P. & Pulido, J.I. (coord.): *Estructura económica del turismo*, Editorial Síntesis, Madrid, pp. 327-366.

Pulido, J.I. (2006b). Sostenibilidad de los destinos turísticos, *in* López, D. & Pulido, J. I. (ed.): *La actividad turística española en 2005 (Edición 2006)*, Centro de Estudios Ramón Areces, S. A. y Asociación Española de Expertos Científicos en Turismo (AECIT), Jaén, pp. 279-295.

Pulido, J.I. (2008) (coord.). "Turismo y Cambio Climático", *Análisis Turístico*, 8: 100-118.

Pulido, J.I. & Sánchez, M. (2009). "Measuring Tourism Sustainability. Proposal of a Composite Index", *Tourism Economics*, 15(2): 277-296.

Quental, N., Lourenço, J.M. & Da Silva, F.N. (2011). "Sustainable Development Policy: Goals, Targets and Political Cycles", *Sustainable Development*, 19 (1): 15-29.

Randolph, J. (2007). "Anti-Globalisation After Seattle, Prague and Genoa", World Markets Centre, URL: *http//www.worldmarketsanalysis.com/pdf/g-indexreport.pdf* Accessed 21 September 2007.

Redclift, M. (2005). "Sustainable Development (1987-2005): An Oxymoron Comes of Age", *Sustainable Development*, 13: 121-227.

Riera, A. (dir.) (2009). *Libro Blanco del turismo de las Islas Baleares. Hacia una nueva cultura turística*, Conselleria de Turismo-Govern de les Illes Balears, Universitat de les Illes Balears, "Sa Nostra" Caixa de Balears, Cambra de Comerç de Mallorca, Mallorca.

Rodríguez, G. (2007). "Anexo I. Principales hitos institucionales –NNUU, UE y España- sobre sostenibilidad y turismo", *Estudios Turísticos*, 172-173: 287-296.

Sharpley, R. (2003). *Tourism, tourists and society*, ELM, Huntington.

Sharpley, R. (2009). *Tourism Development and the Environment: Beyond Sustainability?*, Earthscan, London.

Sinclair, M.T. & Stabler, M.J. (1997). *The Economics of Tourism*, Routledge, London and New York.

Sinclair, M.T. (1998). "Tourism and Economic Development: A Survey", *The Journal of Development Studies*, 34 (5): 1-51.

The Economist Intelligence Unit (2009). *The Austere traveller. The effect of corporate cutbacks on hotels*, Amadeus IT Group, S.A., Madrid.

Tribe, J. (2005). *The Economics of Recreation, Leisure and Tourism*, Elsevier, Oxford.

United Nations (2010). *World urbanization prospects: The 2009 Revision*, Press Release, United Nations, Department of Economic and Social Affairs, Population Division, New York.
URL: *http://esa.un.org/unpd/wup/Documents/WUP2009_Press-Release_Final_Rev1.pdf* Accessed 10 January 2011.

United Nations World Tourism Organization (UNWTO) (2010). *UNWTO Tourism Highlights. 2010 Edition*, UNWTO, Madrid.

United Nations World Tourism Organization (UNWTO) (2008). *Climate Change and Tourism: Responding to Global Challenges*, UNWTO and UNEP, Madrid.

United Nations World Tourism Organization (UNWTO) (2005). *Turismo, microfinanzas y reducción de la pobreza*, UNWTO, Madrid.

United Nations World Tourism Organization (UNWTO) (1995). *Tourism 2020 Vision, UNWTO, Madrid.*

Vanhove, N. (2005). *The Economics of Tourism Destinations*, Elsevier Butterworth-Heinemann, Burlington.

Viner, D. & Nicholls, S. (2006). "Climate change and its implications for international tourism", En Buhalis, D. & Costa, C. (eds.): *Tourism Management Dynamics: trends, management and tools*, Elsevier Butterworth-Heinemann, Burlington.

Vujakovic, P. (2009). *How to Measure Globalisation? A New Globalisation Index (NGI)*, WIFO Working Papers, No. 343, Österreichisches Institut für Wirtschaftsforschung, Wien.

World Travel and Tourism Council (WTTC) (2005). Progress and priorities 2005-06. World Travel and Tourism Council, United Kingdom.

Yeoman, I., Hsu, C., Smith, K.A. & Watson, S. (ed.) (2010). *Tourism and Demography,* Goodfellow Publishers Ltdm, Oxford.